African Architecture

AFRICAN ARCHITECTURE

EVOLUTION
AND
TRANSFORMATION

NNAMDI ELLEH

McGraw-Hill

New York   San Francisco   Washington, D.C.   Auckland   Bogotá
Caracas   Lisbon   London   Madrid   Mexico City   Milan
Montreal   New Delhi   San Juan   Singapore
Sydney   Tokyo   Toronto

Library of Congress Cataloging-in-Publication Data

Elleh, Nnamdi.
    African architecture : evolution and transformation / Nnamdi Elleh.
        p.   cm.
    Includes bibliographical references and index.
    ISBN 0-07-021506-5
    1. Ethnic architecture—Africa. 2. Vernacular architecture—Africa. I. Title.
  NA1580.E44 1996   96-13634
                                                     CIP

McGraw-Hill

A Division of The *McGraw·Hill* Companies

ISBN 0-07-021506-5

The sponsoring editor for this book was Wendy Lochner, the editing
supervisor was Penny Linskey, and the production supervisor
was Suzanne Rapcavage. Interior design and composition: Silvers Design.

This book was printed and bound in Hong Kong through Print Vision, Portland, Oregon.

To my family and special friends whose moral and spiritual support has been invaluable:

Chancellor John Schroeder, Sandra Schroeder, S. W. and Iris Winogrond, Jonnie Dvorak, Scully Stykes, Kristine and Donald Nesbitt, Professor Donald and Barbara Neuman, Bob Greenstreet, Kevin Forseth, Gil Snyder, Joe Stagg, Richard Falk, Carol and Bill Becwar, Mrs. Anne S. de Luengas, Muhammad Daniel Vandi, Annette Lott, Norman and Judy Lasca, Rachel and Tom Glennon, Mrs. Patricia and Lenny Ochogu, Nurudeen Amusa, Denise Manley, Professor Ali Mazrui, Professor Udọ Kultermann, and Allan Persinger.

CONTENTS

Part 2   North Africa: The Maghreb and Egypt

Part 3   Central and East Africa

Part 4   South Africa and the East African Islands

Part 5 West Africa: The Sudan

Part 6   Modern Architecture, Urbanism, and Urbanization in Africa

PREFACE

How does one teach African architectural history in the American academy? Scholars in European and African universities are also looking for answers to this question. I intend this book as a beginning to the engagement of this issue.

Architectural historians have shied away from writing a history of African architecture because the subject is vast, and no one knows exactly where to begin and where to end. This book addresses the methodological problem by defining what I see as the three major roots of African architecture, and by using these definitions as underpinnings for an elaboration on the architecture of each region and country in Africa. This book therefore tries to provide a comprehensive account of the evolution, transformation, and development of African architecture.

There are scholars who have given up the notion of a detailed historical analysis of African architecture because contemporary historiography has presented Africa as a continent without history, and because they subscribe to culturalist overemphasis on distinct cultures of the multiple ethnic groups of Africa. *African Architecture: Evolution and Transformation* recognizes the need to differentiate between the various ethnic groups of Africa, but takes advantage of the social and cultural histories which in one way or another ultimately connects the ethnic groups to one another to lay a solid foundation on which African architecture can be studied.

Rather than dwell on the colonialist divide and rule strategy which has permeated and overcome substantive analysis of African architectural history, this book engages the same colonial strategy in identifying the unifying elements in African architectural history and theory. In addition, this book utilizes climatic, regional, religious, cultural, artistic, and technological differences as elements of both vernacular and metropolitan architectural articulation for each region and locality.

The organizing structure is closely tied to the Triple Heritage Concept pioneered by Professor Ali Mazrui—the identification of indigenous, Western, and Islamic dimensions of African culture. The book is sensitive to the vastness of the African continent. I address this problem by dividing the book into six parts. Each part is developed to demonstrate how a region relates to the Triple Heritage Concept. Readers who are interested in learning about North African architecture can do so without having to read the whole book, and the same thing applies to the architecture of the other regions of the continent. In addition, readers who want to read about the architecture of specific countries of Africa can also do so without reading the whole book.

The Introduction will be important to most readers. It lays the groundwork for the whole book by introducing the Triple Heritage Concept for African architecture. The Triple Heritage Concept explains how indigenous African culture, Islamic culture, and Western culture come together at different stages to create a cultural history for Africa, and this cultural history is replicated in Africa's architectural history.

The study of the relationships between architecture, urbanism, and urbanization is still lacking in Africa. *African Architecture: Evolution and Transformation* also lays a groundwork on which these vital areas of architectural scholarship can be investigated in Africa. These three critical aspects of contemporary architectural history are the subjects of Chapters 18, 19, and 20.

The author is aware of the scope of this continental project and welcomes critiques and criticism. We are at a stage where scholars can no longer give excuses that the greatest shortcoming in African history is the fact that outsiders—especially colonialists—who had vested interests on a distorted African history, wrote what is available to us. While that is a fact, the time has come for Africanist scholars around the world to take the destiny of Africa–focused scholarship in their hands. The information is available, so what is needed is the will to undertake such projects and to submit them to scholarly criticism.

The Triple Heritage Concept has not previously been applied to the study of African architecture, and the history of African architecture has never before been written on a continental perspective. For this reason this book is written as a reference for both practicing architects and architectural history faculty at different levels of educational establishments. It combines architecture and history at a level that covers African civilization studies and is written with multiculturalism in mind. The language is straightforward and references have been included in order to meet the intellectual curiosity of people in universities and colleges.

Nnamdi Elleh

ACKNOWLEDGMENTS

African architectural history is a unique discipline to which people from many parts of the world have contributed; thus, it is readily accessible to everybody, but that opportunity has not yet been exploited, so it remains a mystery. To study African architecture is to go on an intellectual and spiritual journey which takes one to the distant past, back before 6000 B.C. This intellectual and spiritual journey exposes the reader to the various peoples of Africa, the landscape and climate, the vegetation, the cultures of the people, the early houses of the people of Africa in the caves of the Sahara Desert, the beginnings of monumental architecture on the continent, the religions of the people, and all the sociopolitical factors which shaped the various communities of Africa. Above all, the author wishes to remind readers that *African Architecture* opens a new forum of architectural discussions. It is hoped that the ideas posited in this book will be studied with harmony and open-mindedness.

It would have been impossible for me to write this book without the pioneering work of Professor Ali Mazrui, whose television series, *The African, A Triple Heritage*, gave birth to the theme of this book. I was about to conduct a case study on traditional African architecture when the series was featured on public television. The clarity of that program helped to define the theme of this book.

In turn, this book provides only a glance at the vast subject matter that could evolve from an investigation of Africa's architecture. The Triple Heritage Concept of Africa extends beyond politics to unique area such as architecture. That which remains to be analyzed far outweighs what has been analyzed and documented on this subject. Thus, this book presents an overview of historical African architecture as well as a sense of what can be done in Africa now, and in the future.

Actually, the concept of history in African architecture itself is not new. Rather, the problem lies in the fact that African architecture has only been studied at the regional and traditional levels with no reference either to antiquity or to contemporary architecture. Modern architecture, urbanism, and urbanization are all new topics that have not been explored in the context of Africa. This comprehensive and pioneering book, *African Architecture*, explores these new ideas within the context of the past and at the same time utilizes the most up-to-date information. I hope that readers and scholars will be inspired to investigate the subject further after reading this book.

Finally, this book meets the needs of multicultural education for secondary schools, colleges, and universities in the United States, and the increasing demand to bring other viewpoints to the classroom. Several schools of architecture around the country are already teaching the history of architecture from the viewpoints of non-Western cultures. I pay homage and respect to these scholars and practitioners in Africa and other parts of the world whose books and articles have begun to focus attention on African architecture: Professor Udo Kultermann, Olukemi Majekodunmi, Susan Denyer, J. C. Moughtin, Labelle Prussin, Peter Garlake, Professor David Aradeon, Suzan Aradeon, Gwendolyn Wright, Professor F. A. Abloh, Dr. J. B. Falade, G.W.A. Owusu, Professor Jan Vansina, Catherine Coquery-Vidrovitch, Fathy Hassan, David Hughes, Terri Plater, Baldwin Smith, Baj Bleguad Andersen, Basil Davidson, Picton-Seymour Desiree, Felix Dubois, Raphel Ekop, Jean-Paul Bourdier, Trint Minh-ha, G.J.A. Ojo, Margaret Piel, Professor Ali Mazrui, Dr. Michael Anda, Dr. Atamie-Abaraneye Obuoforibo, Dr. F. Funsho, Robert L. Easter, Michael A. Rogers, Jack Travis, Ronald E. Garner, Cheryl McAfee, Robert D. Washington, R. Steven Lewis, Felicia L. Hurst, William W. Adams, Tiffany Johnson, Andrew D. Chin, William J. Stanley, Ikechukwu Orji Daniel Iyang, and others whose names have not been mentioned here. These scholars and the varying views they espouse have been invaluable to African architecture as a discipline.

African Architecture is a team effort to which many people have contributed, especially the faculty and selective academic departments at the University of Wisconsin–Milwaukee. I am most grateful to Chancellor John Schroeder for his support. The faculty and academic staff of the School of Architecture and Urban Planning, University of Wisconsin–Milwaukee formed a historical academic army that helped to put this book together for Africa and the rest of the world: especially Professor Bob Greenstreet, Dean, School of Architecture and Urban Planning, Professor Kevin Forseth, Professor Don Hanlon, Professor Gil Snyder, Paul Mass, Professor Joe Stagg, Professor Tony Schnarsky, Professor Harry Van Oudenallen, Professor Jerry Weisman, Professor Sherry Arentzen, Professor Ernest Alexander, Mary Bates, Professor Jeff Ollswang, Audrey Maynard, Dennis Manley, Brian Wishne, Bill Huxhold, Thomas Hubka, Susan Wistrop, Professor Mike Utzinger, Professor Rick Jules, Professor James Shields, Professor Doug Ryhn, Professor David Reed, Peter Park, Janet Tibbetts, Simuncak Joan, Larry Witzling, Sherba Annabelle, Sandra Schroeder, Mark Roth, Professor Gary Moore, Sammis White, Professor James Dicker, Bonnie Harris, Dawn Miller, Ira Harris, Heather Day, Dee Pesek, Ernest Heftner, Anita Heftner, Carlos Trejo, and especially Paul Olsen, who prepared the photographs. I would also like to thank the staff at Golda Meir Library and the American Geographical Society, University of Wisconsin Milwaukee for their excellent services and support in fishing out research materials. Dr. Christopher Baruth, Jovanka Ristic, Susan Peschel, Howard Deller, Sharon Hill, Yvonne Bode, Helen Gray, Herta Nottelmann, Dean M. Aman, Jennifer Thelen, Jim A. Baxter, Dina Shohaib, Dr. Ruth Williams, Sara Zimmerman, Maribeth Stumph, Christine Omran, Jill S. Dittrich, Dina Shohayib, Yassir Elshashtawy, Mary Bates, Jeff Lackney, Malika Bose, Susan Field, Poly Taylorboyd, Dean Erland Olfe, Bud Haidet, Dr. J. Fries, Steven Antrim, Ron Hunter, Greg Carper. I would also like to thank my students for their support: Olofu Agbaji, Craig Green, Erica Young-Agbaji, Biron Jackson, Mark Mitchelle, Patric Easterline, Tim Ricks, Ray Perine, Mark Briggs, Corey Stettam, Eugene Sims, Hughes Michael, Ju Dawn Evans, Jen Lowe, Susan Chitka, Joe Sosan, Abimbola Odubiyi, Godwin Afoefi, Taiwo Amusa, Kahinde Amusa, Brandi Amusa, Lanre Amusa, Gace Amusa, Nurudeen Amusa, Matricia Patterson, Shannon LaRon Smith, Jutiki Smith, Walter Wilson, and Moyumi Takasuka.

Thanks to Dean Carmen Witt and her staff: Jim Hill, Ben Letwin, Merry Demske, Laura Murphy, Pat Prishman, Professor Udo Kultermann, Dr. Michael Anda, Dr. Funsho Fagbohun, Dr. Jessy Glass, Tabzeera Dosu, Emmanuel Dosu, Allan Persinger, Professor Mensah Aborampah, Professor Ron Edari, Professor Belgrade Smith, Professor Diane Pollard, Professor Cheryl Ajirotutu, Professor Frank Wilson, Paula Arnt, B. T. Sheth, Lenny Zubrensky, Ruth Zubrensky, Steve Zubrensky, Michael Zubrensky, Professor James Peoples, Larry Bell, Judy Brudd, Roberto Nodal, Cynthia Jill Cherny, Cynthia Bilmeryer, Jeff Hancox, Jeff Cartier, Diane Martin-Cartier, Marie-Helene Kana-Cox, Audrey Godwin, Tidwiler Sean, Deeta Bernstein, Joan Haas, Joe Haas, Libin He, Susan Otto, Portia Cobb, Neil and George Kendrik, architect Isaac Blair, Professor David Hughes, Benhard and Tina Brekke, Connie Crabb, Masato Sawaki, William Velez, Trinette Harris, Carolyn Ealy, Wilmer Ealy, Betty Ealy, Martha Ealy, and Mona Ealy, Dr. Ernest A. Wakefield, Heather McClure, Martle Freeman, Samuel Eyo, and Buake Fonfona.

I am also indebted to the following people for the help they rendered during the course of this project: Obinna Nwosu, Gabriel Agu, Akuma Ukaegbu, Ephraim Ozoemela, Nnamdi Udo, Nnamdi Henry Methu, Christopher Ezuma, Chima Igbo, Ifeanyi Agu Nnanna, Kalu Nnanna, Ikechukwi Jerry Orji, Leo Ngwaba, Omenihu Ngwaba, Chidi Ngwaba, Uzoma Ngwaba, Chief M. M. Owuma, Mr. Enekwa, Abera Gelan, Sefa Damte, Levi Uwasomba, Ignetious Okoronkwo, Emmanuel Enebelu, Elekwachi Eme, Gerald Obioma, Ndubuisi Ogele, Chief Eyee, and Kiathy Nelson-Ellison, Fidelis and Deen Omegbu, Alfred Iringeri, Tom and Winnie Dineen, Pauline Jascur, Anwana Eneifiok, Gabriel and Nikki Okafor, Judy K. Lloyd, Caprise E. Compton, Amy I. Powell, Keith Brown, Janel Hetland, Paul Williams, Sherlley Davidow, Caroline Hart, Mathew Kostev, Olanrene Ladipo, Mika Imai, Amy Parish, and Amy Green.

My gratitude to Chioma Elleh and my family members for traveling around to collect photographs for this project: Chief Joseph Kadumeh Elleh, Charity Elleh, Felisha Elleh, Egwuma Elleh, Joe Elleh, Ejikeme Elleh, Olupapa Elleh, Destiny Elleh, Cheta Elleh, Chibudom Ishiuka Elleh, Emeka Chukwuemeha Elleh, Lily Elleh, Benice Elleh, Helen Okwukou Elleh, Gloria Okwukou Elleh, Sylvanus Elleh, Ino Ochogu Elleh, Fawe Elleh, Major Elleh, Sylvaline Elleh, Queen Elleh, Princess Domaz Wilbourn, Dee Wilbourn, Lena Taylor, Jacques Taylor, Rodney Lott, Ricky Lott, Schanara Lott, Gbadegesin Bamidele, Kolade Bamidele, Tayo Bamidele, Lorelle Semley, Christopher Nwonye, Benedicta Nwonye, Ndidi Okonkwo, Una-Unoaku Okonkwo, Motolani Ogunleye, Claudia Orugbani, Clinton Orugbani, Rochelle Vandi, Nyadeigoi Vandi, and Kenyeih Vandi.

I am most grateful to Joyce Miezin whose patience and professional leadership helped to bring this manuscript to fruition. I cannot thank Judy Lasca enough for spending many hours editing this book. I have been a headache to the staff at the Africana Library, and the Special Collections at Northwestern University, Evanston, Illinois, but they have always responded to my demands with kindness. Especially, Patricia Ogedengbe, David Easterline, Daniel Britz, Angela Johnson, Reinessa Neuhalfen, Shayne Mette, Russel Maylone, Scott Krafft, Sigrid Perry, Susan Lewis, Rochelle Elstein, and Sharon Smith. Thanks to the faculty at the Department of Art History, and the staff at the Program of African Studies (P.A.S), Northwestern University, Evanston, Illinois, for their support—Professor Hollis Clayson, Professor Whitney David, Professor Sandra Hindman, Professor Ikem Okoye, Professor Angela Rosenthal, Professor Larry Silver, Professor Michael Stone-Richards, Professor David Van Zanten, Professor K.O. Wercmeister, Professor David Mickenberg, Professor Carl W. Condit, Professor Betty I. Monroe, Shane Smith, Chris Kahler, Beth Zopf, Maura Costa, Sylvester Ogbechie, Aron Vinegar, Bronwen Wilson, Rebecca Parker, Vivian Rehberg, Nina Rowe, Ming Tiampo, Jennifer Lewin, Sarah Miller, Natalie Adamson, David Areford, Michael Batterman, Wendy Bellion, Sarah Betzer, Sheila Crane, Jane Friedman, David Getsy, Amelia Rauser, Jane Guyer, Akbar Virmani, Rosean Mark, Karyn Hernandez, and Maureen Okoli. Thanks to editors at McGraw-Hill Professional Books—Wendy K. Lochner, Penny Linskey, and all the staff who worked on this project. I wish to mention that while I have received much help and many suggestions when I was working on this project, all the faults in it are no one else's but mine.

INTRODUCTION

Africa gives the architectural historian and anybody who enjoys art and architecture an opportunity to study architectural history from a perspective that celebrates human history and the achievements of various world civilizations. The location of the continent in relation to Europe, Asia, and North and South America made Africa a magnetic center for human interaction and dissemination of culture since ancient times. The most common interactions are those among the indigenous cultures of African peoples and those imported from the Arabian Peninsula and Europe. Such cultural legacies are also reflected in the architecture of the continent. The presence of three major cultural factors in African architecture creates enormous problems for the architectural historian due to the lack of written records documenting the degree of interaction among these groups.

However, the architectural historian and readers in general still benefit by undertaking studies of this scope in spite of the complexity because such studies tell us more about ourselves and give credence to the oneness of humanity in our spiritual beliefs and historical origin. Architecture, as an art and science that shapes the environment, is one of the methods utilized by humanity in the elevation of the human spirit, and there are more ancient monuments in Africa representing the human search for eternal life than on any other continent. It is, therefore, no coincidence that Africa, where three major cultures converge, tells us more about our past than do most parts of the world. Hence, the results of L. S. B. Leakey's excavations at Olduvai Gorge transcend time. They are evidence of the historical origin of humanity, not just skeletal remains. The hypotheses and theories advanced by archaeologists from this material help us analyze the patterns of architecture and technology from the various regions of the continent and explain their relationship and influence on other areas of the world.

The history of African architecture is a complex and vast topic to cover in one book because of the continent's size. Africa has an area of about 11,700,000 mi^2, more than three times that of the United States, including Alaska. About 80 percent of the continent lies within the tropics and has more distinct peoples and cultures than any other continent.

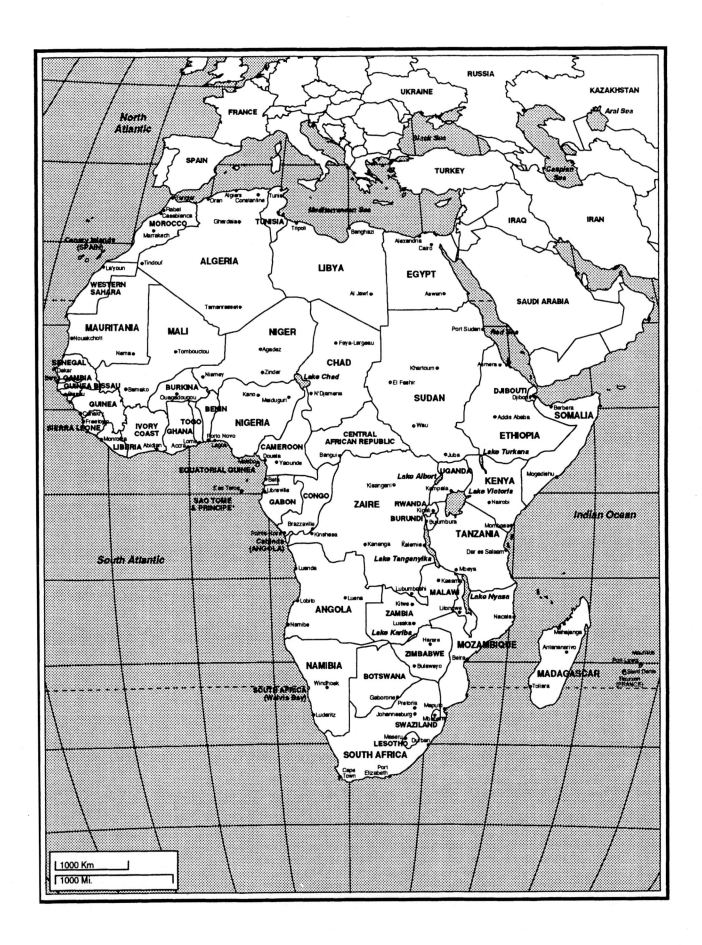

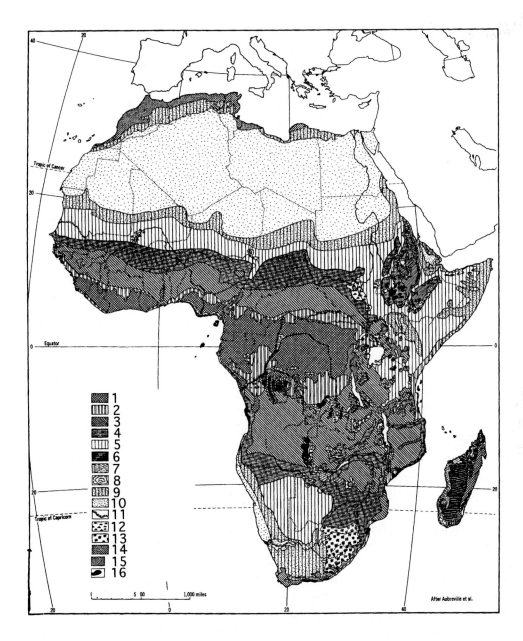

Fig. I.2 Vegetation
distribution in Africa:
(1) tropical rainforest,
(2) forest-savanna mosaic,
(3) relatively moist woodlands
and savanna, (4) relatively dry
woodlands and savanna,
(5) wooded steppe, (6) grass
savanna and grass steppe,
(7) dry deciduous forest and
savanna, (8) thickets,
(9) subdesert steppe,
(10) desert, (11) mangroves,
(12) swamps, (13) temperate
and subtropical grass,
(14) mediterranean vegetation,
(15) montane grassland and
undifferentiated,
(16) evergreen forest.

The complexity shrouding African architecture is partly due to variations in landscape and climate that influenced settlement patterns and building culture all over the continent. Africa has over 50 countries and at least five major geographical zones based on rainfall and vegetation (see Figs. I.1 and I.2). Geographers have identified different geographical zones in Africa, though with some variation. William A. Hance (1975) listed the following: tropical rainforest, forest-savanna mosaic, relatively moist woodlands and savanna, relatively dry woodlands and savanna, wooded steppe, grass savanna and grass

Fig. I.1 (Opposite) Political map of Africa.
(Chioma Elleh)

steppe, thickets, subdesert, desert, mangroves, swamps, temperate and subtropical grass, mediterranean vegetation, montane grassland, and undifferentiated and evergreen forest. Building construction in Africa is determined to a great extent by the distribution of natural building materials and climate.

The desert vegetation regions, for example, are more arid with less moisture, lots of dust, and hot, dry temperatures that are usually characterized by high intensity sunlight. The evergreen forests are usually characterized by extreme rainfall, hot, humid weather, and stable temperature ranges. These contrasts gave or contributed to the manner in which traditional African societies used and continue to use building materials and the way architecture developed in different regions. Buildings in dry regions are more likely to have sun-dried brick as primary cladding material than buildings in the forest zones that utilize both sun-dried brick and timber. The earthwork found all over Africa is commonly referred to as "mud houses" because the adobe work is not done in the traditional Western building method or the walls are raised when the brick material is still wet. This has a negative connotation that distracts from the quality of the finished houses. African architecture is a product of many factors including geography, cultural heritage and assimilation, developmental policies, religious crusades, and political conquests.

PROBLEMS IN AFRICAN HISTORY

There are many benefits in undertaking studies of African architectural history on this scale, but major problems still confront historians who write about the continent. Scholars such as Collins (1968), Seligman (1968), Lucas (1968), and Meyerowitz (1968) have recognized the significance of such problems in African history.

The first problem is that of ancient Egyptian origins and their influences in Africa. The study of this problem ranges from religious influences to architecture, agriculture, kingship customs, and linguistic influences. One school of thought believes that ancient Egypt was entirely a European civilization with Asiatic influences, whereas the other camp insists that Egypt was an indigenous African civilization that was Europeanized toward its later years.

Henry (1965, 23) stated that "some historians would like to give Egypt back to Africa and to re-examine its history, starting from the South, and not from the North or North-West." Professor Bernal (1987, 250) commented that "racism was, from the beginning, an important factor in the downplaying of the Egyptians and the dismissal of the Ancient Model, and after 1860 it became the overriding one." On the other hand, Egypt was excluded from the rest of Africa when it became popular to associate the country with the development of Western civilization.

There is a presumptuous belief that Africans do not have the ability to build any magnificent structure and that any architectural monument in Africa is of Euro-Asian origin. Most eminent 18th- and 19th-century European historians and philosophers advanced this concept without restraint. In 1854, Georg Wilhelm Friedrich Hegel observed that, "Africa is not an historical continent; it shows neither change nor development, and whatever may have happened there belongs to the world of Asia and Europe...." (Davidson 1992, xvi; Garlake 1990, 28). Attitudes like these persisted into the mid-20th century. Even as late as 1961, the British historian Hugh Trevor Roper wrote, "At present there is no African

history: there is only the history of Europeans in Africa, the rest is darkness..." (Garlake 1990, 28).

To placate this historical viewpoint, the 18th- and 19th-century Western historian often excludes some parts of Africa, adopting the convenient opinion that Africa is a "dark continent illuminated only along the Nile Valley and the North Coast by people who were at least partially Mediterranean" (Pothorn 1982, 122). North Africa has been excluded from studies of African art and architecture even in recent times because of its exposure to the Mediterranean and its traditions of *iokoumenical* art, from the Greek expression *oikoumenikos* meaning "the whole world." But as Professor Jan Vansina (1984) points out, we cannot amputate half of Africa and then call a portion of what remains "African art" and architecture. In addition, Diop (1974, xiv) states that passing ancient Egyptian civilization as a purely Mediterranean achievement while discussing African history is like trying to "write the history of Europe without referring to Greco-Latin antiquity and trying to pass that off as a scientific approach."

Emotions run high among Pan-Africanist scholars who believe that ancient Egypt was a Black African civilization. These Pan-Africanists believe that "the history of black Africa will remain suspended in air and cannot be written correctly until African historians dare to connect it with the history of Egypt" (Diop 1974, xiv). On the other hand, there are Eurocentric historians who believe in the Aryan model. These historians recognize and believe in the glamours of Pharaonic Egypt, the Phoenicians, the ruins of Minos and Mycenae, Greece, and Rome without giving any credit to their black African Egyptian origins. To these historians, it is unthinkable for the crown jewels of Western civilization—Greece and Rome—to have African roots (Bernal 1987, 224). Contributions of Africa to the development of Western civilization should not be taken for granted because "they were simply the result of the fact that—as everyone knows, Plato, Pythagoras and Orpheus had taken their ideas from Egypt" (Bernal 1987, 118). Therefore, any relationship between Mediterranean art and African art points to the fact that there is a long history of cultural exchange between Africa and the West. The cultures have been assimilated very deeply on both sides to the extent that it is sometimes difficult to tell what cultures originated from Africa and those that originated from Europe.

According to Bernal (1987, 189), in the 18th century four major forces encouraged the destruction of African history in Europe. They are: Christian reaction, the rise of the concept of progress, the growth of racism, and Romantic Hellenism. The forces reinforced the historical viewpoint that Africa south of the Sahara has no history by down-playing the significance of Egyptian culture to world civilization. In addition, the changed structure of Egypt's racial composition after hundreds of years of European and Arabian immigration allowed its European admirers to claim that it was essentially and originally white. The concept of progress condemned Egyptian antiquities and scientific achievements by designating Egypt a relic of the past which has no place in the growth of modern civilization. On the other hand, the relics found in Greece were admired and uplifted as progressive culture and examples for the advancement of European culture and civilization. Bernal (1987, 190) concluded that "racism and `progress' could thus come together in the condemnation of Egyptian/African stagnation and praise of Greek/European dynamism and change."

This conflict of opinions does not erase archaeological and historical facts that substantiate the Africanness of the Old and Middle Kingdoms of ancient Egypt and of the inevitable cultural and racial mix that followed the Alexandrian conquest of 333 B.C. in the Later Kingdom. This cultural mix is also reflected in the architecture of the continent and is further supported by written documents from classical history. "In classical times the Egyptians were seen as both black and white or yellow; Herodotus referred to them as having black skins and wooly hair" (Bernal 1987, 242). Therefore, it is plausible to conclude that many of the most powerful Egyptian dynasties based in Upper Egypt—the 1st, 3rd, 4th, 11th, 12th, and 18th—were made up of Pharaohs whom one can usefully call Negro. In all likelihood, this segment of problems in African history will be resolved along lines similar to Bernal (1987, 437): "I am happy to be in the excellent company of Dubois, Mazrui and others who, while they do not picture all Ancient Egyptians as resembling today's West Africans, do see Egypt as essentially African."

The second major problem is that of the migrations and the peopling of Africa south of the Sahara Desert by Bantu and Nilotic language speakers. The origins of the Bantu and the Nilotic language speakers are yet to be resolved. Linguists and other social scientists have conflicting hypotheses. This linguistic problem also relates to the disputed origins of Africa's medieval empires such as those of Ghana, Kilwa, Aksum, and Zimbabwe. The question is whether these empires developed indigenously or because of outsider immigration.

The question of immigration becomes an issue in African history wherever a major civilization is found. Different kinds of obviously contradicting racial terminologies are often applied while discussing such African civilizations, and the conclusion often drawn is that the civilization is due to outside influence. The Portuguese and Germans attributed Great Zimbabwe to Asians when they first got there in the 15th century. The civilization of Aksum in Ethiopia has been ascribed to Arab immigrants even when there is no record or date of Arab immigration to Aksum at the beginning of the civilization. Three major foreign immigrations to Africa are on record and can be readily verified. The first was by the Greeks after the Alexandrian conquest of 333 B.C. The Greeks flocked to Africa in large number and worked hard to become African citizens so that they could be accepted by the indigenous African people, including Alexander the Great who adopted the African god Amon-Ra as his father in order to legitimize his ascendancy to the kingship of the African kingdom of Egypt. The next major settlement of Europeans in Africa was from 146 B.C., after Roman conquest of Carthage and Egypt, until about 100 years later in 40 B.C. We know of Roman settlements by the monuments they left in Africa. Finally, there was the major Arab immigration in mid-7th century A.D. after Islam was founded, and it was obviously the beginning of Arabization and Islamization of North Africa.

The Persian conquest of Egypt in 525 B.C., the Turks in 16th century A.D., and the French under Napoleon at the end of the 19th century should also be mentioned. There is also the union of the Queen of Sheba and King Solomon which resulted in the black Jews of Ethiopia or the Falashas. There is absolutely no record that shows Arabian immigration to Ethiopia besides the Muslim migration in the 7th century, long after Aksum had been in existence.

In spite of these documented historical facts, there are scholars who insist that "the history of Ethiopia may be said to begin in Arabia" (Perham 1968, 290). Perham stated that there is a Hamitic group in Africa, who are also known as Cushites. They include the Gallas, Somalis, Danakil, and Kaffas, and they began the Aksum civilization after they migrated from Arabia. These groups named by Perham can be found in more than one place in Africa. Perham goes on to note that linguistic affinity between the Semites and Hamites makes them Europeans: "Both groups are Caucasian and thus belong to the same branch of the human race as the great majority of Europeans. For this reason the Hamites are sometimes called Eurafrican" (Perham 1968, 290). Finally, Perham describes the Hamitic Ethiopian, especially those who have "not been modified by the mixture of Negro blood," as having well cut noses, curly hair, long heads, and "a general Caucasian appearance, the color varying between brown and black" (Perham 1968, 291). Having manufactured all these "Eurafricans," Perham concludes that Aksum must be attributed to them because the Negroes couldn't have been able to build such a civilization. Hence, Aksum is seen not as an African civilization, but as an Arabian civilization in Africa.

Margery Perham is not the only scholar who advocates the Arabian genesis of Aksum. Scholars like Buston (1967, 22) and Ulendorff (1960, 49) do as well. Evidence of cultural exchange between Aksum and people from South Arabia cannot be dismissed totally because the Horn of Africa had always been a major trading center since the period of ancient Egypt when Egyptian merchants went to Punt for spices, incense, gold, ivory, and other goods. Regardless, it is not enough to explain an immigration wave that never took place. Such propositions only succeed in diminishing the achievements of the African people.

In addition, scholars often explain the relationship between ancient Egypt and the surrounding civilizations in terms of colonizer and the colonized or Egyptian races (colonizers) versus other African races (colonized). This is a militarist explanation of relationships that were actually tribal wars, and its purpose is to isolate Egypt from the plethora of ancient African civilizations. There is a serious problem with the militarist approach—it does not consider the concept of historical continuity in Africa as it does in European history.

For example, Roman colonization of Greece is not perceived as a superior race (Romans) colonizing an inferior race (Greeks); rather it is analyzed as the continuity of European history. All cultural exchanges between Rome and Greece are European. This method of regional relationship analysis should be applied to the relationship between ancient Egypt and her neighbors such as Aksum, Punt, and Meroe.

Finally, there are the problems of slavery, precolonial Africa, and colonialism. The debate centers on the question of how much damage was done to Africa by slavery and colonialism, or whether colonialism itself civilized Africa. Leo Frobenius (Haberland 1973, 58), a German explorer who traveled in Africa at the turn of the century, cites European merchant reports of black Africa from the 15th to the 17th century as a "flowering civilized culture" with beautiful cities and lots of wealth. He saw slavery and colonization as instruments of oppression and underdevelopment that also required a rewriting of history. The New World needed slaves, something Africa had in abundance, and the traffic in human beings was necessarily difficult to explain. "It demanded justification. So the Negro was transformed into a semi-animal, an article of trade. So the term *Fetish* (a Portuguese word for *Feticeiro*) was invented as the symbol of the African religion (Haberland 1973, 58).

The issue of slavery widens the dimensions of problems in African history. Africans residing outside the continent get caught in the debate because they rightfully recognize that they are African diaspora and that the interpretation of their history in the New World depends to a large extent on a clear understanding of their historical origin. The keynote speech and other presentations at the 23rd (October 7–10, 1993) Annual Conference of the National Organization of Minority Architects in the United States focused on "Afrocentric Architecture and the African Diaspora." *Newsweek* magazine's cover story on September 23, 1991, began with the question WAS CLEOPATRA BLACK? written in bold, 1-in letters over a glittering portrait of Empress Cleopatra. The article went on to discuss "Facts or Fantasies, A Debate Rages Over What

to Teach Our Kids About Their Roots." These few examples underscore the significance of the problems in African history and how they have spilled over into academic issues affecting nations outside the continent of Africa.

It is important that, within the framework of a verifiable thesis, society at large be educated on the subject of Afrocentricity in architecture and in other fields of study as well. Afrocentricity will lose its legitimacy if used only as a tool for the advancement of an exclusive ethnocentric agenda instead of as a curriculum open to all who are interested. In addition, as in all other fields, Afrocentricity should be open to debate and criticism because such exchange will advance our knowledge of the subject. Afrocentricity must not become a dogmatic belief in the advancement of an academic antithesis to the forefront as an alternative approach to history. Those who advocate this approach would be as wrong as their predecessors who rigged history to further personal agendas, and the subject itself would become fertile ground for the exploitation of chaotic, bogus ideas by extremists on either end of the spectrum. Therefore, if it is to be accepted and legitimized, the theme of Afrocentrism must be embracing rather than divisive.

These problems relate to architecture because architecture is one of the most visible symbols of statehood and civilization. As a result, the questions of who built what, who migrated from where, whether ancient Egyptians were African, and whether slavery and colonialism retarded the development of architecture are significant in African history and make the subject more complex.

Political residues from these problems have been obstacles to the study of the history of African architecture. Especially in Africa, architecture as a profession, architects themselves, and the general public all lose in this complex situation. Lewis (1987, 43) posits a remedy: "The answer of what could architects do lies in the answer to what could architects be…in their wider applications of creative thinking." The ongoing debates clearly suggest that there are obviously historical inconsistencies and omissions in need of review and inclusion in existing architectural scholarship. A starting point would be to retrieve and study the omitted information and to find new meanings and hypotheses that would advance the study of architectural history. African architecture gives us this opportunity.

THE BEGINNING OF NEW THINKING IN AFRICAN HISTORY: THE "AFRICAN PLACE"

The Canadian Universal and International Exhibition of 1967 was an important occasion that gave African countries a place among the nations of the world. Unlike other exhibitions,

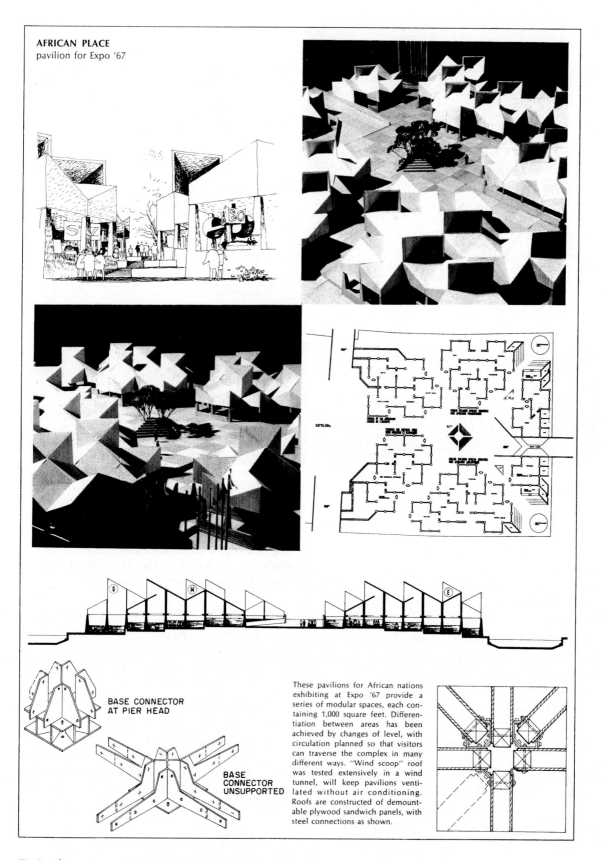

AFRICAN PLACE
pavilion for Expo '67

BASE CONNECTOR
AT PIER HEAD

BASE
CONNECTOR
UNSUPPORTED

These pavilions for African nations exhibiting at Expo '67 provide a series of modular spaces, each containing 1,000 square feet. Differentiation between areas has been achieved by changes of level, with circulation planned so that visitors can traverse the complex in many different ways. "Wind scoop" roof was tested extensively in a wind tunnel, will keep pavilions ventilated without air conditioning. Roofs are constructed of demountable plywood sandwich panels, with steel connections as shown.

Fig. I.3 Plan, section, perspective, and model of African Place pavilion for Canadian Expo 1967. (John Andrews International)

Fig. I.4 *African Place pavilion. 1967.* (*John Andrews International*)

which represented African countries as European colonial estates, the Canadian Corporation for the 1967 World Exhibition established African Place (Figs. I.3 and I.4), a complex for African countries to express their sovereignty and cultures. Mali, Senegal, Guinea, Madagascar, Tanzania, Kenya, Uganda, Gambia, Sierra Leone, Malawi, Niger, Togo, Cote d'Ivoire, Benin, Burkina Fasso, Gabon, Cameroon, Chad, Central African Republic, Republic of Congo, Liberia, Burundi, and Zaire (former Belgian Congo-Leopoldville) took part in the exhibition.

According to John Andrews, chief architect of the African Place, "In this showplace of nations, Africa has her rightful place (Andrews 1967, 2)." Andrews gave the participating African nations separate exhibition spaces defined by changes of levels between each pavilion and by special entrances for each country. For these young nations struggling to find their national identity, this was an opportunity to exhibit national flags and icons free of the supremacy of the national flags and icons of their former colonizers.

LAYING A FOUNDATION FOR THE HISTORY OF AFRICAN ARCHITECTURE: THE TRIPLE HERITAGE CONCEPT

Scholars around the world are beginning to look at African architecture with interest, and publications are now trickling in from many directions. Still, it is difficult to discuss African architecture as a subject because the publications continuously conflict with one another.

Professor Ali Mazrui's concept of "the African, a triple heritage," however, is comprehensive enough to provide the foundation for studying African architecture. His concept embraces all the components that form African history: indigenous, Islamic, and Western. African architecture from ancient times to the present mirrors these triple cultural legacies and cannot be understood without this realization.

Contemporary Africa's triple heritage of indigenous, Islamic, Western legacies is just the modern culmination of a much older triple heritage—the heritage of indigenous, Semitic and Greco-Roman influences in Africa. The ancient Semitic strand has now narrowed and focused more firmly on Arab and Islamic influences; the ancient Greco-Roman strand has now expanded to encompass wider European and American intrusions. (Mazrui 1986, 81)

This book extends these three major components of African heritage to the field of architecture by identifying major historical epochs and landmarks that can help readers gain an understanding of African architecture. Some of these issues are outside the scope of this book, but it is necessary to review them in order to give a comprehensive understanding of the roots of the triple heritage of architecture and of how deeply these separate cultures have permeated African culture and its built environment.

This triple cultural heritage is embedded in the conscious and unconscious minds of the African people and is manifest in art, music, religious ceremonies, politics, and architecture. For example, I recently witnessed a Nigerian wedding in which the bride was a devoted Muslim and the groom a devoted Catholic. The groom, who has a doctorate in political science, and the bride, who holds a master's degree in mass communications, were first married traditionally, according to the customs of the Igbira people of middle-belt Nigeria, in their homeland. The groom paid his dowry as required by the Igbira culture, and an elder of the extended family presided over the wedding, poured libations, and made incantations to the spirits of the ancestors to bless the couple. Next, they had a large wedding in a Catholic church, even though the bride was still a devoted Muslim. She did not see any contradiction in keeping her Muslim faith after wedding a Catholic devotee—the groom. The occasion demonstrated that Africans are culturally immersed in three identical, but separate, cultures that are sometimes difficult to distinguish. By virtue of being Africans, this well-educated and talented couple automatically inherited three cultures: indigenous African, Islamic, and Judeo-Christian. Their wedding ceremonies were both traditional and highly identified with the West, demonstrating that Mazrui's concept of a triple heritage is an African reality. Many urban landscapes and customs as well as historical documentation testify to its accuracy. The triple heritage culture can be traced to its origin in early settlements in Africa.

The development of agriculture around the Nile Valley led to the development of built settlements. Most of those early settlements grew as cloisters of homes around chieftain houses, tribal totems, and shrines, as can be found in several parts of Africa today. Geometrically designed towns began to surface much later. The city for the dead built by Pharaoh Senwosret

in the 12th Dynasty and the well-preserved cities of Tell al-Amarna (Akhenaten) and Kahun (Fig. I.5) are examples from the remote past. Altogether, Africa presents a variety of urban landscapes. The existence of cities like ancient Benin in Nigeria and the fascination of the imperial kingdoms of the Congo Basin with the geometrically planned city must be noted. Most of the capital cities of the Congo Basin were moved due to shifting cultivation and leadership changes, but the chief architects re-created the plans of the original capital wherever it was relocated. A good example is the Kuba capital in the Congo. Vansina (1984, 59) notes that "although the Kuba capital was not permanent, precise measurements for every street, and for the positioning of every public building in or out of the palace, of every plaza, of every private compound, were kept as a plan by the architects, recreating similar effects wherever the capital went."

In southern Africa, numerous stone walled defensive enclaves existed both as seats of governments and as military garrisons and homesteads. These early walled towns shared some fundamental characteristics with their Central African,

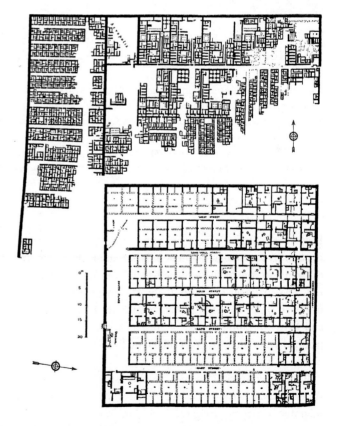

Fig. I.5 Plans of the cities of Tell al-Amarna by Amenhotep IV, 1372–1354 B.C., and Kahun by Senwosret II, 1906–1888 B.C. (E. Baldwin Smith and D. Appleton-Century Company)

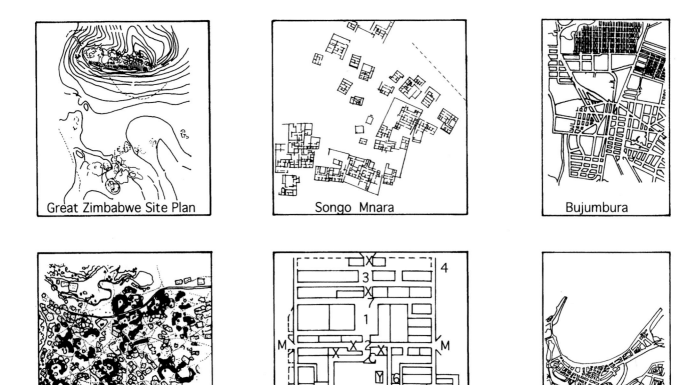

Fig. I.6 Plans of triple heritage cities of Africa. Left to right: Great Zimbabwe, Zimbabwe (indigenous, 1000 A.D.); Songo Mnara, Kenya (Islamic influence, 15th century A.D.); Bujumbura, Burundi (early 20th century, Western influence); a typical Tswana village with Kgotlas, Botswana; Kuba capital Nsheng (indigenous, 19th century) (1) great square; (2) square of the crossroads; (3) square mbweengy; (4) square of the crown council; (5) square of the royal dynasty; (6) royal drum; (7) yon drum; M markets; C Daily council square; Y private council square; Z harem square; and Luanda, Angola (20th century, Portuguese-Western influence).

East African, and West African counterparts until the introduction of the foreign cultures of Islam and Christianity. At this juncture the triple heritage becomes clear (Figs. I.6 and I.7). The character of the southern African cities reflects the presence of an indigenous African culture, Islamic culture, and Westernization and is often marked by geometrically planned cities that are very different from the indigenous cities.

Based on historical documents, the Semitic strand of the African triple heritage culture began with Abraham who migrated to Egypt during the New Kingdom (about 1640 to 1230 B.C.) with members of his family, 70 altogether. He lived in Egypt, prospered, and enjoyed privileges afforded to all Egyptians. Many of his grandchildren held important positions at the Royal Court.

This ancient marriage between Africa and the Israelis leaves many visible cultural strands that are manifest in African architecture and religion. The Falashas of Ethiopia, who descend from King Solomon and the Queen of Sheba, also demonstrate the long history of cultural and intellectual exchange between Judeo-Christendom and Africa. For example, Ben-Jochannan (1988, 24) draws our attention to the fact that most, if not all, of the teachings of King Solomon were copied from an ancient collection of poetry by indigenous African kings. The Book of Proverbs, which we attribute to King Solomon, came from the teachings and poems of Pharaoh Amen-em-ope (1405–1370 B.C.). A comparison between verses from Pharaoh Amen-em-ope's poems and those of King Solomon's Proverbs, Chapter XXII, verses 17–29, demonstrates this connection. The reader should be

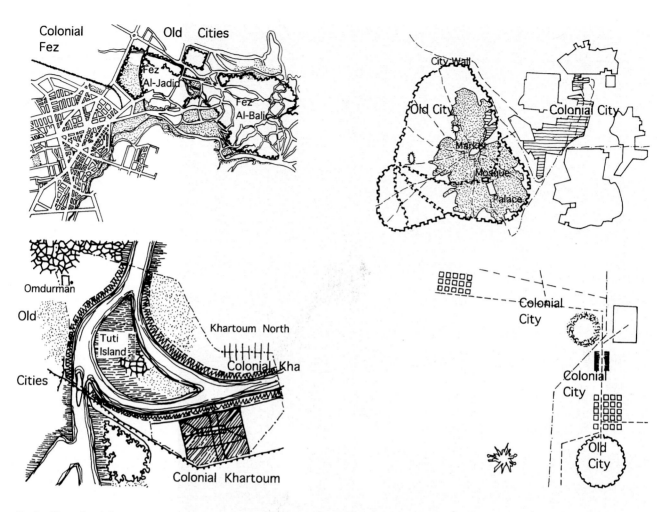

Fig. I.7 *Plans of triple heritage cities of Africa with indigenous, Islamic, and Western sections. Left to right: Fez, Morocco; Kano, Nigeria; Khartoum, Republic of Sudan; Zaria, Nigeria.*

aware that these verses may be in slightly different words depending on which translation of the Bible is used.

THE TEACHINGS OF AMEN-EM-OPE, PHARAOH OF EGYPT (1405–1370 B.C.)

Give thine ear and hear what I say and apply thine heart to apprehend; it is good for you to place them in thine heart, let them rest in the casket of the belly...

A scribe who is skilful in his business findeth himself worthy to be a courtier.

PROVERBS OF KING SOLOMON (976–936 B.C.)

Incline thine ear, and hear my words, and apply thine heart to apprehend; For it is pleasant if thou keep them in thine belly, that they may be fixed upon thy lips...

A man who is skilful in his business shall stand before kings.

Recent foreign policy decisions by the Israeli government have acknowledged the triple heritage and ancient connection between Israel and Africa in the most pragmatic manner. The Israeli government carried out several major airlifts code-named "Operations Moses and Solomon" between 1988 and 1991 to move some Ethiopian Jews [Falashas] to Israel before the collapse of the Marxist government led by Colonel Mengistu Hail-Mariam. Pankhurst (1992, 567) writes that "in Ethiopia, the two religions, Christianity and Judaism, blended in a manner virtually unknown elsewhere in Christendom." He cited the fact that every Ethiopian church has a tabot, the symbolic representation of the Mosaic Ark of the Covenant, and several records of kings from the Ethiopian chronicles who claim descent from King Solomon.

In later times, Byzantine Christians aggressively stamped out all aspects of traditional African religion practiced in classical Egypt before the spread of Christianity and the coming

Fig. C.1 Luxor, Egypt. Hagaag Mosque built on the ruins of a church inside an ancient African temple of Amon-Ra. Building materials and construction techniques were taken from the African temple for the construction of the demolished church and mosque. 600 A.D. (Yasser Elshashtawy)

of Islam. The destruction of ancient African religion in Egypt was carried out in the name of Christianity, which looked down on Egyptian religion as pagan worship and idolatry. Christians considered the giant ancient temples of Egypt as threats to their faith and erected a Christian monastery in the Temple of Amon at Luxor (Fig. C.1). Stones were quarried from the temple for the construction of the monastery, where a prototype temple was built to serve Christian needs.

The corruption and excessive flexibility of the new Christian faith were distasteful to Prophet Muhammad who preferred Mosaic law over the liberal laws of the Christian Church. He, therefore, patterned Islam mainly on the Old Testament. In a rage, the Muslims pulled down the monastery in the Temple of Amon to build the Hagaag Mosque, thus completing the African cultural triangle: an indigenous African temple of the sun god houses a Judeo-Christian monastery, which later becomes the foundation of a mosque for Islamic worship.

It is important to mention that modern Christianity in Africa is largely a product of 19th- and 20th-century European missionaries, except in Ethiopia where ancient Coptic Christianity is the widely accepted practice. Its roots

Fig. I.8 A tomb for Ngouan Amakou at Apprompronou, Cote d'Ivoire. 1975. The angels and the policeman holding a pistol are influences of the West on African art and architecture. (Janel Hetland)

are in Greco-Roman via Judeo-Christian Antioch, Roman imperialism in North Africa, and later European Columbian expansionism. According to Professor Mazrui (1986), Ethiopian Christianity is the oldest in black Africa and the most unusual because it incorporates Judaism and Christianity as the first Jewish Christians did immediately after the death of Christ.

This triple heritage is completed by the traditional aspects of African culture, which are rooted in ancestor worship. Ancestor worship believes in life after death and the omnipresence of ancestors as divine beings and mediators between humanity and the Supreme Being, the Universal God who alone rules the universe with all his powers. Ayisi (1979) said that one function of the ancestor cult is the prescription of appropriate rites for contact with ancestors and the spirit world. This belief in the spirit world does not negate the belief in a Supreme Being. For example, the Ashanti of Ghana have religious ceremonies that invoke several intermediary spirits of the ancestors but still recognize and venerate a Supreme Being who is above all deities and animates them all. This is actually a later version of the concept of monotheism, which the Ashanti took with them from Egypt and the rest of the Nile Valley as they spread across the continent. According to Meyerowitz (1968, 35), "The cult of the King as the Son of the Sun-god among the Akan (of Ghana) is evidently derived from the Middle Kingdom, for their Sun-god Nyankopon has all the characteristics of Amon-Ra of Thebes." Lucas (1968, 34) advances Meyerowitz's observations by stating that "the names of most of the Yoruba deities are survivals of the names of Egyptian deities. This is the case also with West African tribes," while Seligman (1968, 25) concludes that "this view does not imply that all the features common to Ancient Egypt and present-day Negroes are

Fig. I.9 Dodassue, Cote d'Ivoire. A tomb for Kouadio Dongo. An angel and a policeman pray and guard the shrine while the drummers call the spirit of the ancestor. The lion is not just a symbol of power but also a tribal totem. (Janel Hetland)

instances of borrowing; on the contrary, I hold that many common customs are but expressions of wide diffusion of old Hamitic blood and ideas."

Africans see no contradiction in the triple heritage triangle. They pragmatically adopted it and adapted to it in all aspects of their lives to varying degrees, depending on whether they lived within a predominantly Christian, Muslim, or traditional society. For example, some mausoleums in eastern Cote d'Ivoire (Figs. I.8 and I.9) incorporate Christian, Judaic, Islamic, and ancestral symbolism. It is interesting to note that these mausoleums were designed and built by local artisans who did not receive formal architectural training but had a good understanding and acceptance of the cross, the holy angels of Christianity, the star and the crescent, and the ancestors to whom they dedicate the grave and pray for protection and guidance. The fundamental issue here is that the triple heritage of Africa is a cultural reality that influences the lives of Africans and forms a strong foundation for studying the history of African architecture.

THE BOOK

African Architecture provides a comprehensive account of the evolution, transformation, and development of African architecture. It covers historical, traditional, and contemporary African architecture by looking at the various cultural groups of Africa from ethnic, climatic, political, regional, economic, religious, and historical viewpoints.

This book defines and identifies the three major roots of African architecture: indigenous; Islamic, which arrived in North Africa in 700 A.D.; and Western, which arrived in Africa first in 146 B.C. when Rome invaded Carthage and subsequently in early 1300 A.D. when the Portuguese sailed around the west coast of Africa in search of a trade route to the Orient. This is one of the first books to look at African architecture as an area of study from historical and theoretical perspectives. The subject matter covers the entire continent and explains why there are various forms of African architecture.

ORGANIZATION

African Architecture is organized in six parts. Each part has chapters which deal with related topics. Emphasis is given to the urban design of major cities and to the character of the architecture in cities. The reader is given a brief history of the architecture of African countries from the ancient to the contemporary. This book takes into account the fact that African architecture cannot be discussed in a single volume because

of the large area and time frame involved. However, the most available information is utilized to give the reader a clear understanding of African architecture from earliest times to the present.

PART 1: DEFINING AFRICAN ARCHITECTURE

The main purpose of this section is to define African architecture. The scope of the history of African architecture is presented by tracing its traditional, Islamic, and Western origins.

PART 2: NORTH AFRICAN ARCHITECTURE

The objective of Part 2 is to elaborate on the architecture of North African countries. Emphasis is on the cities and their urban designs, especially civic centers that are landmarks. Chapter 4 covers the architecture of Morocco; Chapter 5 discusses the architecture of Algeria, Libya, and Tunisia; Chapter 6 is about the architecture of Egypt. The existence of indigenous, traditional African architecture from Egyptian antiquities to the architecture of modern times, the influence of Islam from 700 A.D., and the infiltration of Western architecture from imperial Rome to the more recent medieval contacts give North African architecture a triple heritage root. The Mediterranean nations of Morocco, Algeria, Tunisia, Libya, and Egypt are predominantly Islam, but this does not make their architecture the same. Each country's architecture is unique because of different historical experiences.

PART 3: CENTRAL AND EAST AFRICAN ARCHITECTURE

This section focuses on the traditional and modern architecture of Central and East African countries. Emphasis is on history and urban design. Chapter 7 focuses on Djibouti, Ethiopia, Kenya, Somalia, and the Republic of Sudan; Chapter 8 discusses Burundi, Rwanda, Tanzania, and Uganda; and Chapter 9 discusses Central African Republic, Congo, Gabon, and Zaire. East African architecture expresses the culture of its people. Its strong Arabian influence is adapted to the climatic elements and styles with the best combination of available resources.

PART 4: SOUTHERN AFRICAN ARCHITECTURE

The emphasis in this section is on the architecture of southern African countries, especially the urban design of major cities in southern Africa. This section also has three chapters. The strong presence of people of European ancestry in southern Africa stopped the spread of Islamic culture further south and embraced a highly Westernized culture that has no relationship to the indigenous architecture of the region. The Republic of South Africa has one of the highest concentrations of Victorian architecture on the African continent, and its contemporary architecture embraces all the ideals of modernism. Chapter 10 discusses Angola, Malawi, Mozambique, and Madagascar; Chapter 11 discusses Botswana, Namibia, Zambia, and Zimbabwe; and Chapter 12 covers Lesotho, the Republic of South Africa, and Swaziland.

PART 5: WEST AFRICAN ARCHITECTURE (THE SUDAN)

The objective of this section is to explain the architecture of the West African region, which is also known as the Sudan. In West Africa, there are more followers of Islam than Christianity. For example, Nigeria is a country with a large Muslim population in the north and a large Christian population in the south. Both alien cultures converge in the middle belt of the country at the River Niger to strike a balance that clearly accentuates the triple heritage concept with indigenous cultures. Architecture in West Africa follows the same pattern. It is strictly West African, and its mosques are unique and different from those in North Africa. Chapter 13 covers Mauritania, Mali, Niger, and Chad; Chapter 14 discusses Gambia, Guinea-Bissau, Guinea, and Senegal; Chapter 15 covers Sierra Leone, Liberia, Cote d'Ivoire, and Burkina Fasso; Chapter 16 discusses Ghana, Togo, Benin, Cameroon, Sao Tome and Principe, and Equatorial Guinea; and Chapter 17 covers Nigeria.

PART 6: MODERN ARCHITECTURE AND THE PROBLEMS OF URBANISM AND URBANIZATION IN AFRICA

This final section of the book focuses on the problems of modern architecture, urbanism, and urbanization in Africa and has four chapters. Chapter 18 covers the problems of urbanism in African cities. Chapter 19 discusses the problems of urbanization in Africa. The term *urbanization* in this chapter is defined as the process by which a city expands. In other words, urbanization determines urbanism. Size, density, and heterogeneity of a city are the independent variables in the urbanization process that determines urbanism. Chapter 20 concentrates on how modern architecture is influencing both urbanism and urbanization in Africa. Modern architecture here refers to any architecture in Africa influenced by the Industrial Revolution in Europe, using standardized mass-produced component parts, and having simplified building form and structure based on function. Much of this material deals with styles of architecture that were influenced by the European architectural movement between 1920 and 1933. It is important to note that modern in this case also includes contemporary architecture and the constantly changing forms that are being built all over the continent today. Chapter 21 concludes the book.

The purpose of *African Architecture* is to lay a foundation for the study of African architectural history and to provide information for professionals practicing in Africa. This book is not designed to solve all the problems facing architects in Africa but rather to raise issues that present and future African architects should keep in mind while practicing on the continent.

1

DEFINING
AFRICAN
ARCHITECTURE

chapter 1

TRADITIONAL AFRICAN ARCHITECTURE

The purpose of this chapter is to show that traditional African architecture is the first segment of African architecture. The roles of history and politics in shaping the architecture of Africa are also analyzed with respect to other relevant factors. The travel of Islam across the Sahara Desert, for instance, and the journey of modern Christianity to Africa have much to do with Africa's triple heritage architecture. It is believed that in its most modern understanding the triple heritage is fully manifest in Nigeria and the Republic of Sudan. Professor Mazrui (1986, 81) states that "the cultural history of Africa is captured in the transition from the triple ancient personality of North Africa and Ethiopia to the triple modern personality of Nigeria and Sudan."

This chapter focuses on various forms of traditional African architecture from antiquity to the present.

1.1 WHAT IS TRADITIONAL AFRICAN ARCHITECTURE?

Traditional African architecture has roots that can be traced back thousands of years despite the fact that most of the historical events that shaped African building culture are not documented. The words *traditional African architecture* evoke several images for architects and nonarchitects alike, regardless of nationality and education. It is easy for readers to associate terms like *Western architecture* with the image of Classical Greek architecture, Roman architecture, Medieval European architecture, Gothic architecture, baroque, Victorian, modern, and postmodern architecture, but traditional African architecture has never been associated with structures designed by trained architects. Current practicing African architects often lack information on this subject; hence, they cannot fully understand African architecture and are unable to incorporate and interpret it in the changing skylines of African cities.

African architecture consists of more than huts with grass roofs. It reaches back to the monuments of ancient times, to cities of the Middle Ages, and includes construction activities of contemporary times. Human settlements in Africa are as old as the history of the human species. So far, the earliest known evidence in the world for the existence of humanity and the emergence of human settlement has been found in East and Northeast Africa.

Early settlements in Africa are believed to date from the Neolithic period, when human beings learned to use hand-made tools to till the ground and establish early forms of agriculture. According to Shillington (1989, 18), "between 5000 and 4000 B.C. permanent settlements of full-time farmers became established in the valley of the Nile, with their farming techniques adapted to the river's annual flood."

Some of the earliest settlements in Africa were cave settlements scattered all over the Fezzan and the Tassili in the Sahara Desert. Knowledge of these early human habitats comes from cave paintings which have been found since the 1850s to the present time. The Tassili cave paintings show true early forms of human communities in Africa, and they cannot be dismissed as accidents because "over thirty thousand examples are known, half of them in the Tassili" (Willet 1971, 45).

The Fezzan and Tassili caves reveal information about the environment and the lifestyles of the people who left the paintings. Some of them have been dated as early as 5750 B.C. Some show efficient transport systems such as a chariot drawn by galloping horses (Fig. 1.1). Cave painting and engraving are not restricted to the Sahara. Many are found in South Africa, some of which date earlier than those in the Sahara.

The cave paintings also convey information about life in the Sahara region before the rivers and lakes of the Sahara began to dry forcing people to move closer to the Nile basin. The migrants who left the Sahara in search of water and settlement took their cave painting tradition with them. Accordingly, Professor Vansina (1984) stresses that the influence of Saharan art and engravings on ancient Egyptian graphic art should be taken seriously in the study of ancient Egyptian or African arts. Ancient Egyptian graphic art borrowed heavily from the paintings of the Sahara, which preceded and also ran parallel to it during most of its traditions.

The making of ancient Egypt began with the Pharaoh in Upper Egypt who unified Upper and Lower Egypt in about 3200 to 2900 B.C. (Fig. 1.2). "The first event of historical importance known to us is the unification of two prehistoric kingdoms, or rather subjugation of Lower Egypt by the Upper Egyptian ruler who tradition designates as Menes, while archeological sources seem to call him Narmer" (Abu Bakr 1981, 85).

The newly found state by King Narmer evolved as a government machinery that collected taxes and supervised farmers and irrigation projects. The kings of Egypt, or Pharaohs, used the excess wealth from taxes to build eternal monuments. Historians believe there were at least 30 dynastic Pharaohs in

Fig. 1.1 Tassili, Sahara Desert. A cave painting showing a chariot. Before desiccation in 6000 B.C.

Fig. 1.2 Menes (Narmer), the first African king (Pharaoh) of Egypt. He united Upper and Lower Egypt in about 3200 B.C. (Presence Africaine Editions)

Egypt spread over the period 3100–332 B.C. The three periods of ancient Egyptian unity and strength are referred to as the Old Kingdom (2685–2200 B.C.), the Middle Kingdom (2040–1785 B.C.), and the New Kingdom (1570–1085 B.C.).

There are other intermediate periods in Egyptian dynastic rule. For example, the period of King Narmer (also known as Menes) (3100–2700 B.C.) is generally known as the archaic period. It marked the beginning of Egypt as a state. Approximate dates for a later period are 1100–300 B.C., when the Greeks under Alexander the Great invaded Egypt. This was the foundation of the Ptolemaic dynasty, which ended about 40 B.C. when Rome conquered Egypt under Julius Caesar. Traditional African architecture in archaic Egypt did not begin with the pyramids: It began in a most humble way with thatched dwellings that continues today. It is a general misconception that the only thing built by ancient Egyptians were colossal stone pyramids. Nothing could be further from the truth, especially during the archaic period when Egypt was developing.

1.2 KAMITIC GENESIS OF THE EARLY HOUSES OF AFRICA

Ancient Africans in Egypt called their country *Km't* (*Kmit* or *Kemet*), meaning the "Black Land" (Cenival 1964, 10; Jordan 1976, 26; Mertz 1966, 39). African architecture originated from the Black Land after the desiccation of the Sahara Desert.

Upper Egypt (the south) was called the Red Land, while Lower Egypt (the north and delta area of River Nile) was called the Black Land. However, the country as a whole was formerly called the Black Land after the Nubian king, Narmer (Fig. 1.2), subdued Lower Egypt and unified both kingdoms into one country in about 3100 B.C. The era of King Narmer provides us with samples of some of the earliest types of traditional African architecture.

The name Black Land also derives from the annual floods of the River Nile which deposit tons of silt at the delta in Lower Egypt. The silt made the soil around the Nile Valley fertile and helped in the development of agriculture in the region. That is why Herodotus described Egypt as "the gift of the Nile."

Therefore, Kamitic (Kemetic) architecture in this context means the architecture of all the black (Km't) people of the Black Land from ancient times to the present. This is because their cultures have roots in the early settlements along the River Nile Valley after the desiccation of the Sahara Desert.

Ancient Africans built their first homes after they left the caves of the Sahara and settled along the Nile Valley where the fertile grounds allowed them to develop a booming agriculture. This shift to agricultural stability was indeed a posi-

tive change engineered by the desiccation of the Sahara and bringing benefits that influenced the development of art, architecture, astronomy, irrigation, and ancient medicine, along with the science of embalming the dead. Grand architecture did not develop immediately in ancient Egypt. The early settlers of the Nile Valley were mostly nomadic hunters who lived in caves because they had no knowledge of architecture. The first houses in the Nile Valley were very simple and impermanent, and they supplied all the fundamentals of Egyptian architecture. Smith (1938, 191) states that the early houses were primitive compared to the monumental architecture that developed later and consisted of "the hut, the round hut, the hoop-roofed house, and the rectangular house with either a Khekher or reed parapet." Initially, these were all built with pliable materials, and it was not until much later that plastered mud, brick, and timber were introduced into the construction.

Smith (1938) also indicates that the need for religious temples and tombs arose after fundamental shelter needs had been met and that the first temples were shelters for the divinity, originally houses for the living that were gradually transformed to religious uses with new significance. Later records corroborate Smith's suggestions. The transformation of Prophet Muhammad's own house into a mosque during the beginning of Islam in the later part of the 7th century A.D., for instance, supports the notion of temples evolving from human dwellings. The next few paragraphs describe early ancient Egyptian house forms.

THE TENT: The migrating nomads in the Nile Valley initially built tents for houses. The tent consisted of one or more poles hung at first with skins, then with matting, and finally with patterned fabrics. The earliest appearance of this shelter in Egyptian art occurs on the mace of Narmer (Menes), where

Fig. 1.3 The tent is one of the earliest houses of Africa. King Menes (Narmer) sits on a royal chair on a raised platform. (D.Appleton-Century Company Incorporated .)

Fig. 1.4 (Top) A reconstructed
throne of an Aksumite king,
Ethiopia. (Bottom) Shrine of
Nyakang, Fenikang in Nilotic
Sudan, which resembles hut
clusters in ancient Egypt.

the king sits on a royal chair on a raised platform under a tent (Fig. 1.3).

THE HOOP-ROOFED HOUSE AND THE ROUND HUT: These were also made of bundled reeds bound together to form a hoop roof at the top (Fig. 1.4). The circular hut of interwoven reeds also relates to the hoop-roofed house. An ebony table of King Menes dating from 3100 B.C. has a woven thatch house carved on it. Smith (1938, 57) concludes that the existence of hoop-roofed houses "in Egypt is supported by the widespread persistence of the circular and thatched house throughout Africa." In addition, the reliefs of the mortuary temple of Queen Hatshepsut at Deir al-Bahari depict round houses such as are common all over Africa today. They are in the tradition of the dwellings of the people of the ancient kingdom of Punt, which was located in present-day Somali

and Ethiopia. Indeed, ancient Egyptians believed their ancestors "originated from Punt" (Davidson 1971, 33; Smith 1938, 20). In the early dynastic period, the round hut was primarily used for grain storage, though its application as a shrine can be seen in the shrine of the God Mene. In addition, round-hut granaries can still be seen in various parts of West Africa (the Sudan). Aksumite churches in Ethiopia were built as round huts, and some of the ancient thrones of the kings of Aksum and other African civilizations also had round plans (see Fig. 7.10).

THE RECTANGULAR HOUSE: This represents the last phase before the creation of the eternal monuments. During this stage, the Egyptian house evolved from tent houses through circular and oval huts to rigid rectangular houses. The transition from oval to rectangular indicates a change in building

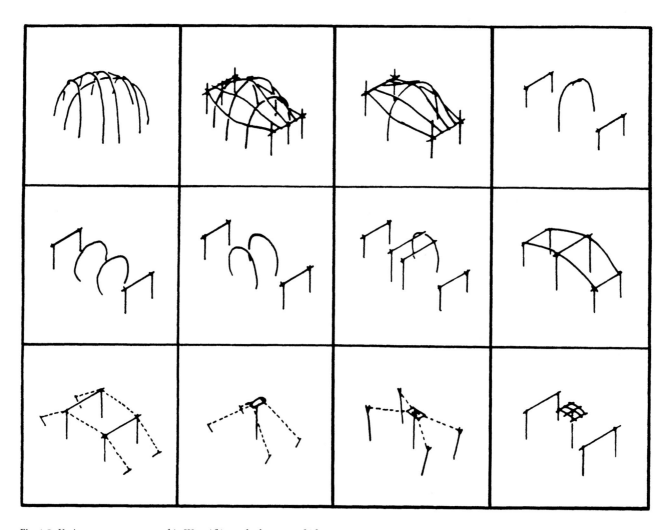

Fig. 1.5 Various tent structures used in West Africa and other parts of Africa. (Labelle Prussin and University of California Press)

technology that goes beyond responding to the circular building form with pliable materials to the construction of a sturdy form with rigid materials. Smith (1938, 21) writes that the ancient Egyptians acknowledged this technological transition at Aniba in Nubia between 2250–1650 B.C. It is important to note that several rural communities in Africa have house forms similar to those in ancient Egypt.

Traditional architecture in Africa can be advanced and incorporated into contemporary buildings if its roots in antiquity are understood. Scholars (Denyer 1978; Hull 1976; Pothorn 1982; Prussin 1986) classify traditional African architecture as: tents Sudanese style, impluvium style, hill style, beehive style, kasbahs, ghorfas, and underground structures. The viewpoints advanced on the issue of ancient architecture in Egypt and its relationship to architecture in the rest of Africa indicate that most of the house forms which constitute

traditional African architecture have roots in Egyptian antiquity. Ancient migrations and the climatic needs of the regions settled by various groups have indeed modified some of the ancient forms into unique styles, as demonstrated below.

Tent structures were used by the ancient people who emerged from the caves of the Sahara and are still in use by present-day nomadic communities, whose lifestyle and economic activities are seasonal. These structures are often constructed and furnished by women, while the men hunt and tend to their animals. Their popularity in nomadic communities is mainly due to flexibility and ease of construction. Prussin (1986) illustrates various tent structures used in West Africa and also in other regions of the continent (Fig. 1.5).

The Sudanese style refers to a variety of rectangular adobe buildings with courtyards, found mostly in the savanna, sahel, and desert regions of West Africa, an area also known as the

Sudan. These are mostly two-story buildings with flat roofs, large pylons, and openings on the roof for ventilation; some are made with baked bricks.

Impluvium style describes the common homes found in forest areas of West Africa. Characteristically, four houses face one another and enclose a courtyard. They are often thatched, either separately or together, as is the case in Ashanti, Benin, Ibos (Igbos), and Yoruba houses (Fig. 1.6).

Hill style is a rather general term applied to house patterns found on hilly settlements around Africa because of the similarities they exhibit regardless of location. It is believed that they all have a common origin from whence migrating tribes diffused them on hillside settlements throughout the continent. According to Denyer (1978), it seems unlikely that such marked similarities could all have originated separately. Some of the similarities include: hillside location, the use of stone in house foundations, terracing, house walls, round-plan houses with diameters less than height, earth superstructures with thatched roofs, socioeconomic factors such as agriculture, and indoor livestock keeping.

The beehive style covers a wide range of house types that utilize pliable materials for structural framing, including reeds, grasses, leaves, woven mats, and animal skins, among other materials. These houses are mostly round in plan and often dome shaped. One exception is the Mousgoum homes of northern Cameroon in which the round plan is maintained, but the dome projects upward into a cone, and the superstructure is constructed from clay materials instead of leaves and grasses. Some authors describe them as the sand castles of Africa. Mousgoum styles are also in other countries of West Africa: southern Chad, Cote d'Ivoire, Burkina Fasso, northern Togo, Benin, and Ghana.

Kasbahs are Arabian imports from Yemen during the periods of Islamization and Arabization of North Africa. Common in Morocco, Algeria, Tunisia, and Libya, these are multistory earth and brick structures that grow higher and wider as the extended family needs more room. In Morocco, they are designed as family or village fortifications.

Ghorfas are multistory, barrel-vaulted stone storage chambers constructed with either stone, sun-baked brick, or furnace-baked brick. They are usually built around a courtyard to permit natural lighting, but access to the chambers themselves is difficult because they were designed to serve the function of storage as well as that of refuge in time of war.

Underground structures in Africa take a variety of forms. Sometimes people create living spaces within caves, but most cultures burrow underground to construct new structures. These are mostly rectangular in plan, and their major structure is a roof supported by falked branches and rafters that are covered with earth. A few cave dwellings can still be found in Algeria, Tunisia, Burkina Fasso, Ethiopia, and Tanzania.

Scholars do not agree on the issue of the origin of most of these traditional structures. So far, Smith (1938) is one of the few scholars who clearly sees a strong relationship between the ancient houses of Egypt and those found south of the Sahara Desert. Moughtin (1985, 154) notes the similarities in styles between the building forms of Egyptians and the older mosques of Hausaland, but feels they should be understood as similar but independent solutions to similar roofing problems. He also states that the influences of Pharaonic Egypt on West Africa should be viewed as speculative because of inadequate evidence. He writes:

The roots of Hausa architecture are lost in antiquity, but it is possible that it shares a common ancestry with the great buildings of Pharaonic Egypt. Some of the early pre-dynastic hieroglyphics depict houses with small pinnacles similar to the Zankwaye that decorate Hausa buildings. The whole character of the Egyptian house drawings resembles that of the architecture of both present day Nubia and Hausaland....

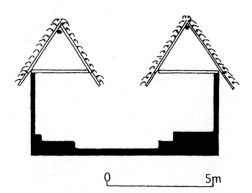

0   5m

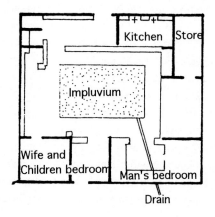

Fig. 1.6 Impluvium house style in Africa (Igbos, Benin, Ashanti).

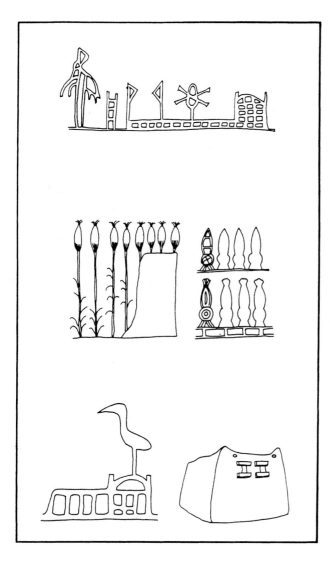

Fig. 1.7 House types and elements from ancient Egypt that are also common in Hausaland, Nigeria.

Moughtin demonstrates his point with sketches (Fig. 1.7) from E. B. Smith depicting house forms and hut shrines in predynastic Egypt, reinforcing Smith's observations without reaching a decisive conclusion.

In *Hatumere: Islamic Design in West Africa*, Professor Labelle Prussin (1986, 103) describes the view that traditional African architecture originates from ancient Egypt as a "North African attribution" that rests on a somewhat fragile interpretation of African history derived from Egyptian heritage. In her view, it is speculation that the Songhay peoples migrated westward from the valley of the Upper Nile into the Upper River Niger bend in West Africa, bringing with them a style reminiscent of the monumental tapered pyramidal walls and earthen construction that characterize Egyptian dynastic architecture. She makes it clear that this view was advanced by early European travelers who were confronted with monumental building types in West Africa but found it difficult to accept that West Africans developed such structures. It is important to mention that Professor Prussin reached her conclusion out of a genuine desire to differ from scholars who propose that Africans are incapable of developing indigenous structures. However, she overlooked a vital historical architectural link in the process. The dilemma is more apparent in a review of the works of Dubois on this subject.

Felix Dubois (1896), a French explorer, gives detailed descriptions of buildings in Jenne, Mali, and states that they are without any doubt the works of descendants of ancient Egyptians who migrated to a new country in the Sudan. He states that the fathers of the Songhays of Mali probably took part in the construction of granite and sandstone palaces and temples for the Pharaohs of Egypt but later became content with clay, a material in abundant supply in their new country. However, Dubois was not able to make a leap beyond the dominant trend in the thought of the times when he described the way the bricks were baked before application to the buildings. He makes a distinction between the Negroes and the Songhays as two different sets of people. In his view, the Songhays were from ancient Egypt and had a superior culture to the Negroes in the Songhay countryside. Dubois says that the Negroes did not make their bricks as cleverly as the Songhays. They fashioned their banco in irregular balls and applied them to buildings without mortar. On the other hand, the Songhays made regular sun-baked bricks of different shapes; flat, long, and rounded. These were set with mortar, covered with special rough-casting, and appear as if cut from one enormous block of stone. "They defy the heaviest tornadoes of rain and wind in an astonishing manner, and with some repairing, which consists of entirely renewed rough-casting, they last for centuries" (Dubois 1896, 148).

Dubois also indicates that ancient Egyptian habitations were characterized by the presence of enclosed courtyards with plastered walls, the predominance of mostly two-story buildings with surmounted terraces, and the use of pylons and obelisks to decorate the houses of the rich (Fig. 1.8). He also mentions how ancient Egyptians resolved roofing problems by using outward projecting planks covered with brushes and clay, while the summits of the walls were finished with densely woven reeds, and concludes that "the same method of construction are pursued in the buildings of Jenne; all these are to be found, with others that are veritably stupefying when seen in the heart of the negro country" (Dubois 1896, 148). Lastly, Dubois makes it clear that the Arabs brought the use of window shorters to the region and expresses a concern that they might destroy the Egyptian character of the town of Jenne

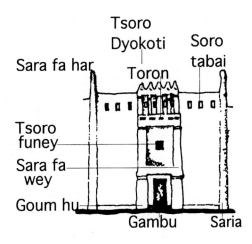

Fig. 1.9 Mali. *The facade of a Songhay house.* (Labelle Prussin and University of California Press)

Fig. 1.8 *Mali buildings similar to those in ancient Egypt. (Top) The ancient palace of Ahmadou at Segu transformed into a fort. (Middle and bottom) Houses at Jenne.* (Dubois, Greenwood Publishing, and Negro University Press)

with the introduction of Islamic art. Dubois gives further architectural descriptions of the houses of Jenne as follows:

> Above all, the houses of Jenne display that essential characteristic of Egyptian art—the pyramidal form, which represented solidity to

those ancient architects. The walls of the oldest constructions have a slight inward inclination, and possess no windows, or only the roughest sketch of them. Light and air enter through openings cut in the ceiling or roof. In all the negro habitations the roofs are rounded to carry off the deluge of winter, but here they are flat, like those of the valley of the Nile, where rain is scarce. The Songhays knew no more how to construct an arch than did the Egyptians. The summits of their dwellings are ornamented by those triangular battlements which may be seen on the palaces of Ramesses Meiamoum. The pylon, which is another characteristic of Egyptian architecture, gives access to the dwellings of Jenne, and forms, too, a motive of decoration, the facade of the houses being adorned with great buttresses of pylonic form....In short, the effect of the whole, its harmonious proportions, the symmetrical distribution of its ornamental motives, and its massiveness, unmistakably proclaim the art of Egypt. (Dubois 1896, 150)

It is interesting to observe that Dubois insists on drawing a distinction between Negroes and the people of Songhay because he had no doubt that the latter descended from ancient Egyptians. Hence, Songhays were not Negroes. But if the Songhays were not Negroes then and today, who else could be a Negro, or was Dubois only trying to be consistent with the traditional portrayal of Africa as a continent without history? Regardless, his architectural descriptions of Jenne are consistent with the writings of Smith (1938) who observed that most Egyptian dwellings from the First Dynasty to the New Kingdom had roof ventilators and parapets such as those found in most parts of Nubia today. A good example is the house of Neb-Amun, which he painted in his tomb at Thebes. In addition, Prussin (1986) suggests that some Songhay architectural terms and those of the Hausas in north-

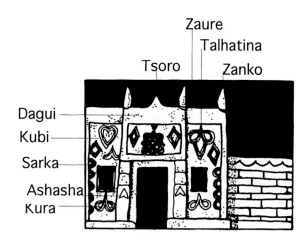

Zaure
Talhatina
Tsoro
Zanko
Dagui
Kubi
Sarka
Ashasha
Kura

Fig. 1.10 Zinder, Nigeria. Facade of a Hausa building showing features identical to Songhay buildings and ornamentation derived from other local mediums. (Labelle Prussin and University of California Press)

ern Nigeria (Figs. 1.9 and 1.10) reveal origins of a common construction lexicon.

Denyer (1978) attributes this similarity in building patterns and techniques to ancient migrations around the Sudan and the Nile Valley from the 2nd millennium B.C. She also emphasizes that similarities have been found between the culture of the Yorubas in southwestern Nigeria and that of the ancient Egyptians.

1.3 TRIPLE HERITAGE RELIGIOUS SYMBOLS AND THE EVOLUTION OF MONUMENTAL ARCHITECTURE IN AFRICA

Religion has always been one segment of cultural expression which elevates humanity beyond existential limits and places it within the realm of supernatural concepts. In ancient African tradition, architecture was one of the instruments of human transcendence to the world beyond by overcoming death through the preservation of the body. The simple idea of the worship of the sun god Amon-Ra evolved into an architectural concept that shaped the ancient world as well as our modern urban landscape beyond the imaginings of the ancient African kings who aspired to pierce the sky with their obelisks and pyramids.

George Hart (1986, 4) describes Amon-Ra as the "primeval deity and supreme god of the Egyptian pantheon." Several monuments and temples were dedicated to this god by Pharaohs of various dynasties. Indeed, he was often depicted anthropomorphically on a throne like a Pharaoh, and many

Pharaohs cast themselves as the children of Amon to demonstrate their divinity. For example, a relief in Queen Hatshepsut's temple at Deir al-Bahari shows the impregnation of her mother by the god Amon, the same god who commanded Tuthmosis III (Fig. 1.11) to extend the boarders of Egypt by conquering the Middle East during the 18th Dynasty.

Several temples dedicated to this supreme being still stand among the complex of temples at Karnak, which were built during different dynasties. The 6000-m² Great Hypostyle Hall with its 134 columns is the most grandiose of all within the Karnak complex. Pharaoh Tuthmosis III also built Akh-Menu Hall to celebrate his jubilee. Queen Hatshepsut erected a 90.2-ft (27.5-m) tall obelisk weighing 302 tons to symbolize and celebrate Amon as the sun god. It is interesting to note that the hieroglyph on the shaft of this obelisk clearly emphasizes that Amon, the father of Queen Hatshepsut, directed and personally supervised the erection of this obelisk. The obelisk and its inscriptions symbolically captured the essence of the religious feelings of Queen Hatshepsut and her royal birth by a divine god, Horus. This is demonstrated by two short verses from the shaft of the obelisk (Breasted 1962, 129):

Her father Amon established her great name; Makere upon the august Ished tree; her annals are myriads of years, possessing life, stability, and satisfaction. Son of Re, Khnemet-Amon, Hatshepsut, beloved of Amon-Ra, king of gods————. [When] she celebrated [for] him the first occurrence of the royal jubilee, in order that she may be given life forever.

Beloved of Amon. Her majesty [fem.] made the name of her father established upon this monument, and abiding, when favor was shown to the King of Upper and Lower Egypt, the Lord of the Two Lands, Okheperkere [Thutmose I], by the majesty of this god, when the two great obelisks were erected by her majesty [fem.] on the first occurrence; the lord of the gods said: "Thy father, King of Upper and Lower Egypt, gave command to erect obelisks, and thy majesty [fem.] will repeat the monuments, in order that thou mayest live forever."

The worship of the sun god had been in practice since the Old Kingdom, and at one point, this was the most dominant god both in Lower and Upper Egypt and in the heart of Nubia where several temples were dedicated to him. It can be stated that the worship of the sun god in ancient Egypt led to the concept of monotheism and to an architectural metaphor which propagated that concept, while entrenching itself in the building programs of the monarchs who administered and advanced the idea. This monotheism is also one of the critical ancient links between the preexisting supernatural beliefs of life after death, which fertilized and nourished the construction of the early pyramids of the Third and Fourth

Fig. 1.11 Egypt. Pharaoh
Tuthmosis III, son of a Sudanese
woman, who expanded the
Egyptian empire during the 18th
Dynasty. 1504–1450 B.C. (Presence
Africaine Editions)

TRADITIONAL AFRICAN ARCHITECTURE   *29*

Dynasties and the evolution of Judiasm, Christianity, and Islam. The concepts of eternal life and heaven feature prominently in Christianity and Islam.

In the ancient African kingdom of Egypt, Amon-Ra was often identified with the god Osiris, the god of judgment who guarded the gate to eternal life and who alone had the power to make humans inherit eternal life and also cause women and men to be born. A prayer by Pharaoh Tuthmosis III (Fig. 1.11), son of the Sudanese woman and husband of Queen Hatshepsut who founded the 18th Dynasty, gives a deep insight into the divinity of Amon-Ra, Osiris, and their intrinsic influence in the concept of eternal life in Judiasm, Christianity, and Islam. Ben-Jochannan (1988, 2) presents the following extract from Chapter CLIV of the Book of the Dead:

Homage to thee, O my divine father Osiris, thou hast thy being with thy members. Thou didst not decay, thou didst not turn into worms, thou didst not rot away, thou didst not become corruption, thou didst not putrefy...I shall not decay, I shall not rot, I shall not putrefy...I shall have my being, I shall live, I shall germinate, I shall wake up in peace...My body shall be established, and it shall neither fall into ruin nor be destroyed off this earth.

New architectural symbolism began to emerge in ancient Africa during the time of the Queen of Sheba in Ethiopia and King Solomon in Israel (c. 976–936 B.C.). The worship of the sun god Amon-Ra and the serpent which features highly on Egyptian totems and crowns was already in practice before 976 B.C. The obelisk was a common medium of representation for the sun god, while the cobra featured not just on the crown of Upper and Lower Egypt but also in buildings such as the step pyramid of King Zoser in the Third Dynasty. As a protector of the king, the cobra was symbolically represented on the walls of the Zoser complex (Figs. 1.12 and C.3).

There are ancient Ethiopian documents which record the denunciation of the sun god of Egypt and Ethiopia and the adoption of the God of Israel. In the Kebra Nagast (Chapter 28), the Queen of Sheba declares: "From this moment I will not worship the sun but the creator of the sun, the God of Israel" (Ullendorff 1960, 98). The cobra also features highly on Ethiopian art as it did in ancient Egyptian art. "This motif finds expression in traditional art, where to this day the story of King Solomon and the Queen of Sheba is depicted as beginning with the reign of the serpent" (Ullendorff 1960, 98). The serpent cult is known as Arwe in Ethiopia, and it was believed that the first king of Ethiopia was a serpent. These ancient beliefs have not disappeared. In middle-belt Nigeria and parts of Ibo Land, Nigeria, the snake cult is still in practice, and the snake is revered as the grand ancestor of the tribes. Serpents like the cobra and the python are not killed in these parts of

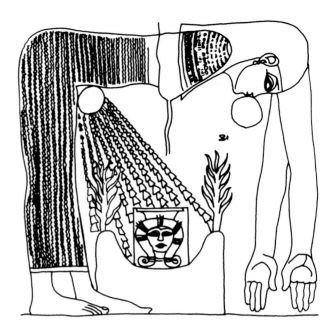

Fig. 1.12 Egypt. (Top) "The temple of Denderah depicted in the center of the horizon and bathed in the rays of the sun which the goddess of the heavens brings forth in the morning." Cenival 1964. (Bottom) A Ptolemaic bas-relief depicting a Pharaoh about to erect a pair of obelisks in the presence of Horus who holds an ankh (a cross or sign of life) in his hand. (Cenival)

Nigeria even when they crawl into living quarters. They are carefully removed by priests and taken to the woods.

The triple heritage architecture of Africa and its symbolism were expanded with the coming of Christianity to Ethiopia in the middle of the 4th century A.D. during the reign of Queen Candace. "According to tradition, the beginnings of Christianity in Ethiopia date back to the Apostles, i.e., there were then a few Ethiopian believers. In the Acts of the Apostles 8.26–40, the eunuch of Queen Candace went to Jerusalem to worship and was baptized by Philip the Deacon. The Ethiopians returned home rejoicing" (Sellassie 1972, 97).

To understand the new images and their functions in Christian buildings, a review of the parallels between Christianity and many ancient African religions is necessary. Some scholars consider these parallels as evidence of African triple heritage culture and genesis of Judaism, Christianity, and Islam (Champollion 1814; Diop 1974; Bernal 1987; Finch et al. 1988), but the focus in this study is on the architectural

implications of such religious beliefs and symbolism. While anthropologists, archeologists, clergies, rabbis, and historians continue to debate this topic, further research of the subject will demonstrate that African architectural history tells us more about ourselves and gives credence to the oneness of humanity in our spiritual beliefs and historical origin.

The following summary is a review of this vast subject and it gives meaning to the arts and architecture of Africa before and after the Christian era. The point of departure in this synopsis is that Osiris and Horus are one because "the king (Pharaoh) identified himself at death with Osiris, and his heir became Horus, the avenger of Osiris" (David 1982, 107) and Osiri-Horus are the later archetype of the Christian Jesus Christ.

OSIRIS-AMON-RA-HORUS (SINCE 3100 B.C.)	JESUS CHRIST (SINCE CHRISTIAN ERA)
Horus was an infant child conceived by a spirit and born of the virgin mother Isis (Finch 1988, 37; Hart 1986, 88).	Jesus Christ was conceived by a Holy Ghost and born of Virgin Mother Mary (Matthew, Chapter 1, 18–25; Luke, Chapter 1, 26–38).
The birth of Horus was announced by Thoth, the messenger of the gods, the scribe, and patron god of hieroglyphics.	The birth of Jesus was announced by angel Gabriel.
In the Egyptian Zodiac, Horus is December 25th. "The sun begins to rise from its 'cave' around midnight on the eve of December 25th and can be said to be 'born in a cave.' Between 2410 and 255 B.C., on the morning of December 25th, the constellation Virgo, 'the Virgin,' was on the eastern horizon as the sun rose and so the sun could be said to have been 'born of the Virgin'" (Finch 1988, 37) (Fig. 1.12).	Christmas, the celebration of Jesus Christ's birthday, is December 25th.
Set, the god of chaos and evil, was Horus's antagonist (Hart 1986, 194).	The Christian Satan was derived from the Egyptian *Set*. In the Egyptian language, Set means evil force and *an* adds emphasis (Finch 1988, 36).
Set accused Horus of being a bastard child because he had no living father, while he (Set) accused Isis of harlotry.	Satan, the antagonist of Jesus Christ, tempted him, while Joseph, the husband of Mary, accused her (Mary) of harlotry.
Horus was a cosmic god represented as a falcon.	Jesus, the Son of God, is identified by a Holy Ghost in the form of a dove at baptism.
Horus as the son of Ra rises as a sun which overcomes the forces of darkness (see Fig. 1.12). "Thoth decreed that he should be	Jesus, the solar archetype of Horus, is the light which overcomes evil by washing away sins (darkness), and most Christian art por-

called the `Light-giver, who cometh forth from the horizon'...; hereupon Horus commanded Thoth that the winged sun-disk with uraei should be brought into every sanctuary wherein he dwelt and in every sanctuary of all the gods of the lands of the South and of the North, and in Amentet, in order that they might drive away evil from therein" (Budge 1969, 483).

trays Jesus ascending to heaven with rays of sunlight shining over Him.

Osiris, the father of Horus, was the holy spirit which impregnated Isis, his sister, who gave birth to Horus.

The Holy Ghost, God, impregnated the mother of Jesus Christ, Mary.

Osiris was murdered by Set, his brother's enemy, but was awakened from death by his son, Horus.

Jesus was crucified by the Roman soldiers but rose from death after 3 days.

Osiris is the lord of eternity, the judge of the dead, and no one receives eternal life without his approval. "The Egyptians of every period in which they are known to us believed that Osiris was of divine origin, that he suffered death and mutilation at the hands of the powers of evil, that after a great struggle with these powers he rose again, and he became henceforth the king of the underworld and judge of the dead, and that because he had conquered death the righteous also might conquer death..." (Budge 1959, 61).

Jesus is the son of God, and no one goes to the Father (eternal life) without passing through him. "Christ became a Savior with a perceptible likeness to the dying-and-rising gods of the Mysteries, Osiris, Adonis and the rest" (Ashe 1976, 34).

The ankh, known as "crux ansata" (Finch 1988, 46), is the ancient African symbol of life which unites the masculine and the feminine images.

The cross on which Jesus was crucified is shaped like the African ankh.

Osiris's body was anointed before it rose from death. In Egypt, the *krst* or *karast* means the anointed mummy of Osiris which rose from death (Finch 1988, 49).

The word Christ is a Greek translation of Kristos, which means "the anointed." This word has its roots in the Egyptian *krst*.

Osiris's body was mourned by his wife-sister, Isis, and her sister, Nephthys (Fig. 1.13).

Jesus Christ's body was mourned by Mary and His kinswoman Martha. Both also mourned the death of Lazarus before Jesus woke Lazarus from the dead.

Lazarus is an Egyptian word with roots in azar, which was also a name for Osiris. Lazarus means to rise or "come forth" (Finch 1988, 52). It means "Osiris come forth."

Jesus woke Lazarus up in the presence of Mary and Martha by saying "Lazarus come forth" (John, Chapter 11, 1–44).

Virgin Isis, the mother of Horus—sister and wife of Osiris—can be compared to the Virgin Mary. As the mother of Horus, Isis was also known as Hathor (Hart 1986, 76). In literary translation, Hathor means "mansion of Horus," from the Egyptian root word *Het*.

Mary is a derivative of an ancient Egyptian expression and its literal translation is "the beloved." "The only figures with any interest as antecedents are those offered by Egypt and Egyptian Judaism, the Anath-Neith-Wisdom complex of deity. As mother and virgin, and still more as perpetual virgin, Mary does have affinities in that quarter. Moreover, the Egyptian themes appear in her cult later. She becomes Queen of Heaven like Anath" (Ashe 1976, 172).

Isis was often represented holding the infant child Horus. Isis, as the virgin goddess, was still worshiped in Africa in the 4th century A.D. before the Christians destroyed the cult (Hart 1986, 102; Mazrui 1986, 46)

Isis evolved into the Black Madonna and the Holy Infant, a nativity made popular by the Roman legions who worshiped Isis but later converted to Christianity and kept the same icons. The Black Madonna and the infant child can still be found in some Catholic churches in Europe today. For example, "The Black Madonna of Einsiedeln is not just an isolated entity, but carries a religious and psychological significance with archetypal grounding. She is one of about four hundred other Black Madonnas throughout the world. Most renowned among these are Our Lady of Czestochowa in Jasna Gora, Poland, and Notre Dame de Montserrat in Spain, including Our Lady of Guadalupe in Mexico" (Gustafson 1990, xii).

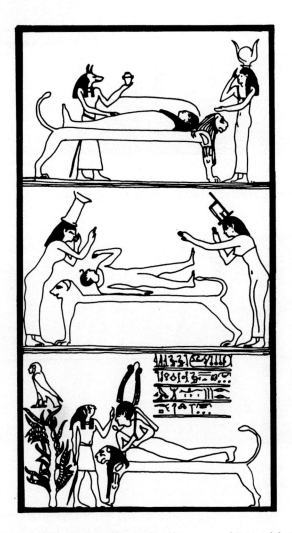

Fig. 1.13 Egypt. (Top) Anubis anointing the mummy of Osiris while Isis gives directions. Middle: Isis and Nephthys mourn the death of Osiris. (Bottom) The soul of Osiris on an Erica tree, while Horus commands Osiris to rise from the dead.

This synopsis demystifies the psychology and the beliefs which governed the design of temples, tombs, and palaces in Africa from ancient times through the beginning of the Christian era to this day. It has been mentioned that ancient Africans in Egypt learned how to build monumental structures long after their ancestors left the caves of the lush Sahara Desert, and architectural technology was highly advanced by the beginning of the Third Dynasty, but the Africans in Egypt maintained some religious beliefs from the archaic period and applied them to construction in the Old Kingdom. David (1982, 126) observed that "the great stone temples of historic Egypt retained all the elements which were already in the reed shrines of the Predynastic Period, in which the chieftain had made offerings to the local deity."

The beliefs from the predynastic period found expressions in walls, columns, beams, and several other surfaces and component elements of the houses, temples, and tombs. Cenival (1964, 90) notes that "the pillars of the temples were the features which best lent themselves to the interplay of symbols…" The pillars represented some of the major plants in ancient Egypt, namely, the palm, the papyrus, and the lotus, which has strong theological significance. The predynastic religious town of Buto was represented by the palm. The papyrus represented Lower Egypt where it grows in abundance, and its religious importance highlights how young Horus was born by a mother only and was hidden in the marshes of the papyrus. The papyrus was incorporated into the architecture of the Step Pyramid of King Zoser, which dates to the Third Dynasty (Figs. C.2 and C.3), in order to represent King Zoser as the son of Horus. At the time of creation, the rising young sun Amon-Ra (Horus) was supported by the lotus plant. At Abu Simbel, there are several Osiride pillars at the Temple of Ramses II, 19th Dynasty (1250 B.C.). These columns emphasize the belief that the king will rise from death in the likeness of the risen mummy of Osiris. The walls of most Egyptian temples and tombs served both techtonic functions and symbolic functions, whereas the cosmic beliefs were permanently represented and stored. The role played by the goddess Hathor, Osiris, and Anubis in the tomb of Amenophis II is brought to our attention by Erik Hornung (1990, 55):

> Hathor is the only goddess appearing on the pillars of the tomb of Tuthmosis III's successor, Amenophis II, along with the gods, Osiris and Anubis. On the walls of the tomb of the latter king's son and heir, Tuthmosis IV, Hathor is depicted as often as both the other gods together. The classic trinity of the most important gods of the dead has thus been established, each related to a very different aspect of the Beyond. Each raises the same ankh sign, symbolizing life, to the pharaoh's nose. This gesture incorporates the gods' powers of animation, sustaining life in the Beyond and bringing about repeated resurrections, true to the promise of the Pyramid Texts: "Rise, for you are not dead!"

Christian belief in the resurrection is strongly rooted in the ancient African concept of "Rise, for you are not dead!" This idealization of death as a temporary step has a ripple effect in the design of churches in Africa and around the world. Most church interiors and exteriors are designed to reflect the sign of the ankh (the cross) (see Fig. 7.7). Some of the best preserved Christian icons are in the medieval rock-cut churches of Lalibela in the mountains of Ethiopia. The ankh, which becomes the cross, and the sacred altars for the gods and priests are now for choirs, Christian clergies, and bishops. Another lasting legacy of religious symbolism in Africa can be seen in the layout of the ancestor compound. The ancestor compound is first a temple for the worship of the ancestors who had passed to the world beyond and are entombed in the compound. As a holy place, the children of the ancestors commune with the ancestor whose presence also offers protection for the living. In other words, the ancestor compound is also a communal temple, where the spirit of the ancestor is preserved and worshiped. Utilitarian needs have inspired some modification of the ancestor compound, but its link to ideas from the past cannot be ignored.

The introduction of stone architecture by King Zoser in the Third Dynasty was done in the spirit of preserving the body so that it would be reborn or germinate again. In this case, the relationship among a religious belief, the king, the god worshiped by the king, and the house of worship was inseparable. In fact, architecture became the most important medium for expressing the concept of oneness or monotheism and eternity. The Step Pyramid of Zoser, the Great Pyramid of Cheops, the Great Sphinx, the Funerary Temple of Queen Hatshepsut (Figs. C.2 to C.7), and many others

Fig. C. 2 Saqqara, Egypt. The tomb complex of Pharaoh Zoser. Third Dynasty, 2700 B.C., by architect Imhotep. (Yasser Elshashtany)

Fig. C.3 The Cobra Wall of the south tomb of the Zoser complex. 2700 B.C.(Yasser Elshashtany)

Fig. C.4 Gizah, Egypt. (Opposite, top) The Great Pyramid of Cheops. Fourth Dynasty, 2530 B.C. (Yasser Elshashtany)

Fig. C.5 Gizah, Egypt. (Opposite, bottom) Right backround: The Great Pyramid of Cheops. Front: The Great Sphinx which Chefren built to portray himself as a great African king. Fourth Dynasty, 2500 B.C. (Yasser Elshashtany)

Fig C.6 Deir al-Bahari, Egypt. Funerary temple of Empress Hatshepsut. 18th Dynasty, 1520–1484 B.C. (Yasser Elshashtany)

were constructed to preserve the body for the life after. It was only natural that the need for huge temples and tombs came after the need for fundamental shelter had been met.

Fig C.7 Karnak, Egypt. Avenue of the Rams at the Temple of Amon. (Yasser Elshashtany)

1.4 THE BEGINNING OF DYNASTIC ARCHITECTURE IN AFRICA

Dynastic architecture began in ancient Egypt during the Old Kingdom, especially from 2900 to 2200 B.C. just before regional princes began to destroy temporarily the empire Menes had united. The architecture of majestic tombs and temples was being built with strong emphases on religious and burial rituals. Burial customs in ancient Egypt were not too different from burial customs in most parts of Africa today. Usually a 6-ft-deep grave and a chamber on one side of the grave are excavated to receive the body. The side containing the body is bricked up to form a small room, while the rest of the grave is filled in. The pyramids, funerary temples, and tombs are also the most visible cultural expressions of a belief in the comforts of the material world. The dead are equipped with supplies for the life after. This materialistic philosophy has made funerals the most expensive celebrations in most parts of Africa, such as Nigeria. Relatives of the deceased spend a

Fig. 1.14 Egypt. Pharaoh Zoser, the African king who commissioned Imhotep to build the Step Pyramid at Saqqara.
Third Dynasty, 2700 B.C. (Presence Africaine Editions)

Fig. 1.15 Saqqara, Egypt. Section of the Step Pyramid of Zoser. 2700 B.C.

lot of money to stack the graves of the dead so that they would lack nothing in the life after. Africans no longer build pyramids, but they carry on a custom they learned long ago from their ancestors. There is no doubt that "the tombs of the Pharaohs were very much more elaborate but worked on the same principle" (Macquintty 1965, 27; Smith 1938, 61).

Under the direction of Imhotep, the Nubian architect who built the Step Pyramid for King Zoser (Figs. 1.14 and 1.15), architecture made the transition from simple structures built with pliable materials to stone buildings. Traces of the old construction methods can still be seen in the Step Pyramid. The blocks used in the Step Pyramid were small, and the embedded columns and ceiling joists were stone copies of the bundles of plants and beams used in earlier construction (El-Nadoury 1981, 178). In addition, the Egyptians developed garden designs with pools, bridge construction, dams, and city planning, as in the city of Kahun during the reign of Sesostris II in the 12th Dynasty.

1.5 THE GREAT PYRAMID OF CHEOPS (KHUFU)

This colossal structure remains one of the seven wonders of the ancient world. Its huge mass and the area of its base could comfortably accommodate "the cathedrals of Florence, Milan, and St. Peter's, as well as Westminster Abbey and St. Paul's" (Smith 1938, 96). Cheops (Khufu), the great builder and master administrator, achieved his goal in the Fourth Dynasty (Fig. 1.16), and nothing built in ancient Egypt surpassed it.

The triad complex of the Pyramids of Mycerinus (2470 B.C.), Chefren (2500 B.C.), and Cheops (2530 B.C.) marked the climax of great pyramid building in ancient Egypt. Each was

encased in carefully dressed stone that has almost disappeared, except on the top part of the Pyramid of Chefren. These pyramids (Fig. 1.17) were not constructed exactly alike; however, their basic plan can be illustrated by the Pyramid of Cheops. Unlike the Step Pyramid of Zoser built during the Third Dynasty, the king's burial chamber in the Pyramid of Cheops (Figs. 1.18 and C.3) is located in the middle of the monolith, while the queen's burial chamber is below it. As shown in the plan, several smaller pyramids and mastabas surround the three great pyramids. These were for the king's staff and members of the royal family and cults. The king's burial chamber consists of a caballed vault which is pierced at oblique angles on two sides by two holes that run from the chamber to the surface of the structure. These vaults are exits for the eternal living spirits of the dead.

The accuracy of the masonry work in this great pyramid is debated among engineers who recognize the expertise involved in creating such a colossal structure with very little margin for error. The stunning aspect of this great monument is the weight of the monoliths which "average two and a half tons, while a few weighed thirty tons" (Smith 1938, 96). All engineers and Egyptologists who have studied this pyramid recognize the ingenuity involved in hoisting monoliths of limestone and granite weighing so much to the height of 479 ft (146 m). The ancient Greek historian Herodotus (5th century B.C.) gave one of the earliest accounts of the construction of Cheops's Pyramid (Shillington 1989, 25):

In the building of the Great Pyramid, King Cheops (Khufu) brought the people to utter misery, for he compelled all the Egyptians to work for him. The stone were quarried in the Arabian mountains and dragged to the Nile. They were carried across the river in boats and then dragged up the slope to the site of the pyramid. The people worked in gangs of a hundred thousand men, each gang for three months. It took them ten years to build the road along which the stones were dragged and to build the underground chambers on the hill whereon the pyramid stands. These were to be the king's burial places.

The pyramid itself was twenty years in the making. Its base is square, each side eight hundred feet [about 244 m] long, and its height is the same [actually about 150 m]. The whole is of polished stone and most exactly fitted; there is no block of less than thirty feet [9 m] in length.

This pyramid was made like a stairway with tiers, courses or steps. When this, its first form, was completed, the workmen used levers made of short wooden logs to raise the rest of the stones; they heaved up the blocks from the ground on to the first tier of steps; when the stone had been so raised it was set on another lever that stood on the first tier, and a lever again drew it up from that tier to the next. The upper part of the pyramid was the first finished off, then the next below it, and last of all the base and the lowest part. There are writ-

Fig. 1.16 Egypt. Pharaoh
Cheops (Khufu), the African
king who built the largest
pyramid during the Fourth
Dynasty. 2530 B.C. (Presence
Africaine Editions)

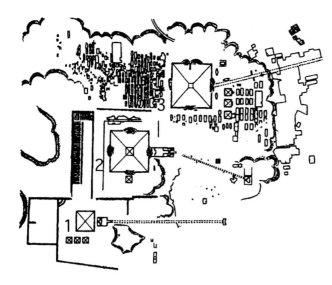

Fig. 1.17 Gizah, Egypt. Plan of the pyramid complex: (1) Mycerinus; (2) Chefren, and (3) Cheops. Fourth Dynasty, 2530–2470 B.C.

ings on the pyramid in Egyptian characters showing how much was spent on purges and onions and garlic for the workmen. According to the interpreter who read the writing these things cost as much as sixteen hundred talents of silver.

Herodotus's record has been very useful, but engineers still don't agree totally on how the huge monoliths were lifted. However, it is quite clear that what he meant by "the upper part of the pyramid was the first finished off" refers to the polishing of the caisson which was left rough at the time of quarrying and transportation until the stone was placed where it was desired. The masonry operation began from the base which was on desert bedrock. The masons cleared all the sand on the site before laying the foundation.

Not all Egyptologists agree with the suggestion that the monoliths may have been raised by means of tackle and pulleys. Fitchen (1978, 3) notes that the massive and sometimes colossal monoliths precluded the possibility of suspending their dead weight from ropes. Instead, blocks of stone were lifted, either by wedge or lever or rocker, by jacking operations. Fitchen's hypothesis suggests that the size of the stone determined what device was utilized in raising a monolith to its desired height and position. For example, the rocker device would be suitable for medium-sized monoliths of a few tons, but much heavier monoliths that could not be lifted by the device would require heavier mechanisms. He suggested the balance beam as a possibility. Here is Fitchen's (1978, 3) description of the rocker device:

The rocker (for raising medium-sized blocks of a few tons in weight) was a strongly built assemblage of wooden pieces consisting of two

runners (flat above and curved to a large radius below) that were linked by a number of stout rods in a pattern which allowed wooden levers to be inserted between two of them at either end in order to rock the device and its load, first one way then the other. As the device was rocked back and forth, slabs of wood (the shims) were positioned under the raised runners alternately to left and right; and in this way a practiced team could raise blocks quickly and with the minimum of danger to any of the work—or the workmen—below them.

As for heavier monoliths, a balance beam, a device that works on the principle of the steel-yard, is used. To use this device, a horizontal beam must be raised above the ground on a fulcrum. The fulcrum is set beneath one end of the beam instead of the middle so that the beam can rock freely. The short arm of an unequally set beam gains a great deal of mechanical leverage to lift within a limited distance when rocks are loaded on the long arm of the beam. Several balance beams like this could be used simultaneously to lift heavy monoliths.

Barocas (1972) sheds more light on this subject by suggesting the use of ramps. He envisions four ramps made of earth and rubble built on the four sides of the pyramid as the stone block levels of the pyramid began to rise. The stone blocks were hauled up three of these ramps on sleds, while the fourth ramp was used to bring down the empty sleds. "At various stages in the process of transporting the stones from the quarry and on up the pyramid, rollers and lever-like prying tools were probably used" (Barocas 1972, 27). The ramp was eventually built to the peak of the pyramid where the cap-

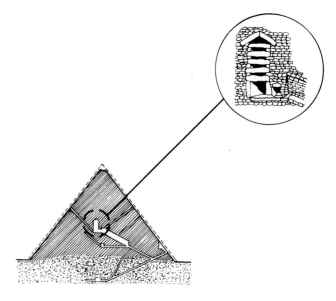

Fig. 1.18 Gizah, Egypt. The Pyramid of Cheops and the king's burial chamber.

stone was put in place. At this point, the workers would begin to work downward to smooth the surface of the pyramid and to remove the ramp.

Generally speaking, constructing a pyramid involves three major steps: quarrying the stones, transporting them to the site, and erecting the stones to the desired positions. These are the key components that have puzzled engineers and Egyptologists who have dealt with the construction problem. The process of erecting obelisks has given insight into these mysterious constructions that took place thousands of years ago. A large unfinished obelisk (41.78 m) left at Aswan provides the "exact method of quarrying large monuments" (Badawy 1987, 100). According to Badawy, the initial stage of quarrying involves heating the rock, cooling, and pounding with dolerite balls to create a fissure. A separating trench 2.5-ft (0.75-m) wide was then cut downward in the rock by men squatting in contiguous compartments 2-ft (0.6-m) wide. These men continued to pound left and right of a middle vertical line marked on the stone with a sequel of triangles that indicated the level of their progress. The fissure was controlled by constant inspection while the pounding was going on. At the bottom of the fissure, tunnels were cut at intervals to be filled with packing, wetted to cause more fissures. The remaining parts gradually separated from the parent rock.

Inscriptions left by heads of such operations indicated a good safety record for this ancient method of quarrying obelisks and monoliths. Badawy (1987, 100) writes: 1000 men of the palace, 100 quarrymen, 1000 soldiers, 50 oxen, 200 asses (Kanofer, Ninth, and Tenth Dynasties), 10,000 men to extract a block for a sarcophagus, further transported by 3000 sailors to the Nile (under Mentuhotep IV): "not a man perished, not a trooper was missing, not an ass died and not a workman was enfeebled." The obelisks were transported to construction sites on barges during the rainy season when the Nile is flooded. The next stage was the erection of the obelisks. It has been hypothesized that this may have been accomplished by filling the excavated location site with sand, which was gradually removed from the base until the obelisk tilted to its permanent position. This hypothesis was advanced by Petrie who suggests that "a granite beam weighing 55 tons (Khufu), or an obelisk of 30 meters could be raised by tilting it up on 2 piles" (Badawy 1987, 103).

Some scholars hold the view that the pyramids may not have been built with slave labor, and that Cheops was not the cruel slave driver portrayed by Herodotus. Rather, the pyramid is viewed as the achievement of a successful king who was a great administrator. Smith (1938, 99) believes that "unquestionably the King was an energetic and successful organizer." Those who share this view consider that it was a good move for the king to put 100,000 men to work during the rainy season when the Nile was overflooded and farm work temporarily suspended. However, it is difficult to erase the Hollywood image of starved slaves toiling to lift monoliths of stones onto rising pyramidic piles. The Pyramid of Cheops has remained a great mystery, even to early 18th-century explorers such as Napoleon, and it will continue to remain so indefinitely because the ancient Egyptians left no detailed written records describing their construction process.

Labib Habachi (1984) has written extensively about the pyramids, obelisks, and their influence on modern skyscrapers. His book *Obelisks of Egypt: Skyscrapers of the Past* portrays the obelisk as the root of the modern skyscraper. Several texts exist of Pharaohs boasting that they erected obelisks which reached, pierced, or mingled with the sky. In addition, cities such as London, Paris, Rome, and New York, the city with more modern skyscrapers than any other, also have obelisks that have been transported from Egypt. Professor David Hughes (1993) suggests that through the obelisk Africa's impact on the modern skyscraper was symbolic and typological as far as form is concerned. Obelisks were located at places of worship and centers of power during religious rites, just as modern skyscrapers are at the centers of our cities and symbolic of corporate success and power.

1.6 THE IMPACT OF WARS AND CONQUEST ON THE HISTORY OF AFRICAN ARCHITECTURE: THE CASE OF THE PTOLEMIES AND THE CITY OF ALEXANDRIA

This section concerns the architecture of the last dynasty (Ptolemies) of Egypt, then a nation beleaguered by siege from surrounding major powers. The Ptolemaic dynasty intrinsically changed the face of Egypt from a traditional African population to its present ethnic composition. The city of Alexandria was founded on the site of an ancient Egyptian city, Raqote. Alexander the Great built his new city after his conquest, but then he was buried at Memphis. However, General Ptolemy, who usurped power and inherited Egypt as his province, brought Alexander's body back to be buried in his city a few years later.

The ancient city of Alexandria is a living monument to all of humankind who were attracted to Egypt by the magnet of its wealth. Alexandria began with the Persians in 525 B.C. and ended with the brief reign of Alexander the Great who forged a new destiny for imperial Egypt by 332 B.C. by ushering in the Ptolemaic dynasty, a period also identified as Hellenistic Egypt. The most famous ruler of the last dynasty was Empress Cleopatra. Macquintty (1976, 91) suggests that "the

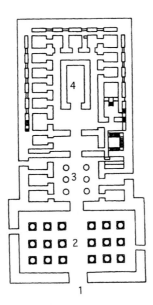
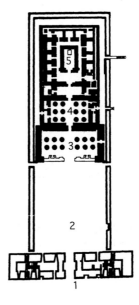
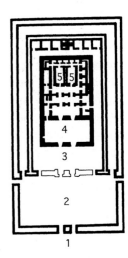

Fig. 1.19 Egypt. (Left to right) Plan of the Temple of Hathor at Dendra; plan of the Temple of Horus at Edfu; and plan of the Temple of Haroris and Sobek at Kom Ombo.

(Barocas & Grosset & Dunlop)

Ptolemies were Macedonian Greeks who had no previous ties with Egypt." Cleopatra VII grew up in a world controlled by the Romans, "and she, like her father, realized that her only chance of survival was to collaborate with them" (Macquintty 1996, 104). Regardless of her ancestry, Cleopatra was an African princess. More than 250 years of the reign of her family dynasty in Africa with strong assimilation policy rightfully confirms her identity. It is important to understand the nature of the relationship between the Greek conquerors and their African subjects in ancient Egypt because this relationship determined the extent of the Ptolemaic innovations in architecture there. The Greeks were anxious to be seen as Africans, rather than as Greeks and ruling conquerors, because they knew this was the only way that Africans would accept their rule. Alexander the Great was aware of this from the moment he conquered Egypt, and he took steps to become African by adopting an African god as his father.

According to Bernal (1987), Alexander the Great clearly considered himself to be the son of Amon, one of the ancient African gods. He quickly hurried to consult the god's oracle at the Libyan oasis of Siwa. The oracle told him that he was the god's son, and from then on he was portrayed on his coins as a horned Amon. This was, in an ironic way, the beginning of the ancient Greco-Roman strand of African triple heritage.

Cultural interaction between the Egyptians and surrounding cultures goes back to the Mesopotamians, Assyrians, Babylonians, Persians, Nubians, Greeks under Alexander, Romans, and later Islamic conquerors. At this juncture, it makes more sense to view Egyptian history in the later period as a composite of cultural activities from different parts of the world, and even more so as African history. Those who

shaped the destiny of Egypt at that time should not be seen as white or black, but as African, though perhaps of different ancestry. There was too much crossbreeding between the natives and the foreigners to leave room for such distinctions, especially since the Greeks had a policy of assimilation in all aspects of Egyptian life (Diop 1974, 5; Macquintty 1965). Alexandria, or el-Iskandariya as it is known in Arabic, became the center of knowledge and the capital of the Ptolemaic dynasty and of Hellenistic culture.

While the Ptolemies were holding onto power, Greek immigrants were exporting African culture to Greece and Rome in a gradual manner that figured in the development of Western civilization. Building technology was transferred from Africa to Rome and incorporated in a non-Egyptian style. Most of the time, components and elements from great Egyptian temples such as the sphinxes were used. "Objects like these, and numerous smaller pieces, were also exported, no doubt through Alexandria, to be used in Roman temples of Sarapis and Isis, or in the grounds of Hadrian's Villa at Tivoli and Diocletian's palace at Split" (Baines and Malek 1980, 169).

It is difficult to access the building program of the Ptolemies due to the presence of Persians and Romans. For example, most of the necropolis areas contain burial chambers with Greco-Egyptian influences. The adoption and worship of Egyptian gods often meant the preservation and sometimes renovation of existing temples to meet immediate needs. The Temple of Hathor at Dendra, Temple of Horus at Edfu, and the Temple of Haroris and Sobek at Kom Ombo (Fig. 1.19) were built by the Ptolemies. These structures share the traditional linear plan that often has a general enclosure wall, a major linear entrance, a large open courtyard, a colonnaded vestibule, a hypostyle hall, and sanctuaries.

Alexandria is not just an ancient city. It is also a modern city with many high-rise buildings, overhead bridges, and all other conveniences found in major urban centers of the world. Muslim impact in the Middle Ages is apparent. Later Turkish, English, and French influences are all highly visible, as is the case in many North African cities.

1.7 TRADITIONAL ARCHITECTURE IN SUB-SAHARAN AFRICA

Traditional African architecture does not end with the wonders of the Nile. The study of the African architectural portfolio therefore includes the grand wonders in Egypt, Ethiopia, the Meroetic Pyramids in the Sudanese Desert (Fig. 1.20), the ruins of the citadel states of East Africa, the grand castles of Zimbabwe, the architecture of the ancient cities of Benin, Timbuktu, Kano, and other medieval cities of the empires of

West Africa, and of course the 19th-century planned cities of Kuba. These are the realms of traditional African architecture and the first component of the triple heritage architecture of Africa. The pyramids in Egypt are known all over the world, but of the other wonders in Africa little is known.

In Ethiopia, there are many sunken churches carved out of solid rock, a typical example being Saint George's Church. Some of the churches were carved out of mountains about 8000 ft above sea level. They are so mysterious that "The local people in Lalibela cannot believe their own ingenuity. Instead, many believe that angels descended from heaven to help carve out the sunken churches. And many native people are convinced that God Himself was the grand architect" (Mazrui 1986, 221).

Donahue (1979, 4) calls Saint George's Church at Lalibela the "eighth wonder of the world." There are many such churches carved into solid rock 8000 ft above sea level in the mountains of Ethiopia (see Figs. 7.5 to 7.9). Three of these wonderful churches are discussed in Chapter 7. Additionally, the Ethiopian monarchy was one of the longest in Africa, and

Fig. 1.20 Republic of Sudan. Pyramid of the North Cemetery at Meroe. 250 B.C.–350 A.D. (Edition Leipzig)

successive kings left numerous monuments including the obelisk at Aksum (Fig. 1.21).

In East Africa, Kenya, Tanzania, Mozambique, and Uganda, there are many monuments built from stone. These monuments attest to the existence of empires or states that were organized beyond the agricultural societies of Africa. According to Professor Mazrui (1986), the theme of gloriana was founded by dynastic empires of Africa which also believed in using stone and brick to erect durable testimonies to their lifestyles.

In West Africa, there were many medieval empires with well-built capital cities. Ghana, the Land of Gold and the first of these medieval empires, was already known to the North African world by the end of the 8th century. Other empires were Mali and Songhay. The latest and last of the empires to fall, in 1897, was Benin Empire whose hire still reigns as a traditional ruler in Benin City, Nigeria. Kumbi Saleh was considered the capital of ancient Ghana, and Timbuktu was the capital of Mali.

Benin City, the capital of the Benin Empire, was an urban center before the Portuguese arrived in the mid-1400s. According to Ryder (1969, 24), "Portuguese ships first reconnoitered that part of the West African coast which now lies within the boundaries of Nigeria some time between 1469 and 1479." Udo Kultermann (1969, 15) also writes that, when the Portuguese arrived in Benin around 1500, they found a city-state which was a nautical mile long from gate to gate; the inhabitants were prosperous and experienced in metalworking. Professor Kultermann's findings agree with the writings of Dapper, a 16th-century Dutch explorer and merchant (Davidson 1991), and also with the findings of Leo Frobenius mentioned earlier in the introductory section "Problems in African History."

Further south, in Zimbabwe, the stone houses are part of traditional African architecture. The falcons of imperial Pharaonic Egypt are manifest on the great walls of this complex.

It has been mentioned in the introduction that African architectural history is complete only when the whole continent is taken into consideration. The architecture reviewed in this chapter clearly constitutes indigenous African architecture. The most common forms of traditional African architecture, however, have not changed very much. Small houses, "huts," built with pliable materials can be found in North,

East, South, and West Africa. However, these are hybrids of much earlier forms that evolved in the Nile Valley when societies began to develop and farming became a profession.

1.8 THE RELATIONSHIP BETWEEN ANCIENT EGYPTIAN ARCHITECTURE AND ARCHITECTURE SOUTH OF THE SAHARA DESERT

This is the least studied aspect of African architecture in spite of the fact that several scholars have found connections between elements in ancient Egyptian architecture and those in architecture south of the Sahara Desert.

Ethiopia is a starting point for this study because of its proximity to ancient Egypt and the overlap of ancient Egyptian civilization and other African civilizations in the region. Ethiopia became a Christian nation in the mid-4th century A.D., and several Christian churches reminiscent of ancient Egyptian monuments were built from the Christian era onward. The essential elements in the plans of the churches could have been handed down to the Christian converts by pre-Christian civilizations of Ethiopia such as Aksum.

It is true that several Egyptian Christians moved to Ethiopia at the beginning of Muslim domination of Egypt and the rest of North Africa in the 7th century A.D. But that migration alone does not explain the similarities between pre-Christian Ethiopian architectural monuments and those in ancient Egypt. One valid explanation is that the monuments were built by the descendants of ancient Egyptians who fled southward (Upper Egypt) as different conquering armies came to the region from abroad, especially the Alexandrian conquest in 333 B.C. No exact date has been fixed with regard to the beginning of Aksum civilization, but there are scholars who favor its existence in about 1000 B.C., while others place it much later at 300 B.C.

There are architectural monuments in the ancient African kingdom of Aksum, Ethiopia, that remind us of ancient Egypt. They include obelisks, temples, and palaces. The tallest obelisk in the world, though no longer standing, is in Aksum. The multistory obelisk is 108 ft (33 m) tall, and it differs from the Egyptian obelisk because instead of inscriptions it has false doors, windows, columns, projecting monkey-head, and other elements reminiscent of Aksumite building tradition. Sellassie (1972, 61) notes that "in erecting the Stelae (obelisks) most probably the Ethiopians employed the Egyptian method for raising obelisks. If this is so, it implies certain links with Egyptian art and techniques" (see Fig. 1.21).

The fundamental plan of an Egyptian temple was synthesized from the plan of Egyptian domestic architecture. The

Fig. 1.21 (Opposite) Aksum, Ethiopia. One of the standing obelisks carved to represent Aksumite building tradition in stories. 300 B.C.–300 A.D. (Richard Pankhurst, Leila Ingrams. Ethiopia Engraved by Kegan and Paul International)

elements in the plan consisted of the fenced-up forecourt, porticoed vestibule, great (hypostyle) hall, and a chamber or sanctuary. The Egyptians often arranged these elements in linear order with hierarchal emphasis on the function of the spaces. Hence, the linear arrangement shaped Egyptian temples into rectangles (see Fig. 1.19).

In Ethiopian churches, the vestibule is present but not always porticoed. The great (hypostyle) hall becomes the nave, and the chamber or sanctuary remains the same as the Holy of Holies accessible only to the officiating priests. The fenced-up forecourt which commences the linear procession in an Egyptian temple is much more formal compared to the Ethiopian forecourt which becomes the surrounding courtyard in some of the rock-cut churches like Saint George's (see Fig. 7.7).

In Ethiopia, the most typical church buildings in the countryside are round (see Fig. 7.10), but they retain the rigid spacial arrangement of vestibule, nave, and sanctuary. Pankhurst and Ingrams (1988, 25) observed that:

> The round church, the most typical in the country as a whole, was divided into three concentric sections. The outer one, called the Qené Mahalet, was a circular corridor in which laymen would stand and pray. The second passage-like area, nearer the interior, was the Maqdas, reserved for officiating priests, while the third section, the Qeddus Qeddusan, or Holy of Holies, was a chamber in the very centre of the building. This sanctuary, into which none but the clergy could enter, housed the altar, as well as the all-important tabot, or altar slab, which symbolised the Ark of the Covenant given to God by Moses.

The similarity between the churches of Ethiopia and temples of ancient Egypt is more striking in the plans of rock-cut churches from both civilizations. The site and the nature of construction required modesty in the arrangement of the plan, so the fenced forecourt is missing from both the Egyptian and the Ethiopian rock-cut building plans. In addition, both plans are squares. The plan of the Peripteral Temple of Queen Hatshepsut (1520–1484 B.C.), the plan of the rock-cut Temple of Ramses II (1301–1235 B.C.), and the plan of the rock-cut Temple of Horemheb (1342–1314 B.C.) can be seen as earlier prototypes of ancient Ethiopian churches and temples (Fig. 1.22). The 4th-century Church of Maryam of Seyon (see Fig. 7.4) at Aksum, Ethiopia, is clearly a much later version of ancient Egyptian temples such as the Peripteral Chapel of Senwosret I.

The most distinguishing aspect of Aksumite architecture from Egyptian architecture is wall treatment that has horizontal timber reinforcements and outward projecting wooden stumps known as monkey-head. These are aspects of Ethiopian architecture that need to be researched properly,

and the presence of monkey-head support systems in the architecture of the Sudan (West Africa) indicates that there is an ancient link between the Sudan, Ethiopia, and the cultures of Egypt as Dubois (1896) and several scholars have indicated (see Fig. C.55). In the Sudan, toron (1.9) are outward positions that serve both structural and maintenance functions. The relationship between the toron and the monkey-head support systems in Ethiopian buildings needs to be investigated. The fact that ancient Egyptian houses also have toron suggests that ancient Ethiopians modified the toron to meet the structural needs of their buildings.

The evolution of the ancestor compound that surrounds a central courtyard should be analyzed not just as a primitive instinct for mutual defense and association but also within the context of its historical evolution from the earliest settlements

Fig. 1.22 Egypt. (Left to right) Peripteral Chapel of Senwosret I, Karnak; Peripteral Temple of Amenhotep III, Elephantine; plan of Peripteral Temple of Hatshepsut, Buhen; plan of a rock-cut temple, Garf Husein; plan of small rock-cut temple of Ramses II; and plan of rock-cut Chapel of Horemheb, in quarries of Sisila. (Barocas & Grosset & Dunlop)

along the Nile Valley and its influence on the design of tombs and temples in ancient Egypt and the rest of Africa. The need to investigate the evolution of such forms underscores the significance of Ethiopia and the Republic of Sudan as the gateway to the analysis of the relationship between ancient Egyptian architecture and architecture south of the Sahara Desert.

Ancient Africans in Egypt left few records about their construction method, so the information available on their domestic architecture comes from grave excavations and illustrations on the walls of palaces, temples, and tombs. Several models of ancient African houses have been recovered from graves and tombs in Egypt and Nubia. These models are called "soul houses" because they were placed in the graves to house the souls of the departed. Scholars (Badawy

1966, 12; Smith 1938, 19) believe that soul house models represent actual house forms in ancient Egypt. "It seems probable that all the features of these models are copied exactly from actual houses (Smith 1938, 19)."

A brief comparative analysis of the architectural elements of the soul houses and houses in other parts of Africa reveals astonishing similarities. This analysis considers the fact that ancient migrations, Islamic influences, Western influences, and changes in customs have also modified the houses in present-day Africa. Nonetheless, the fundamental architectural elements that highlight the Kamitic (Kemetic) genesis of the houses of Africa are readily visible.

Understanding the depth of the relationship between ancient Egyptian architecture and architecture south of the

ARCHITECTURAL ELEMENTS IN ANCIENT EGYPTIAN HOUSES	ARCHITECTURAL ELEMENTS IN MOST PARTS OF AFRICA
In ancient Egypt, clay houses (mud or adobe) and brick houses were very common. The rich were more likely to use brick (Badawy 1966, 16).	Walls made of clay (mud or adobe) are still very common in most parts of Africa. There are also walls made of brick as they were made in the ancient times (Dubois 1896, 149; Smith 1938, 20).
Vaulted roofs and flat roofs were very common in ancient Egypt. These vaults were sometimes ribbed on their interiors with timber and reed. The types of ribs used in several parts of West Africa (see Figs. 13.5 and 13.6) give insight into how ancient Egyptians made some of their domes.	Vaulted roofs are still common in most parts of the Sudan (West Africa). They form entry vestibules to enclosed compounds and courtyards. The Hausas and the Songhays still use vaults for their entry vestibules (see Figs. 13.7 and C.83).
Egyptian houses had ventilators on their rooftops and terraces.	Houses that use rooftop ventilators are still common in several parts of West Africa. For example, Dongon house types have ventilators on rooftops just as several adobe structures in Jenne and Hausaland do (see Figs. 1.23, 1.25, 13.3, 15.10, 15.11, C.83, and C.85).
Badawy (1966, 17) said that ancient Egyptian houses always had external stairs: "They mostly rise along the left side wall in the court or feature flights of steps built on half an arch, sometimes on a curved plan. They lead to the upper floor directly or through a trapdoor" (see Fig. 1.24).	Several houses in the Sudan (West Africa) have stairs similar to those illustrated by Badawy. There is no doubt that Islam has modified and influenced house decoration in Africa, but the indigenous building elements are still very visible (compare Figs. 1.24 and C.54).
Badawy (1966, 17) confirms that "A hood-molding is sometimes found over the doorway and occasionally the door posts are indicated as projecting and battered." Ancient Egyptian windows had bars over them. They also had hood-moldings, projecting sill, and are set high up as illustrated by Figure 1.23.	The doors and windows found in Songhay and Hausa architecture are typical examples of doors and windows found in ancient Egyptian houses. Traditional Hausa houses built in the 1970s (see Fig. C.85) still have all the typical door and window elements in ancient Egyptian houses. The similarity between Hausa architecture and typical Egyptian houses can no longer be

described as coincidental when studied carefully. Figures 1.9, 1.10, 1.23, 1.25, 13.3, C.55, C.57, C.58, and C.85 have demonstrated that there is a strong indigenous and archetypal relationship between ancient Egyptian doors and windows and the doors and windows of the Sudan (West Africa).

Enclosed courtyard has always been a very important aspect of ancient Egyptian architecture. In palaces, temples, and tombs, the enclosed forecourt comes before different enclosed courtyards. The courtyards had high religious and fellowship functions as places of gathering and socialization.

The ancient courtyard and forecourts of Egyptian architecture survive as the ancestor compound. Ancestor compounds are the most common form of dwellings in most African villages and indigenous cities because they facilitate the daily rituals of fellowship and solidarity with the spirit of the ancestor. Most African tribes still bury their chiefs and revered personalities in the compound as a way of preserving the cult of the ancestor and the extended family solidarity.

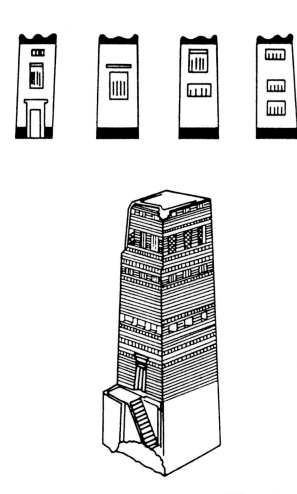

Fig. 1.23 Egypt. Elevations of a house model of Amenemet, and an axonometric of an ancient Egyptian house type.

Sahara Desert will require intense effort by architects, archeologists, anthropologists, art historians, historians, and other social scientists. Such combined effort by scholars from different disciplines should use Ethiopia and the Republic of Sudan as strategic starting points. Recent studies by interdisciplinary teams are already producing results. For example, the archeologist, Professor Friedrich W. Hinkel (1991, 222) states that: "The characteristic peculiarity of Meroetic architectural design is the practice of joining harmonic rectangles which determine the outer limits of the plan. The `Inner Harmony' of the Egyptian type of sacral building develops into an `Outer Harmony' principle in Meroetic times."

The archeologist, P. L. Shinnie (1991, 49), supports Professor Hinkel's suggestions by indicating trade between Egypt and people south of the Sahara "dates from the Old Kingdom when important caravans traveled south from Aswan to exchange Egyptian manufactured goods for the exotic products of Africa." This is a confirmation of the trans–Saharan trade routes which continued in Roman times and later to the Medieval period in Africa. David O'Connor (1991, 145) states that the sizes of Nubian kingdoms and their interactions with ancient Egypt "were much larger and more powerful than has been allowed for, and that our perspectives on the historical relationships between Egypt and Nubia need to be accordingly adjusted." This ancient relationship was a major process of economic and cultural diffusion in Africa, including building traditions and styles. Horton (1991, 264) emphasized that "the Nile Valley allowed communications between the Sahel-Savanna and Mediterranean North Africa.

Fig. 1.24 Egypt. *Restored perspective of a house with courtyards. A stairway leads to the terrace from the left side of the courtyard.*

Fig. 1.25 Egypt. *(Left) Restored perspective of a house from a tomb. (Right) Restored perspective of the house of Nakht.* (A. Badawy)

Whoever controlled Nubia controlled this corridor, and with it the prosperity of Egypt." Recent discoveries of freestanding structures and graves in Nubia (Sudan) that postdate 3000 B.C. and future studies in this field would clearly support the notion that there is a strong architectural relationship between ancient Egypt and Africa south of the Sahara.

chapter

WESTERN ARCHITECTURE IN AFRICA

This chapter explores the two phases of the introduction of Western architecture into Africa. The first occurred during the Roman Conquest of North Africa, which constitutes the beginning of Western architecture in Africa because subsequent foreign invaders and occupiers of North Africa did not bring any new building styles or construction methods with them. Instead, they followed the existing status quo, especially in places like ancient Egypt.

The second arrival of Western or European architecture began about the mid-14th century. Traditionally, the Arabs were the go-betweens for supplying slaves to the southern European countries of Portugal and Spain. The Arabs also purchased ivories, gold, spices, and other commodities from African dealers who utilized the trans-Saharan trade route that ran from West Africa through the desert to North Africa. In order to maintain their monopoly of the lucrative trans-Saharan trade, the Arabs made it impossible for

Europeans to reach the gold mines of medieval African empires. Nonetheless, Europeans heard many stories about the gold mines of Tumbuktu and the riches of the Sudan. In addition, the Portuguese wanted a sea route to India through the West African coast.

It is important to perceive architecture as a cultural form that can be diffused in distant places through trade links and other forms of social interaction. The process of tracing ancient trade links between Africa and Europe also unfolds the triple heritage architecture and explains the existence of Western colonial cities and building types in Africa. The Portuguese are given credit for opening trade links between Africa and Europe several centuries after the end of Roman domination; however, the Portuguese did not initiate the European desire to go around the West African coast. According to Panikkar (1963), Herodotus wrote about Phoenician explorers who were sent by the Egyptian King Neco to circumnavigate Africa and of a Carthaginian crew under Hanno who were sent to do the same. Herodotus also said that Libya, the ancient Greek name for Africa, was washed on all sides by bodies of water except where it connects with Asia. According to Herodotus, "the Carthaginians also tell us that they trade with a race of men who live beyond the Pillars of Heracles...." (Panikkar 1963, 15).

How far along the West African coast Hanno traveled with his men is not clear. The existence of ancient Roman architectural ruins both along coastal cities of Morocco and further inland can be explained by earlier Roman occupations instead of later European influences. However, Hanno's mention of gorillas and streams of fire flowing into the sea indicates he got as far as the rain forest regions, possibly Sierra Leone. There are, however, no architectural ruins dating to Hanno's time in that region. Regardless, because the Romans stayed longer on the continent, traded with people of the interior throughout the desert, and also sent several expeditions southward to suppress rebellious Berber tribes, they had more knowledge of the Sahara and West Africa than did the Greeks.

In later times, the French and the Portuguese simultaneously declared themselves the first to sail along the Gold Coast, although investigation indicates that both claims were inaccurate. Rather, there were early expeditions dispatched by the great Italian houses to the West African coast. The unsuccessful voyage of the Vivaldi brothers who never made it back in 1292 has been reported (Panikkar 1963, 125). A Genoese, Banzaretto Malocello, who discovered the Canary Islands, made his voyage after the Vivaldi brothers. In 1402, the Frenchmen Jehan de Bethancourt and Gadifier de la Salle took control of the Canaries. Maciot de Bethancourt, a descendant of Jehan de Bethancourt, sold the Canaries to Count Ennque de Guzman of the Castilian court in 1418. This caused a conflict between the Castilians and the Portuguese, who then took it as a challenge to lead the way to Africa, the Land of Gold, as it was then known in Europe. The vital point here is the recognition that the Portuguese and other European powers that came after them consciously or unconsciously packaged architectures from their homelands in diplomatic portfolios and trade supplies and gradually deposited and diffused them along the West African coast. What began as a trading expedition would escalate to colonization centuries later, resulting in the diffusion of a new form of architecture that owes its heritage to Greco-Roman civilization. "Trade was opened up with the modern Ghana and, in 1482, "a fort was built on the site of the later castle of Sao Jorge da Mina" (Blake 1969, 98). Colonial urbanization in Africa was the product of economic relations, social relations, and cultural exchange. Catherine Coquery-Virdrovitch (1991, 34) says that "the earlier forms of colonial urbanization consisted of camps, forts, military settlements," which served as exchange centers and outposts of coercion and domination for larger economic objectives.

A short period of withdrawal by France, due to civil war, left the door open for the Portuguese, especially Prince Henry, who wanted the gold of the Gold Coast and needed a sea route to the East Indies. By the mid-16th century, the Portuguese had gone around the West African coast and established trade centers with the Africans, mainly in slaves, gold, spices, ivories, and oil. The Portuguese embarked on great building activities from Ghana to Lagos and beyond the Angolan coast all the way around the Cape. "For fifty years, holding a monopoly, they traded without hindrance (1480–1530). After 1530, however, their exclusive rights were questioned by other powers, first by France, and later, by England and Holland" (Blake 1969, 14). This new competition among the Europeans along the West African coast heralds Africa's second dark age following the collapse of the Egyptian empire. According to Donahue (1979, 5):

> Real trouble began for the Africans with explorations from the West. Diego Cao (or Cam) sailed from Portugal to the mouth of the Congo River in 1484; in 1490, Diaz sailed around the cape of Good Hope; and, finally, Vasco da Gama made his famous trip to India the same way. Followers of these explorers robbed and plundered the African cities; the natives who were not prepared for war lost their property and their homes.

Later in the 19th century, Benin City was one of the cities that was plundered after the oba had killed some British invaders. Admiral Rawson captured the city of Benin and sent the royal guards fleeing; the city's treasures were looted and sent to England. Oba Ovonramwen tried in vain to protect his crumbling palace and kingdom. He was persuaded to leave the city when the enemy was already at its gates. His subjects left with him, so the British occupied a city without inhabitants. Two days after the conquest, a great fire swept through Benin City, carrying away in its flames the remains of an epoch (Ryder 1969, 290).

The European powers established several trading centers along the West African coast long before the fall of Benin. As usual, the traders brought new culture and technology. The homes of wealthy European traders were modeled after prototypes in their homelands. For example, in 1480, King John II of Portugal commanded his general on the Guinea coast to build a fort in Mina, Gueani. "Thus fortified, the commander, Diogo d'Azambuja set out with 600 men, on board a fleet of ten ships and two barges" (Blake 1969, 99). The stoneworkers, masons, and carpenters, all Portuguese, began work after Diogo d'Azambuja was given a site on which to build his fort by the West African king of Caramansa. Within a few weeks of landing, the Portuguese erected several structures: Their building site was surrounded with a defensive wall. A chapel was erected, and the castle, known originally as Sao Jorge de Mina but later changed to Elmina Castle, is now in Ghana (Fig. 2.1). This 15th-century fort became a standard for most of the European forts built in Africa afterward. It had defen-

Fig. 2.1 Ghana, West Africa. Elmina Castle (formerly Sao Jorge de Mina). By Diogo d'Azambuja. 1482 A.D.
(United Nations Educational Scientific and Cultural Organization (UNESCO))

sive walls, bastions that faced all directions, was armed with several cannons, and above all was primarily located for easy access to the ocean. The walls were very thick and the surveillance towers were equipped with cannons. In 1637, the Dutch captured this castle after almost 200 years of Portuguese occupation.

The Western contribution to the triple heritage of African culture and architecture is intertwined with the introduction of Christianity. The Europeans came with the Bible to proselytize the Christian religion to the Africans. It is important to note that Christianity was already thriving in Africa, especially in Ethiopia, Egypt, and parts of the northeastern Sudan before the age of explorers. However, the coming of Islam in the 7th century stopped Christianity from spreading further south. "According to the Coptic Church, Christianity was brought to Egypt by Saint Mark himself" (Mazrui 1986, 47), one of the apostles. In that case, it was a Semitic injection that continues ancient cultural exchange between the Israelis and Africa.

The advent of Christianity also meant that a foreign architectural culture was in the making in West Africa. The ancient Roman strand in North Africa finally found a way to the heartland of Africa after several centuries. The importation of foreigners to build slave depots and administrative and residential quarters began the importation of new styles of architecture into Africa, a phenomenon which spread gradually. Christians came at different times and from different countries and different sects. For example, the Catholics tried to transplant Catholic churches, while the English advertised their Anglican church. Different trading companies brought their parent country's architectural heritage and hybrids.

The following section briefly highlights the styles of Western architecture that have been imported into Africa from about 146 B.C., when Rome occupied North Africa, to the present time. It is important to mention that Western transfers of architectural styles to Africa from 146 B.C. to the present represent multiple layers of historical epochs. It would be impossible to separate the various layers in a single volume. Nonetheless, the major styles that currently dominate Western architectural influence in Africa are discussed. These include contributions from the Romans, Portuguese, Spaniards, British, French, Germans, Belgians, Dutch, and the imports of the Emancipados (returned emancipated slaves), as well as the contributions of Western and African architects since the end of World War II, through the years of independence, to the present time.

2.1 ROMAN ARCHITECTURE IN AFRICA

Roman architectural implants in Africa were the direct result of conquest and imperialistic territorial expansionism, and they mark the first major introduction of Western architecture on the continent. Roman building activity in Africa began with the twilight that gradually ushered out Pharaonic Egypt. By 700 B.C., Egypt was in its late period, and the series of events that would install foreign kings and queens on her Pharaonic throne was beginning to ferment. Egypt had reigned with its native African kings and queens for over 2500 years and no longer had the energy to defend itself from other competing powers.

Egypt's isolation from the world ended with the invasions of the Assyrians under Assurbanipal (667–610 B.C.), who installed his son, Psammetichus I, on the throne. Nebuchadnezzar II, the Babylonian king, mounted an unsuccessful attack on Egypt in 601. Cambyses (525–522 B.C.), the Persian king, conquered Egypt and began the 27th Dynasty. He was succeeded by Darius I. Finally, Alexander the Great, the king of Macedonia, marched his troops into North Africa to conquer Egypt in about 333 B.C., after the Persians had ravaged and colonized the native population for over 200 years. Alexander died and was replaced by Ptolemy, son of Lagus, who established the Ptolemaic dynasty (30th and last).

West of Egypt, in the area that is present-day Tunisia, was the Phoenician city-state of Carthage. The name Carthage is derived, through Latin, from the Phoenician *Kart-Hadasht*, meaning "new city," which might imply that it was deliberately intended to be more than a convenient stopping point on the route to Spain. The original homeland of the Phoenicians is now Lebanon, and the major cities were Sydon and Tyre. The Phoenicians had a long tradition of trading activity in the Mediterranean. Carthage, a stopping point on the way to Spain, eventually grew to be a city-state, especially after the collapse of the homeland of the Carthaginians to the great Babylonian army and subsequently to the Persians.

Carthage was already a strong independent city-state with a strong economic and military force in the Mediterranean by about 580 B.C. It had influence over southern Spain because of mineral resources, which made the city a rival to Rome. Rome and Carthage remained enemies for about 100 years. The three wars between them are known as the Punic Wars, from the Latin *bella punica*. The first Punic War began in 264 B.C.

when Rome wanted to gain control of Sicily. Hannibal, the son of Hamilcar Barca, tried to invade Rome from Carthage through the Alps on his elephant infantry mobile army, but he was defeated by Rome after a significant loss. The end of the second Punic War set the end of the Carthaginian empire in motion. Rome began "the third Punic War against Carthage in 149 B.C. with the goal of destroying Carthage entirely, due to irrational fears about its possible revival. The city was razed to the ground in 146 B.C." (Warmington 1980, 237). Most of what is left of Carthage today are ruins. Some beautiful mosaics, columns of buildings, and stumps of arches that are still standing tell much about this magnificent city before its destruction.

The arrival of Rome marked the beginning of Western architecture in Africa as a recycled classical concept originally from Egypt to Greece, then Rome, and back to North Africa with new flavor. At El Djem, Tunisia, a colosseum constructed in the 3rd century A.D. rivaled the one in Rome and could seat over 30,000 spectators (Fig. C.8). The ancient town of Sufetula, Sbeita, still has remains of temples executed in Greco-Roman classical style. The porticos, columns, and the craftsmanship reflect ingenious Roman engineering (Fig. C.9). Roman antiquities can be found all over North Africa in countries like Morocco, Algeria, Tunisia, Libya, and Egypt. Some ancient African cities such as Leptis Magna and Ptolemais were converted to military garrisons. The Romans built theaters, basilicas, bathhouses, triumphal arches, and villas in many cities of North Africa. In city planning, the Romans applied the refined Greek city plan to North African cities such as Leptis Magna and Ptolemais, a principal city of Cyrenica. As the name suggests, Ptolemais dates from the reign of the Ptolemies in ancient Egypt.

Two of the major factors in the Ptolemais's city plan are the grid and the distinction between major roads and feeder roads. The grid runs north, south, east, and west with the major roads, but the feeder roads all run north-south. Major monuments and public buildings were placed next to major roads. In Ptolemais, the triumphal arches were placed over the major carriageway at an intersection. It has been suggested that the triumphal arch was constructed in a style similar to the triumphal arch in the Forum of Theodosius at Constantinople. The columns of the triumphal arch are essentially Corinthian, while the square plan was commonly adopted for most houses, as demonstrated by the plan of the Ptolemaic city bathhouse, which dates to the Byzantine period.

The Romans did not limit their building activities to the North African coast. They colonized as far as Upper Egypt and further into the heartland of the Sahara Desert and the Sudan. The Roman kiosk next to the Meroetic Lion Temple

at Naga is a good example (Fig. 2.2) and demonstrates how far the Romans went into the heartland of Africa and their desire to learn about ancient African religions. This kiosk marked one of the limits of Roman territory in the Sahara and gives credence to the fact that the Romans bought merchandise from the caravans of the trans-Saharan traders. It also became an architectural diffusion contact and, as is demonstrated in later chapters (Part 5), this Roman building activity influenced some construction styles and techniques still practiced in parts of West Africa.

The arrival of Islam in the early 7th century led to the fall of Byzantine Rome and to the rise of a new form of architec-

Fig. 2.2 Naga, Republic of Sudan. The Roman kiosk built next to an ancient African Lion Temple. 400 A.D.
(Edition Leipzig)

ture as well as to the end of the first phase of the introduction of Western architecture into Africa. Islamic movements in parts of southern Europe, especially Spain, isolated Europeans from Africa for several centuries, until the age of the great sailors and explorers. The Portuguese led the way at this time, described in this book as the second coming of Europeans to Africa. The Greeks and the Romans were the dominant players in the first coming, although the Greeks, unlike the Romans, ruled Egypt without introducing new architectural elements.

2.2 PORTUGUESE ARCHITECTURE IN AFRICA

The Portuguese brought medieval European fortress architecture to Africa. Their sphere of influence was primarily along the West and Southwest African coast. The dominant theme of Portuguese architecture in Africa was that of defense. Portuguese forts were designed to withstand attacks

from the natives, rival slave hunters, and pirates from other European countries. Some of the prominent features are high towers for guards and surveillance, thick and high masonry walls with gun turrets, large storage spaces and dungeons for slaves, and almost all living quarters located within the main defensive wall. The most prominent of the Portuguese castles is Sao Jorge, built between 1480–1482, and now known as Elmina Castle.

One of the highest concentrations of European forts and castles in Africa is along Ghana's 350-m Atlantic coast. Ghana was most attractive to the European powers because of the large quantities of gold exported from there since the time of the ancient Ghana empire. At least 30 forts and castles were built along the coastal lands of Ghana. The forts also became depots for goods awaiting shipment to Europe and the Americas. The second fort built by the Portuguese was Fort Axim, in 1516 A.D. The Danes captured it in 1642, and the English subsequently took it from the Danes in 1872.

Much of what we know about the architecture of the Portuguese forts in Africa comes from Portugal, especially from the works of the architects who designed them. Castle Elmina and Fort Axim are no doubt examples of military architecture conceived with the whole purpose of keeping what is meant to be kept inside the fort on the inside and, conversely, what is meant to be kept outside the fort on the outside. Elmina Castle and Fort Axim may have been built under the direction of a Languedocian, Diogo de Boytaca, who some authors identify as Diogo d'Azambuja (Kubler 1972) and who was a key player in the design of "Portuguese fortifications in Africa and the Orient" (Blake 1969, 99).

Geometry had a major influence on the Portuguese architects of the time. Walls were treated as cellular structures and functioned as barriers, passages, spacial volumetric, and above all, as impregnable obstacles. Following the trend of architecture in Portugal at that time, Elmina Castle and Fort Axim reflect the Portuguese plain style in which the excesses of the Manueline era were being discarded for simpler purist architecture. Altogether, the Portuguese began a new type of irreversible cultural architectural marriage between Africa and Europe, which still lingers today.

2.3 ENGLISH ARCHITECTURE IN AFRICA

English imports to Africa cover a wide range that includes forts, Gothic (Figs. C.88 and C.89) and Victorian styles, and English cottage houses. Each marks a stage of English intrusion into the continent's history. The English legacy begins with the age of exploration and the scramble for gold and continues through the age of colonization and independence (1600–1960), 360 years that changed the continent's architectural history.

The English followed in the footsteps of the Portuguese in that their first architectural construction in Africa was a fort. "A hilltop site near Kormantine was allocated to the English for the purpose of building a small fortified lodge, which was destroyed by fire in 1640" (Hutchinson 1979, 100). The Dutch took this site from the English several years later. Fort Carolusburg was completed by the English in 1665, and its name changed to Cape Coast Castle by 1690. In 1691, the British started Fort Dixcove and completed it in 1697, exchanged it with the Dutch for another fort in 1868, but got it back in 1872. James Fort, originally started by the Portuguese, was taken and renovated by the English in 1673.

The settlement of the southern parts of Africa by people of English and Dutch origin brought other kinds of English architecture to Africa, including commercial buildings, religious buildings, administrative buildings, residential structures, and multifunctional facilities such as parks. Picton-Seymour (1977, ix) states, "The discovery of gold and dia-

Fig. 2.3 Cape Town, South Africa. Standard Bank, Adderley Street. Designed by Freeman. 1880. (Desiree Picton-Seymour and A.A. Balkema Uitgewer)

monds in South Africa provided an impetus for the material manifestation of rich and flamboyant buildings."

In Cape Town, South Africa, the Standard Bank building on Adderley Street is one of the late 19th-century (1880) English architectural landmarks. In spite of some renovations, this classical building still retains most of its original design by Freeman. Its columns are Corinthian. According to Picton-Seymour (1977) the Banking Hall rises two stories and the

Fig. 2.4 Cape Town, South Africa. Saint George's Cathedral, Wale Street elevation. Designed by Banker and Masser. 1900 A.D. (Desiree Picton-Seymour and A. A. Balkema Uitgewer)

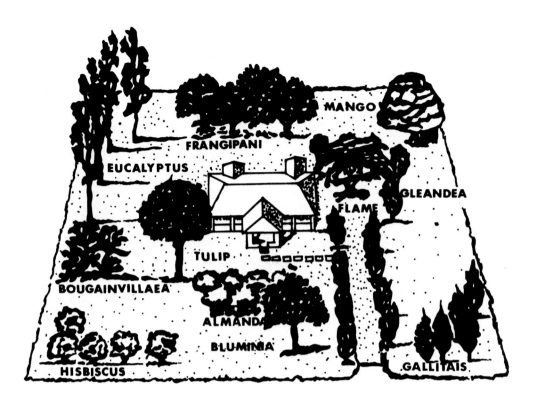

Fig. 2.5 Kaduna, Nigeria. English house layout at the exclusive European Quarters, now Government Reserved Quarters. (W. T. W. Morgan)

interior furniture is mostly mahogany. Unlike the Standard Bank, Saint George's Cathedral in Cape Town follows the Gothic style (Figs. 2.3 and 2.4) as do similar structures in many African countries.

Colonization of several countries in Africa by the English extended their architectural import beyond medieval castles. They also built residences and schools to train their clerks who were employed by their multinational corporations, such as the Niger Delta Company. The residences were mostly prototypes of Victorian houses designed for temporary accommodations. One factor that influenced English construction in Nigeria, Sierra Leone, and Ghana is that the British had no intention of settling down in those places. Their primary objective was commercial, so many homes were designed as temporary structures that would later be abandoned. This fact is clearer when one compares the elegant and permanent structures built in South Africa where the Dutch and a good number of English settled.

Colonization brought English architecture in Africa to a bureaucratic standardization. Except for the mansions designed for the governors of their colonial provinces and the administrative buildings, the English were obsessed with re-creating their country villages abroad. Hence, they stipulated rigid cardinal rules for the surroundings and layout of houses of their colonial administrators (Fig. 2.5). The garden layout was very formal and took advantage of tropical evergreen shrubs, trees, and the shade they provided to the buildings to reduce heat. Moreover, the English believed in segregated quarters for the servants in their colonies and built their houses accordingly. In contrast, this policy was debated a great deal by the French who wanted to assimilate Africans into their culture as a channel for the consolidation of the greater France abroad.

2.4 FRENCH ARCHITECTURE IN AFRICA

The first slave fort built by the French was on St. James Island at the mouth of the Gambia and Senegal Rivers. Commercial exploitation was the main concern of the French. The Dutch and the English tried to drive the French out of the region. The Dutch, for instance, burned down a French trading station just 1 month after its completion. However, by the early 19th century, the pursuit of commerce led to territorial ambitions and the need to create a greater France. This finally culminated in the partitioning of Africa in 1897 and the adoption by France of a colonial policy of assimilation under which the French pursued a liberal attitude toward their colonies. French architects working in the colonies had assimilation in mind, but its full meaning was an obstacle to implementation, except on an experimental basis in a place such as Dakar, Senegal. Therefore, the French had to act in a covert manner so as not to rouse public resentment and rebellion by the colonial citizens, causing procolonialists like Marrast to write that "we conquer the hearts of the natives and win their affection, as is our duty as colonizers" (Wright 1991, 1).

Underneath this liberalism lies an inherent desire to re-create the home environment in the colonies. This desire was accomplished on a grand scale in major African cities planned by the French: Fez, Casablanca, Dakar, Cairo, and Abidjan. In the city plan, they wanted to create extensions of Paris abroad and a greater France with a great culture worthy of global emulation. This was of such importance to the French people that the French colonial architectural program was based on a doctrine of urban assimilation. French citizens and literary guards were aware of this policy, and they did not hesitate to celebrate it whenever it was applied and accomplished successfully. "One novelist, for example, praised J. H. Collet de Cantelou, director of the Architectural Service of Madagascar in the 1930s, because he has asserted authority in directing new buildings, just as [the colonial administrators] are directing the economy…" (Wright 1991, 3).

Colonial urban planning policy at the turn of the 20th century also became an outlet for the French to express themselves and cure the ills plaguing major French cities, especially Paris. It was, in a way, an experiment for curing the problems of overcrowding, industrial pollution, prostitution, and other social nuisances by testing the "medicines" abroad first before using them at home. Consequently, the boulevards of Paris and their diagonal intersections were exported to the urban centers planned in Africa. While there was a modest respect for the cultures of the colonial people in the way the buildings were executed, there was a celebration of France in the way the larger urban ambiance was being shaped. For example, the Palace of Justice in Casablanca retains an Islamic flavor with tender columns and triad arches, but it sits in a city that looks like nothing indigenous to Morocco. Another example can be found in the Tetuan railroad station in Rabat (see Fig. 4.1). The two towers that define the symmetry of this building are of Frankish origin, but a new vocabulary has been added to it, and the treatment of the entrance with a horseshoe-shaped arch gives the building an Arabian look. This process of giving buildings a new look by adding or subtracting certain elements later becomes known as Arabisances in the North African colonies. Neither the cities of Dakar in Senegal nor Banjul in Gambia look like a traditional sub-Saharan African city because of the way they were executed by French architects and planners.

2.5 DUTCH ARCHITECTURE IN AFRICA

The Dutch began their building program at Ghana with the construction of a lodge in 1642. The lodge was expanded to a

Fig. 2.6 Pretoria, Republic of South Africa. Traditional Dutch architecture. (American Geographical Society Collection, The University of Wisconsin-Milwaukee Library)

fort 10 years later and called Fort Ussher. The English took over in 1782 but returned it to the Dutch 3 years later. The Dutch abandoned it in 1816, but returned in 1830. Finally, it was transferred to the English in 1868. It is one of the forts currently in use as a prison by the Ghanaian government. Another Dutch fort taken by the English in 1782 but later returned is Fort Senya Beraku. Today, it serves as a guest house for tourists. One of the last forts built by the Dutch is Fort Leydsaanheid, which currently serves as a district police station for the Ghanaian government. The French did not hesitate to bombard Fort Amsterdam when they had the opportunity. It was all part of the scramble for gold and the struggle for commercial and territorial dominance.

The most significant contribution of the Dutch to African architecture is not the slave forts they built but the Victorian style and native Dutch style architecture that the settlers built around the cape coast of South Africa. The dominance of Victorian architecture in southern Africa stems from the influence of the time, that is, the application of iron in building construction and finishes during the Industrial Revolution. In addition, the Europeans who went to South Africa settled in large numbers, especially the Germans, Dutch, English, and French. Victorian and Gothic buildings in South Africa were built as permanent structures, not as mere commercial outposts as in other parts of the continent (Fig. 2.6).

2.6 ORTHODOX CLASSICISM MEETS MYSTICAL VILLAGE FORTRESSES

South Africa has a distinctive history as far as African architecture is concerned because the country has more European settlers than any other African nation. The balance of the triple heritage architecture swings heavily in favor of Western style architecture in South Africa. Unlike most multicultural societies, where several cultures gradually fuse into one another in the most unconscious manner, gradual changes take much longer than usual in the Republic of South Africa, and in most cases, powerful interest groups work very hard to promote change.

Several South African architects have taken part in the search for a cohesive national identity and political stability. A limited number of citizens were constantly in touch with the industrial and cultural changes going on in the Western world. In the 1930s and 1940s, a group of young South African architects in Johannesburg was devoted followers of Le Corbusier. Most of them believed in the social ideals of the modern movement and its possible far-reaching implications in helping to liberate humanity from abject poverty. However, they

Fig. 2.7 Maputo, Mozambique. House of the Three Giraffes. Amancio de Alpoim Guedes. (Udo Kultermann)

were powerless and had little room to express their feelings through their works. They resorted to metaphorical expressions which could only be decoded by those who knew them well. This group includes Stanley Saitowitz, Vaughn Bovuswlo, and Amancio Guedes, among others. Most were trained in the United States and the United Kingdom. Wilhelm O. Meyer, who attended the University of Pennsylvania and graduated in Louis Khan's master's class of 1961, demonstrates a unique ability in his work and clearly declares himself a son of two worlds by synthesizing the most intrinsic aspects of architecture that belong to the West and Africa. His work, and that of Julian Elliot, Amancio Guedes, and many others, is derived from a measured cultural rainbow of architectural repertoire that illuminates the inquisitive mind. This rainbow spectrum ranges from orthodox Western classicism to modern architecture and fortified African town layouts.

In all cases, these individuals accept a dual personality that is molded by both a rigid rationalist Western culture and a mystical traditional African environment with its innocent ambiance. These elements betray each other in a complementary manner. The fact that South Africa is, by all accounts, an industrialized country and that architects who practice there make maximum and efficient use of its resources and building technology could fool the untrained eye into thinking that all European built structures in South Africa are *purely Western*. That is not necessarily the case because many buildings in southern Africa respond to the genius loci of the African environment under the cover of a Western facade.

For example, Professor Pancho Guedes is not only an architect but a painter and a sculptor as well. His works are influenced by mystical, traditional African art, along with Cubism and Renaissance art. There are very few architects who can speak as many languages and dialects of architecture with comfort and professional fluency in this age of specialization. Yet, Guedes speaks the language of classicism, the Renaissance, and modernism and, in each case, relies on his African roots for inspiration. Each project bears a theme and leaves unforgettable, mesmerizing images drawn from an inexhaustible source of energy. Their size is modest, but each radiates a captivating presence that echoes the African theme of the past 30 years. Pancho Guedes has built enough houses in Mozambique and other parts of South Africa to fill a sizable town. He has described his works as *Stiloguedes*, a term he defines as follows:

> *Stiloguedes is my most idiosyncratic style, my royal family as it were. It is a bizarre and fantastic family of buildings with spikes and fangs, with beams tearing into the spaces around them, invented as if some parts are about to slip off, and come crashing down, with convulsive walls and armored lights. The plans of the Stiloguedes buildings are simple, quite straightforward and functional. It is the sections that are contorted, decorated and full of exaggerations. It is the sections and their reflections on the facades that are the architecture. They stretch that mysterious relationship between plan, section and facade and turn these works into strange apparitions. (Guedes 1985, 68)*

Stiloguedes are expressed in projects like the House of the Three Giraffes, a house with concrete tent roofs and three long-necked chimneys (Fig. 2.7). At Prometheus, an apartment block is cantilevered from a central row of pillars. The inspiration is from one of Picasso's 1928 drawings. Other projects include the Smiling Lion, the Sapial Bakery, House Boesch, and the list goes on. Guedes's greatest asset is his chameleonlike flexibility. At House Boesch, the organic character of Frank Lloyd Wright's houses is well detailed with meticulous conviction, while the Standard Bank of Mozambique is a masterfully executed edifice in Renaissance classicism. Guedes has a strange but effective way of telling the African story.

Wilhelm Meyer elaborates the duality of the South African theme in a formalist mannerism that mirrors the work of his predecessors at the turn of the 20th century, while searching for the ideal meaning of African gloriana and its place in the industrial age. His recent addition to the Johannesburg Art Gallery, which Sir Edwin Lutyens began in 1911, a mere 25 years after Johannesburg was planned, was executed as a continuity of Lutyens's design. His projects at Rand Afrikaans University and the 1979 Verwoerdburg urban development design reflect a less formal approach to his syncretic vocabulary.

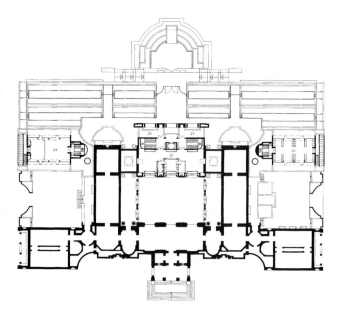

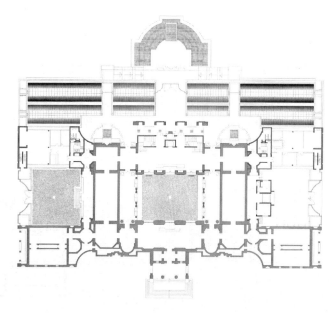

Fig. 2.8 and 2.9 Johannesburg, Republic of South Africa. Lutyens's Art Gallery extension. (Top) Ground floor plan. (Bottom) First floor plan . 1983. (Meyer Pienaar Smith Architects & Urban Designers)

Meyer had to resolve the formidable challenge of completing Lutyens's conception, which was not realized originally. It was indeed necessary that he pay accurate attention to Lutyens's original intentions because the gallery is one of several South African historical landmarks. According to Meyer (1984, 2), the main significance of the Johannesburg Art Gallery in the stream of work produced by Lutyens is his

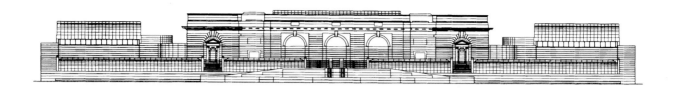

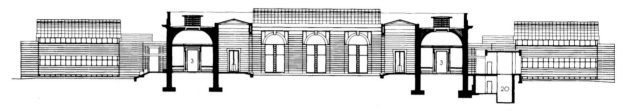

Fig. 2.10 Johannesburg, Republic of South Africa. Elevation of Lutyens's Art Gallery extension. 1983.
(Meyer Pienaar Smith Architects & Urban Designers)

complete move into the classical idiom for public buildings, later to mature in his magnificent, regal design for the Viceroy's House in New Delhi, India. The gallery did not take full advantage of its location in Juobart Park, so there was no dialogue or connection between the gallery and the park. This was one of the issues that confronted Meyer. In addition, the client wanted a large, naturally lit exhibition space that could be easily subdivided with screens.

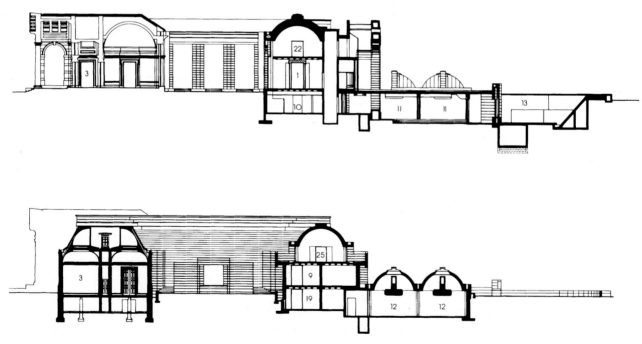

Fig. 2.11 Johannesburg, Republic of South Africa. Elevation-sections, Lutyens's Art Gallery extension.
1983. (Meyer Pienaar Smith Architects & Urban Designers)

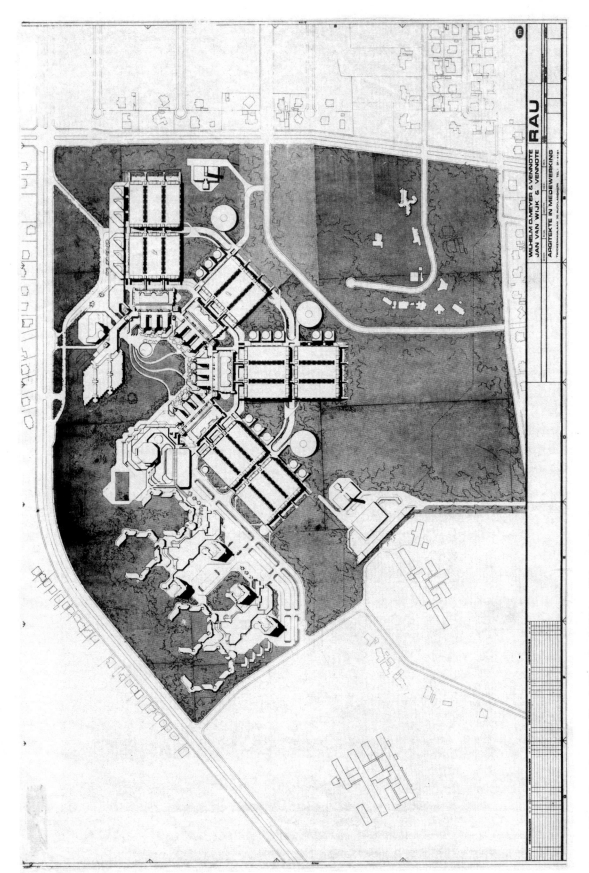

Fig. 2.12 Johannesburg, Republic of South Africa. Rand Afrikaans University. Site plan. 1975. (Meyer Pienaar Smith Architects & Urban Designers)

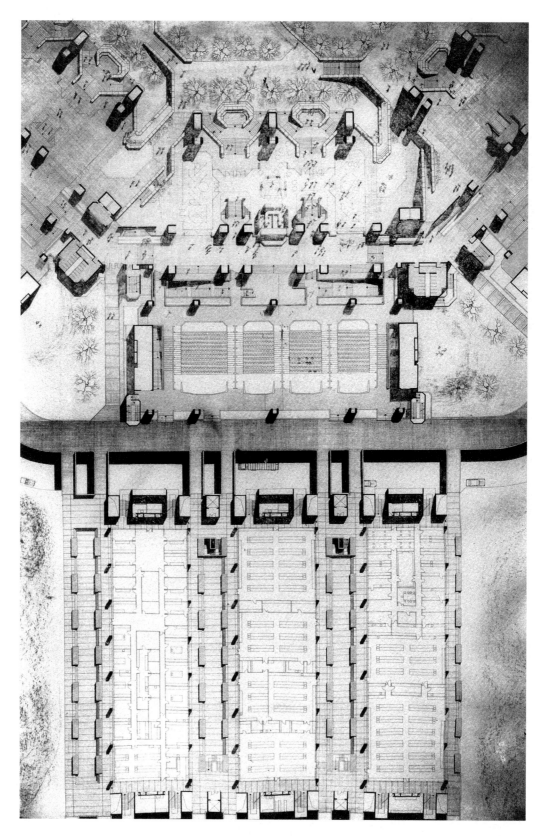

2.13 *Johannesburg, Republic of South Africa. Rand Afrikaans University. Ground floor plan of one
segment: Central open court, student spaces, walkway, lecture theaters, and laboratories. 1975. (Meyer Pienaar
Smith Architects & Urban Designers)*

Fig. 2.14 Johannesburg, Republic of South Africa. Rand Afrikaans University. Aerial view from the east.
1975. (Meyer Pienaar Smith Architects & Urban Designers)

In order to meet the client's needs and reconcile the park and gallery, the extension was partially placed below ground level to form a threshold platform as a foreground to the original building (Figs. 2.8 to 2.11). The park "flows up" over the terraces formed by the underground extensions onto the new copper roof of the gallery. This roof is purposely allowed to tarnish so that the resulting verdigris will blend with the green park vegetation. The original portico remains the major point of access, while a new covered portico receives visitors from the park into the new foyer, from which access is gained into the existing exhibition hall and the new lower level gallery.

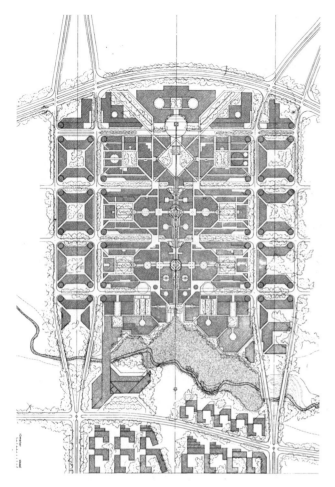

Fig. 2.15 Verwoerdburg, Republic of South Africa. Site plan. (Meyer Pienaar Smith Architects & Urban Designers)

ical heart of the university, without looking like a building site for years to come. The university core encloses an inner-landscaped space and garden that are encircled by an uninterrupted walkway. This walkway begins at the main entrance, the library, and links all the colleges, administrative, and extracurricular departments of the university (Figs. 2.12 to 2.14). The construction is mostly in posttension concrete, and the influences of Louis Khan can be seen on the library and on the rest of the complex.

The housing complex was similarly conceived as a small village adjoining the academic campus and was executed in load-bearing brick construction. Meyer continues the village format in Verwoerdburg urban design. Using an artificial lake as a focal feature, a labyrinth of low buildings was carefully knit together into self-contained compounds with landscaped courtyards to reflect a rural ambiance (Figs. 2.15 and 2.16). These projects maintained an eclectic discourse with the South African landscape but were not limited by it. Rather, they exploited modern technology to attain their full potential.

Critics and scholars must be attentive to this marriage between traditional African architecture and modern technology or else they will not recognize it, as they are not used to seeing it in that light. The images of the past have become unconscious blindfolds that can prevent one from recognizing ongoing trends. Meyer's approach to architecture in Southern Africa is best summarized with the following excerpt from a speech he presented on July 13, 1991:

I like architecture to which response can be on many levels—not only on the physical level via as many senses as are available but also on the remoter subjective, contemplative level to do with moods, symbolism, images, the breathtakingly new, daring, calm, fresh, full of discovery, memories, reminiscences. To be all these things it must speak of its place in time—its landscape and its culture, meaning the essence of the layers of its past as also the aspirations of a possible future interpreted through the creative visions of its maker. (Meyer 1991, 5)

In contrast, Meyer took advantage of the landscape and an indigenous repertoire to create modern compounds, which are ringed like traditional Ndebele, Tswana, or Zulu kraals, at Rand Afrikaans University. Indigenous South African habitations and villages were often designed as self-contained fortresses, in concentric order, as exemplified by the enclosures of Great Zimbabwe (see Figs. 11.12 to 11.17 and C.39). These projects reflect what Meyer (1984, 5) considers an "ultimate marriage between irreconcilable qualities of inevitability in its logical solution to the situation, as well as the magic of a pure creation in art, tribal or otherwise." Meyer took advantage of the tradition to resolve both the logistics of developing the campus over a long period of time and arranging infrastructures on the campus in an order that enhanced centralization and compactness. According to Meyer, the radial form of the university fulfilled the client's requirement that the first phase of construction should complete the phys-

2.7 GERMAN ARCHITECTURE IN AFRICA

Germany had only a brief colonial presence in Africa because its territories were taken by the British and the French as a result of World War I. The Germans built Fort Fredrickburg in 1683 in Ghana but abandoned it in 1705. The Dutch took

Fig. 2.17 Cameroon. German colonial building constructed on stilts like traditional houses in the region. 1890s.
(Dipl-ing Wolfgang Lauber)

possession of this fort in 1725 and renamed it Fort Hollandia. The solid, square stone building with its heavy, Germanic masonry belonged to the Brandenburgers, a German trading company. Christiansborg Castle, the largest of all the European castles in Africa, is also of German creation. Still in excellent condition, it served as the seat of government during colonial British administration of Ghana for over 30 years, until 1960 when Ghana became a republic.

Nevertheless, the Germans left several monuments that remind everyone of their brief tenure in Cameroon, Togo, Namibia, and Tanzania. Although the Germans were in these colonies, only from 1884 to 1914, they had intended to stay on a permanent basis and made ambitious plans to develop them with German engineering. Some of the orderly, heavy architecture still in use testifies to this fact. The Germans tried unsuccessfully to gain access to the growing foreign trade of the 19th century in Africa until they finally established bases in the Cameroon, Namibia, Tanzania, and Togo, toward the end of the century. However, there were additional motivations for them to make the most of their colonies.

The fear of overpopulation in Germany made it necessary to establish possible areas for immigration. Like all the other European powers, Germany also wanted cheap sources of raw material for the maturing, industrial complexes in their homeland, as well as new markets for their manufactured goods. Unlike the British for whom profit, with little intent to settle, was the main motive in tropical Africa, the Germans' intent was both to settle and, above all, to make a profit. As a result, they took their planning and development seriously. They built permanent, rather than temporary, structures.

In 1986 and 1987, a joint Cameroonian and German professional team of architects was able to study and record with accurate drawings the state of some of the existing German buildings in the Cameroon. Among these is the colonial administration building constructed in 1886 on the shores of the river. This building is so strategically located that it has a view of the river, the sea, the nearby Fernanda Po Island, and the towering, 13,000-ft Cameroon Mountain. The site was originally selected for the cool breezes coming from different directions. Its foundation is on volcanic rock from the mountain, and the walls are of masonry brick. Iron girders and wood are used for the floor and the roof, respectively.

Like most of the other colonial powers, it did not take the Germans long to learn the climatology of Cameroon and then to copy some of the building methods used by the natives. In this regard, it became common practice to mount buildings on stilts (Fig. 2.17), as in these pictured colonial houses built at the turn of the century for the staff who managed the plantations. Today, they are still in use by the Urban Planning Authority of Cameroon.

2.8 THE IMPORTS OF THE EMANCIPATED SLAVES: BRAZILIAN, CREOLE, SPANISH, AND MORE VICTORIAN ARCHITECTURE IN AFRICA

Upon the abolition of the slave trade, some of the free men and women moved back to Africa bringing with them technical skills acquired from the West. Two countries in West Africa, in fact, were carved out just for the resettlement of freed slaves from the Americas, Brazil, and Europe, especially southern Europe. The British resettled many slaves in Sierra Leone, while the Americans resettled many in Liberia. Freetown in Sierra Leone and Monrovia, named after President Monroe of the United States, in Liberia were the major centers of resettlement.

Some of the returnees also settled in Lagos, Ibadan, Abidjan, Banjul, Dakar, and all the other major West African coastal cities. Those who came from Brazilian plantations built houses with skills and forms reminiscent of those they found in Brazil. Some scholars now refer to them as the Brazilian Houses of West Africa, and there are many such

houses in Lagos, Port Harcourt, and Ibadan in Nigeria. Those who came from Spain and Portugal brought the Spanish style, while those who came from the islands of Jamaica brought Creole styles. Some of these houses were three or more stories. "The three-storied houses are typical in Creole style, erected in the nineteenth century by ex-slaves and typical of early Banjul, Freetown, Liberian coastal towns and of Lagos" (Church 1980, 229).

In reality, there is not much difference between Creole, Spanish, and Brazilian styles. They all have Portuguese and dominant Spanish influence, since Brazil was a former colony of Portugal. Consequently, the Brazilian style is a prototype of Portuguese architecture in Brazil. On the other hand, the slaves from the United States came back with a distinctive style. They brought prototypes of Victorian styles from Georgia. The buildings are predominantly in Monrovia, a typical example being the home of President Joseph Jenkins Roberts of Liberia (Fig. 2.18). The slaves freed from England also brought back a style unique from the Brazilian, Creole, and Spanish styles, but similar to the Victorian architecture from England. A good example of this

Fig. 2.18 Monrovia, Liberia. The home of President Joseph Jenkins Roberts. 1840s. (Reuben K. Udo & Africana Publishing Company)

Fig. 2.19 Freetown, Sierra Leone. The first building of Fourah Bay College. Early 1900s. (Reuben K. Udo & Africana Publishing Company)

is the original building of Fourah Bay College, Freetown, Sierra Leone (Fig. 2.19).

2.9 POST-WORLD WAR II IMPORTS: THE INTERNATIONAL STYLE, A GIFT TO INDEPENDENT AFRICAN STATES

World War II left England and its competitor, France, both weakened. The Union Jack—the English flag that symbolized the "sun that never sets on the English empire"—began to tear apart as one of the largest empires ever built by humanity faced rebellious citizens in all corners of the globe. England could not afford to police the empire effectively any longer. By 1945, India was already moving toward independence. By 1960, almost all the English colonies in Africa had achieved independence.

But the young emerging nations had no infrastructure, and 400 years of underdevelopment caught up with them. They had to build new capitals, new schools, and hospitals, but their traditional architecture had been neglected for those 400 years, and no skilled builders or craftspeople were trained by the colonizers before they left.

A group of students from the colonized countries had gone to England and France to study architecture and other trades and later returned to rebuild their countries; however, their professional training did not consider their background historically and architecturally significant. These architects were left to seek out their own identities and apply them in their construction efforts. Unfortunately, not only were they uneducated about their own culture, but they were also indoctrinated by the dominant Western culture that had swept through the world and set the standard of operation and execution of projects visually, aesthetically, symbolically, and structurally.

Fig. 2.20 Lagos, Nigeria. The Crusaders House. 1950s. (Udo Kultermann)

The foreign trained architects lacked sensitivity to the cults of ancestor worship in Africa and to the different arts which they generate. So these professionals had to learn the basic vocabularies of traditional African art from the unadulterated artists who had been trained by indigenous artists. In Nigeria, some of those architects include former Vice President Alex Ifeanyi Ekwueme, Femi Majekodunmi, Oluwole Olumiyiwa, among many others. The early projects executed by these architects were less eclectic with traditional African architecture than their later works. For Oluwole Olumiyiwa, the search for indigenous identity began with the Crusaders House at Lagos (Figs. 2.20 and 2.21).

In Europe and the United States of America, the reconstruction of the war-battered facilities was still in progress. Le Corbusier's idea of the house as a machine and Mies van der Rohe's transparent structuralist expressions of the international style were becoming increasingly popular. The European and American architects who came to build in the new independent African nations were highly influenced by the socialist movements of the time, and their ignorance of traditional African architecture did not make it easier for them because some of them felt that Africa had no history, except in the northern areas. Prussin (1986, 4) states, "or that such attitudes have severely limited the development of any

real understanding of the subject is obvious, even more important, they reflect the deep seated historically evolved patterns of theoretical misconception and misinterpretation."

This helps to explain why the international style is the dominant character of most African cities today.

chapter

ISLAMIC
ARCHITECTURE
IN AFRICA

This chapter explains the third aspect of African triple heritage architecture and is a journey through time and space from the Arabian Peninsula in 640 A.D. to the present. The fall of the Eastern Byzantine Empire and its North African provinces meant the rise of Islam with a new form of a house for God, Allah.

This chapter begins and ends with the spread of Islamic architecture in North, East, and West Africa. It will be noted that Islamic influence is not strong in southern Africa where Christianity and European settlements prevented its spread. It can be concluded that the further north one goes the more Islamic the continent becomes, and African architecture follows this geographical distribution.

3.1 THE SPREAD OF ISLAMIC ARCHITECTURE IN NORTH AFRICA: THE EARLY PERIOD

The growth and expansion of what we now know as Islamic architecture began with the birth and spread of Islam. Muhammad, the Great Prophet who founded Islam, lived from 570 to 632 A.D. Islam and Islamic architecture spread through most of Asia Minor and the Mediterranean basin 100 years after the death of the Prophet.

Because of its strategic location, Northern Africa has witnessed more conquests and occupations than most regions of the world. Egypt and its neighbors, for example, were conquered and occupied several times by differing foreign armies. This was the military passage and garrison for the superpowers of the ancient world. "During the first millennium B.C., for example, the country was a province of one foreign empire after another—Assyrian, Persian, and finally, under Alexander the Great, Macedonian. Alexander's General Ptolemy founded a dynasty which maintained itself for three centuries before capitulating to Rome" (Hill and Golvin 1976, 19).

Byzantine Rome treasured its southern provinces of North Africa because they were one of the major sources of grain.

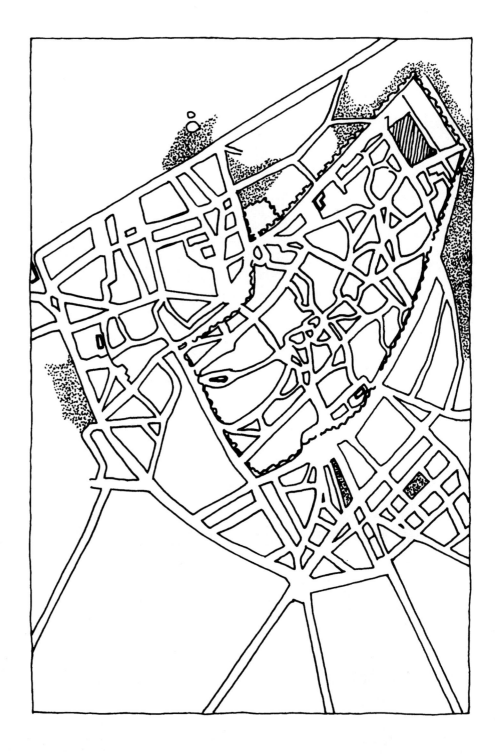

Fig. 3.1 Qayrawan, Tunisia. A triple heritage town showing the ancient city within the wall with the European planned areas outside the wall. Founded 663 A.D.

Tunisia, then known as Tripolitania, was one of the major centers of grain production. Emperor Constantine II had difficulty controlling his North African provinces because his governors there rebelled against him. Subsequent repression of the North African provinces only weakened the emperor's ability to control the provinces. He was, therefore, not in a position to stop the invading Arabs from the Arabian Peninsula. Aside from this, Byzantine control of its North African provinces was not complete. The Byzantines controlled the cities, while the Berbers controlled the villages. The Berbers, who had no love for their imperial masters in Constantinople or for the urban-dwelling governors in North Africa, had no desire to fight for the defense of Byzantine provinces in their homeland. Therefore, when Egypt fell to the Arabs in 641 A.D., nothing stood between the Arabs and the rest of the Byzantine provinces of North Africa.

Fig. C.10 Qayrawan, Tunisia. Great Mosque. Gallery. 800 A.D. (American Geographical Society Collection, The University of Wisconsin-Milwaukee Library)

Fig. C.11 Qayrawan, Tunisia. Great Mosque. Glazed tiles. (American Geographical Society Collection, The University of Wisconsin-Milwaukee Library)

Fig. C.12 Qayrawan, Tunisia. Great Mosque. Filigree in stone. (American Geographical Society Collection, The University of Wisconsin-Milwaukee Library)

Fig. 3.2 (Below) Qayrawan, Tunisia. Great Mosque, north facade of the main prayer hall facing the sahn and the minaret. 836 A.D. (1) Mosque. (American Geographical Society Collection, The University of Wisconsin-Milwaukee Library

The arrival of Islam in North Africa began as a raid on Ifriqya, present-day Tunisia, with a defeat of the Byzantine army at Sbeitla in 647 A.D. Caliph Uthman b. Affan authorized Abd Allah b. Sa'd to lead the expedition from Egypt, but this invasion was unsuccessful and Abd Allah b. Sa'd withdrew. "It was not until 663–4 A.D. that the real Muslim conqueror of North Africa, Uqba b. Nafi al-Fihri, arrived and founded Qayrawan, a fortress city at the end of the desert" (Hiskett 1984, 3). The garrison was defended from the Berbers by Arab tribesmen, and it was from there that Uqba b. Nafi al-Fihri waged *jihad* (Islamic holy war) against the Byzantine rulers and the Berbers until his death in 682 A.D. Qayrawan (Figs. 3.1 to 3.3 and C.10 to C.12) became the site of one of the major

mosques which would influence the architecture of North Africa from the 9th century onward.

The Qayrawan mosque was founded on an old Roman Byzantine construction site that has been rebuilt several times, with one of the major reconstructions in 836 A.D. The mosque has a major courtyard within its walls. Three of the walls have arcades, and the fourth is the facade of the sanctuary. According to Hutt (1977) and Hoag (1977), the Qayrawan mosque dates from the Aghlabid period and served to introduce many elements which subsequently became an integral part of North Africa's architectural repertoire. Hoag (1977, 64) also suggests that the mosque, finished in 836 A.D. by Ziyadat Allah, had a 236-ft-wide prayer hall "with sixteen aisles of seven bays each flanking a much wider mihrab aisle." This plan is referred to as the T-plan, and it dates back to the al-Walid's mosque at Medina.

The city of Qayrawan has characteristics of several ancient North African cities. There was a high defensive wall with bastions, and movement to and from the city was highly controlled. The walls were necessary for the defense of the town because the Berbers did not readily accede to the invading Muslims. The dominant features in the town are the wall and the Great Mosque, along with streets closely bound together to facilitate neighborhood and interpersonal contact. The streets outside the perimeter of the wall, on the other hand, were laid by imperial France, and the difference is unmistakable. The former is closer to the indigenous model, whereas the latter is dominated by Western influence. In this case, the triple heritage model is still a reality.

Fig. 3.3 Qayrawan, Tunisia. Great Mosque, mihrab aisle. (American Geographical Society Collection, The University of Wisconsin-Milwaukee Library)

Fig. 3.4 (Below) Cairo, Egypt. Plan of al-Azhar Mosque. 970–972 A.D. (Gabriel Okafor)

3.2 INTERMEDIATE AND LATER PERIODS OF THE SPREAD OF ISLAMIC ARCHITECTURE IN NORTH AFRICA

This is the period of the Fatimids through the Saladins (Ayyubid dynasty) to the periods of the Turkish Mamelukes and the Ottomans (from 969 to 1517 A.D.). Many scholars treat each of these epochs independently for convenience, due to the large timeframe and the number of caliph dynasties involved.

The rise of the Fatimids in the 10th century was made possible by a combination of forces. First was the death of Uqba b. Nafi al-Fihri, founder of Qayrawan Fortress, followed by the arrival of his successor, Hassan b. al-Numan, who fought many battles against the resisting Berber tribes. Second was the death of the Berber prophetess, al-Kahina, the soothsayer who challenged Muslim authority. Her death helped to reduce the tension between the conquering Arabs and the Berbers who increasingly converted to the Muslim religion in large numbers.

The converted Berbers liked the religion, and a radical camp believing in orthodox Islam began to emerge among them. By the late 9th century, this radical camp joined with Abu Abd allah al-Shite who regarded succession to the caliphate as belonging exclusively to the descendants of the Great Prophet's son-in-law, Alib Abi Talib. Fatima was the wife of Alib Abi Talib and the daugter of Prophet Mohammed. She and Alib Abi Talib and his Berber armies

sacked the reigning Aghlabid governor in Qayrawan and established a dynasty known as the Fatimids. The Fatimids marched eastward and captured Egypt in 969 A.D. under the leadership of Caliph Muizz.

According to Briggs (1974) the first mosque erected by the Fatimids was al-Azhar (Figs. 3.4 to 3.6) at Cairo, and the first city was al-Kahirah in 970 A.D. Al-Azhar's pattern may have "originated from Hagia Sophia, in Constantinople" (Hoag

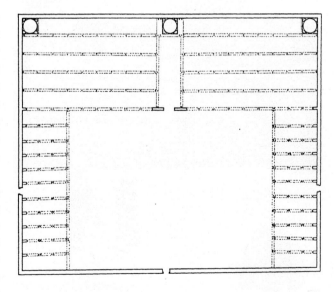

Fig. 3.5 *Cairo, Egypt. Al-Azhar Mosque. Prayer hall facade. 1131–1149* A.D. *(Keith Brown)*

Fig. 3.6 *Cairo, Egypt. Al-Azhar Mosque. Facade of the prayer hall facing the interior court. (Yasser Elshashtawy)*

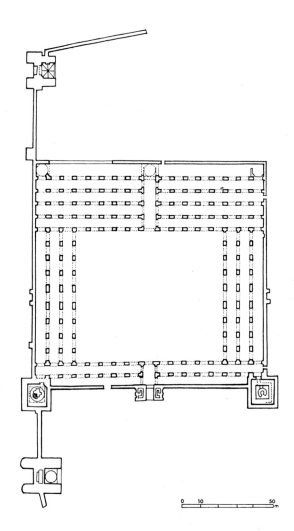

Fig. 3.7 *Cairo, Egypt. Plan of al-Hakim Mosque. 990–991 and 1002* A.D.

Fig. C.13 Cairo, Egypt. Al-Rifa'l interior. 1911. (Yasser Elshashtawy)

1977, 136), but influences from the Ibin Tulun Mosque, also in Cairo, are more visible. Al-Kahirah is more of a fortified citadel than a city. It covers an area of 1200 yd². Additionally, the Mosque of al-Hakim must be added to the list of achievements of the Fatimids (Figs. 3.7 and 3.8). The Mosque of al-Hakim (990–1013 A.D.) "was erected on the model of Ibn Tulun, and on a comparable scale" (Kuhnel 1966, 68). It had large brick piers around the courtyard and a winding minaret.

Following the Fatimid dynasty, Saladin or al-Malik al-Nasir Abu'L Mustafar Sala ad-dunya wa'd-din Yusuf Ibn Ayyub fought many wars with the Crusaders. He ruled in Cairo from 1171 to 1182 and left an indelible mark on the city. For instance, he built the Great Citadel that still dominates the city of Cairo and has innovations that later affected "the finest Arab monuments of Cairo, if not indeed of all the Muslim world" (Briggs 1974, 78). These innovations are a citadel for military defense, the maristan (hospital), and the

madrasa (school). The Mosque of Sultan Hassan is an example of the architectural program of Saladin. Saladin built his schools to suppress the teachings of the Fatimids. After the

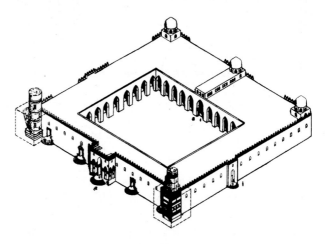

Fig. 3.8 Cairo, Egypt. Al-Hakim Mosque 990–991 and 1002 A.D.

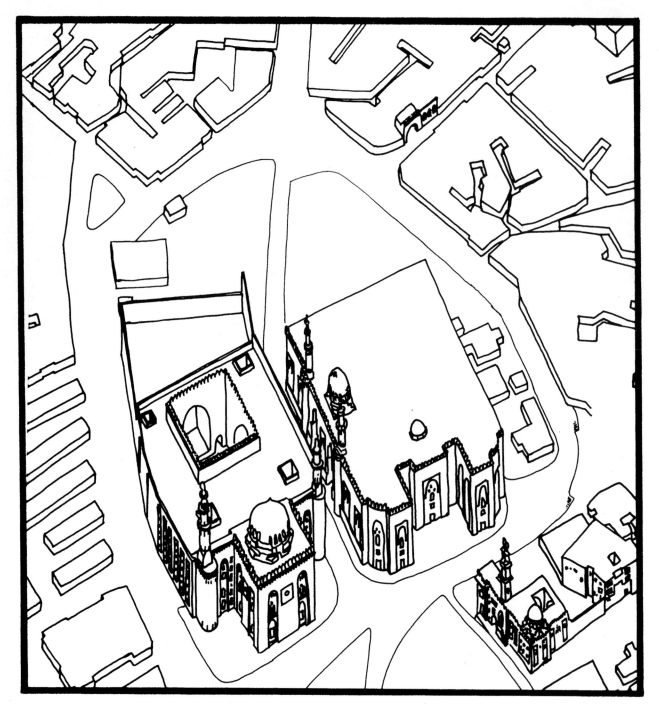

Fig. 3.9 Cairo, Egypt. Salah Ad-Din Square. Left: Sultan Hassan Mosque-Madrassa. 1362 A.D., Right: Mosque of al-Rifa'l. 1911 A.D. (Keith Brown)

middle of the 13th century, some of these Madrasas were converted to mosques, often having completed the mission of stamping out the teachings of the Fatimids, by adding minarets which gave them a new identity. Next to Sultan Hasan stands the Mosque of al-Rifa'l (Fig. 3.9), built in 1911 by Princess Khushyar, the mother of King Ismail, as a family mausoleum, and completed by her grandson Khedive. While there are differences between these two buildings, the influences of Sultan Hasan Madrassa on al-Rifa'l (Fig. C.13) cannot be ignored. For example, in al-Rifa'l, the central bay facing Saladin Square is an inverse of the two side bays of the facade of Sultan Hasan Madrassa facing the same square.

Egypt was the center of the Mameluke period of Islamic art in North Africa. Mameluke is the name given to Turkish slaves imported to Egypt as soldiers during the Middle Ages. The Mamelukes rebelled against their masters and gained power and influence after Saladin. Initially they were the sultan's bodyguard. The Mamelukes built many mosques and palaces for themselves and their masters in Egypt.

Residential housing design in medieval Cairo had common principles for people of all classes and differed only in scale and decoration. These common principles included: a living room or hall (qa'a) as the core, with auxiliary rooms that together formed a unit; privacy as a major factor, achieved by the use of curved entrances, vestibules, and punched wooden screens on windows, both in men's quarters and in the harem; unlike in many Islamic countries, residential architecture in medieval Egypt was highly extroverted. Windows faced toward major streets, as in the Palace of Amir Bashtak. Because of this, a city of the Mameluke period, inherited from the Ayyubids, had special medieval characteristics that were visible both in residential buildings and in public buildings such as mosques. The Mamelukes inherited the walled city of the Fatimids and the new royal city built by Saladin. Mameluke influence on Islamic architecture in North Africa was later interwoven with the influence of a new invading army, the Turks.

By the 16th century, the Turkish empire was a major force in Europe and had already projected its might to the East. The Ottomans became Arabized, and this cultural fusion produced new elements not just in politics and religion but also in the architecture of North Africa. "The fusion produced new architectural forms combining Turkish clarity of expression with the North African concern for interior space..." (Hutt 1977, 22). It is possible to say that "if creativity ceased in later periods, a distinctive North African style had been achieved which has validity in world architectural terms" (Hutt 1977, 23).

3.3 THE SPREAD OF ISLAMIC ARCHITECTURE IN EAST AFRICA

East Africa had always maintained contact with people living east of the Indian Ocean in China and the nearer Arabian states. The Islamization and Arabization of the East African people encouraged more trade among the coastal towns and the nations of the Indian Ocean, thereby facilitating the devel-

opment of a triple heritage culture. "The coastal towns and settlements were always completely dependent on the trade of the Indian Ocean" (Gerlake 1966, 1). However, they were politically and culturally self-contained. They maintained a maritime relationship with the West and the East without rejecting their culture. It is believed that prior to the 19th century, the East African cultures and religions were primarily local phenomena under the leadership of local intellectuals.

East Africans sold gold and ivory to Swahili or Arab traders who lived around the East African coast. The coastal region covers over 1000 mi from Somalia in the present-day Horn of Africa to Kilwa in present-day Tanzania. In addition to this, there were local craftsmen who helped in the development of the East African coastal cities and citadels. As a result, most of the mosques and Islamic buildings in East Africa were built by master builders who were competent artisans having knowledge of structural and building composition.

Islamic architecture on the East African coast is homogenous in five basic elements: technique of construction, ornamental and decorative detail, the composition of mosque mihrabs, mosque planning, and the planning of domestic buildings. Most of the structures were made of coral limestone and had highly developed interior spaces that included flat roofs, domes, gables, and vaults. The walls were usually plastered. Overall, a clear synthesis of African and Arabian culture utilized available construction resources to develop a purely indigenous East African Islamic architecture. The fusion of Arabian and Islamic architecture gives the planning of East African towns a simple format like that found in traditional African villages.

The streets are a maze of winding paths dictated by the location of different buildings in the medieval style. A good example is the town of Songo Mnara, where houses have a basic plan and are located in such a way that many houses share a common courtyard. This indicates the communal aspect of extended family planning. Most of the houses had inner courtyards surrounded by windowless walls used for domestic activities as a part of private outdoor space. Some houses had access to the roof for family relaxation, and the houses were often separated by narrow alleys, as is the case in many medieval cities.

Larger houses and mosques have more elaborate courtyards. Sometimes a complex has several courtyards, as in the case of the now ruined Husuni Kubwa complex (see Figs. 3.10 and 3.11). Husuni Kubwa, which means the "large fortified house" in Swahili (Gerlake 1990), was built in the island town of Kilwa in the 13th century. The complex had several courtyards for different functions, with a distinct progression from the private to the public courtyards. One of the king's private courtyards had a sunken pool; next to it was the

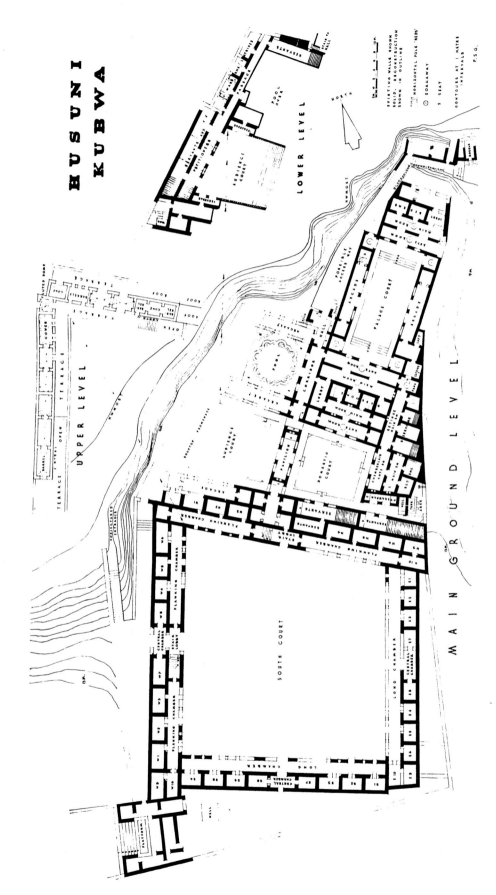

Fig. 3.10 Kilwa, Tanzania. Grand plan of the Palace of Husuni Kubwa. 13th century A.D. (Peter S. Garlake, Oxford University Press)

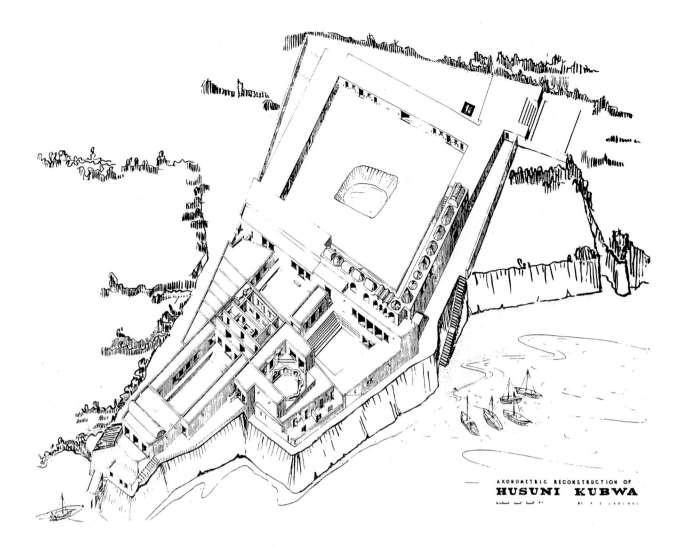

Fig. 3.11 Kilwa, Tanzania. Reconstruction drawing of the Palace of Husuni Kubwa. (Peter S. Garlake, Oxford University Press)

audience court with seats and night lamps. A series of arcades overlooked the audience court. A line of vaulted rooms with barrel and conical domes stood above the arcade. Husuni Kubwa was located on the edge of a cliff and was completely walled around. It was a multifunctional building that made a strong statement about the one man who lived there.

The ruins of Husuni Kubwa demonstrate the glorious years of Kilwa, Tanzania, before it was looted and torched by the Portuguese. A few brief accounts exist of the town before it was burned. In 1331, Ibn Battuta wrote, "Kilwa is one of the most beautiful and well-constructed towns in the world" (Davidson 1991, 143). A German traveler in the company of ·d'Almeida, the Portuguese general who burned Kilwa, wrote in 1505, "In Kilwa there are many strong houses several stories high. They are built of stone and mortar and plastered

with various designs" (Davidson 1991, 104). In 1517, Duate Barbosa wrote that "Going along the coast from this town of Mozambique, there is an island by the mainland which is called Kilwa, in which is a Moorish town with many fair houses of stones and mortar" (Davidson 1991, 159).

3.4 THE SPREAD OF ISLAMIC ARCHITECTURE IN WEST AND SOUTH AFRICA

The story of the spread of Islam in West Africa is similar to the story of its spread in East Africa. There was already an existing trade link between North and West Africa through the Sahara Desert. The trans-Saharan trade gave Islam a route to West Africa, and in return, it made towns along the trade

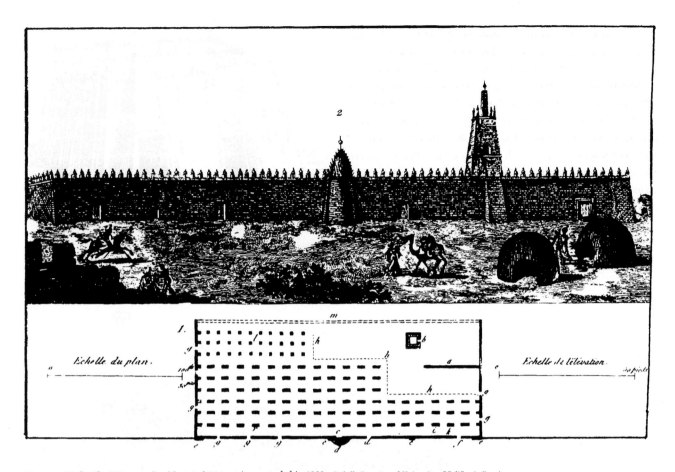

Fig. 3.13 **Mali.** *The Djinguere Ber Mosque (1324 A.D.) as recorded in 1828.* (Labelle Prussin and University of California Press)

route prosper due to a larger volume of trade between North and West Africa.

Some scholars believe that the trans-Saharan trade route goes back to the time of Carthage, Rome, and the Byzantine Empire. This trade route has been a major conduit of gold, ivory, and food supplies from West Africa to the North African empires. The gold trade seduced the Arabs, who had established forts in Ifriqiyya (now Tunisia), into staging long expeditions to the west coast. "One such slave raiding expedition seems to have been organized between 734 and 740 A.D. by the then governor of Afriqiyya Ubayd Allah b. Al-Habib" (Clarke 1982, 8) and placed under the command of his son and one of his generals. The success of this expedition inspired the governor of Ifriqiyya in 745 A.D. to order wells to be dug along the trade route from southern Morocco across the western Sahara to West Africa.

Fig. 3.12 **Halwar, Senegal.** *Mosque built in indigenous style with ancient pylons and pillars reminiscent of ancient Egyptian construction. The original mosque was rebuilt before the mid-19th century.* (Jean-Paul Bourdier)

Trade expanded because of the new water resources along the route, and the North African merchants sent more slaves, gold, and foodstuffs in exchange for clothes, horses, and salt. Some of the Northern African merchants, Arabs and Berbers alike, began to settle in the cities of the ancient empires of West Africa along the trade routes. Some of the principal routes were from Tahert in modern Algeria to Gao in West Africa. Tahert was established in 770 A.D. Sijilmasa, a Moroccan city founded in the second half of the 8th century, had a route that led to ancient Ghana. Another route led from Cyrenaica in North Africa to Borno-Kanem in present-day northern Nigeria. These ancient trade routes also became the route for Islam.

In West Africa, the mosque as a building type is accepted wholeheartedly by the North Africans, but its structure is reborn in a new form that is essentially West African. In this case, the Arabian mosque is absorbed by African traditions and gives new meanings that radiate African ancestral mysticism in an organic form. In West Africa, the mosque takes precedence over the domestic house. A good example is the 17th-century Mosque of Futa Toro, although it is not the oldest mosque in West Africa. According to Aradeon (1989, 124), "the cylindrical kitchen tower which projects above the level of the terrace living spaces possesses only one light source." A multipurpose perforation on the upper portion of this cylinder serves both as a source of light and as a vent for smoke coming from the ground floor. This feature can also be seen on the Mosque of Halwar (Fig. 3.12). It is, therefore, important to recognize that "With respect to the West African mosque, many features are West African; buttressing systems, parapet pinnacles, projecting pickets, a conical mihrab, and in the case of the Dyula mosque, a conical minaret" (Aradeon 1989, 121). This is now known as the Sudanese style.

Fig. 3.14 Senoufo, Cote d'Ivoire. Traditional housing. (Labelle Prussin and University of California Press)

Fig. 3.15 Segou, Mali. Entrance pylon of the house of Madani, "the son of Ahmadu, ruler of Segou at the time of French conquest in 1890." (Labelle Prussin and University of California Press)

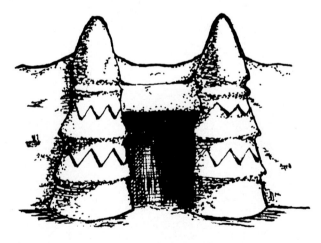

Fig. 3.16 Gurunsi, Burkina Fasso. Three different entrance portals.
(Labelle Prussin and University of California Press)

Many West African kings accepted Islam during the Middle Ages and made expensive pilgrimages to Mecca. One account describes the return of King Mausa Musa, a medieval emperor of the Mali empire. Prussin (1986, 150) notes that King Mausa Musa commissioned the Djinguere Ber Mosque in 1324–1327 A.D. in Timbuktu (Fig. 3.13), believed to be one of the oldest mosques in West Africa. The great Mosque of djenne in Mali is discussed in detail in Chapter 13.

In North Africa, Islam brought reformatted Byzantine buildings back to life and gave them new meanings and structure. Thus, the old Western legacy left by the Romans went through an evolutionary process with the coming of Islam. On the other hand, Islamic buildings went through another evolutionary change in West Africa by adopting ancestral features. Moughtin confirms this view by emphasizing that the similarity between the reed arches of the Sudan in the Lake Chad basin and some of the arches used in Egyptian Islamic architecture is not a coincidence because they suggest much earlier forms of reed architecture in the Nile Valley (Moughtin 1985) and they share similarities with Dongon architecture.

Dongon rectangular houses are characterized by vertical recesses, narrow openings, and monumental portals that give a feeling of loftiness. The Senoufo, the Palacca of the Ivory Coast, and the Gurunsi of Burkina Fasso also have house types with such features (Figs. 3.14 to 3.16). Studies conducted on houses with similar characteristics in Old Cairo city (Mameluke) suggest that the prototype for this architecture was probably Pharaonic Egypt (Ali Ibrahim 1984, 47). In this case, it is clear that living units had more vertical than horizontal expansion and were usually one or two stories. Samples of Pharaonic houses from the Old Kingdom confirm this proposition and also support the view that the ancestors of Songhay people and several other ethnic groups migrated from ancient Egypt.

Another aspect of Islam and Islamic architecture in North Africa is the dual dynamic of cultural assimilation which it fostered in the 7th century. People who formerly saw themselves as Africans took on a new cultural identity because of Islamization, the religious conversion to the creed of Muhammad, and Arabization, the linguistic assimilation into the language of the Arabs. In time, the great majority of North Africans came to see themselves as Arabs.

2

NORTH AFRICA:
THE MAGHREB
AND EGYPT

4

THE ARCHITECTURE OF THE KINGDOM OF MOROCCO

his chapter reviews the architecture of Morocco, covering a brief history of Morocco, its people, and its cities, especially Rabat, Fez, Casablanca, and Marrakesh. Today's Morocco is a composite of thousands of years of history beginning with the early settlers, to the Berbers, the Carthaginians, the Romans, the Arabs, and the impact of Western powers—Britain, Germany, France, and Spain—in the late 1800s before becoming a protectorate of France. Morocco was an independent state before the scramble for Africa, but colonial rivalry, fueled by commercial and territorial ambitions, contributed to its colonization and the influences of Western architecture.

Morocco's strategic location and its proximity to southern Europe at the Strait of Gibraltar made it attractive to the colonists (Fig. 4.1). Despite local resistance, each wanted to be in control of the territory.

An Anglo-French commission responsible for dividing Africa between England and France reached its decision during the early part of the 20th century. Germany was being increasingly outmaneuvered at this time, and the events leading up to World War I were already building up.

The British decided to recognize Morocco under France's sphere of influence in exchange for French recognition of Egypt within the British sphere. The Italians were aligned with Libya, while France was increasing its grip on Algeria and Tunisia. Sub-Saharan Africa was also being divided into colonial labor and commercial estates. France received a large portion of the Sahelian regions, while the British were more interested in the ever-green Niger Delta region which makes up present-day Nigeria. The French were satisfied with a settlement that awarded them a million square miles of desecrated Sahel and desert. "At the time of the settlement, Lord Salisbury had sarcastically referred to the area as 'what a farmer would call very light sand,' adding, 'we have given the Gallic cock an enormous amount of sand, let him scratch in it as he pleases'" (Allison 1988, 116).

The French used the murder of a French citizen in Casablanca in 1907 as an excuse to invade the city and establish their colonial rule over the entire country. It was the beginning of modern Western influence on the architecture of present-day Morocco and the continuation of ancient Greco-Roman imperial legacy.

Fig. 4.1 The Maghreb and Egypt. (Gabriel Okafor)

Arab influences on the architecture of Morocco began in the 8th century. It is important to understand the significance of the various Arab and Berber dynasties because they form the chronology that many scholars use when explaining different styles of Islamic architecture in Morocco. The original headquarters of the Islamic world after the death of the Prophet were in Damascus but moved to Baghdad when the Umayyad dynasty in Damascus was overthrown by the Abbasids. One of the surviving Umayyad princes, Abd al Rahman, fled to Spain and founded an independent caliphate with its headquarters at Cordoba. North Africa was ruled from the headquarters of the Abbasids caliphate at Baghdad from 750 A.D. to the end of the 8th century. Built by the Aghlabid dynasty, the Qayrawan Mosque in Tunisia, Ifriqiyya, dominated North African Islamic architecture until the time of the Fatimids. However, in the 7th century, a major event permanently split Islam into two sects. The event was masterminded in Morocco by converted Berber Muslims, known as the Kharidjites, who were overzealous and demanded to be part of the ruling elite, instead of maintaining an Arab ruling monopoly. However, the Kharidjites were unable to form a cohesive state or build a major Islamic monument because they fought too much against one another.

From 786 A.D., the Idrisids ruled Morocco and established the Sharifian rule. Sharifian tradition holds that descent from Prophet Muhammad is a qualification for political power. Next came the Hilalians, a dynasty established by Arab tribesmen, who migrated to Morocco between the 12th and 14th centuries. The Hilalians differed from the other Arabs who established earlier dynasties in that they were mostly rural people.

Some scholars draw distinctions between the Arab and Berber dynasties. The Almoravids, the Almohads, and the Marinades were some of the important Berber dynasties. The Almoravids, also known as Sanhajas, became the *marabouts,* a religious brotherhood devoted to conquering unbelievers for the faith, and they later played a significant role in the spread of Islam in West Africa. They built fortified enclaves known as *ribats* for their warrior monks and from which to operate their raiding expeditions. The ribats would later become important representations of medieval architecture in North Africa. The Almoravids were very dogmatic and were inspired to fight for their religion by Ulama Abdullah Ibn Yasin who had come from Mecca. By 1ᴜ56 A.D., they had conquered Marrakesh, Algiers, and in 1086 A.D., they crossed into Spain.

By 1130 A.D., the Almohads were beginning a campaign against the Almoravids. Because of the Sufi cult, which venerated their leaders who were mystics, not just learned men, the Almohads contributed to the proliferation of tombs. The tombs of the Sufi leaders became shrines and holy places of pilgrimage. The most important contribution of the Marinades is the city of Fez.

European intrusions returned in late 1399 with the occupation of Tetouan by the Castilians. In 1415, the Portuguese occupied Centa, while the Ottoman Empire dates from 1518 to 1830. An awareness of these stages is helpful in the study of the various styles of Islamic architecture in North Africa.

4.1 TRADITIONAL ARCHITECTURE OF THE KINGDOM OF MOROCCO

Most Moroccans are Berbers whose ancestors have lived in the region for centuries before the foreign invasions. The Berbers were already in the region before the Romans arrived and even before the Phoenicians who settled there and traded with southern Spain. Like people in other parts of Africa, the Berbers are not unique in having several dialects which divide the population into subgroups. The three principal dialects are Masmuda, Sanhaja, and Zanata, and they correspond to the three major subgroups.

The Berbers have a rich heritage based on family life and unity. Their traditional values revolve around the extended family, with elder leadership and decision by popular consensus. "Berber virtues are loyalty to the ethnic group, namely dignity of bearing and physical courage" (Landau and Swaan 1967, 16).

As in most African countries, the dual existence of village life and urban life is also present in Morocco. In this case, the majority of rural dwellers are Berbers. Ancestry is a major bonding factor for the family. Members of the same lineage live together with absolute loyalty to the family and a close family structure that can be easily observed in the architecture of their homes, kasbahs. Farming is the main occupation. Some Berbers are nomads who move their animals according to the seasons, grazing in the lowlands during winter and in the highlands of the Atlas Mountains during the summer. It is common for people of the same ancestry to migrate together and look out for one another's interests. Leadership at the local level is always elected, and the Berbers would have no tolerance for dictatorship. Years of occupation by foreign conquerors have taught them to be free and culturally attuned to

elected leadership. Disputes among people usually break out along ethnic lines and are often exploited by opportunists who use ancestry to gain advantage over their opponents.

The triple heritage concept is once again manifest in Moroccan architecture by virtue of its indigenous past, its Arab presence, and its colonial past. The Romans originated Western influence in the region, before later intrusions by the Spanish, British, Germans, and French who colonized Morocco until it became independent in 1956. Colonization did not destroy some of the indigenous house types such as the tent and the kasbah. On the other hand, it did not develop them either.

THE TENT

The tent is one of the earliest forms of architecture to have played a major role in the housing of certain populations in Morocco. It was adopted due to its functional and practical

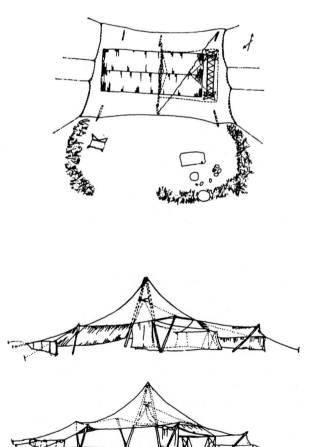

Fig. 4.2 Morocco. Plan and sketches of tent structures showing day and night conditions.

Fig. 4.3 Morocco. Tent structure. (American Geographical Society Collection, The University of Wisconsin-Milwaukee Library)

applications to climatic and cultural needs. Nomads who travel long distances during the course of a year find it useful. The role of women in constructing and maintaining tent architecture should be understood. Many nomadic cultures leave the responsibility of making and furnishing shelters to women, while the men tend to their animals in the field. Professor Prussin (1982, 18) emphasized that, "In the world of Nomadism, it has traditionally been the women who have borne the responsibility for creating, erecting, maintaining and dismantling the domestic environment, whether it be a tipi, a yurt or a black skin tent."

The plans for tents are usually fixed. It is easier to make small changes than large changes. Nomads sometimes weave their tent covers or use tanned animal skins. It is also common for them to obtain new tent materials from markets or by barter with sedentary populations. In southeastern Morocco, Tekna tents (Figs. 4.2 and 4.3) are sometimes made with woven cloth and camel skin; these tents are adjustable to provide shade and comfort, depending on the time of the day.

A caravan of nomads often consists of members of one extended family from a common lineage. They pitch their tents near water wells along defined seasonal paths. The transport of the tent material is usually on camels. Duly (1979, 34) states that "Nomadism (or transhumance) is not the aimless wandering it may appear; the pastoralists are in fact slaves to their cattle, and must continually judge when and where to move their herds in order not to exhaust the mean pasture available."

KASBAHS

Morocco does have other forms of indigenous architecture besides tents. There are kasbahs which are "Frequently ten or more stories high and built out of packed clay and air dried bricks, kasbahs are common especially in the southern valleys of the Atlas Mountains" (Porthon 1982, 123). Usually built to house many families of one ancestral origin or one large patriarchal family, kasbahs have thick walls that insulate their interiors from excessive thermal variation. Only the more prestigious buildings have windows on the top floors. Porthon (1983, 123) suggests that some kasbahs were built progressively upward as the family grew larger. Kasbahs are common in the high Atlas Mountains, the middle Atlas, and the desert regions of Morocco.

The architecture of kasbahs is unique. They evolved out of the defensive necessities of the times, especially during the Arab settlements of the mid-7th century and the constant invasion by Berber groups. The Berbers themselves also raided each other, so it was natural to design defensive shelters. Kasbahs are, therefore, forts uniquely built in indigenous Moroccan styles. They can be made of stone or earth (clay), and their interiors are sometimes well furnished with tiles and glazed stones. The entrances are usually well decorated with Arabic, Berber, and Moorish symbols.

In the Dra Valley region, some villages consist of walled forts with several family units living within the confines. As Shirley Kay (1980, 147) states, "This is the heartland of Berber

Fig. C.14 Tinerher Oasis, Morocco, consists of several kasbahs. (American Geographical Society Collection, The University of Wisconsin-Milwaukee Library)

kasbahs, the region where at every turn, one sees decorative family fortresses carefully built of mud and chopped straw with towers and crenelated battlements, or fortified villages, Ksour, with equally decorated towers and entrance gateways." A kasbah becomes a ksour when an entire village lives within its walls and shares common defense fortifications (Fig. C.14). In this case, there are usually several extended families who own their kasbahs. The effects of the chaos brought by conquering Arabs and by the intergroup wars were minimized by the development of kasbah architecture. In the 16th century, kasbahs were used to fend off Portuguese invaders along the coast of Morocco.

Some kasbahs are still constructed in the traditional method. Hired laborers may be used, but most of the builders are blood related. Large amounts of wet clay, sometimes mixed with straw, are set in a mold and are built up as part of the wall, as opposed to the traditional method of baking bricks and using them on walls after they are dry. The wall is sometimes plastered over and given a smooth surface; this is an easy medium to work with in terms of wall decorations and other kinds of surface treatment.

4.2 RABAT: THE CAPITAL OF MOROCCO

Rabat is both a modern and an ancient city. Any visitor to the city would notice this ambivalence of time, the coexistence of the past and the present. As a modern city, it is a product of the imperial French ambition to create a greater France. But Islam and its struggle to anchor its roots deep into the bedrock of African soil gave it another personality, thus adding more historical layers to the resilient indigenous Berber culture. Finally, there are the ruins of the crumbled Roman Empire. Colonization during Roman and French times has one thing in common: imperial vested interests executed with overwhelming military occupation. In each case, two independent foreign cultures came into contact with each other not out of choice but by imposition. This latter fact shaped the cultural destiny of Rabat and is highly visible in the architecture and urban design of the city.

Military occupation always maintains its own ideology, a blueprint or master plan that occupiers follow to accomplish their agenda. The name Rabat is derived from *ribat*, a stronghold or monastery for Muslim monks. The ancient Roman city of Chella was the site of the monastery which became a holy place and a necropolis for the royal family. By its holy status the ribat influenced future sultans to build sacred monuments in the vicinity. Ya`qub al-Mansur was the first sultan to put a major landmark near the ribat. "To mark the victories of the Moroccan armies over the Spanish in the battle of Alarcos, Ya`qub al-Mansur set out in 1196 A.D. to build the mosque still known by its minaret, the *Tour Hassan*" (Landau and Swaan 1967, 147) (Fig. 4.4). Ya`qub al-Mansur was following the example of his grandfather who had built a ribat for his military garrison near the site of the necropolis. It is suggested by Landau and Swaan (1967) that Ya'qub al-Mansur used the city of Alexandria as his model for Rabat, or Ribat al-Fath (stronghold of victory).

As far as architecture is concerned, the incomplete minaret of Hassan Mosque remains a major landmark and dominates the city. Built in the Almohad style, its enormous base suggests that it would have been one of the tallest minarets if it had been completed. The gate of the Ouadiah Kasbah is another edifice that shows the Islamic style of the Almohads. This majestic gate symbolizes Ya'qub al-Mansur's desire to make Rabat his capital. This gate is concerned more with aesthetics than with defense; therefore, its construction is intended more for visual consumption than for physical security. The horseshoe-shaped gate is exotically carved in ocher masonry. It is decorated with a series of vaulted chambers in successive order from the outer court to the inner court. This gate derives from that of the ancient capital of Meknes (Fig. C.15), with its impressive tile work. It displays a pattern found in many Moroccan and North African holy cities and shrines. Although Rabat had ceased to serve as the capital for centuries following dynastic power struggles, it was made the capital of modern Morocco by the French in 1912.

Colonial decisions are usually in the colonizers' interests, no matter how disguised or whatever motive they may have. Moving the capital of Morocco from Fez to Rabat is an example of one of those decisions. As resident-general and head of the French army in Morocco, General Lyautey had the power to make any decision regarding the administration of the colony with which he had been entrusted. One of his first decisions was to transfer the capital from Fez to a coastal city on the Atlantic shore because he was uncomfortable with Moroccan resistance in Fez. This gave him the impetus to make a fast decision. Rabat had to be prepared to serve as the

Fig. C.15 *Meknes, Morocco. Gate of Ouadiah Kasbah.* 1191 A.D. *(American Geographical Society Collection, The University of Wisconsin-Milwaukee Library)*

center of administration for Morocco. For Lyautey, this meant building a new city next to the old one, while preserving the latter. Here lies a duality, the conflict that inevitably arises when old and new, and two culturally separate elements, are brought together. As Taylor (1984, 16) phrases it, "the arrival and penetration by these European powers of local or regional institutions—political, social and cultural—brought about situations of confrontation between the new and already existing."

What Wright (1991) describes as Lyautey's cultural preservation and exploitative goals for Morocco surfaced as he tried to preserve the culture and character of the old Rabat while

Fig. 4.4 *(Opposite) Rabat, Morocco. Minaret of Tour Hassan.* 1196 A.D. *(American Geographical Society Collection, The University of Wisconsin-Milwaukee Library)*

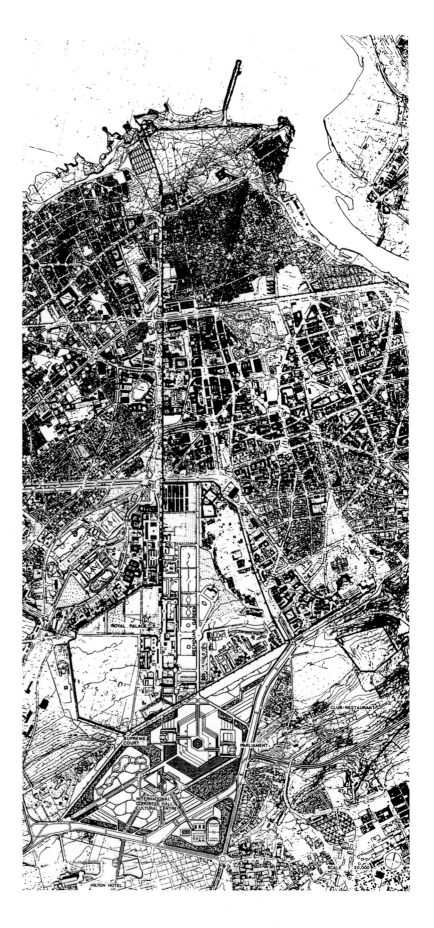

Fig. 4.5 Rabat, Morocco.
1978 master plan. Designed
by Kenzo Tange Urtec. (Kenzo
Tange)

Fig. 4.6 Rabat, Morocco. Royal Palace. (American Geographical Society Collection, The University of Wisconsin-Milwaukee Library)

building a modern city for industrial exploitation of the country. This approach gave Rabat the dual character of a modern city with a memorable past.

Different scholars hold different views on Lyautey's projects, which were executed by Henri Prost. The existing 1913 plan held that the old walled city, *medina* in Arabic, remain in tact with only a few major roads around it. By 1920, the plan met Lyautey's desire to preserve both the old and the new city. This can be seen as a success. In addition, it helped to establish the circulation system in the new city. Applying modern urban design techniques to Rabat produced an "impressive" (Abu-Lughod 1980, 157) and "compelling" master plan (Wright 1991).

One of the criticisms of the 1920 plan is that it left no room for the old city to expand in a natural way. This is, in fact, why Henri Prost deliberately surrounded it on all sides with the new city. Above all, too much preference and concession were made to the European inhabitants at the expense of native Moroccans. As a result, Moroccans had to move out to squatter settlements in the outskirts of town because the new

city could not accommodate immigrants from the rural areas. This implies that the new city was not planned with the pur-

Fig. 4.7 Tetuan, Morocco. Railroad station. (American Geographical Society Collection, The University of Wisconsin-Milwaukee Library)

pose of accommodating the Moroccans in the first place but for the colonials themselves.

A postcolonial master plan prepared by Kenzo Tange and the Urtec in 1978 completely rearranged the city and gave it a central focal point (Fig. 4.5). This is where the early plans differ from the later one. The Parliament Building, the Supreme Court, and the existing Royal Palace (Fig. 4.6), the branches of the Moroccan government, are grouped together and connected visually in the new document. An existing garden in front of the Royal Palace, known as Mechour Garden, forms a connecting corridor between the Supreme Court, the Parliament Building, and the Royal Palace. The 20th-century Royal Palace and other buildings in several Moroccan cities such as the Tetuan (Fig. 4.7) have been executed in the Arabisances style. Thus, while the building plan and function are essentially Western, the facade and other decorative elements symbolically utilize Arabian and Islamic images. This was the colonial's way of respecting the indigenous architecture of their North African colonies. The concept of Arabisances is discussed in detail in Chapter 5.

In an era of political upheaval, Kenzo Tange found it prudent to protect the government buildings from the people. He achieved this by barricading the Parliament Building and the Supreme Court with a forest and an artificial lake. This desire of Tange's to protect the bureaucrats from the governed achieves fruition at Abuja, Nigeria, as is shown in Chapter 17.

4.3   CASABLANCA

Casablanca is probably the best known Moroccan city abroad because of the film *Casablanca,* even though the movie was not filmed there. It is also the first port of entry by colonial France in the process of controlling the destiny of Morocco in the 20th century. France invaded Casablanca in 1907 under the pretext of protecting its citizens. Thus, Casablanca has a special meaning for colonial France because it provided the French with a foothold in the country. The French government always wanted to present Morocco as a successful foreign policy coup, and Casablanca was one of the showpieces. It was particularly important to Lyautey that Casablanca developed into a successful story. In fact, the writing on his tomb bears his aspirations for Casablanca and Morocco as a whole: "To be one of those in whom men believe, in whose eyes thousands seek command, with whose voice roads are opened, countries populated, and cities built" (Hoisington 1984, 74). It was this inner conviction that inspired Lyautey to convert Morocco from an agrarian to an industrial country

for France. This also meant that a new city was to be added to the two old medieval medinas.

The medieval medinas grew out of old settlements peopled by ancient Phoenicians, Romans, and later the Portuguese, who named it "Casa-Branca (white house)" (Johnson 1970). The Portuguese destroyed and abandoned their city in 1468. The sultan of Morocco built a new city on the site. Three-hundred years later in 1770, the city was called "Dar el Beida (Arabic for white house)" (Johnson 1970). It was the Spaniards who translated this last name to Casablanca. This ancient past gives Casablanca an indigenous and Islamic influence as well as constant encounters with the Western world. This time it was under Lyautey, who was determined to make it a modern city. Once again, Henri Prost was given the task of shaping the destiny of Casablanca. Gwendolyn Wright (1991, 102) describes the Casablanca scheme as follows:

> Prost organized the city in a fan pattern around the Place de France and its two economic poles: the port, which tied Casablanca to Europe, and the railway station, which tied it to the interior of the country. From these nodes he defined zones for particular functions within the ville nouvelle: administration and commerce in the center; elite residential and recreation areas (racetrack and beaches) to the west; industry and European working-class residential district to the east; military and health-care services along the southern periphery.

In the end, Casablanca looked more like a French city than an Arab city. The meaning of modern city in Morocco translates as a rejection of Arab medina. Prost's initial sketch of the Boulevard du IV Zouaves in Casablanca was based on his vision of what a European city would look like instead of what an Arab medina should be in modern times. The city grew rapidly at the peak of French influence in North Africa, and many Europeans migrated to Casablanca during World War II. Several French businesses were opened and land speculation around the outskirts of the city was rampant. The influx of immigrants from Europe and from the countryside greatly increased the population, which expanded from only 20,000 in 1907 to 1.5 million in 1968 (Johnson 1970). Today, Casablanca is a modern city with one of the largest shanty towns on its outskirts because the population rapidly outgrew the new city.

Casablanca's architecture from 1915 to the present is a fusion of Western and Arabian motifs. For example, Joseph Marrast's design for the law courts drew heavily from the indigenous Iwan decorative style. Carved stone, ceramic tile, and green tile are used to embellish the walls and the roof. The largest mosque in the world, King Hassan Mosque, was completed in Casablanca in 1993 at the cost of $1 billion.

Fig. C.16 Fez, Morocco. Aerial view. (American Geographical Society Collection, The University of Wisconsin-Milwaukee Library)

King Hassan II Mosque is an architectural edifice of a monumental proportion. The mosque seats in a 9-hectare (22.5 acres) area divided as follows:

Area 1: Mosque, minaret, and madrasa (school)

Area 2: Parking lots, courts

Area 3: Underground walkway

Area 4: Museum and library

The mosque consists of a major prayer hall, an ablutions room, moorish baths (*hammams*) and underground parking structure. The central part of the major prayer hall has a mobile ceiling which can be removed. The 200-meters- (218.72 yds) tall minaret is the tallest in the world. The amount of material required for the construction of this edifice was enormous. It took 300,000 sq meters (983,606.56 sq ft) of concrete; 40,000 tons of steel; 250,000 tons of Moroccan marble covering an area of 220,000 sq m; 30,000 sq m of plaster, and 30,000 workers in various aspects of the building industry to execute the gigantic project. With all this, the

mosque is capable of accommodating 25,000 worshipers inside and 80,000 worshipers on the platform. This mosque is the fulfillment of a royal wish as shown below from the extract of a speech given on July 11, 1988, by His Majesty H. M. King Hassan II:

I want there to be a great and beautiful achievement whereof Casablanca would be proud till the end of times. I want a mosque to be built here alongside the sea, a magnificent temple of God, a mosque whose high minaret would indicate the way to Safety, that is the way to Allah....

4.4 FEZ

Fez is another Moroccan city born of Marinades Berber dynastic leadership during the Middle Ages. By 1248 A.D., the founder of the Marinid dynasty, Abu Yahya Abu Bakr, had defeated the Almohads dynasty and occupied the city of Fez. The Marinids conquered the Almohads not necessarily for the advancement of Islam, but for the sake of power. On the other hand, their wars against Christian Spain were for both religious and socioeconomic reasons (Landau and Swaan 1967).

The location of Fez is ideal for the growth of a city. The region has a large supply of fresh water, enough rain to support agriculture, a balanced seasonal fluctuation, and natural quarries for construction materials. Fez has a distinct character from all other Moroccan cities because of its triurban conurbation. It is made up of old Fez (Fas al-Bali), new Fez (Fas al-Jadid), and the European modern city designed by Henri Prost. Both old and new Fez are medieval cities, but they differ in function. New Fez was founded on March 21, 1276 A.D. (Landau and Swaan 1967) by Sultan Abu Yusuf, who was tired of the old city and wanted a more luxurious place for his dynastic reign. New Fez was built within a walled city of about 200 acres. The great Mosque of Qarawiyin, which still dominates the landscape of the city, was inaugurated in January 1279 A.D.

Qarawiyin Mosque measures 177 by 111 ft. The prayer hall follows a T-plan with seven aisles perpendicular to the direction of prayer (qibla). The extreme aisles on either side run parallel to both the prayer hall and the inner courtyard, the sahn. The tiled courtyard is faced by horseshoe-shaped arches on plain columns.

Fez Jadid, the royal city, is a double-walled military bastion. It has few gates and a moat filled with water diverted from Wad Fez. The original design did not consider mounting cannons on battlements to strengthen its defenses as cannons were not yet invented. The walls were later reinforced toward the end of the 16th century to accommodate and support cannons.

The layout of modern Fez shows two kinds of city planning. Both Fez Jadid and Fez Medina have identically strong African-Arabian labyrinths of dense clusters of houses and streets that define public, semipublic, private, and semiprivate spaces (see Fig. I.7). In each case, the clusters define strong cultural and climatic responses. On the other hand, colonial Fez under France shows a strong resemblance to contemporary, rational European town planning models. Strong diagonals make up several city squares and display a strong zoning layout. There is a large structural gap between Fez Jadid, Fez Medina, and colonial Fez. The first two are identical, but neither relates to the colonial city. This has been justified as a preservation approach to town planning in a traditional society.

4.5 MARRAKESH

Marrakesh was already a major urban center under the Marinid dynasty before the Sa'dian dynasty took over and reinstated the city as the capital. The Sa'dians were the descendants of Prophet Muhammad who migrated from Arabia to Morocco in the 12th century.

Marrakesh is also one of the nine cities designed by Prost under Lyautey. The ancient wall of the medina makes it a unique entity from the modern town. Kutubiyya remains one of the most impressive landmarks in the old city. This 12th-century mosque boasts a 77-m minaret and a 17-aisle prayer hall perpendicular to the direction of Mecca. The minaret is built from sandstone. Unlike the old medieval city with narrow winding streets, the new French town of Marrakesh has broad streets and boulevards lined with trees and flowers.

5

THE ARCHITECTURE OF ALGERIA, TUNISIA, AND LIBYA

The discussion in this chapter covers Algeria, Tunisia, and Libya. These countries are, like Morocco, in the Maghreb, and they all share identical history. Their common boundaries with the Mediterranean Sea and proximity to southern Europe make them military centers of activities from the West and the East. Major Western architectural impact began in the region with the Romans in 146 B.C., while the major impact from the East began in the middle of the 7th century A.D. following the Islamic conversion of nonbelievers in the region. These conquests from the West and the East influenced architecture in the region to form the triple heritage of African culture.

Two distinct styles of architecture are added to the indigenous elements of the region: the classical style brought by the Romans and the Islamized mosques, citadels, and palaces developed by the Arabs. It is easy to recognize that Roman imports into the region clearly retain their Greco-Roman origin when viewed through one of the traditional methods of determining architectural styles: columns and entablatures, capitals, pillars and pilasters, doorways, windows, pediments and gables, facades, towers, and ground floor plans.

Islamic calligraphy and its ability to occupy a central position in the visual arts of Islam bring most Islamic arts under a common umbrella. This poses a slight problem when it comes to distinguishing the various styles of Islamic architecture. As mentioned earlier, scholars have preferred to look toward various dynastic rules in North Africa as guides when separating the various Islamic styles in the region. For example, Hutt (1977, 16) indicates that the Qayrawan Mosque built during the Aghlabid period influenced many major buildings in the region. Qayrawan Mosque initiated the final transition of Christian buildings to Islamic buildings in North Africa as the Arab settlers converted some Roman churches, temples, and palaces to mosques. The pointed horseshoe-shaped arches indicate a mixture of Eastern and Western motifs in a religious building. In this instance, other component parts such as the square minaret had multiple functions at the early stages. The principal function was to call followers to prayers, but minarets also served as lighthouses for ships and caravans and as watchtowers for approaching enemies. Hutt (1977, 16) sums up the common characteristics of the early mosques as consisting of quadrooned domes before the mihrab, shell squinches, T-plan, horseshoe and polylobed arches, and square minarets.

Unlike the Greco-Roman antiquities and the Christian places of worship converted to mosques, styles of architecture by later colonial powers in North Africa cannot be classified by countries or political regimes. The traditional format of using major building components still applies. A new concept known as Arabisances or Arabization of Western architecture comes into play. Here the agents are not Arabs or North Africans, but colonials such as the French in Morocco and Tunisia, the Italians in Libya, Ethiopia, and Somalia, and the British in Egypt. Some scholars contend that Arabisances is truly "a symptom of the evolution of colonial politics and a sympathy felt by numerous French architects for the Arab world and culture" (Baudez and Béguin 1980, 41). The underlying factor here is a pacification approach to colonial domination to reduce the fear of North Africans that the colonials had come to dominate their culture. This is the view given to the colonized African, but people in the "mother country" are presented with a different story that portrays Arabisance as an exotic culture that is becoming an appendage of their own. Thus, the colonies are places where the citizens of a great colonial nation can go for holidays, jobs, and exploration. A balanced view considers Arabisance to be a bridge between two different cultures such as the new city of Rabat in Morocco and the existing ancient medina.

Arabisance was achieved through the process of Arabization by the simple addition of decorative or symbolic Arabian motifs to buildings that are essentially European in plan and conception. The Palace of the Dey of Tunis at the 1867 Paris Exhibition is an Arabized baroque building. Its horseshoe-shaped arched columns and window trims are as visible as the inherent baroque elements that echo its French origin. Skanes Palace (Fig. 5.1) in Monaster, Tunisia, is a two-story building with a formal plan that has no relationship with the traditional Tunisian building, yet the treatment of the windows, entrances, and solar protection mechanism becomes motifs of cultural exchange. Some of the applications, such as the window shades, are necessitated by the climate, but they assume new meaning or become decorative elements when juxtaposed with alien motifs.

Baudez and Béguin (1980, 49) contend that Arabisance was accomplished in Africa through three principal "vectors": public buildings, indigenous habitat, and foreign schemes. Public buildings, however, were the major vectors. They had French plans and compositions but were decorated with Islamic motifs. These include administrative buildings, post offices, hospitals, and police stations. The indigenous habitats had more positive effects in that they inspired French archi-

Fig. 5.1 Monaster, Tunisia. Skanes Palace. (American Geographical Society Collection, The University of Wisconsin-Milwaukee Library)

tects such as Prost to reconcile imported concepts with internal structures of the Arab town. However, they had limited success. The term *foreign schemes* refers to the Arabia style, which was used by wealthy Europeans in the colonies for their homes. Local builders leaned toward the precedents set by these villas, and a sincere concern for indigenous North African forms began to emerge beyond the decorative stage. The modern movement and its desire to strip architecture of the vestiges of the classical times, coupled with the unlimited freedom to borrow building motifs regardless of the context, gave the villas a unique form that blended with North African landscapes. Moroccan, Algerian, Tunisian, Libyan, and Egyptian architecture in 19th- and 20th-century colonialism were all influenced by Arabisance.

Another significant factor is that French imperialism in Africa in the late 19th century coincided "with the emergence of architectural and urban planners trained at the Ecole des Beaux-Arts who produced numerous master plans for cities in Africa, Asia, and South America" (Taylor 1980, 53). This in itself provides insight into the spirit behind French architects' experimental projects in Africa, and it is accurate to say that these early experimental projects by Prost and Lyautey were a prelude to Le Corbusier's city of 3 million people. Africa was, therefore, an experimental ground where the French tested urban planning schemes before they applied them to their own cities. Their success, in terms of the speed with which they were accomplished, was due to the fact that almost all of the projects were carried out under military governors. The governors of the colonies had absolute power to execute any project in the interest of France. The freedom of not having to go through legislative debates before embarking on a project enabled the military planners to execute many projects in North Africa in a short time.

5.1 ALGERIA

Morocco provides a good overview of what to expect in Algeria. As one of the countries in the Maghreb, the Algeria of today is shaped by thousands of years of history. Some of the most beautiful cave paintings are in the Tassili n' Ajjer. "They are the most complete existing record of a prehistoric African culture and among the most remarkable Stone Age remains to be found anywhere" (Rinehart 1986, 5). The cave paintings depict a culture that bloomed in a well-watered Sahara with lots of game until about 6000 B.C. when weather changes caused the Sahara to desiccate. The cave dwellers left the region and migrated east, south, and west of the Sahara in search of water and better grazing grounds.

Carthage comes into the picture when Algeria is discussed. Its commercial enterprises around the coastal towns of the Mediterranean and the coastal cities they built were a prelude to Pax Romana after the Punic Wars in 146 B.C. What is left of the old African city-state and the ruins of the Roman cities bear witness to the years of Roman glory and to how extensive the empire was. These are souvenirs for historians who have written extensively on Rome and the significance of its North African provinces. The provinces were the breadbasket of imperial Rome, so Roman presence was intended to be permanent. In later times, the Turks, Portuguese, and French all had an impact on the architecture and cultures of Algeria because of their conquests and colonization.

The French left an 8-million-franc bill for grain import unpaid for nearly 30 years, telling the Dey-Hussein they would pay only if the Algerian government stopped patronizing pirates and slave dealers in the Mediterranean. It is reported (Rinehart 1979, 28) that the Dey called a French consul in Algiers, Algeria, "a wicked, faithless, idol-worshiping rascal and slapped him in the face with his fly-swish" during an exchange in 1827. This was the excuse for which the French were waiting. Charles X of France called for an apology and gun salutes to the French flag. When the Dey refused to comply, a naval blockade was imposed on Algeria which was finally invaded in 1830 when France realized that the blockade had no impact on the Dey. The Dey fled to exile to save his neck. From then on, the architecture and culture of Algeria were intertwined with France's colonial policies.

5.2 THE PEOPLE AND TRADITIONAL ARCHITECTURE OF ALGERIA

Algerians are mostly Berbers and Arabs, but intermarriage over the centuries makes physical distinction between the two groups difficult. There are rural dwellers and urban Algerians.

According to McMorris (1979), the major Berber groups are the Kabylie of the Kabylie Mountains east of Algiers and the Chaouias of the Aures range south of Constantine. Kinship remains the major strand that binds traditional family institutions which are passed down from one generation to the other as extended families. There are nomadic and sedentary Berber farmers in the rural areas, and their architecture reflects their family closeness. However, farming and land tenure utilize a complex mix of traditional Berber law, Islamic law, Turkish law, and French colonial input.

Lebbal (1989) has identified several forms of housing in the Aures of Algeria, including tents, gourbis, cave dwellings, and subterranean dwellings. Gourbis are a step above tents. They are not mobile, often consist of one or two rooms under a roof, and are made of earth materials or shrubs. Cave dwellings are structures carved into caves, while subterranean dwellings are found underground. The physical environment of the Aures shapes the kinds of housing in the region. The steep cliffs and long ridges protect those who dwell there from the harsh environment and from invading enemies since the landscape is not easily accessible. The Berbers have always taken refuge in the region since Roman times. Unlike the coast, with its Mediterranean climate, the Aures has extreme weather seasons, cold winters and hot summers. Housing in the region is adapted to the terrain and the dictates of the seasons.

Like most traditional societies where people share their space with one another, animals, and agricultural products, the Aures house also adopts these general functions for its Berber inhabitants. A clear distinction is made between public and private domains, usually achieved by the application of walls that define the domain of one family as separate from those of others. The entrance for animals usually differs from the ones people use and can be easily distinguished. The animal entrances are usually on the sides of the walls and are often much lower in height. The space for animals is clearly distinct from the living space for humans, where there are barriers to keep the animals out.

Most houses have entrance spaces and verandas that lead to the intimate sections of the house. "Some dwellings have a cellar and a kind of entrance hall, known as *skifa*, for preserving the intimacy of the house" (Lebbal 1989, 29). The skifa serves as a multifunctional space for cooking, for receiving guests, and for sleeping. Figure 5.2 shows a shawia house in the Aures. Some houses have courtyards, storage areas, guest rooms, and a terrace.

Indigenous building technology in the Aures utilizes earth, stones, and timber. Stone buildings are more difficult and expensive because of weight, transportation, and lack of skilled masons. Earth houses are more common. Earth is used for foundations, walls, load-bearing structures, roofs,

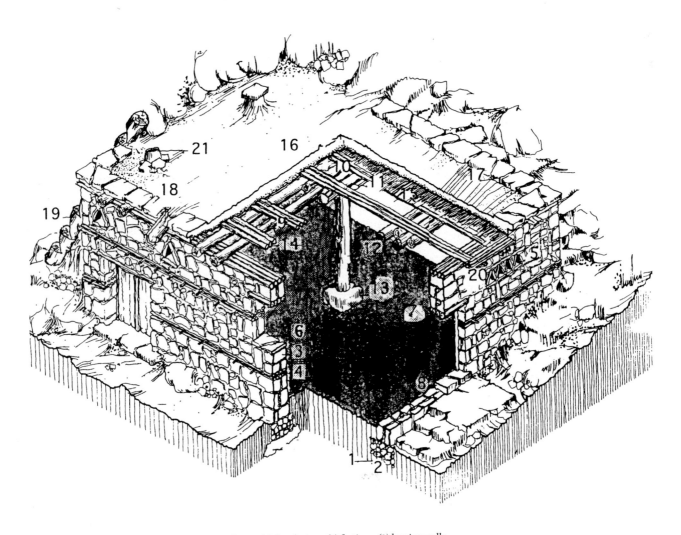

*Fig. 5.2 Aures, Algeria. Sketch of a shawia stone house: (1) foundations, (2) footings, (3) bearing walls,
(4) lacing timber, (5) openings, (6) windows, (7) lintel, (8) threshold, (10) roof structure, (11) hsasat,
(12) hagidith, (13) hazruthon-hagidith, (14) joist, (15) palm stems, (16) terrace surface, (17) stone border,
(18) rainwater spout, (19) ladder, (20) roof projection to protect the entrance, (21) opening in the ceiling.*

fences for privacy or security, and for plastering surfaces. Usually family members lay out and build their own houses as communal work. Labor is divided; some mix the clay, some supply straw, some transport material to the construction site, and others raise the walls. Usually, a house can be completed within a relatively short period. One day to two weeks is common, depending on the availability of family labor and supply of building materials.

5.3 CITIES OF ALGERIA: ALGIERS AND SIDI BEL ABBES

The French created 20 colonization centers in Algeria in 1843. Algiers and Sidi bel Abbes are among these towns. Algiers is an ancient city redesigned by the French to suit their colonial needs. It still retains some of its medieval character in spite of 18th- and 19th-century additions of wide boulevards, high-rise buildings, and shops that give a visitor the feeling of being in a French city such as Paris. Long colonnades of corridors line the sides of some major streets in an attempt to give Algiers the feeling of an Arab medina. The resulting urban character is a trio composed by an indiscriminate fusion of Berber, Arab, and French culture.

One of the remarkable Islamic medieval monuments in Algiers is the Great Mosque built around 1096 A.D. (Fig. 5.3). Horseshoe-arch columns form the aisle arcades, and there are eleven aisles of five bays in the mosque. Architecture in Algiers, however, is not limited to the Middle Ages, nor to the work done by the French during 130 years of colonial rule.

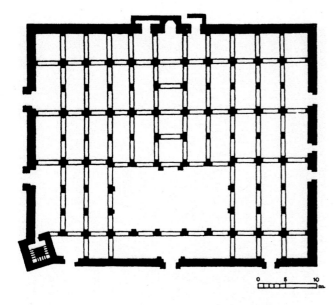

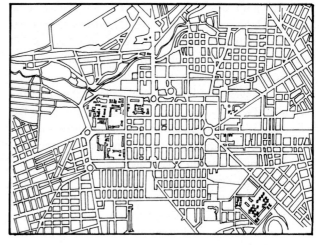

Fig. 5.4 Sidi bel Abbes, Algeria. 1980 plan.

Fig. 5.3 Algiers, Algeria. Plan of the Great Mosque. 1096 A.D.

Postindependence construction has been going on due to the large economic expansion generated by vast sums of petrodollars. Some of the projects realized since the 1970s include Algeria's International Air Terminal in 1976, the International Business Center, and the Civic Center. Kenzo Tange's plan for the Algiers International Airport expanded an existing structure to one with an annual passenger capacity of 5 million people. "The main theme of the design of the Algiers International Airport was shortening the time passengers must spend traveling from the check-in place to the aircraft or from check-out place to taxis or private vehicles" (Tange 1979, 10). Tange also used the vaulted shell roofs of the airport to symbolize aircraft fuselages because of their similarity in shape. Oscar Niemeyer's proposals for the Algiers Business and Civic Centers are reminiscent of his work in Brasília. Both projects are offshoots of the superblock works he completed in the Brazilian capital.

Sidi bel Abbes (Fig. 5.4) is an example of a town whose destiny was shaped by a French colonial program. A significant fact about Algerian cities is that most were designed by military engineers whose primary objective was defensive fortification. The French established their 20 colonization centers in Algeria and embarked on rebuilding dilapidated Turkish towns with urgency. This included road construction, bridges, dams, waterholes, and farm centers for greater France through the colonial settlers. Each colonization center was regarded first as a military garrison, then as an economic center.

"In 1838 the director of engineering in Algeria sent the heads of the different towns a circular giving advice for the establishment of plans for new towns" (Malverti and Picard 1991, 214) with specific instructions to make security a priority. In 1847, the town of Sidi bel Abbes was presented by French military engineers as the model center of colonization (Malverti and Picard 1991). The presentation justified the conditions under which the town was created, and it showed the use of landscape to create a regulated city plan. For Sidi bel Abbes, orders came from Paris in 1847 to the commander-in-chief of Algeria specifying the construction of public buildings, fortifications, distribution of plots to settlers, and construction of roads and grids to coordinate the whole town. The governor in Paris insisted on the need for a nearby plateau on the chosen site to be "securely occupied, in order that no part of the surrounding land should be out of sight and for a crenelated wall to be raised, flanked by fortifications and preceded by a ditch" (Malverti and Picard 1991, 215). The realization that this was a time of territorial fights and occupations of forts among the European powers explains Paris's paranoia and insistence on fortifications for the city of Sidi bel Abbes.

In accordance, the engineers conceived the town as a fortification before adding sections for civilian colonists. The wall made it possible to regularize the streets and blocks. A 25-m-wide boulevard ran through the town east and west linking the military camp to the civilian section. The military camp was equipped with a large parade ground, while two small ones were built in the civilian quarters. All roads were designed for military convenience to all sections of the town. Two wide roads ran parallel to the main boulevard on either side of the town, and a major artery road ran north and south crossing the town.

The town was designed entirely for the convenience of the settlers with no consideration for the Algerians in a grid pattern that gave the settlers the feeling of being in Europe. Sidi bel Abbes was one of the only towns not to include buildings for the ethnic chiefs within the town wall.

Some changes have been implemented as shown in the 1980 plan (Fig. 5.4). The wall that regulated the town has been discarded and is replaced with wide boulevards on most of its length, while the east-west termini in the original plan have become nodes for main diagonal motorways that extend through the town north and south. The implication here is that Algerian cities have French landscapes dotted with buildings that politically sympathize with the Arab culture because they were all planned by the French. This is a paradigm shared by Tunisia and Libya in their own distinctive ways and a true example of the African triple heritage architecture.

5.4 TUNISIA

Writing about the architecture of Tunisia is like constructing a long bridge that spans centuries of events and the ancient ruins they have left for study. Crossing the bridge requires an understanding of the common fate that the countries of the Maghreb share with one another. Early Arab conquerors of the Maghreb called it *jazirat al Maghreb,* Island of the West, because it is bounded on the north by the Mediterranean Sea and on the south by a large sea of sand, the Sahara Desert. Tunisia is a gateway to the west of the Maghreb, Morocco, and it is also a crossroad to the Arabian Peninsula. Tunisia became independent in 1956, after 75 years of French colonial rule.

Tunisia has experienced over 3000 years of differing governments, beginning with the Carthaginians, the Romans, Byzantine Rome, Muslims, Turks, Italians, and finally the French, who conceded in 1956. The name Africa was given only to Tunisia by the Romans, but the name later became synonymous with the entire continent. Roman intrusion into Africa began in 146 B.C. with the defeat of Carthage. The territory was occupied by Rome and reorganized as Proconsular Africa. Proconsular Africa was governed by a civilian governor appointed annually by the Roman senate. In 46 B.C., Julius Caesar deposed the king of Numidia, a territory next to Proconsular Africa, because of personal grievances against the king who supported Pompeii during the civil wars. Caesar attached parts of Numidia to Proconsular Africa. Carthage was rebuilt as a Roman city and the capital of the province by Caesar's orders. It was also a major Christian center from the 2nd century A.D. through the Byzantine period until the Arabs

Fig. C.17 Carthage, Tunisia. Mosaic on a pavement. 500 B.C. (American Geographical Society Collection, The University of Wisconsin-Milwaukee Library)

came with Islam in the mid-7th century. In 693 A.D., the city fell to Arab conquerors who called the region Ifriquiya from the Roman name Africa.

Tunisia has one of the richest collections of Byzantine and early Christian mosaics in the world. "Among the hundreds of mosaics unearthed in Tunisia, a considerable number date to the fourth through sixth centuries, by which time North Africa was thoroughly Christianized" (Alexander 1983, 8). It was popular for rich landlords to decorate their ceilings, walls, and floors with traditional themes and mosaics. Alexander (1983) observes that "the repertory of Christian symbols was limited and stereotyped" to sanctified areas of a church. The mosaics were located in places where they could not be walked on—the sanctified choir, apse, and baptistery. However, the themes in other areas of the church represented daily occasions and typical family events (Fig. C.17).

The beautiful mosaics were completed by master mosaicists who planned carefully before laying out their work. Alexander (1983) believes the technique of laying the mosaics and adjusting the compositions for a house and for a church were the same. Differences between the two are in plan and purpose. In houses, the mosaicist did not have to implement comprehensive composition for the entire structure. Entryways, peristyles, and bedrooms were distinguished slightly by type of mosaic or by size. On the other hand, the mosaicist had to adopt a comprehensive approach that would unify key component parts of a church from the entrance to the nave, aisles, altar, and raised apse.

5.5 TUNIS

This city dates from the Carthaginian period, but it became the administrative capital and replaced Qayrawan in the late 9th century. Built on the west bank of a lake, the city has grown into a twin city of old and new. The Roman cities were gradually replaced with different building types and urban layouts from the mid-7th century. Churches were replaced by mosques, while the square gridirons of the Roman cities were replaced with the monolithic and dense labyrinths typical of African and Arab urban landscape. The dense streets of the old city provide a city life that cannot be replaced by the new because they are natural environments for shops (souk or bazaar) and other kinds of social activities (Fig. 5.5). The great Mosque of Tunis dominated the city before the French planned city came into being. However, ancient Tunis has not remained immune to modernization. Pre- and postindependence development schemes have taken their tolls. Major highways have cut through the city to make room for government secretariats and office buildings. O. C. Cacoub specifically designed vehicular access through the ancient city by creating a wide boulevard that runs through the heart of the city.

The traditional city (medina), the ruins of Roman cities, Arabian, and later Turkish and French construction give major African cities such as Tunis their triple heritage charac-

Fig. 5.5 Tunis, Tunisia. A souk. (American Geographical Society Collection, The University of Wisconsin-Milwaukee Library)

Fig. 5.6 Monaster, Tunisia. An austere mosque. (American Geographical Society Collection, The University of Wisconsin-Milwaukee Library)

Fig. C.18 Monaster, Tunisia.
The ribat. 9th century.
(American Geographical Society
Collection, The University of
Wisconsin-Milwaukee Library)

ter. In recent times, Shiite puritanical approaches to Islam based on the philosophy of humility, absolute equality, and an egalitarianism regulated by the Holy Koran have gradually been reflected in mosque construction. The flamboyant ornaments that garnish many ancient mosques and holy shrines are increasingly under scrutiny as satanic distractions to the worship of God. Monaster, Tunisia, has some of these plain mosques. They reflect the humble philosophy and plainness of the believers, both in daily activity and in dressing codes (Fig. 5.6). This is an invocation of the spirit that inspired medieval Islamic monks to build fortresses such as the great 9th-century ribat at Sousse and the 10th-century ribat at Monaster. Monaster is an ancient city with walled battlements mounted with small square towers. A tall round tower called the nador dominates the ribat (Fig. C.18). Some of the ancient masonry techniques used for ornamental purposes can still be found in various parts, especially at remote oasis, outside the major cities (Fig. C.19). These patterns of brick decoration are derived from traditional Berber patterns in rugs and other textile fabrics. Architectural skeuomorphism (the process of borrowing architectural ornaments from nonarchitectural sources) is very ancient in Africa and has always been used in the embellishment of specific parts of buildings. The application of natural forms found in vegetation to the decoration of column capitals goes back to Egyptian times, and several ethnic groups still practice this tradition.

5.6 LIBYA

Libya is located in the Maghreb and became independent from Italy in 1951. Libya has played an active role in the history of North Africa since 2700–2200 B.C., when some early records of Berber tribes were mentioned in Egyptian records. The defeat of Carthage in 146 B.C. and the imperial reorganization of the region by Julius Caesar increasingly Romanized the region. Some strategically placed cities bloomed both as Roman military garrisons and as commercial centers for gold coming from the African interior for shipment to Rome. Lucrative profits from olive oil encouraged the commercialization and financial investment in agribusiness in African cities along the Mediterranean coast. Leptis Magna was one of those well-placed cities.

Leptis Magna benefited both from the olive oil trade and the trans-Saharan trade. Mathews and Cook (1963) note that caravans came northward from the regions of the Niger and Lake Chad with precious goods strapped tightly to the lumbering camels. Leptis Magna was already a rich commercial center before the Romans came, but the Romans redesigned the city. The presence of many colonists and the city's increasing wealth from agribusiness inspired its citizens to engage in gigantic building projects.

During the reign of Augustus Caesar, a wealthy citizen named Annobal Rufus financed the construction of many civic centers in Leptis Magna, including the market and the

Fig. C.19 Tozeur, Tunisia. Brick decoration derived from Berber carpets and textile patterns. (American Geographical Society Collection, The University of Wisconsin-Milwaukee Library)

*Fig. 5.7 **Leptis Magna, Libya.** Aerial view looking east. "In middle distance is the Wadi Lebda with the harbor at its mouth to the left. The Forum Vetus is at left center, with the Theatre, the Market, and the Chalcidicum grouped in the lower left. In the center can be seen the Forum of Severan times with the Basilica and, to the right, the Nymphaeum. In the center right are the Hadrianic Baths and the Palaestra, with the Arch of Septimius Severus in the lower right." (University of Pennsylvania Press)*

theater (Figs. 5.7 and 5.8). The theater was completed west of the market in 1–2 A.D. It was built in the standard Roman semicircular form. The builders excavated the rock on the site to form the cavae of the auditorium. A seating area for dignitaries was demarcated from the main audience by a semicircular low manhole screen. The lower half of the auditorium was subdivided into six sections running down from five major entrances. Six other steps led to the top seating areas from the middle of the auditorium, while a colonnade of marble columns wrapped around the upper edge of the supporting wall.

By the time of Emperor Tiberius (14–37 A.D.), Emperor Trajan (98 A.D.), and Hadrian (117 A.D.), Leptis Magna had become a highly Romanized African province of Rome. The people of the city enjoyed all the rights of Roman citizenship, and conversion to Christianity was becoming increasingly popular. "By the beginning of the second century,

Christianity had been introduced among the Jewish community, and it soon gained converts in the towns and among slaves" (Berry 1989). The prosperous years were interrupted when vandals came into the region through Spain in 429 A.D., but the Byzantine General Belisarius drove them out in 533 A.D. The returned Byzantine imposed too many taxes on the population, creating an unpopular government that had control only over the North African coastal cities, leaving the interior to rebellious Berbers who continued to challenge the weakened empire.

Finally, the Muslims came in 670 A.D. and sacked whatever was left of imperial Byzantine-Rome. It was then that the Arabian and the Berber dynasties began in the region, followed by the Ottoman regency period, and finally, the Italian

*Fig. 5.8 (Opposite) **Leptis Magna, Libya.** Stage of the theater seen from the southeast entrance. (University of Pennsylvania Press)*

Fig. 5.9 Kabao, Libya. A section of the qasr.

colonization that ultimately led to Libya's independence. The historical background of each country clearly highlights the triple heritage of African architecture.

One of the most distinctive architectural structures in Libya is the fortified storehouse where a family stores grain and takes refuge in time of siege. These storehouses are composite organic honeycomb cells added to over a period of time by different families. The qasr at Kabao (Fig. 5.9) displays a communal effort for common interest and trust within a traditional society. Sometimes, castles (*qasr*) are built with stones in order to be impregnable, but more often than not they are built with earth material in the adobe style.

5.7 TRIPOLI

Tripoli, the largest city and the capital of Libya, could also be described as a twin city, the old city and the later Italian colonial city. In the old section, the narrow winding streets are not dictated by any order; rather they evolved organically over a period of time. According to the Libyan General Committee for Participation in the World of Islamic Festival (1976, 5), the old city of Tripoli has been rebuilt often. The Roman city was surrounded by walls, and in medieval times the gateways were strengthened to ensure greater security. The walls enclose the city in an irregular triangle, with one side thrust into the sea to protect the harbor. Security around the city is strengthened by a moat around the peripheries of the city wall. Old Tripoli is dotted with a few castles outside the city wall for early warning signs, the most famous of them being Al-Saraya al-Hamra Castle. It is believed that Al-Saraya al-Hamra Qasr dates to Roman times but has been renovated and remodeled by various dynastic rulers of the city. The winding streets are also places of social activities such as markets (*souk*).

Tripoli reveals the triple heritage architecture of Africa in many ways. The ancient wall has features of both Roman times and later Ottoman domination. Tall minarets of various mosques loom over the city skyline to emphasize the strong presence of Islam. The Mosque of Darghut and its unique multiple half-disc roof structure add to the presence of Islam in the city. The application of Islamic calligraphy to doors, windows, lintels, and mosaic decorations is all part of the triple heritage. The architecture of the Romans mixed with the architecture of the natives and Muslims in a way that made the triple heritage a reality, but with a much stronger Islamic presence.

6

THE
ARCHITECTURE
OF EGYPT

his chapter concentrates on the architecture of medieval and contemporary Egypt. Egyptian antiquities which predate the periods of Islamic conquest of North Africa have been discussed in Chapter 1 as part of indigenous African architecture. The concern of the triple heritage history at this moment is to investigate the process of Arabization and Westernization in the architecture of Egypt.

6.1 MEDIEVAL CAIRO

Like many North African cities, Cairo is a dual city with an ancient and modern section. Changes have been taking place in the medieval parts of the city to meet the increasing urban needs of today and the future. Egypt, with a population of 40 million people, is inhabitable mostly along the Nile Valley and Delta region, and over 9 million people reside in Cairo, nearly one out of every four Egyptians. As a result, Cairo is a dynamic city with a constantly changing ambiance. This dynamism pushes the city to adopt the character of a modern metropolis, while maintaining its antiquities more than any other city on the face of the earth.

"The site of present day Cairo was most likely farmland for the Pharaohs during the eras of the pyramid buildings" (Aldridge 1969, 8). The Pharaohs planted vegetables that fed the engineers who built the pyramids. However, ancient Cairo was not just a plantation. It was also the center of ancient religions that paved the way for present-day Christianity and Islam through several centuries of evolution of religious philosophy. Egypt and Abyssinia (present-day Ethiopia) became Christian nations very early during the Byzantine period and were strongholds of the Coptic church. Greek was the official language in that era due to the cultural influences of the Ptolemaic Hellenistic period.

The Christian works of Saint Mark, who was martyred about 62 A.D. began to decline with the Diocletian oppression between 284 and 303 A.D. Emperor Constantine and Theodosius finally adopted Christianity as the official religion by 380 A.D. The works of the Apostles and the Coptic church came into conflict with Islam 300 years later, and Egypt fell into the hands of the Muslims in 640 A.D. From then on, the neoplatonic philosophy that took root in Alexandrian Egypt under the Ptolemies and their Hellenistic culture began to decline in the same way as the Christian Coptic Byzantine church did.

The successor of Prophet Muhammad was known as a caliph. Caliph Abu Bakr succeeded the Prophet at his death in 632 A.D. and was succeeded 2 years later by Caliph Omar who continued the expansion of Islam to the West. Caliph Omar conquered Alexandria, the booming seaport capital of Egypt, through General Amir who preferred Cairo as a place for his tent. He withdrew to the less unruly city of Cairo and created a buffer between himself and the Byzantine Christians he had just conquered. However, that did not last long. By 641 A.D., Amir was the sole master of the city he had conquered. He founded a mosque near the Roman citadel of Babylon at Cairo and laid out the new town of Fustat (*the tent*), bringing about the dawn of the age of great citadel buildings of which Cairo boasts some of the best in the world.

6.2 FUSTAT, ASKAR, AND KATAI: THE ABBASIDS DYNASTY AND THE BEGINNING OF AN ISLAMIC CITY IN AFRICA

An ancient Roman city, Fortress (Babylon), was to give way to Fustat. Emperor Trajan built Babylon for security and as a seaport for the shipment of grains to Rome (Fig. 6.1). Amir built his house in the vicinity of the mosque, while his followers and deputies built their houses around his in the winter of 641–642 A.D. The original mosque was simple. It was built with mud, brick, and palm tree trunk supports. The wall finishes were not plastered, and strewn pebble was used for the floor. It had no minaret, just a mihrab. Amir was ordered to remove an unfinished pulpit by Caliph Amar who had accused him of elevating himself above others (Aldridge 1968, 42; Russell 1962, 36). The original mosque was only 90 by 57 ft, but it was rebuilt and enlarged several times over the centuries.

The city of Fustat prospered because of a reopened canal that was originally built by Trajan to link the Red Sea. From the day the Trajan Canal was reopened, Fustat began to replace Alexandria as Egypt's capital. Increasing Arab immigration from the Arabian Peninsula meant more trade and prosperity in Fustat. The buildings in the new settlements took precedence over the Roman fortress city Babylon. They were mostly two- to four-story buildings. Building materials came from old Pharaonic monuments and any other buildings that were destroyed; some Coptic churches and monasteries were also destroyed as Fustat grew into a booming capital city. That is how the foundation for medieval Cairo began during the Omayyad dynasty. This dynasty was so named after Caliph Omar, the supreme ruler of the Islamic world who rose to the caliphal office in 634 A.D.

In 750 A.D., 118 years after Prophet Muhammad's death, a radical group that claimed descent from the Prophet's uncle Abbas, overran the caliphate of Omar and seized power. General Saleh, who took over Fustat, did not want to begin his leadership in an old city founded by a people he had just subdued. He moved north of Fustat and founded the royal quarters of el-Askar, meaning "the soldier" in Arabic. This military camp grew into a township with its own palaces. It was soon connected to Fustat with rows of houses and gardens, which continued to boom as a commercial center. A surge of political rebellion by the Egyptians and Arabs against the Abbasid caliphate brought a new element into play, the introduction of Turkish slaves and mercenaries into Egypt to suppress local rebellions. They did a good job at it, but their powers also rose with it.

It must be emphasized that Baghdad remained the headquarters of the whole Islamic world in its early stages. In 832 A.D., Harun al Rashid, the spiritual and sole leader of Islam in Baghdad, sent his son Mamun to Egypt to suppress local rebellions. Mamun went to Egypt with a Turkish slave (Tulun) who was given to him in 815 A.D. Tulun served well in Mamun's court in Egypt and became powerful. In 868 A.D., Tulun's son, Ahmad Ibn Tulun, succeeded his father in Egypt by appointment from Baghdad, but he later made Egypt an independent caliphate from Baghdad.

Ibn Tulun cleared an ancient site north of Fustat and Askar and built a new capital where he began to prosper as the sole ruler of Egypt. The new town was divided into special *katai's* (districts) for the different populations who lived there. The city housed his mercenaries in different districts and contained many administrative buildings, palaces, extensive gardens, and a large hippodrome. The great Mosque of Ibn Tulun was built at the center of the new city. The Tulinid dynasty was short-lived because the Abbasids reconquered Egypt in 905 A.D. Aside from the mosque, everything was burned to prevent other slaves from taking power.

The Mosque of Ibn Tulun (879 A.D.) is one of the most prized masterpieces of Islamic monuments (Figs. 6.2 and C.21 to C.22). It was built in the tradition of the Abbasid's mosque in Samaria where Ahmad Ibn Tulun was educated. The principal material is well-fired red brick garnished in stucco. The plan is rectangular and measures 400 by 459 ft. The inner court is surrounded by rows of arcades, and the present minaret was placed off-center during the 13-century renovation by Lajin. The symmetrical plan was borrowed from earlier mosques in Baghdad, while the arcades on piers

Fig. 6.1 Islamic Cairo, Egypt: (1) Attaba Square, (2) el-Hakem Mosque, (3) el Akmar Mosque, (4) al-Azhar Mosque, (5) Abdeen Palace, (6) al-Mo'ayed Mosque, (7) the Blue Mosque, (8) el-Rifa'l, (9) al-Sultan Hassan Mosque (Madrassa), (10) Ahmed Ibn Tulun Mosque, (11) Citadel, (12) Amed Ibn Kalaoun Mosque, (13) Muhammad Ali Mosque, and (14) El Gawhara Palace.

(Janel Hetland)

Islamic Cairo

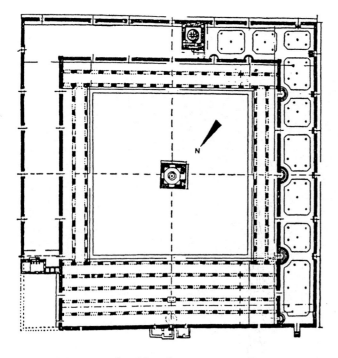

Fig. 6.2 Cairo, Egypt. Plan of Ibn Tulun Mosque. 876–879 A.D. (Janel Hetland)

are reminiscent of the great mosque in Samaria. According to Hoag (1975, 56), the present stone minaret was part of a reconstruction by Lajin in 1296 A.D. The ornamentation on the soffits of the arches was carved in stucco, and it represents a mix of different styles imported from Samaria. These styles were later applied to various mosques in the Islamic world.

The cities of el-Askar and el-Katai ceased to thrive after the Abbasid reconquest. Their decline began slowly and they were later absorbed as appendages to the thriving Fustat, which was becoming an attractive metropolis before the Fatimid dynasty began and halted its growth. At this juncture, it is useful to mention that the Fatimids founded al-Kahira and the Great Mosque of al-Azhar which was mentioned in Chapter 3. The followers of the descendants of the Prophet's sons-in-law rose up and marched eastward to conquer Egypt, installing a radical Shiite Islamic sect dynasty which preceded the rise of Saladin.

One of the monuments of the Fatimid period was the al-Hakim Mosque. It was begun in 990 A.D. by the Fatimid Caliph al-Aziz, and his son, al-Hakim, finished it in 1002 (Figs. 3.7 and 3.8). Although over 100 years older than Ibn Tulun Mosque, it takes precedent from there. The mosque has three domes and a peculiar minaret that does not resemble any other in Egypt. Hoag (1975, 141) also says that al-Hakim's original design had at least thirteen entrances, all symmetrically arranged and three of them monumental.

The map of old Cairo is dotted by more than 100 great monuments from the Middle Ages; the Abdeen Palace, el Akmar Mosque, al Mo'ayed Mosque, the Blue Mosque, and el

Fig. C.20 Cairo, Egypt. Ibn Tulun Mosque. 876 A.D. (Terri Plater)

Fig. C.21 Cairo, Egypt. Ibn Tulun Mosque with minaret derived from the Great Mosque at Samaria. (Terri Plater)

Fig. C.22 Cairo, Egypt. Ibn Tulun Mosque, northeast ziyadah. (Yasser Elshashtawy)

Rifa'il Mosque are a few examples. Within Saladin's citadel (1176–1183), the military museum, Muhammad Ibn Kalaoun Mosque, Muhammad Ali Mosque, and el Gawhara Palace stand out. The Mosque of Muhammad Ali (1830–1857) was built in the style of the great mosque in Istanbul (Fig. C.23). It is one of the most imposing monuments in Cairo, with a 52-m-high interior dome. King Muhammad Ali exchanged an ancient obelisk that is now in Paris with an ornate clock from King Louis Phillippe of France. Saladin, the founder of the Ayyubid dynasty, destroyed the Fatimid dynasty in 1171 A.D. and began work on the citadel to defend Cairo from the Crusaders.

Christian Coptic Cairo, near Roman Fortress, or Babylon, should also be mentioned (Fig. 6.3). Early Christian

Fig. C.23 Cairo, Egypt. Muhammad Ali Mosque. (American Geographical Society Collection, The University of Wisconsin-Milwaukee Library)

Egyptians, like their Muslim counterparts, made use of Egyptian temples for their churches. Later churches were built through the efforts of the Coptic community as a whole. Five outstanding churches are still well preserved: Saint Sergius (Abu Sarga), Saint George (Mari Girgis), Saint Barbara (Kadisah Burbarah), the Hanging Church (el-Muallakah), and the Virgin (el-Adhra). A Jewish synagogue, a monastery, and a convent still stand in the region. The form of the churches was derived from the Roman basilica. This is true mainly for the nonmonastic churches, which were often domed, had double colonnaded interiors, and a semicircular apse at one end. The Coptic churches were conservative and unimposing in order to avoid attention and provocation from the Muslim community which increased its violence toward the Coptic community in the middle of the 7th century. They had no bell towers either because bells were forbidden under Muslim law. The inside of the churches has the following divisions: entrance hall or narthex, nave, chancel, side aisle, and sanctuaries. The naves are usually separated on either side by columns that are joined by continuous architraves. In contemporary times, some churches built in Egypt take precedent from traditional form. The earliest house form, the round hut, has inspired the design of some churches such as the Catholic church shown in Figure C.24.

Medieval Egypt went through several changes under different dynastic leaders: the Umayyids dynasty which began after the death of the Great Prophet, the Tulunids (868–905), the Fatimids (969–1171), the Ayyubids (1171–1250), the Bahri Mamelukes (1250–1382), the Circassian Mamelukes (1382–1517), the Ottoman regency (1517–1805), and finally

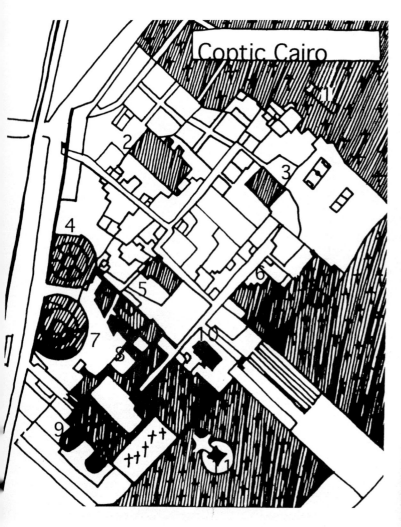

Fig. 6.3 Cairo, Egypt. Plan of Coptic district: (1) Greek Orthodox church, (2) Saint George's Convent, (3) Saint George's Church, (4) Saint George's Church and Monastery, (5) Saint Barbara Alley, (6) Saint Barbara's Church, (7) Babylon fort, (8) Coptic museum, (9) the Church of the Virgin (al-Moualega), (10) Jewish synagogue, (11) Greek Catholic church. (Janel Hetland)

Fig. C.24 Cairo, Zamelek district, Egypt. Catholic church. 1986. (David Hughes Photos)

the Muhammad Ali dynasty (1805–1952) when Egypt became independent.

Modern Egypt, and subsequently modern Cairo, owes its nature and present structure to the Muhammad Ali dynasty. Muhammad Ali began as a governor of Egypt and was accountable to Istanbul, but he followed the history of previous dynasties and made himself independent. It was during the regime of his grandson, King Khedive Ismail (1863–1879), that Cairo became increasingly Westernized, and ambitious projects were financed with foreign loans. Britain used the debts as an excuse to occupy Egypt from 1882 to 1956. The last of the Alis, King Faruk, ruled Egypt until 1952 during the revolution. Before then, his grandfather had converted a sec-

tion of old Cairo into a Parislike area on the bank of the River Nile.

6.3 MODERN CAIRO: THE PARIS OF NORTH AFRICA

History is a continuum of events: The leap from medieval Cairo to modern Cairo brings a new dimension of architectural history to Egypt. Cairo, with its Pharaonic past, has been attracting many people since ancient times. The 19th century was no exception, especially the middle of the century when the Western world was experiencing the Industrial Revolution. The United States was tangled in the Civil War, which changed the way warfare is executed, while European powers remained neutral, waiting for the outcome in order to align themselves with the victor. In Africa and other parts of the world, Europeans were competing with each other for territorial domination and all the riches that were to be made from it.

As usual, the main European contestants were the French and the British. The French were courting the Egyptians with their Gallic charm, as well as with a bribe to build the Suez Canal, in return for Egypt's agreement to be a protectorate of France. The British used a combination of Union Jack gunboat diplomacy, accumulated wealth from other imperial pillages of weak nations, and their Oxbridge Victorian aristo-

cratic charm to outmaneuver the French. At first totally opposed to the Suez Canal, the British had to have it once the French completed it after 10 years of construction using Egyptian money and labor. In the end, the British succeeded—they had Egypt and the canal.

Inside Egypt, the Muhammad Ali dynasty ruled. Sometimes Egyptian kings were happy to be the precious bride that every major power was trying to wed, but most of the time they were in distress, fighting off the maneuvering imperial sharks that dressed in grooms' suits. These sharks were determined to bite off the kingdom of Egypt to satisfy their appetite for territorial expansion. History was being made in the field of architecture while the Muhammad Ali dynasty was bargaining away the future of Egypt with the imperial powers. Joseph Paxton raised Victorian architecture to its zenith with the construction of the Crystal Palace at

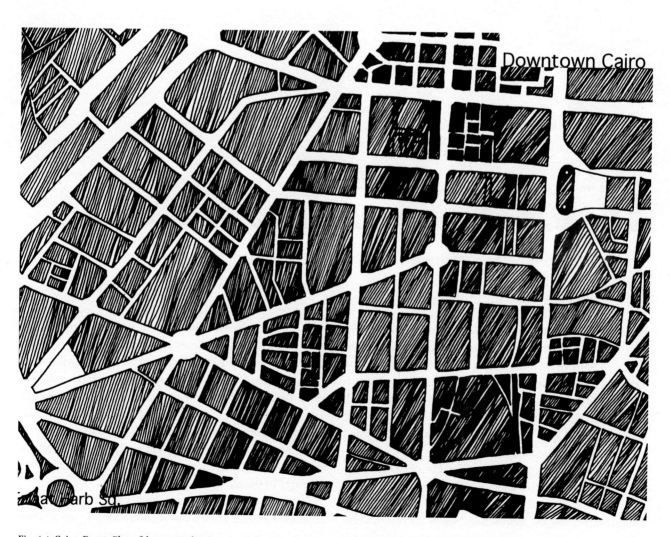

Fig. 6.4 Cairo, Egypt. Plan of downtown district.

Fig. 6.5 Cairo, Egypt. Talaat Harb Square. (American Geographical Society Collection, The University of Wisconsin-Milwaukee Library)

Hyde Park in 1851. Bibliothèque Nationale was built in Paris, to be followed many years later with the regularization of the streets of Paris by Baron Haussmann, making way for the increased output of industrial products coming out of French factories. "By this time Egypt was ruled by Khedive Ismail, Muhammad Ali's grandson, and it was in Ismail's time that the accumulated store of European affluence did its best and its worst for Cairo" (Aldridge 1969, 197).

King Ismail was educated in France and traveled extensively to other parts of Europe. Once he became king, his ambition was to create a Paris on the bank of the River Nile. Another factor was the approach in 1869 of the commissioning of the Suez Canal, the major engineering achievement

that opened a much shorter route between the East and West, rather than the journey around the West African coast. Important world dignitaries were expected in Egypt for the occasion. Ismail turned to Baron Haussmann, the man who made Paris the most charming and romantic city he had ever seen. With this decision, the sacred medieval medina of Cairo that took centuries, many wars, and an infinite amount of human ingenuity to create was cut in two, into the east and west. Boulevard Muhammad Ali and Clot Bey were the main carriages to the old city (Figs. 6.4 and 6.5).

Downtown Cairo has many boulevards that intersect at roundabouts and major squares of the kind found in Paris. The incentive to give the city a Parisian look was carried out

Fig. 6.6 Cairo, Egypt.
Headquarters for Islamic
Affairs. 1990. (Yasser
Elshashtawy)

in a scheme that gave free land to rich Egyptians and Europeans in return for erecting a house worth at least 30,000 francs within 18 months. The rich gladly obliged and built villas in large numbers, many by Europeans who numbered 85,000 out of a population of 300,000 in Cairo in 1872.

According to Aldridge (1969), the king built an opera house for the opening of the canal. Verdi was commissioned to write an opera for the occasion. Because *Aida* was not com-

pleted in time, *Rigoletto* was performed instead on November 1, 1869, the day the canal was opened. French Empress Eugenie, the Crown Prince of Prussia, Henry of the Netherlands, Prince Louis of Hesse, and a large entourage showed up for the occasion. The rush to see the new Paris of Africa continued until the following year when the Prince of Wales (Edward VII) and his princess paid an official visit to Cairo. It was a year of "Arabian Night" life. As Aldridge (1969,

Fig. 6.7 (Opposite) Cairo, Egypt. Window detail, Headquarters for Islamic Affairs. (Yasser Elshashtawy)

Fig. 6.8 El-Marb Cairo, Egypt. Modern apartments. 1990. (Yasser Elshashtawy)

Fig. 6.9 Cairo, Egypt. City of the dead, where private tombs have been converted to living quarters. (Yasser Elshashtawy)

199) put it, "The year of the Canal opening, 1869, was an astonishing one for Cairo. Life for the rich and the foreign became one long festival of balls, banquets, theaters, operas, races."

Haussmannization of Cairo continues to this day. The central business district looks more like Paris than anything in a traditional Arab medina. The buildings lining the corners of Talaat Harb Square stand out with their Parisian architectural styles and motifs. Even in suburbs like el-Maadi and Helliopolis, boulevards and streets run at diagonals. In addition, houses and public buildings show influences of Arabisance as in Morocco, Tunisia, Algeria, and Libya.

Arabisance is always a response to one major factor in Egyptian architecture: The relationship between house openings and light is highly controlled. This is true in traditional Egyptian houses, and window articulation remains a major element in modern Egyptian architecture even when the surfaces of the wall have been stripped of classical and medieval decorative motifs. Public buildings also respond to this ves-

tige of traditional decoration as shown in the Headquarters for Islamic Legal Affairs and Culture Building (Figs. 6.6 to 6.8).

Cairo is still a growing city, and migration from rural areas makes it difficult to cope with the increasing population. A necropolis, "the city of the dead," has been annexed by homeless families into a city of the living. Here, tombs made for the dead are now homes for thousands of families (Fig. 6.9), without the permission of the owners whose relatives lie there. The city's problems were further escalated by a major earthquake, measuring 5.9 on the Richter scale, which struck Cairo shortly after noon on October 12, 1992. From early reports, the death toll was high, and medieval Cairo was not damaged as much as some of the newer areas. It was the newly constructed private apartments and commercial buildings that sustained most of the damage. The Egyptian government introduced new building codes when it became obvious that the buildings that were damaged in the earthquake were poorly constructed.

3 CENTRAL AND EAST AFRICA

chapter

7

THE ARCHITECTURE OF DJIBOUTI, ETHIOPIA, KENYA, SOMALIA, AND THE REPUBLIC OF SUDAN

Djibouti, Ethiopia, Somalia, Kenya, and Sudan are located in the Horn of Africa (Fig. 7.1). In Djibouti, Kenya, and Somalia, the fusion of Arab and African culture has produced a unique people and language called Swahili, one of the most widely spoken languages in Africa. The politics of 19th-century colonization created most of the differences that can be seen in many East African countries. These differences are really cultural exaggerations that were designed to facilitate the divide-and-rule principle. Boundaries and states were instruments for colonial exploitation and for the convenience of administering the "estates," as they were viewed, during the scramble for Africa. To the colonizers, national boundaries were determined by strategic and economic values. Ethiopia and its neighbors were already Christian states by mid-4th century A.D., with large Coptic communities, before Islam began to penetrate and dominate the region in the 9th century. Somalia, Kenya, and Djibouti were gradual-

ly Islamized, whereas Ethiopia and parts of Egyptian Nubia resisted this influence. There is strong evidence of the existence of the triple heritage culture in this region, especially in Sudan, where ancient religious conflicts continue to overshadow the political, cultural, and economic life of the country. The competition between the English and the French split people arbitrarily into English or French enclaves within this area. In the Horn of Africa, British Somaliland, French Somaliland, and Djibouti are products of such colonial, monopolistic competition. An ancient nation like Ethiopia retains most of its heritage due to the unsuccessful attempt of the Italians to colonize the people.

The Horn of Africa continues to be a hot spot because of its strategic geographic location and consequent vital connection to the Suez Canal and the Red Sea link to the Indian Ocean, the shortest route between Europe and Asia. The pattern of colonial architectural influence seen in North Africa is also prevalent in the Horn and the rest of East Africa.

7.1 DJIBOUTI

France formally occupied Djibouti in 1888. The principal ethnic groups in Djibouti are the Afars and the Isas. Other inhab-

Fig. 7.1 Central and East African countries. (Gabriel Okafor)

itants of the country include Arabs, Somalis, Ethiopians, Chinese, Indians, Jews, and Sudanese. In spite of this plural ethnic constitution, the population of Djibouti remains under 1 million people. The Afars and the Isas are ethnic groups also found in both Ethiopia and Somalia.

Djibouti has an 800-km coastline which serves as a gateway from the Indian Ocean to the Red Sea. Ethiopia surrounds the country along its northern, western, and part of its southern border, while Somalia surrounds the rest of the southern border. The country is hot and humid year round with an average temperature of 85°F. The landscape is arid, with little rainfall. France wanted to have a presence in the region to gain military and economic advantages. Leonce Lagarde, a French military commander of the territory, made treaties with local chiefs, collected taxes from the people, and used the money to expand his mission in the region and organize Djibouti into a colonial country. A railroad extension from Djibouti to Addis Ababa in 1889 attracted many inhabitants to the country. The European population grew to 200 out of 10,000 local residents. Lagarde was ready to incorporate a city by this time, so he joined resources with the railway company to design the city.

The city grid (Fig. 7.2) follows the narrow landscape. The seaport area and the railway station became the most developed parts of the new town. With the exception of the buildings constructed by the French, houses in Djibouti follow the traditional East African coastal architecture style. A major element is art deco, predominant in plaster work and carved doors and windows. The traditional coral building method which dominates major East African cities such as Kilwa, Zanzibar, Dar es Salaam, and Lamu is the major source of the architectural repertoire of Djibouti. The plaster work on the walls of traditional buildings is quite delicate, and the motifs are of traditional vegetation and of characters from Islamic

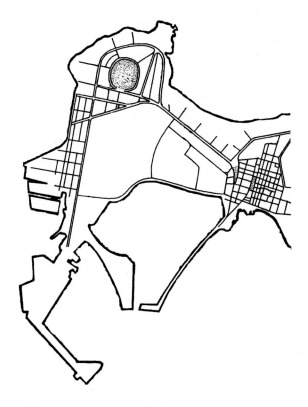

Fig. 7.2 Djibouti city plan.

writings. In a way, the triple heritage reached its fullest balance in Djibouti because here it not only produced a people whose heritage is a blend of African and Arabian, but also a culture that mirrored the distinct features found in the people themselves.

Unlike the buildings in traditional African styles, colonial buildings were essentially Arabisances because they included African, Islamic, and Western motifs in the same buildings. In Djibouti, buildings are arranged in courtyard style to preserve indoor and outdoor spaces for different occasions and for privacy. Unlike most North African cities, there is no traditional city beside modern-day Djibouti because the French were able to lay their grids when the town's population was small.

7.2 ETHIOPIA

The role of Ethiopia as a link between Pharaonic Egypt and sub-Saharan Africa has been discussed in Chapter 1. This section provides detailed information on some of the pre-Christian and medieval architecture that connects Ethiopia to Pharaonic Egypt and sub-Saharan Africa. The building programs of modern Ethiopia are also discussed here.

In Ethiopia, the triple heritage swings from a predominantly Muslim community to an orthodox Judeo-Coptic Christian community adopted by the people since the 4th century A.D., when they had strong ties with the Byzantine imperial church.

Ethiopian architecture in the Middle Ages bears no resemblance to anything elsewhere. Its roots stem from the indigenous pre-Christian era in the ancient kingdom of Aksum. The records of German explorers who have reconstructed Aksumite palaces verify that pre-Christian era construction techniques in Ethiopia were carried over to the rock-hewn churches of the Middle Ages. These magnificent rock-hewn churches are the only standing remains of medieval Ethiopian architecture, mainly because of their stronger construction. Their free-standing counterparts have all vanished, although some stumps of their foundation stones remain. Krencker's reconstruction (Fig. 7.3) is based on the foundation remains of an Aksumite palace. The mystery church of Debra Damo and the great pre-Christian stelae of "Aksum in which built-up forms (identical to those used at Debra Damo) are scrupulously imitated in solid stone" (Buxton 1970, 52) provide good descriptions of ancient building methods in Ethiopia (Fig. 1.21). These stelae of Aksum show multistory towers as high as 13 stories. The stelae have sculptured doors with all accessories, a latch at the base, and are carved to precision. The process of hewing the giant stelae and transporting them posed as difficult a problem as that faced by the ancient Egyptians in constructing their vast monuments and makes one appreciate the ingenuity of the Aksumites. Buxton (1970, 53) summarizes the distinguishing characteristics of the pre-Christian Ethiopian style as follows: In Plan, they all adopted the square with built-up foundations that form solid horizontal plinths or pedestals which rise in steps. Pre-Christian build-

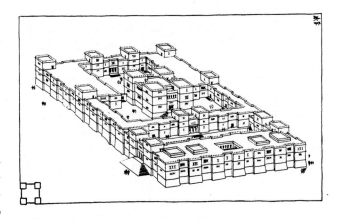

Fig. 7.3 Aksum, Ethiopia. A reconstructed sketch of Ta'akha Mariam's Palace. 300 A.D.

ings in Ethiopia had monolithic columns that were square in shape with bases and capitals that were detailed in different ways from surrounding motifs. The styles of these columns were later used in the construction of the rock-hewn churches during the Middle Ages, 1300s A.D. According to Buxton (1970), this peculiar technique may have been widespread in various parts of the world in early times, but its wholehearted adoption seems to be a special characteristic of the Ethiopian style. Generally speaking, walls of rubble and earth-mortar are reinforced at intervals by means of horizontal timbers placed into the inner and outer surfaces of the wall. In addition, short round timbers penetrate the thickness of the wall; these timbers project beyond the outside wall (the monkey-heads), and a few go completely through, projecting inside as well. The underside of the timber is slotted and fits over a longitudinal timber, anchoring it firmly into the wall. Krencker's diagrams, based on Debra Damo, show the typical wall and window construction very clearly.

Doors and windows are treated as integral parts of the structure but with special horizontal reinforcements. Internal friezes in the rock-hewn churches certainly represent the same method that was applied in Aksumite houses. Buxton (1970, 54) states that such friezes consist essentially of rows of joined-up blind panels constructed exactly like single windows, with the usual corner blocks. The use of beams and panels on the ceilings of the rock-hewn churches can also be traced to the pre-Christian Aksumite palaces. Other elements in the rock-hewn churches that evolved out of pre-Christian Ethiopian architecture are: arches, domes, naves, and roofs. The arrival of Christianity in early 4th century A.D. created a fusion of both the indigenous building techniques and those of the basilica church. The effect of this cultural fusion can be seen most strongly in the interiors of the rock-hewn churches. The Ethiopians borrowed the elements of the Christian basilica to create churches out of traditional building methods and motifs that are uniquely African. In addition, the construction techniques were from ancient Egypt, especially those for the rock-hewn churches and the stelae.

The name Ethiopia was made popular during the Christianization of Aksum. A Greek word meaning "land of people with burnt faces" (Pankhurst and Ingrams 1988, 10), it was later applied to all people of dark skin. Aksum was a major center in early Ethiopian Christian history and dedicated Coptic Christians still visit there on pilgrimages. With the fall of Askum, Ethiopian monks built new churches in the most ingenious ways by hewing them from the living rock. These churches are now called the Churches of Lalibela. Harassment by Muslims and the determination of Ethiopian Coptics to get closer to God were contributing factors in the transformation of solid rocks into houses of God in medieval Ethiopia.

7.3 THE MIDDLE AGES AND THE CHURCHES OF LALIBELA: "A NEW JERUSALEM IN THE MOUNTAINS"

Several reasons account for the fact that Africa's triple heritage architecture has been sustained for so long in Ethiopia, almost as it has always been since ancient times. The town of Adefa, located 8500 ft above sea level, became a sacred sanctuary for a retiring Zagwe king of Ethiopia, King Lalibela, who was deposed by the Solomonic dynasty in the later part of the 13th century A.D. In addition, pressures from the Muslim Fatimid dynasty in Egypt in the 10th century caused many Coptic Christians to flee from Egypt to Ethiopia. Because it was cut off from Byzantine, Alexandria, and Egypt by the Muslims, the Ethiopian church paid more attention to the Mosaic ways of the Old Testament than to the New Testament. Ethiopia's ties with Christianity go beyond the Alexandrian Coptic church to legends associated with the initial stages of the Christian faith itself. According to Hammerschmidt (1970, 44), "it is alleged that the mother of God (*Mary*) with the Christ child lived for a time during their flight from Bethlehem on the Island of Tana Cerges [near Lake Tana in Ethiopia], the very island which is supposed to have harbored for 600 years the Ark of the Covenant which was stolen from Jerusalem before it was brought to Aksum." These are looms of the ancient Semitic strand of the African triple heritage culture, nourished and maintained by Christianity at all levels of Ethiopian life. Above all, the royalty of Ethiopia have been the custodians of the faith since the 4th century A.D.

Therefore, the deposed Zagwe king could not have chosen a more suitable place, nor a better occupation to pursue. The nearly dozen churches erected as a result are among the wonders of the ancient world. In 1521, Francisco Alvares, the chaplain of a Portuguese mission, visited these churches and was afraid to write about them because he doubted whether people in Portugal would believe his detailed descriptions. These churches still cast the same spell of wonder and mesmerize those who visit them today. Each monolithic church is carved out of one solid rock and excavated inside and out with a mathematical precision, representing a building style that is uniquely Ethiopian and can only be found in Ethiopia. It has been mentioned in Chapter 1 that some of the medieval Ethiopian churches owe their construction techniques and styles to ancient Egyptian temples (see Figs. 1.22 and 7.4).

Fig. 7.4 Aksum, Ethiopia. The Church of Maryam of Seyon. Rebuilt in the 11th century on the foundation of a 4th-century building. (Richard Pankhurst, Leila Ingrams. Ethiopia Engraved by Kegan and Paul International)

Historians have wondered about the motives behind the building of these churches. One answer is that God inspired King Lalibela to build them. Others speculate that King Lalibela built the churches in competition with the Solomonic dynasty to win back the favor of his people. In either case, one thing is certain: King Lalibela spent all his wealth constructing these churches and personally worked alongside the workmen. He lived like a monk on a vegetable and root diet and was a changed man at the time of his death. The kings of the Zagwe dynasty are regarded as tyrants by the Ethiopian people, but King Lalibela is regarded as a saint. His great works set him apart from the notorious deeds that became associated with his ancestors.

The largest and one of the most important of these churches is the Church of Beta Madhane Alam (House of the Redeemer of the World). Gerster (1970) indicates that this church, cut from a mass of stone, measures 33.7 m long, 23.7 m wide, and 11.5 m high (Figs. 7.5 and 7.6). The external columns are aligned with the inside columns. The interior plan is subdivided by four longitudinal arcades into five aisles. Each arcade has eight bays unified by a nave. The aisles have flat ceilings, while the nave has a barrel vault. The relief decoration on top of the roof reflects the eight bays of the interior. In the case of Beta Madhane Alam, they are eight arched blind arcades; the window details on the east elevation vary. This church is a duplication in rock of the Church of Our Lady of Zion at Aksum that was destroyed in the 16th century.

The Church of Beta Maryam (Saint Mary's Church) was one of King Lalibela's favorites. He and the royal family attended mass there, and it is presently one of the most frequented churches by Christian pilgrims. This church has a plain exterior that is compensated for by a highly ornate interior. The Church of Saint Mercurius and Bethlehem is no less amazing.

The most beautiful of all the churches in the holy city is Saint Beta Giyorgis (Saint George's Church), the sunken splendor of Lalibela (Fig. 7.7). Tradition has it that this is one of the last churches to rise within the mountain cavities of Lalibela. This monolith was built by King Lalibela to satisfy the demand of the equestrian patron saint of the warlike Ethiopians who appeared in full armor in a vision to the king. The patron saint asked why all the saints had received their churches while he had none. He left footprints of his white horse on the bottom of the pit. It was then that the king decided to build this beautiful wonder. According to Gerster (1970, 107), no description of this church should omit the word "elegant." It is indisputably a well-proportioned testimony to architectural ingenuity and expertise in the working of stone. It was a later work done by sculptors who had mastered the art of stone carving after building several monolithic churches. The early medieval rock-cut church at Dongolo (Fig. 7.8) does show a strong affinity to the Roman basilica.

Ethiopian Solomonic monarchs continued to invest in building construction and in establishing different capital cities each time a monarch began his reign. Emperor Tewodros II moved to Debra Tabor in the 1860s and built the Church of the Savior of the World (Fig. 7.9). Emperor Facilidas moved his capital to Gonder in the northwest province of the country. He built several churches and schools and encouraged his ministers to convert the new city to a commercial center. The Church of Madhane Alam at Gonder and the buildings around it call our attention to the coexistence of both oval and rectangular house forms in Africa. This fortresslike city has similarities with the circular fortresses found in Zimbabwe (Fig. 11.16). In addition, round house forms in Ethiopia (Fig. 7.10) point to the fact that different house forms in ancient Egypt have been diffused to different parts of Africa via Ethiopia and Sudan. The ruins of the Facilidas Castle (Fig. 7.11) still stand as a testament to the glorious years of Gonder. The castle was built in 1640 by an Indian architect. One of the indulgences of the emperors of Ethiopia was the huge gardens around their castles complete with pools and well-equipped zoological collections. This practice was continued until the time of Emperor Haile

Sellassie, whose giant lions became the totem for his kingship, symbolic of the powers of the Lion of Judah. The castle retains only a few characteristics of traditional aristocratic Ethiopian architecture in key elements like the domes of its towers, which are derived from the traditional hut, and the terrace finishes such as those found in the Church of Maryam of Seyon at Aksum. Gonder was a distant prelude to the 20th-century politics of Westernization and the occupation of Ethiopia.

Nineteenth- and twentieth-century imperial politics shaped Ethiopia and influenced its architecture in a radical way that took it far from its glorious roots. Ethiopia is the only country in Africa not colonized by any imperial power, with the exception of a 3-year Italian occupation during World War II. This does not mean that the country was ignored. In fact, Britain, France, and Italy were highly involved in the region in the 19th century, and Italy managed to keep parts of the territory for a few years, although it endured many years of resistance from the people of Ethiopia under the leadership of Emperor Yohannes. Emperor Menelik succeeded Yohannes and declared war against the Italians in 1886 after importing arms from France and Russia. In spite of Ethiopia's independence, the Italians managed to introduce some European architecture for their military officers in the occupied regions. Both the private and the recreational quarters built for the officers conformed to a style that mixed Italian and traditional Ethiopian construction motifs. The sketch of an Italian military casino at Sa'ati shows a house with vertical Roman arches capped with a roof style derived from traditional Ethiopian architecture (Figs. 7.12 and 7.13).

In 1886, after the battle of Adwa, Emperor Menelik founded the present capital of Ethiopia, Addis Ababa, and began the process of modernizing the nation. Official government buildings were built in the Western style from that time on as a process of modernization, one which of course ignored Ethiopia's long history. During the 1960s, when many African countries became independent, Addis Ababa was chosen as the headquarters for the Organization of African Unity (OAU). Present-day Addis Ababa was developed by Emperor Haile Sellassie before the Marxist regime of Colonel Haile Maryam Megistu drastically slowed the pace of progress.

Addis Ababa was not immune to the post-World War II architectural and technological movements that swept the world. African leaders chose a modern style for the Hall of Africa (Fig. 7.14) in Addis Ababa, signifying acceptance of the future and of the technology that would be imported to reconstruct colonially ravaged Africa. Ethiopia's independence made it the logical choice for an all-African capital city. Emperor Haile Sellassie played the dual role of bringing Ethiopia to the forefront of African politics while preserving

Fig. 7.5 (Opposite, top) Lalibela, Ethiopia. Interior view of the rock-hewn Church of Madhane Alam (Redeemer of the World). Late 13th century. (Richard Pankhurst, Leila Ingrams. Ethiopia Engraved by Kegan and Paul International)

Fig. 7.6 (Opposite, bottom) Lalibela, Ethiopia. A facade of the rock-hewn Church of Madhane Alam. Late 13th century by Emperor Lalibela. (Richard Pankhurst, Leila Ingrams. Ethiopia Engraved by Kegan and Paul International)

Bet Giorgis

Fig. 7.7 *(Above) Lalibela, Ethiopia. Aerial view of Beta Giyorgis (Saint George's Church), showing how it was carved from the surrounding living rock. A cruciform structure, the ancient Egyptian sign of the ankh dominates the design.* (George Gerster)

Fig. 7.8 *(Opposite) Dongolo, Tigre, Ethiopia. The interior of a rock-hewn church. Early 13th century.*

(Richard Pankhurst, Leila Ingrams. Ethiopia Engraved by Kegan and Paul International)

Fig. 7.9 (Above) Debra Tabor, Ethiopia. The
Church of Madhane Alam (Redeemer of the
World) built by Emperor Tewodros II. 1864
A.D. (Richard Pankhurst, Leila Ingrams. Ethiopia
Engraved by Kegan and Paul International)

Fig. 7.10 (Right) Tigre, Ethiopia. A round
church at the village of Mishuk. 1988. (Richard
Pankhurst, Leila Ingrams. Ethiopia Engraved by Kegan
and Paul International)

Fig. 7.11 (Above) Gondah, Ethiopia. An 18th-century engraving of Facilidas Castle. (Richard Pankhurst, Leila Ingrams. Ethiopia Engraved by Kegan and Paul International)

Fig. 7.12 (Right) Sa'ati, Ethiopia. Sketch of an Italian military casino. 1890s. (Richard Pankhurst, Leila Ingrams. Ethiopia Engraved by Kegan and Paul International)

Fig. 7.13 (Right) Asamara,
Eritrea, Ethiopia. An Italian
military commander's house.
(Richard Pankhurst, Leila Ingrams.
Ethiopia Engraved by Kegan and
Paul International)

Fig. 7.14 (Below) Addis
Ababa, Ethiopia. Hall of
Africa, the Organization of
African Unity (OAU)
Building. 1960s. (American
Geographical Society Collection, The
University of Wisconsin-Milwaukee
Library)

its royal traditions. Whereas the Hall of Africa represents the future by technological innovation, ancient Ethiopian aristocracy maintained the traditions of the past. Nothing exemplifies this architectural duality more than the gate to Emperor Sellassie's Imperial Palace and the Ethiopian Parliament Building. Unlike the closely fitted lions of the Lion Gate at Mycenae, two Solomonic lions sit apart on top of the classically inspired central bay of the entrance (Fig. 7.15). The two side bays help to define the neoclassicism of the gate. Emperor Sellassie's taste for luxuries is clearly revealed in his Trinity Church. The imperial entrance with its open colonnade was specially designed for one occasion,

Fig. 7.17 (Right) Addis Ababa, Ethiopia. Site plan, Development Center. Aarno Ruusuvuori, 1975. (Architectural Office Aarno Ruusuvuori, Helsinki, Finland)

Fig. 7.18 (Below) Addis Ababa, Ethiopia. First floor plan, Development Center. (Architectural Office Aarno Ruusuvuori, Helsinki, Finland)

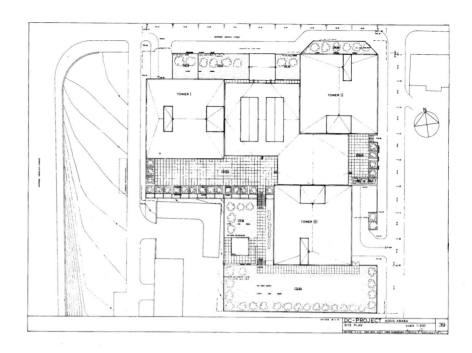

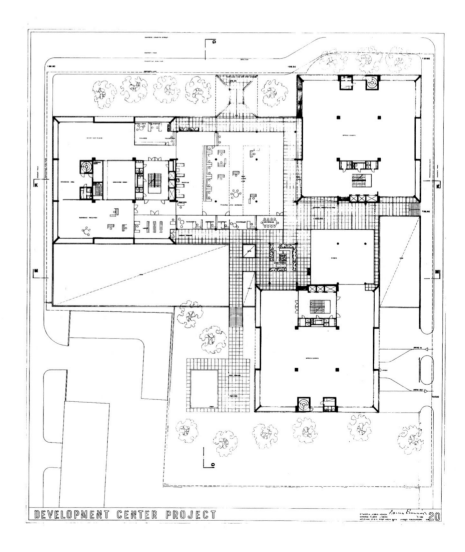

Fig. 7.19 Addis Ababa, Ethiopia. Development Center. Aarno Ruusuvuori, 1975. (Architectural Office Aarno Ruusuvuori, Helsinki, Finland)

the procession during his coronation in 1918. The grandeur of the church and the symbolism of the Solomonic lions at the Imperial Palace gate clearly defined Haile Sellassie's view of his royal lineage as divine and destined to govern Ethiopia for eternity. His ascendance to the imperial throne was, in his view, a mandate to the Solomonic dynasty to bring Ethiopia into the modern world. He expressed this belief in his autobiography: "Thus we ourselves, by virtue of our descent from the Queen of Sheba and King Solomon, ever since we accepted in trust, [in 1916] first the regency of the present, we have set out to the best of our ability to improve, gradually, internal administration by introducing into the country western modes of civilization through which our people may attain a higher level; hence our conscience does not rebuke us" (Sellassie 1976, 5). Emperor Sellassie's descent from the Queen of Sheba and King Solomon clearly highlights the depth of the triple heritage and how strongly many Africans feel about their connection and influence on the Semitic culture.

The term *modernization* has proven a self-defeating ideology for many African leaders because of the simplistic interpretation of the past becoming divorced from the future. This often leads to cultural destruction. In other words, the importation of European Renaissance building styles into Ethiopia was a means of equating the Ethiopian imperial regency to the 20th-century monarchs in Europe who were colonizing the world. That was a misguided policy that traded a great ancient heritage for something very new in the name of development. This philosophy of modernization also explains the emperor's preference for the newly constructed Parliament Building and modern office buildings which completely ignore Ethiopia's rich building tradition (Fig. 7.16).

Underdevelopment is a major obstacle to the full realization of the design intent behind building projects because of the lack of an industrial base for manufactured building components and of skilled manpower. If they are to succeed, architects who practice in such conditions must work out suitable logistics to overcome these problems. They must

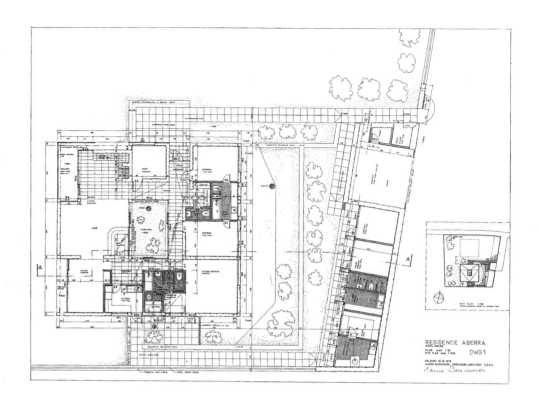

address issues of technology, climate, culture, and finance. The problem is made more complex by the desire of African leaders to make their cities look as Westernized as possible for the sake of modernization.

Aarno Ruusuvuori, a Finnish architect, achieved remarkable results with limited resources. His projects include com-

mercial and private housing initiated by Emperor Sellassie, but completed during Colonel Mengistu's regime. A Development Center project belonging to the Ethiopian Agriculture and Industrial Development Bank was completed in 1975 in Addis Ababa. The building is located downtown near major city landmarks, the Organization of African Unity

Hall (OAU), Emperor Haile Sellassie Jubilee Palace, and the Hilton Hotel, and in a neighborhood surrounded by apartment blocks and medieval monuments. Architect Ruusuvuori was aware of the difficulty of working in the site, considering the kind of solution desired by the Ethiopian government. Ruusuvuori's answer was to design a three-tower structure unified by a common base. The approach to the Development Center building allows generous space for pedestrians at the entrance level (Figs. 7.17 to 7.19), with shades to minimize the sun. The main hall of the bank is placed on the entrance level. There are three towers, each approximately 31 by 31 m². Two towers are six stories, approximately 21.5 m in height, while one tower of nine stories is approximately 31.5 m in height. The towers are connected by a single-story enclosure. Two partially underground levels under the whole complex include car-parking and technical units. The building has on-site cast concrete pile foundations with tie-beams, a reinforced concrete ground slab, and retaining walls. The towers are reinforced concrete superstructures of columns, walls, beams, and slabs. The remaining structures are independent but of similar construction. External facing is mostly smooth-cast finished concrete, with fairface (boarded) finished elevations and staircase blocks. Tinted glass aluminum windows are fitted throughout. To reduce cost, only the bank computer room is air conditioned, and the concrete and reinforced concrete were supplied by local industry. The windows are deliberately inserted further between the column bays to give depth and to reduce solar penetration.

Architect Ruusuvuori also accomplished many residential projects before the Marxist revolution, such as the Aberra House and the Lilibeta House in Addis Ababa (Figs. 7.20 and 7.21). These houses represent a new way of thinking that believes in the future and its idealistic, modern concept. The revolution that wrestled power from the last Solomonic emperor, Haile Sellassie, and his feudal lords was supposed to make life better for all Ethiopians. Instead, it plunged the nation into endless civil strife and literally strangled national development for over 12 years. The collapse of Colonel Mengistu Haile Mariam's government in May 23, 1991, and several years of civil war have taken an enormous toll on the people of Ethiopia and the imperial city of Addis Ababa which Emperor Menelik founded. The city has been bombarded several times since 1991 by warring factions, and the country continues to break into smaller ministates along ethnic lines. The major port city of Masawa has been leveled by intense war, as have other major cities of Ethiopia in the regions of Eritrae and Tigre. It will take time before Ethiopia is rebuilt, but the impact of the war will leave indelible marks on the people and the physical structure of Ethiopian cities.

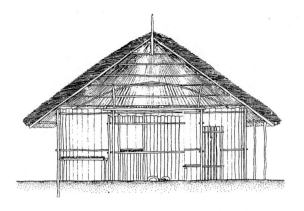

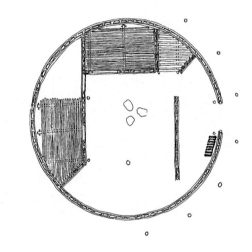

Fig. 7.22 Kenya. Plan and section of a Kikuyu house. (Kaj Blegvad Anderson and Oxford University Press)

7.4 ETHNIC GROUPS AND HOUSE FORMS IN KENYA

Kenya, the safari capital of the world, gained independence from Great Britain in 1963 and became a republic under the leadership of the late President Jomo Kenyatta in 1964. The area known as Kenya was settled by the indigenous Africans (Rinehart 1984) before 1000 B.C. Kenya is one of the countries where the Swahili language developed due to the early interactions between Arab merchants and Bantu-speaking people from coastal East Africa. The Portuguese explored the region in the 17th century, and the British came in the 19th century and colonized the country.

The Kikuyu, the Kipsigis, Maasai, Nyika, Swahili speakers, Luyia, and Galla people are some of the major ethnic groups in Kenya. Culture here revolves along ethnic lines, and the extended family is the center of an individual's loyalty in

Fig. C.25 Kenya. Aerial view of a Kikuyu village. (American Geographical Society Collection, The University of Wisconsin-Milwaukee Library)

small village communities. The Maasai people are nomads whose movements in the grassland depend on the season. They build their houses with pliable materials such as leaves and animal skin. In some cases, stems are bent and tied together to form flat-roofed buildings with round corners. Joseph Thompson, who traveled in the region in the late 1900s, describes the dimensions of the houses as 10.5 ft tall, 9 ft long, and 5 ft wide (Anderson 1977). Traditional architecture among native people does not change quickly. In fact, it is passed down from one generation to the next using technical skills similar to their original forms.

The Kikuyus build their homesteads in villages, a practice that is also found among the Maasai people. The Kikuyu homestead usually consists of several unit houses belonging to members of the same ancestral heritage. Unlike the Maasai, their houses are more rigid. They use communal labor to build a house, and more often than not, a house is completed in one day. Anderson (1977, 82) observes that,

"The materials used for the wall of the Kikuyu houses reflect the adaptation of traditional building material to changing circumstances." The Kikuyus use poles of timber boards for the walls of their houses (Figs. 7.22 and C.25). Usually, the houses are circular in shape, and the roofs are made from poles that are tied together for the rafters and the saplings. In later times, nails were sometimes used both for the walls and the roofs. The rafters meet at the apex, and thatch is used to cover them. Thatch usually insulates the house from intense sunlight because this material does not conduct heat; however, thatch has the disadvantage of impermanence.

The family structure usually determines the arrangement of houses within a homestead. The homestead chief's house or the man's house is usually near the entrance to the compound. The senior wife's house follows a traditional pattern in terms of how things are arranged within. There is a fireplace in the middle, with other furniture arranged around the corners of the house. Usually, only girls sleep in the same room with the women and boys, except when young, sleep in the men's room. There is usually a central courtyard for the homestead, used for cooking and socialization during the hot dry seasons. The courtyard is used most in the evening after sunset. Here women tell folk stories to children to teach them the traditions of their ancestors and to expose them indirectly to the laws of the society, while young adult men have increased contact with older men to learn the process of initiation into manhood.

7.5 CITIES OF KENYA: LAMU, NAIROBI, AND MOMBASA

Lamu is one of the oldest towns along the East African coast, and because its architecture includes a wide range of styles, it serves as a basis for discussion of the architecture of most East African coastal cities. According to Allen (1974), Lamu originated as a seasonal or year-round trading site for the Bantu-speaking people of the interior. In culture, politics, and religion, it was first and foremost an African town. The process of Islamization took place long after the town had prospered and attracted Muslim settlers from the Arabian Peninsula. Further evidence for the African origin of Lamu is the fact that funerary inscriptions on tombs are rare in East Africa, except for those in Arabic after the 19th century. This suggests late Arabian influence on architecture.

The town of Lamu has numerous houses, tombs, mosques, and a few palaces of distinct architecture. Tombs are built in differing styles, reflecting their indigenous African origins. Houses in Lamu were first made of wattle and daub, but later with some stone, especially as the town prospered through trade. There were two-story buildings, but most of the houses were single story. The fundamental house plan was designed for the extended family, with space to accommodate various needs of the family on all occasions. There are usually courtyards surrounded by houses and rooms. Some houses have multiple courtyards which form indoor and outdoor spaces for the residents, while some are specialized rooms for occasions like weddings and funerals. A special space, the *nyumba ya kati,* serves to prepare the body of the dead and remove it from the house through a hole in the back wall. Stucco work and other details are positioned to enhance the mood of an occasion and often are symbolic of affluence and power in the community. The narrow winding streets (Fig. 7.23) of Lamu are also indicative of a traditional culture influenced by surrounding villages. The Swahili culture is a true representation of African triple heritage architecture with an indigenous origin and an Islamic influence.

Nairobi, Kenya, belongs to the class of African cities such as Lagos, Abidjan, Accra, and Cairo that have vast built-up areas

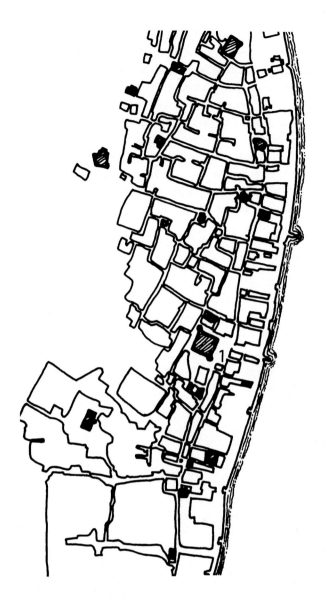

Fig. 7.23 Lamu, Kenya. City plan. (1) Mosque.

predominantly reflective of European urban design models. Nairobi, in particular, is a dual city of well-planned areas as well as settled unplanned areas. Land control around the Nairobi area was established for English settlers and a small number of African elite. The architecture of Nairobi has some hybrid Victorian-style buildings, but the skyline, like that of Lagos and many other major African cities, is predominantly international, with no reference to African culture.

African cities in this category perpetuate a fallacy that there is nothing to be gained from the African village or city layout. Nairobi has functional Cartesian grids that are intercepted by roundabouts at central points, a model commonly used by colonial English city planners in their colonies. Most of the buildings in the colonial districts of Nairobi could be found anywhere in Europe, especially London. Colonial public buildings adhere to Renaissance and neoclassical styles with an English flavor. In the suburbs, rich landlords, mainly of English origin, built Victorian houses with large yards and gardens.

Jamia Mosque in Nairobi (Fig. 7.24) is confirmation of the strong Islamic presence in this region. This mosque is also an East African beacon bordering the Orient, as is expressed in the three huge onion domes on each of its three bays. The solid brick masonry building mixes North African mosque motifs with East African motifs to form something uniquely African.

Mombasa is an ancient city with modern and old sectors. A Portuguese fort built in the 16th century remains a major landmark. The Portuguese established their presence and controlled the East African coast for over 100 years before they decided to build Fort Jesus in 1593. "When the Portuguese realized that it was time to build a fortress in Mombasa, the Chief-Architect of India, Joao Batista Cairato, was called upon to produce the plan" (Boxer and Azevedo 1960, 89).

The Portuguese employed the experience acquired in building forts in West Africa and India to construct a sophisticated bastion. The fortress' plan has not been altered since it

Fig. 7.24 Nairobi, Kenya. Jamia Mosque. (American Geographical Society Collection, The University of Wisconsin-Milwaukee Library)

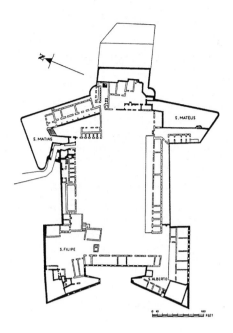

Fig. 7.25 *Mombasa, Kenya. Plan of Fort Jesus. Joao Batista Cairato. 1593.*

was completed. Conceived as a military fortress, Fort Jesus has a nearly rectangular plan with four corner bastions that are specifically designed to give extra protection to the gunners' positions. These bastions were named in homage to specific individuals: Sao Matias to Matias de Albuquerque; Sao Mateus to Mateus Mendes de Vasonelas; Sao Filipe to Phillip II of Spain, king of Portugal from 1580 to 1598; and Santo Alberto to Cardinal Albert, Viceroy of Portugal. The bastions and the walls protecting them were carefully located to ensure maximum gun range (Figs. 7.25 to 7.27).

One interesting aspect of the Mombasa fortress is its anthropomorphic qualities, which echo the humanistic attitude of the Renaissance artists and architects. An essential aspect of military architecture of the period was the creation of plans that enabled soldiers to see, fight, and effectively defend themselves. Fighting is, of course, done with arms, and the two eastern bastions facing the sea clearly symbolize the arms of Fort Jesus, while the protruding rectangle is the head. The tilted bastions to the sides (Sao Matias and Sao

Fig. 7.26 *Mombasa, Kenya. Defensive wall detail, south wall of Fort Jesus.* (American Geographical Society Collection, The University of Wisconsin-Milwaukee Library)

Mateus) were designed to widen the field of fire against an approaching enemy, while the rectangular shape calls for fewer resources to defend the entire structure. "In all respects, therefore, Fort Jesus is an outstanding example of the styles of fortification which had spread over Europe which was taken by the Portuguese to Africa and to the East" (Boxer and Azevedo 1960, 96).

7.6 SOMALIA

Somalia is located on the Horn of Africa; its strategic position on the Indian Ocean makes it a gateway to the East. Somalian history goes back to the ancient time of Punt when it had contact with other contemporary nations because "the ships of enterprising Egyptian, Phoenician, Persian, Greek, and Roman traders visited the Coast of Guban (the ancient land of Punt)" (Rinehart 1982, 5). These ships were in search of aromatic and medicinal resins like frankincense and myrrh, which are harvested from trees on the hills of Somalia.

During the 10th century A.D., this ancient African country received a large influx of immigrants from the Arabian Peninsula. Arab traders who engaged in slavery from Africa to Europe transported thousands of their human cargo through the coastal seaports. In most parts of Africa, slaves were assimilated wholeheartedly as members of the family. Hence, the Arabs and Africans mixed in a way that resulted in a distinctive culture, one which contributes to the African triple heritage culture.

The Somalis were, and still are, predominantly farming people who own a lot of cattle and goats. Life and social organization are rooted in the extended family based on kinship and clans, of which there are thousands. As in many traditional African societies, the extended family gives support to its members, and associations run along family lines to a large extent. The nomads of Somali use tent housing that is portable and mobile. They utilize frames of forked sticks to make pliable structures which are then covered with blankets, animal skin, or mat. The technology is simple and easy to assemble in a relatively short period. Somali nomads move in groups with their families and herds. Camels, donkeys, and horses are the principal modes of nomadic transportation, along with trekking.

Fig. 7.27 (Left) Mombasa, Kenya. Aerial view of Fort Jesus with the Indian Ocean in the background. (C. R. Boxer, Carlos De Azevedo and Hollis and Carter)

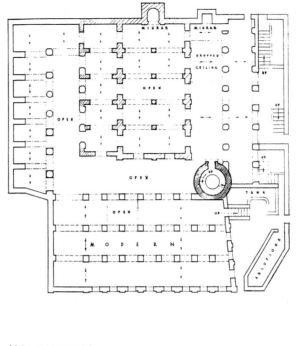

Fig. 7.28 Mogadishu, Somalia. Plan of Jamia Mogadishu. 1238 A.D. (Peter S. Garlake, Oxford University Press)

7.7 MOGADISHU

Mogadishu is the primary city of Somalia. Its significance goes back to the Middle Ages because of its maritime contact with China, Persia, India, other areas of the East African coast. It was also in contact with the hinterlands and, of course, the Mediterranean. Duarte Barbosa, a 16th-century Portuguese traveler, described Mogadishu as "a place of great wealth" (Davidson 1991, 163). The famous 14th-century Moroccan traveler Ibn Battuta described it as endless in size, a place where 200 camels were slaughtered daily to provide for the population. It is clear that Mogadishu had attained an urban structure before Somalia was colonized in the late 19th century.

One of the major goals when constructing a house in the region is to achieve a cooling effect. Adobe is commonly used for construction in urban centers, while oven-baked and sun-dried bricks are also equally used by the wealthy. In the past, the most common building material was coral cement which was collected in shallow waters along the coast. Openings are usually decorated with intricate plaster ornaments typical of most houses along the East African coast. The skyline of Mogadishu is dominated by minarets of mosques from the

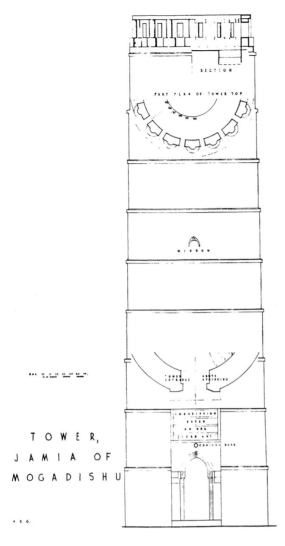

Fig. 7.29 Mogadishu, Somalia. Tower of Jamia Mogadishu. *(Peter S. Garlake, Oxford University Press)*

Cush during the 19th Dynasty. Some scholars, however, are of the opinion that Cush may have begun around 295 B.C. to 350 A.D., producing the Napata and the Meroitic cultures, respectively. One common agreement is that ancient Egypt and Nubia had a high degree of association. Pyramids in the Sudanese desert at Meroe confirm this fact in spite of the differences between the pyramids in Egypt and those in the Republic of Sudan.

The move toward a triple heritage commenced very early with Roman intrusions into Nubian Africa, as demonstrated by the kiosk at Naga (Fig. 2.2). Roman desire to maintain control of its Upper Egyptian province led to the construction of military garrisons next to earlier African sacred shrines. The kiosk borrowed some features from Egyptian temples but retained a Greco-Roman character in its arches and pseudo-Corinthian columns. The triple heritage was completed in the 7th and 12th centuries with the coming of Islam into the region, despite Coptic Ethiopian and Nubian church resistance. The Islamic fundamentalism of the 19th-century Mahdists resurfaced in the 20th century with a holy war between this group and a secessionist Christian South indoctrinated by ancient Christian Byzantium in Coptic manners and beliefs. This holy war is tearing the country apart. No city in Africa wears the symbols of the cultural trilogy—traditional African Egypto-Nubian culture, Greco-Roman and later Western culture, and Islamic culture—more than Khartoum, the capital of the Republic of Sudan.

The popular traditional adobe Sudanese style of architecture, which dominates West Africa, is also found in the Republic of Sudan. The houses, often made of clay and brick, are designed to adapt to the endless semidesert climate which is very hot during most of the year. Thick walls and small

13th century to the present, beginning with Jamia Mogadishu (Figs. 7.28 and 7.29). Architectural details mirror that of Lamu in that they show very strong African influence. Doors, lintels, windows, beams, and facades are specially carved with designs from indigenous and Islamic symbols.

7.8 THE REPUBLIC OF SUDAN

One of the most recent developments in African antiquity is the discovery of what could be the site of the ancient African kingdom of Cush. The ancient city may have been a contemporary of Egypt because it began to develop around 3200 B.C., grew rapidly around 2400 B.C., and reached its zenith from 1750 to 1500 B.C. In about 1500 B.C., ancient Egypt conquered

Fig. 7.30 Khartoum, Republic of Sudan. Traditional house. *(American Geographical Society Collection, The University of Wisconsin-Milwaukee Library)*

openings help in cooling the house (Fig. 7.30). Some of the beams that support the roof project outward, like the monkey-head of Aksumite buildings in Ethiopia and traditional architecture in the Republic of Sudan, resemble those found in Nigeria, Egypt, Tanzania, Ethiopia, and Burundi. Colonialism was capable of subdividing Africa into nation-states based on the European definition of nation at the turn of the century; however, it was not able to redefine the cultures of the people. So traditional architecture in the Sudan transcends the Sudanese border.

7.9   KHARTOUM: A TRIPLE HERITAGE AFRICAN CITY

Khartoum, the capital of Sudan, has an interesting mixture that clearly expresses the triple heritage of African architecture. The most important aspect of Khartoum as an architectural landmark for Africa began in 1898 when the British and the Egyptians captured the Islamic fundamentalist Mahdists and set up colonial rule.

Khartoum is strategically located at the confluence of the White Nile and the Blue Nile. It is a center that strongly encourages commerce between various groups from East, North, South, and West Africa. The union of the two great branches of the Nile gave rise to four towns that form the Khartoum cornubation (Fig. I.7): (1) Omdurman, the original capital of the Mahdists before the Anglo-Egyptian invasion; (2) colonial Khartoum planned by Lord Kitchner; (3) Khartoum North; and (4) a less inhabited core known as Tutu Island. Omdurman is made up of a maze of typical indigenous architecture similar to what one would find in several West African and some North African desert cities. Towns similar to Omdurman are Timbuktu, Old Kano in northern Nigeria, and Old Fez in Morocco, and the architecture can be characterized as a hybrid of Sudanese style.

Colonial Khartoum was planned by Kitchner as a military containment and a reservation for the English colonialists.

Fig. 7.31 Khartoum, Republic of Sudan. The Mahdist's Tomb. 19th century. (American Geographical Society Collection, The University of Wisconsin-Milwaukee Library)

Fig. 7.32 Khartoum, Republic of Sudan. Government building. (American Geographical Society Collection, The University of Wisconsin-Milwaukee Library)

Hence, military functionalism was the major objective that guided the plan. Colonial Khartoum was designed as a European city without any reference to the plans of Omdurman and Tutu Island.

> *The new lay-out was primarily designed to satisfy military requirements, its most striking features being wide thoroughfares and also subsidiary diagonal streets contained in rectangles which divide the town into a fence of Union Jacks containing a number of streets radiating from center points in each rectangle at which machine guns could be set up commanding them. (Collings and Deng 1984, 71)*

Khartoum North is more or less a continuation of colonial Khartoum, though less formal. The militarized Union Jack and diagonals found in colonial Khartoum are absent here. The architecture also maintains the character of the Sudanese style, but with very broad streets that are out of scale with the surroundings. Tutu Island is less inhabited, but it is the oldest settlement in the region. Its location between the confluence of the Blue Nile and the White Nile makes it the core of the three major settlements that form Khartoum. Tutu Island has a much denser labyrinth than Omdurman and Khartoum North.

Khartoum is characterized by intense tropical sunshine and a vast savanna and desert. The Nile is the greatest feature on the landscape, or else it would be a sea of sand. The desert calls for special building layouts to minimize the intensity of

Fig. 7.33 Khartoum, Republic of Sudan. Auditorium at General Gordon's Medical College. Early 1900s. (American Geographical Society Collection, The University of Wisconsin-Milwaukee Library)

the sun. These are achieved through arcades, or clustered houses with narrow footpaths between them. The proximity of these houses to one another allows for some shade between them. Like most desert environments, the major building material is sand, and it is used either as sun-dried brick or as adobe construction material.

The Mahdist's Tomb confirms a strong Islamic presence (Fig. 7.31). Its surroundings adhere to a self-contained Islamic shrine with a courtyard within a fence. The oblong bell-shaped dome gives the tomb a sturdy and stable look on the vast sandy landscape. The Mahdist's Tomb is a success mostly because of the architect's ability to fit the tomb within the vast landscape without exaggerating the scale of the building. The symmetrical composition and the equitable elements help draw attention to the building.

On the other hand, the historical palace of General Gordon, which has served as Sudan's presidential residence, brought a Western Renaissance architectural style that reinstated long-gone Roman intrusions into that part of Africa. The palace is surrounded by arcades that shade the building

(Fig. 7.32). The balconies on the arcade are detailed with Spanish ballustrades. Nowhere is Western architecture better expressed in 19th-century Sudan than the chapel at Gordon's Medical College campus (Fig. 7.33). Most of the buildings are in the classical and Renaissance styles. The pediment, classical columns, and the rotunda of the auditorium, with its inviting steps, make no pretense about the importation of the Jeffersonian campus planning philosophy to Africa. This classical expression, along with the strong Islamic presence through a plethora of Egyptian-inspired mosques, makes Khartoum one of the major centers of the triple heritage of African architecture. The provision of arcades to line several streets in colonial Khartoum should be seen as a colonial sensitivity to climatic need in building construction. The arcades provide pedestrians with shade from the intense sunshine, and they help keep the buildings cool as well (Fig. 7.34).

In summary, the towns that form the Khartoum cornubation clearly express the triple heritage concept. Omdurman has an African desert city character and strong Islamic influ-

Fig. 7.34 Khartoum, Republic of Sudan. Colonial buildings with arcades to provide shade. (American Geographical Society Collection, The University of Wisconsin-Milwaukee Library)

ence. Khartoum North is an African, Western, and Islamic mix in design, its African building character overpowered by broad, endless streets that do not deal with the intense light and the open landscape properly. Colonial Khartoum is primarily an English military containment for privileged colonialists and perhaps a few Egyptian and Sudanese elites. This is true because "when Baily wrote that 'everybody knew everybody' he did not mean that the members of the British community socialised with each other on the basis of equali-

ty, or that there was comingling between British and Sudanese" (Collings and Deng 1984, 74).

In the Sudan, pure and absolute Islam meets Africa proper. Khartoum is thus at the center of several worlds, which also includes the iron grid world of Western functional-spatial determinism that was based on the Union Jack. The directions of the city plan are thus as Islamic as they are Britannic, and the union of African, European, and Islamic architectural vocabularies reinforces the triple heritage concept.

8

THE ARCHITECTURE OF BURUNDI, RWANDA, TANZANIA, AND UGANDA

Burundi, Rwanda, Tanzania, and Uganda are sometimes referred to as the countries of the Great Lakes region of East Africa. Many African kingdoms emerged in this region during the Middle Ages and lasted into the 19th century when European colonialism forged them into colonial states. The Middle Age kingdoms fought with one another in competition for the dominance of the region, especially from 1500 to 1800. However, "the period ends with the rise and expansion of Buganda in the central area and Rwanda in the south as the `super-powers' of the Great Lakes region and, in the north" (Webster, Ogot, and Chretien 1981, 776). Other ethnic groups such as the Heso and the Jie dominated the region.

Within the precolonist kingdoms, leadership was organized around central dynastic rulers who appointed counselors, chiefs, artisans, musicians, and religious leaders to help in promoting the wishes of the king and state. The states were devel-

oping their political culture and identity when colonialism came to the region. "As it was, the colonial invaders came instead, the British to Kenya and Uganda, the Germans and thus the British to Tanzania, the Germans and then the Belgians to Rwanda and Burundi" (Davidson 1969, 219).

Islam moved slowly into Central and East Africa. The Sufi fraternities were the major carriers of trade, including the slave trade. Freeman-Grenville (1991) suggests that, in addition, with the increase of the settlement of Indian traders in Zanzibar after 1801, the Bohoras, Ismaili and Ithua'ashari Khojas, and other small sects built mosques on the coast and later inland. In the late 19th century, Arab traders succeeded in converting substantial followers to Islam in Uganda, Tanzania, and eastern Zaire.

8.1 BURUNDI

Three major ethnic groups dominate Burundi: the Hutus, Twa, and the Tutsi. These groups have remained rivals in the years preceding and after independence (1962) and have consequently dragged the country into repeated violence. Burundi began the 19th century first as a German colony, then British, and finally Belgian. It is one of the small nation-states formed during the power struggle over Africa as a means of pacifying the European powers who had not received what they considered a fair share of the African estates for mineral and commercial exploitation.

Historically, the Hutus farm the land and produce most of the food crops that feed the nation. In contrast, the Tutsi were warrior pastoralists who moved from place to place to find good pasture for their herds. This division of labor between the warrior Tutsi clan and the sedentary farming Hutu clan resulted in a ruling class and the ruled. The Tutsi ethnic group, with a smaller population, dominates and rules the country because of its wealth from cattle. The Twa are scattered among the Hutus and the Tutsi and take sides with either group, depending upon with whom they live.

The location of Burundi at an altitude well above sea level gives it a warm, but not humid, climate. Burundi is situated on the rolling hills of East Africa where the Kagera and Ruvuvu Rivers begin their long journey toward North Africa as tributaries of the River Nile. The hillsides are ideal for the round beehive-style house, with a free-standing structure and thatched roof. Houses are located according to the extended family as is the case in many rural African societies.

8.2 BUJUMBURA: THE CAPITAL OF BURUNDI

Very little has been written on the architecture of Burundi, so studies done in this area should consider the fundamental factors that make up African architecture. The role of the traditional ancestor cult in art and architecture in Burundi needs to be documented. The most critical challenge facing any architect in Burundi is being able to carefully separate layers upon layers of architectural motifs from different cultures—indigenous, Islamic, and Western. These cultures have interacted rapidly with each other since the era of colonialism in the 19th century. Research into the transformation of mythical figures into art and architecture would yield information on the architecture of Burundi because, like many African societies, Burundi has many mythical beliefs which have been incorporated into its art.

Bujumbura (Fig 8.1) is the largest and most important city in Burundi, with a population of 272,000. Its place in a country with little industrial infrastructure cannot be underestimated. Besides being the center of administration, it is also the center of business, culture, transportation, health services, and the like. As a former Belgian colony, the city plays the dual role of Western and African city. La Ville Indigene (the native town) sits next to a small Western-style city designed to conform to rectangular grids.

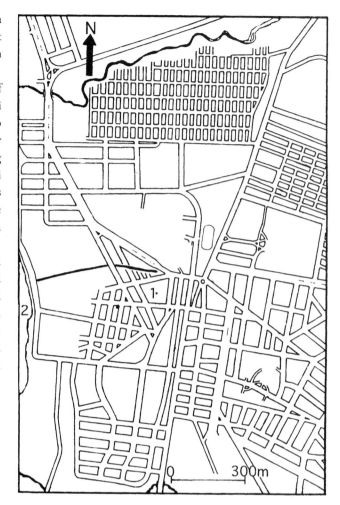

Fig. 8.1 Bujumbura, Burundi. City plan. (1) Mosque.

8.3 RWANDA

The story of Burundi replicates itself in Rwanda. Both were once German colonies. Although the Council of Berlin designated Rwanda-Burundi as a German sphere of interest in 1885, it was not until the 1890s that the German government extended its authority to East Africa. Both colonies became Belgian protectorates after the defeat of Germany in World War I. In addition, the same ethnic groups that make up Burundi also make up Rwanda, so ethnic conflict spills over to Burundi when it takes place in Rwanda.

Rwanda is located on the sloped hills of the East African Rift Valley. The vegetation is dense but not intolerable owing to the altitude, which rises to over 9000 ft above sea level in some parts of the country. Farming and cattle herding are the main occupations of the people, the majority of whom live in rural areas. Extended family plays a major role in the settlement pattern. There is strong loyalty to kinship based on ancestral order. The majority of the people are Catholics and have no difficulty reconciling their ancestral worship and Christian doctrines. The head of an extended family is usually the chief. Normally, he is the elder of the family and lives with his wife or wives and sons and grandsons along with their wives in a common compound.

Traditional architecture is a mixture of oval and square plan structures made from pliable materials. Building is usually done communally and finished in a few days. The traditional architecture of the Hutus or the Tutsi in Rwanda is similar to that of their counterparts in Burundi. Building material is usually obtained locally from the woods. The transition from traditional architecture to European-style buildings is readily visible because new materials such as aluminum used in roofs of traditional buildings with earth walls can be distinguished. Besides being the sign of status and affluence, such new additions also make the house more durable.

Kigali, the capital of Rwanda, is still a medium-size town. It was designed by the Belgians during the colonial era. The existence of a traditional African town, a city planned by Europeans, with churches and a few mosques for the relatively small Muslim community, makes the triple heritage hypothesis a reality even in a less developed country such as Rwanda. The organization of towns in Rwanda mirrors the form in many traditional African towns. The location of the house and its layout are based on sites that pleased the spirits of the ancestors. The Hutus lay their houses according to their ancestral lineages, while the Tutsi who own cattle build less permanent structures depending on the seasons and the places they take their stock for grazing. The beehive style of architecture dominates the style of housing among the Hutus and the Tutsi.

8.4 TANZANIA

The Republic of Tanzania was formed by the fusion of two ancient states, one in the mainland known as Tanganyika and the other an island city-state in the Indian Ocean encompassing Zanzibar and Pemba. Tanganyika and the island city-state were joined to become the Republic of Tanzania in 1964. Tanganyika and Zanzibar have long ties that began in ancient times through trading links in the Indian Ocean between East Africa, North Africa, and the Orient. East Africa was highly involved with the ancient Egyptian traders who sailed to the region via the Red Sea, as is proven by the finding of ancient Egyptian gold coins from the last dynasty (Ptolemy Soter) in Tanzania. In addition, the Roman demand for ivory statues, tables, ornaments, chairs, and ivory stables for the imperial horse indicates that East Africa also had trade connections with the Mediterranean countries. By the 1st century A.D., ivory could only be obtained in the interior of the Upper Nile region of Africa because elephants were being depleted more rapidly around the Lower Nile and Adulis. "Consequently the supply of ivory from the East African coast, though it was considered to be of lower quality than that of Adulis, assumed a greater importance" (Sheriff 1981, 551).

The trade link between East Africa and the international community grew in the Middle Ages, when Arab merchants began to settle along the coast and on the island. A great cultural fusion of Afro-Arabian people was formed to facilitate trade in the region. The result is the Swahili culture which has been mentioned in Chapter 7. East Africa did not restrict its maritime activity to the Red Sea, the Mediterranean, and the Arabian Gulf. Trade was conducted with Far East countries including China and India. According to Sutton (1990), in 1420 A.D., the sultan of Malindi, one of the principal Swahili states of the time, sent a distinctive gift, a giraffe, to the emperor of China. Early contact with Asia is also proven by findings of several porcelain pieces in East African cities such as Kilwa, Zanzibar, and Pemba. The Asian contact added a new cultural dimension to the East African coast, a large number of Indian and Chinese immigrants.

Commercialism led the way to German colonization of Tanzania in 1890, following the inability of the German East African Company to administer the territory properly. "The company's ineptitude led to the German government's assumption of administrative responsibilities in 1890" (Kaplan 1978, 35). Germany, however, was to lose the territory to Great Britain in 1917 following its defeat in World War I.

Several ethnic groups inhabit Tanzania, but the major ones are the Maasai, the Sukuma, the Haya, the Gogo (Ugogo), the Sonjo, the Fipa, the Chaga, the Rundiha, the Luguni, the Ngoni, and the Swahili-speaking Hehe. Each of these ethnic groups belongs to one of the major language groups of Africa: the Cushites from ancient Cush; the Nilotic, or people who migrated southward from the Nile Valley; the Central Sudanic, or people whose ancestors migrated from the regions of Sudan; and the Bantus. These people engaged in pastoralism and agriculture which favored certain crops in the plains of Tanzania and allowed the rearing of cattle.

The Sonjo speak a Bantu language and inhabit parts of the interior districts in northern Tanzania near the border with Kenya. They are mainly agricultural, and their building and social structure revolve around this. The topography of the district occupied by the Sonjo varies from well-watered mountains to desert and plains. The Oldonyo volcano dominates the landscape with its surrounding craters, and its summit has religious significance for the Sonjo. The famous Serengeti Plain extends north and west of these mountains.

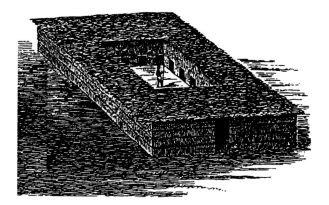

Fig. 8.2 Tanzania. Traditional Gogo house.

There is insufficient rainfall in this area except on higher mountain slopes, and as a result, some areas lack adequate water supply in the dry season. The dominant ethnic group in this region is the pastoralist Maasai with their large herds of cattle. The Sonjo form a Bantu enclave within a Maasai dominated landscape. This means that the Maasai, the Sonjo, and the variety of wildlife on the Serengeti have to supply themselves with water during the dry seasons. The Sonjo have evolved an ancient irrigation system to deal with the water problem during the long dry seasons. "The irrigation system as it now exists is believed to have been first laid out and built at the time the village was founded, as told in myth" (Gray 1963, 55).

In the Sonjo community, social life revolves around the extended family network based on descendants; partners of a monogamous marriage normally live together in a single house. Land for building and farming is communally owned but is given to extended family members by consensus or by the elders. As Gray (1963, 42) points out, "the necessary materials for house building are readily available in the nearby forests and fields, but the construction requires the co-operation of a number of men." A man builds his first house at the time of his first marriage. His father-in-law provides half of the building material, while his extended family members supply the land, labor, and other needed materials.

Sonjo houses often have a circular plan and are made from pliable materials from the vicinity. The round ground plan is marked out with forked sticks that are rigid after being dug into the ground. Beams are placed on the forks in the circle, and other pliable beams are bent over the structure until a netlike frame is achieved. Special stems are used as ropes to tie the beams together wherever necessary. Finally, the entire structure is thatched all over, leaving a pointed apex in the middle of the dome that forms the house structure. It is important to mention that a man is not allowed to marry in the traditional Sonjo society until he has been initiated into manhood by the male cult.

Gogo communities also express their family affinity in the physical layout of their houses. Their animals are kept in a pen in the middle of the compound (Figs. 8.2 and C.26). In recent times, government programs to provide affordable housing in

Fig. C.26 Tanzania.
Traditional Gogo architecture.
(American Geographical Society
Collection, The University of
Wisconsin-Milwaukee Library)

Fig. 8.3 Tanzania. Traditional buildings with modern materials. (American Geographical Society Collection, The University of Wisconsin-Milwaukee Library)

the rural areas have experimented with traditional building designs, but such direct applications and interpretations are limited. Besides, these programs are utilized more as exotic tourist marketing tools than as a genuine search for affordable housing for the poor. The emphasis on commercial profitability removes the incentive to study how such programs can be developed to meet contemporary housing needs (Fig. 8.3).

8.5 THE JOURNEY FROM DAR ES SALAAM TO DODOMA

Dar es Salaam began with the first visit by the Portuguese sailor Vasco da Gama to East Africa in 1498 and with the destruction of the city-states of Kilwa and Mombasa. "By 1506 Portugal had claimed control over the entire coast and over trade on the Indian Ocean" (Kaplan 1978, 17). An Anglo-German agreement in 1886 and Bismarck's decision to convert Tanganyika into a German sphere of influence brought in a new form of economy in the latter part of the 19th century. German control of the area was more resolute and brutal following the official German government takeover of the area from the German East African Company. One of the final results was the evolution, development, and consolidation of urban inequalities like those in Dar es Salaam by the emergence of an underprivileged lower class and highly favored middle and upper classes. Independence from colonialism meant the opportunity to correct its wrongs. Dar es

Salaam was a symbol of colonial oppression in the minds of many Tanzanians.

As would be expected, Dar es Salaam, the former capital of Tanzania, reflects the strong presence of Europeans, Arabs, and Asians in an African city. According to de Blij (1963), the city plan is essentially a legacy of European occupation, and the core of the town reflects the German impact and concessions to Sultan Majid of Zanzibar, who chose Dar es Salaam as the center of his possessions in Africa. Dar es Salaam is located on the coast of the Indian Ocean and has railway links to the inland territories. It displays racial separations and different architectural peculiarities that reflect the European powers who were there at different times, beginning with the Portuguese.

Dar es Salaam was situated on the narrow estuary, Princess Margaret Quay, to facilitate shipping and trade for the sultan of Zanzibar and British traders in the middle of the 19th century. The Bismarck government moved its headquarters from Bagomoyo to Dar es Salaam in 1891 and immediately commenced the construction of buildings. Several were already constructed in the city by 1903 and by World War I, including the large Lutheran church which remains one of the major landmarks of the city, the government offices, a post office, the harbor buildings, hospitals, and residential buildings.

Dar es Salaam is a city of architectural variety. The streets are lined with buildings reflecting Anglo-German and Afro-Arabian influences. It is not uncommon to find Victorian buildings crowned with German pagoda roofs, while the wall surfaces are articulated with decorations derived from Islamic calligraphy. Two- and three-story neoclassical buildings with long arcades line some of the streets in the downtown area. The walls of these buildings are plain, but the arches and Portuguese balustrades used in the articulation of the balconies compensate for their bareness. It is not unusual to get the feeling of a 19th-century European town while walking through some sections of Dar es Salaam. The cathedral near the harbor remains a major landmark. Completed by the Germans between 1903 and the start of World War I, it is a good architectural signature of the German missionaries who built it.

There was an increase in upper-class housing which became a symbol of social status for the elite. Villas with self-contained yards and amenities lined the Dar es Salaam waterfront. Little was done as social pacification for the middle class, who were mostly government workers, and nothing at all was done for the lower class. The disparity between the upper class, the middle class, and the lower-class squatter settlements was so obvious that the Tanzanian government decided to change its image by relocating the capital to Dodoma in the interior after independence.

Dodoma is an attempt to correct colonial social urban injustice and to centralize the capital city for the sake of development. It is important to note that Tanzania, Nigeria, and Cote d'Ivoire have all moved their capitals in recent times for the same reasons, but the outcome has been different for each city. Vale (1992, 47) suggests that "as in Nigeria, the move of the capital represents a departure from an overcrowded colonial port and an attempt to site the national government in the less-developed center of the country." The major difference here is the philosophy and policies guiding the development of the new capital city. In the case of Tanzania, the move was geared toward meeting the needs of the people.

It is very easy to tag the Tanzanian government's decision to move to Dodoma with socialist labels. Vale (1992, 149) believes that "the decision to move the capital to Tanzania's rural heartland is intimately tied to the government's version of an ideal Socialist state." This statement is partially true because it implies a definition of socialism practiced in the former de facto communist and socialist states around the world. The other side of the story is that Dodoma is the Tanzanian government's effort to re-create Ujamaa villages, cooperative compounds based on the principles that have kept and protected extended family compounds. In other words, the philosophy behind Dodoma has more to do with traditional African society and culture than with socialism per se as in the former East versus West ideology. As Vale (1992) points out, the Arusha declaration of former President Julius Nyerere was reprinted in full as Appendix A of the Dodoma

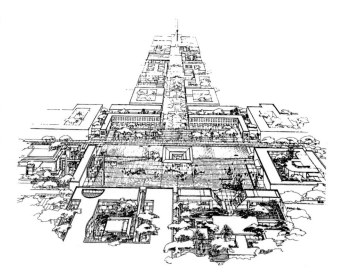

Fig. 8.4 Dodoma. *Perspective of National Capital Center looking north.*
(James Rossant Architect)

master plan. The declaration was essentially about "politics and economics," as both concerned the Tanzanians. In Nyerere's own words: "For the Declaration is about the way in which we shall make a reality of human equality in this country, and how our citizens will achieve full control over their own affairs" (Nyerere 1970, 173). Thus, Dodoma was conceived as the people's forum and as a link between the government and the rural population it was serving. It cannot be overemphasized that its other objective was to end the association of Dar es Salaam with German and British domination of the territory. It should not be surprising that, unlike the Abuja plan in Nigeria, the Dodoma document was a strong deviation from the 20th-century urban design model. At the diagrammatic level, this basic difference may be seen by comparing Abuja's plan, which closely resembles Costa's cross-axial Brasilia, with that of Dodoma, which appears as a polycentric cluster (Vale 1992).

The Dodoma plan is more conservative and people oriented, whereas the Abuja plan is grander but less related to the people of Nigeria. One of the ills of Dar es Salaam is the densely packed buildings and the inability to protect low income citizens of the city. President Nyerere's Arusha declaration clearly stipulates what it means by the principle of self-reliance. All families must have and live close to arable lands to help them grow part of their food requirements. This meant discarding the old Dar es Salaam way of packing people next to one another in buildings without adequate land for gardening. Housing areas were therefore envisioned as being much closer to the village prototype than those, for example, in Abuja (Vale 1992). Dodoma (Fig. 8.4) has a mixture of shopping centers, restaurants, apartments, cultural facilities, and government ministries together on a shared area. But Abuja, like Brasilia, its predecessor, is zoned and each of the aforementioned activities is in a separate location.

Dodoma is equipped with a network of pedestrian pathways, something that grand and luxurious Abuja lacks because it is designed for motor vehicles. Vale (1992) states that the width of the Abuja Mall was chosen to match the grand proportions of the buildings that flank it, to mimic its predecessors in Washington, D.C., and Brasilia, while the width of the Dodoma Grand Mall could easily fit within the width of Abuja's grand secondary streets. It is customary for designed capitals like Washington, D.C., Canberra, New Delhi, Chandigarh, Brasilia, and Abuja to express strong axial vistas, but Dodoma did not conform to this tradition. "Its parliamentary complex reaffirms time worn associations of natural forms with political power" (Vale 1992, 158). Overall,

Dodoma has lived up to its dream of being a traditional African city that reaffirms the values of the people. Abuja, on the other hand, sought to propagate national unity and political power but gave little consideration to the poor people who would inhabit it. Still, available financial resources will be the final determinant of meeting housing needs for low income groups in Dodoma.

Dar es Salaam and Dodoma are not the only cities of Tanzania. The island of Zanzibar and Pemba have some of the best preserved classic architecture of Swahili middle ages and are distinguished by the art deco that garnishes the walls and notches of the buildings. As in Lamu, Kenya, the houses in Zanzibar were built with brick. They are self-contained one- and two-story buildings with gardens, courtyards, servant quarters, walls of coral, and with a prioritized degree of privacy in the location of the master bedrooms, the wives' rooms, and the parlor or living space. In most cases, the verandas are well decorated with plaster work, and careful atten-

Fig. 8.5 Zanzibar, Tanzania.
Plaster decorations on walls.
(Janet Hetland)

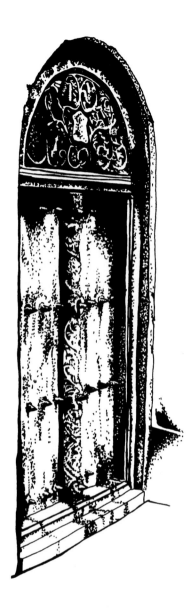

Fig. 8.6 Zanzibar, Tanzania.
Sketch of two carved doors.
(Janel Hetland)

tion is given to the openings which are decorated along the top and down the sides as pilasters (Fig. 8.5). Most of the plaster work and the specially carved doors on the East African coast are carved in situ (Fig. 8.6). Nancy Ingram Nooter (1984, 36) states that two vertical sideposts, a heavy lintel, a two-panel door, a centerpost that ensures proper closure, and a heavy beam threshold at 15–20 cm above floor level are the major features that distinguish Zanzibar doors from all others.

8.6 UGANDA

Uganda is a Swahili term that means "Land of the Ganda," (Room 1994, 193), named after the most numerous ethnic group in the country, the Buganda. That is why

Sathyamurthy (1986, 71) suggests that "the name of Uganda was in fact interchangeable with that of Buganda until the incorporation of the territories which ultimately constituted the Uganda Protectorate." The Uganda protectorate began with the unification of four existing states, Buganda, Bunyoro, Ankole, and Toro, with the addition of smaller states such as Lango, Acholi, Madi, West Nile, Bkedi, Bugisu, Busoga, Teso, Karamoja, Sebei, and Kigeri. Uganda had a colonial experience similar to many African countries. It was declared a British protectorate in 1894, and it became independent in October, 1962. Westernization of Uganda began with the Christian church, but Islam was already well established there. "There is evidence that Muslim traders tried to reach Buganda by the eastern route—from around Mombasa to the east of Lake Victoria and Busoga—as early as the

1850s" (Oded 1974, 23). In this case, the triple heritage architecture is as real as it is in the other African countries that have been discussed in this book. The existence of an indigenous culture, an Islamic culture, and a Judeo-Christian culture has set the stage for another cultural legacy expressed in the architecture of the people. In the case of Uganda, finding the cultural balance among indigenous, Islamic, and Western architecture has always been a complex issue because it is so rooted in religion that the dividing lines have often been mixed up by all the players involved.

As in several parts of Africa, the intense competition between Christianity and Islam in Buganda in the late 1800s also affected architecture. The people of Buganda were torn between choosing Christianity or Islam, and abandoning their traditional worship. The whole community, including the king of Buganda who is traditionally known as *kabaka,* would switch to the religion that had staged the best campaign. Sometimes, this resulted in a stalemate. The kabaka and his subjects would then resort to their traditional religion, condemning both religions and calling Christians and Muslims alike liars and troublemakers. The king often determined which faith was adopted by the community, and his subjects converted to whatever religion the king believed in. The kabaka King Mutesa reigned in Buganda when the reli-

Fig. 8.8 Uganda. Chagga
traditional architecture.
(American Geographical Society
Collection, The University of
Wisconsin-Milwaukee Library)

Fig. 8.9 Uganda. Chagga traditional architecture. (American Geographical Society Collection, The University of Wisconsin-Milwaukee Library)

gious competition between Christians and Muslims was taking place.

The background story of the Islamic and Christian intrusions into Uganda has several implications for the architectural historian. First, there is the problem of what architecture can be considered indigenous and what can be considered foreign, a problem shared by the coastal cities in Kenya, Tanzania, Somalia, and Djibouti. Several stone medieval buildings in Uganda, for instance, are ascribed to foreign influence with a total disregard for indigenous evolution. The tombs of the kabaka have not been problematic as far as distinguishing between indigenous and foreign influence in architecture. These are beehive-type houses made from stems and reeds that rise up to 30 ft (Figs. 8.7 to 8.9). These structures have not been studied and updated until recent times, and the results indicate that there is much to be learned, if traditional African architecture is given the opportunity to develop.

Some recent works by architects who dared to investigate the genius loci of the African environment and the tradition of building bear this out and are beginning to have an impact. In Uganda, the works of Justus Dahinden at Namugongo National Shrine Cathedral and Mityana Pilgrims Shrine demonstrate that traditional African architecture has dynamic metaphors and repertoires that can be exploited to create architecture that is uniquely African and to which users can respond. According to Dahinden (1987), the pilgrimage and parish church of Namugongo in Uganda, East Africa, is a circular building 42 m in diameter (Fig. 8.10), situated on the plateau adjoining the large natural depression of Namugongo. The church stands on the site of what was once a memorial chapel to the glory of the martyred saints of Uganda. The cult of the ancestors and the burial practice which places deceased ancestors in tombs are transferred to

Christianity for the burial of Christian martyrs. The position of the altar is on the exact spot where Saint Joseph Mukasa Balikuddembe died. The circular space, which is redivided in the interior into three segments, is adopted from the parti of the architecture of the people of Chagga (Figs. 8.7 to 8.9).

The success of Dahinden's projects is even more visible at Mityana, however. The Mityana Pilgrims Shrine commemorates the canonization of three African martyrs (Figs. 8.11, 8.12, C.27, and C.28). The church is the focus of an urban complex that includes a school, social center, Carmelite convent, presbytery, parish hall, and health center. The church can be opened to outer courts partially covered with tentlike roofs to serve as a meeting place for the community. Access to the service can be gained from all sides. The significant element marking the main entry is a drum tower that links the inner and outer spaces of the church.

According to Justus Dahinden (1987), the design adapts to the climatic conditions as well as to local culture and in particular to the symbolic consciousness of African people. In this respect, the image of this building is both rational and irrational. The three spherical segments symbolize the three honored martyrs (Fig. C.28) and are arranged around the central common space which is covered by a flat roof with a skylight above the altar. These spherical segments express particular spatial qualities: a baptistery with space for singers, a

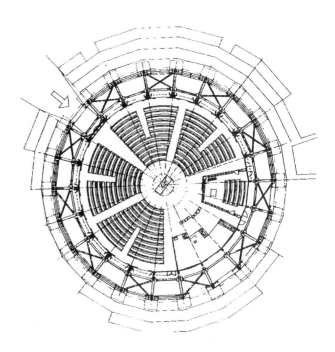

Fig. 8.10 Uganda. Plan of Namugongo National Shrine Cathedral. Designed by Justus Dahinden, 1982. (American Geographical Society Collection, The University of Wisconsin-Milwaukee Library)

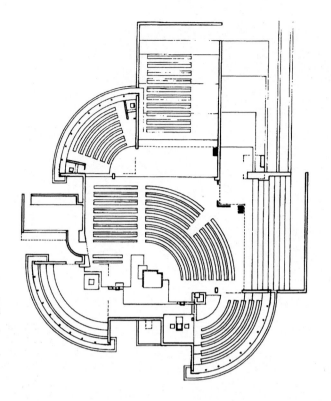

chapel with a tabernacle for the nuns, and a place for confession. These spherical segments are also an ancient Bantu building symbol of marked religious dimension. The response of the design to modern building materials is a vindication of traditional African building design and clear proof that the problem has not been with the architecture but with the hesitation of trained architects to innovate with this form since the Middle Ages.

Kampala, the largest city and the capital of Uganda, is a growing city with a large urban population. Political instability since the time of Idi Amin has slowed progress in the city, but this is now changing. Buildings such as the Uganda National Theater and Cultural Center express Uganda's desire to become part of the modern world. It was completed in the late 1950s before Uganda attained independence from Great Britain. Early public buildings, however, including churches in the city, were built with traditional materials. Logs were used for walls and straw for roofs. In Uganda, African architecture assumed a new complexity brought about by the presence of a large Indian community. Hindu and other Oriental architectural repertoires appear in buildings around the country and in other East African cities, making the classification of African architecture more difficult.

*Fig. 8.11 **Uganda.** Plan of Mityana Pilgrims Shrine. Designed by Justus Dahinden, 1983.* (Professor Justus Dahinden)

*Fig. 8.12 **Uganda.** Mityana Pilgrims Shrine under construction. 1983.* (Professor Justus Dahinden)

Fig. C.27 Uganda. Mityana
Pilgrims Shrine. Architect:
Justus Dahinden. 1983.
(Professor Justus Dahinden)

Fig. C.28 Uganda. Mityana
Pilgrims Shrine. Justus
Dahinden. 1983.
(Professor Justus Dahinden)

chapter

THE ARCHITECTURE OF THE CONGO BASIN: CENTRAL AFRICAN COUNTRIES

he Congo Basin covers an immense area in the heartland of Africa. Many countries lie within this territory, and they are peopled by a multitude of ethnic groups, as is the case in other African countries. Because of the large size of the region, it is important to define it before we proceed. This book uses Vellut's (1981) boundaries for the region.

The area is bounded by the Atlantic coast on the west, Lake Tanganyika and the Nile-Zaire ridge on the east, the Ubangui Savannas on the north, and the plateau separating the Zaire and Zambezi basins on the south. Central African Republic, Congo, Gabon, Zaire, and Angola are within this region. Some scholars describe Angola as part of southwestern Africa, whereas others consider it part of central Africa. Neither distinction disrupts the objective of this book.

This region has a strong ethnolinguistic relationship because of the Congo dialects which spread from Gabon to the

Benguela plateau and from the Atlantic Ocean to well beyond the River Kwango. The kingdoms of the Congo and the Loango once existed in this region. Their success was closely related to the natural resources of the region because its short dry season and long rainy seasons made farming lucrative. "In the fifteenth and sixteenth centuries a single state, Kongo [Congo] held sway over the entire region between the Benguela plateau and the Bateke plateau and from the sea beyond the River Kwango" (Vansina 1981, 546).

9.1 CENTRAL AFRICAN REPUBLIC

The cultural mix between African, Islamic, and Western architecture has been least studied in this part of the continent. Islam was already in the savanna parts of the region by the 1500s, just as the Portuguese were embarking on their expeditions. There is no doubt that a long period of cultural exchange is on record between Africans and Europeans, but the information says little about architecture. Any study of the architecture in this region must begin with the archetypes that form the bedrock of indigenous concepts behind building form. This necessitates a comprehensive search and documentation of all forms of sociocultural and artistic expression,

171

of which architecture is only a segment. In this geographical region, nature and the spirits of ancestors play very important roles in social organization, beginning with the individual and on to the extended family headed by an elder. The organization of the village depends on this structure.

The spirits of the ancestors shape the rites, arts, and settlement patterns. Masks are used to represent both the visible and invisible worlds, and the carved object is often used to represent the stories of the people in different ways. Objects of sacred value are rarely displayed in public, as are objects which make political statements. It is in this latter area that the influence of the West in architecture is felt most strongly. Street paintings in the capital city of Bangui tell stories of the Western influence on African architecture in the most elaborate way, depicting scenes representative of daily urban life but utilizing images that are alien to the indigenous culture.

It is difficult to comprehend Africa's modern history or any lesson about Africa without recognizing that Africa is changing rapidly on a daily basis. In this case, while traditional society exists in the Central African Republic (CAR), the modern industrial society coexists with it, as exemplified by cities like Bangui. Bangui, the nation's capital, has the highest concentration of industry and modern amenities. Critical to this understanding is the realization that the agent of cultural exchange between the agrarian community and the African city belongs to both sides simultaneously.

According to Mamdani (1988), social transformation is an overriding factor in today's Africa. Central African Republic and all other countries in Africa should be studied from this perspective, without losing touch with colonial and Islamic influences. Central African Republic is a former French colony that gained its independence on August 13, 1960. O'Toole (1986) names some of the principal ethnic groups in the country: Gbaya-Manja, Banda, Ubangians, Sara, Zande, and Nzakara. There are also refugees from neighboring Cameroon. With a rather sparsely populated hinterland and only one real urban center, the whole of the landlocked Central African Republic focuses on Bangui for access to the larger world. Like most other African cities, Bangui experienced accelerated growth after World War II, and that growth became even more rapid after independence. The reason for this rapid growth is hardly unique to Bangui. Throughout Africa, people flocked to the city seeking a better life.

According to O'Toole (1986), in the instance of Bangui (Fig. 9.1), what was once a European settler town situated along the Ubanqi River, astride the rapids, is now a bustling city centered around the Place de la Republique and along Avenue Boganda. From earliest colonial times through its three principal urban-renewal plans in 1946, 1967, and 1971, Bangui has remained a highly segregated city. Expatriates and

Fig. 9.1 Bangui, Central African Republic. City plan.

the high-level Central African bureaucratic bourgeoisie live in the center of the city. Here also are the government palace, the ministries, the army headquarters, the embassies, the European commercial areas, and the residences of many of the wealthy, both foreign and Central African. To the west and north of this well-established and carefully constructed area are a number of other planned zones. Planned sections along the Avenue de France and Avenue Boganda that predate independence have such amenities as water and electricity. In these areas, the houses are constructed of blocks and cement on clearly defined rectangular lots and are inhabited by relatively affluent civil servants and middle-income foreigners. Neither these older areas on the semiperiphery of the city nor newer housing areas to the north or east along the river are available to most Central Africans.

Away from the planned center and its semiperiphery, the city is composed of spontaneously created African *kodros*. The most conspicuous of these kodros is Kilometer Cinq and its Mamadou-Mbaika market covering 14,650 m² and including many stores owned by Lebanese, Portuguese, and Hausa merchants. With its dusk-to-dawn bars and dance halls, this section of the city is virtually off-limits to nonkodro dwellers but is the center of urban life for many Central Africans. The city's largest and most important mosque is located in this hub of African-controlled commerce.

9.2 ETHNIC GROUPS AND HOUSE FORMS IN THE CONGO

The name Congo once applied to a huge area that was under Belgian control during the colonial period. Angola, Central African Republic, the Republic of Congo, and Zaire were all once identified by this name. The three major imperial European powers that shared this area were the Portuguese, the Belgians, and the French. The Portuguese controlled Angola and the French controlled part of northern Congo, while King Leopold of Belgium had the remaining and major share. The Republic of Congo gained independence from France in 1960. As in the rest of the Congo, the people here are mostly of the Bantu language group. The capital of the Congo Republic, Brazzaville, is on the east bank of the Congo River. The west bank of the river was in the Belgian Congo

and the site of the capital Leopoldville, now Kinshasa. Kinshasa, now the capital of Zaire, and Brazzaville are twin cities that owe their existence to the large Congo River and share a history of colonial domination, the one by Belgium and the other by France.

People in the Congo vary greatly, from the 4-ft-tall Pygmies to the 7-ft-tall Watusis. Their customs are traditionally rooted in ancestral worship; however, Christianity and Islam have both greatly influenced the lifestyles of these people. The nuclear family with its link to the extended family remains the norm.

Traditional houses are of pliable material built in villages according to ancestor family compounds. Some compounds and towns were well laid out in a different traditional manner. Rather than a labyrinth of endless winding streets, they had broad streets in straight lines (Fig. 9.2), as in the Kuba kingdom. Public plazas and meeting places were clearly defined, and it must be noted that this urban planning design developed indigenously. The transition from indigenous architecture to colonial architecture began with the Portuguese who built forts and other forms of trading stations. The French expanded the Western influence to its crescendo, and its impact is most noticeable in Brazzaville.

Fig. 9.2 Congo. Traditional village layout in the Kuba capital. 1860s. [United Nations Educational Scientific and Cultural Organization (UNESCO)]

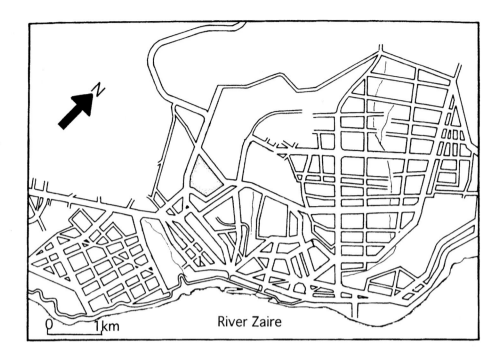

River Zaire

9.3 BRAZZAVILLE

In Brazzaville (Fig. 9.3), the capital of the Congo Republic, the architecture is of an unpretentious colonial appearance in the French modernist tradition. The French architects who worked in Brazzaville saw the city as an extension of France and applied their architectural philosophy, derived from the modern movement of the 1920s led by Le Corbusier, to the city without restraint. In the process, they stripped some buildings of their classical identity, but left the parti and axiality

Roman arches at its base. The arches have been transformed into plain square columns at the point where they meet the lintel. Saint Anne's Cathedral, which remains one of the major landmarks of Brazzaville, adopted a traditional African house repertoire and elements for its design and details (Figs. 9.6 and C.29). The masonry work around its clerestory windows is detailed and reinforced with neo-Gothic elements, with emphasis on re-creating an entryway that looks like those of traditional houses made of less durable materials. Overall, the city of Brazzaville has the look of a French town. Streets that meet at odd angles and buildings that turn triangular corners give the illusion of a European city in Africa.

There is always a disadvantage to this duality and Europeanization of African cities. Low income neighborhoods and inadequate housing provisions always create a traditional labyrinth whose plan contradicts or collides with the European-planned side of the city. Perhaps it is Africa's unique way of asserting itself to colonial administrators.

untouched. The Congo Chamber of Commerce Building (Fig. 9.4) is a good example of this work. Smooth surfaces and crisp edges compensate for the neoclassical details which are lacking in the building. Hotel Brazzaville (Fig. 9.5) originally had

Fig. C.29 *Brazzaville, Congo. Window details at Saint Anne's Cathedral.*
(American Geographical Society Collection, The University of Wisconsin-Milwaukee Library)

9.4 GABON

Gabon, with its capital at Libraville, was once a French colony. It became independent on August 17, 1960. Gabon is bordered in the north by equatorial Guinea and the Cameroon Republic, and in the southeast by the Congo Republic. The total population of Gabon is "between 1.1 and 1.3 million inhabitants" (Barnes 1992, 1), and the Fang is the major ethnic group in the country. In addition, "there are nearly fifty ethnic groups in Gabon belonging to eight major linguistic families: Myene, Kota, Tshogho, Mbele, Benga, Punu-Eshira, Duma and Teke" (Barnes 1992, 104).

Gabon is mostly a Christian nation with Catholics in the majority. Some Gabonese have mixed traditional ancestral religion with Christianity into what is commonly known as *Bwiti.* "Bwiti is referred to by anthropologists as a syncretic religion, that is, one that brings together elements of indigenous beliefs with those imposed by the outsiders" (Barnes 1992, 111). This practice is common in many African countries.

Libraville (Fig. 9.7) is Gabon's largest and the most commercial city, as well as the administrative center of the country. Most Gabonese, however, still live in villages within extended family compounds. Traditional architecture is highly ornamented with carved columns and mythical figures. Some houses are two-stories high with raffia-palm frond roofs. The building materials consist of timber and bamboo stems. The method of weaving the bamboo stems together forms a grid of diagonal or square lattice. Walls are plastered on the inside with clay but exposed on the outside so that the bamboo lattice, which forms part of the building decoration, remains visible. Cooling is achieved through high-pitched roofs of bamboo fronds and grass.

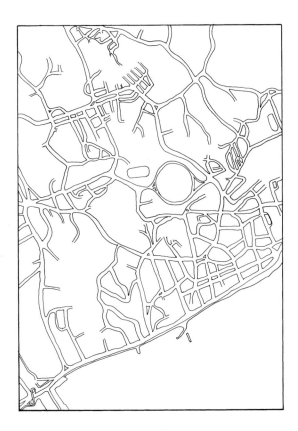

Fig. 9.7 *Libraville, Gabon. City plan.*

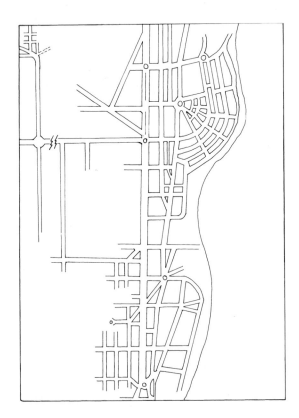

Fig. 9.8 *Kinshasa, Zaire. City plan.*

9.5 ZAIRE

Congo-Kinshasa, a former colony of Belgium, became independent in 1960. Its capital city, Leopoldville, was renamed Kinshasa. "Zaire, as it is now called, ranks high as a supplier of many of the world's natural resources. It is the world's largest producer of industrial diamonds, the second-largest supplier of gem stones" (Crane 1971, 17). In fact, this wealth of natural resources is what attracted the European colonists.

Belgium set out to create a giant empire that would rival everything England and France had acquired in Africa. Leopoldville, named after King Leopold II, became the center of this empire. For King Leopold II, Leopoldville was like a personal estate, an extension of Brussels, which had undergone changes during the mid-1900s. Thus, it was planned like a European city. The main streets are boulevards that proceed from major city landmarks and meet at roundabouts (Figs. 9.8 and 9.9). Public buildings such as the Musée de la Vie Indigene (Museum of African Life) look nothing like African indigenous design. Instead, a Renaissance building with Roman arches is an African museum in name, but it takes on a European design precedent (Fig. 9.10). The Catholic cathedrals built at the turn of the 19th century follow neo-Gothic style (Fig. 9.11). Modernism in Kinshasa takes a

Fig. 9.10 Kinshasa, Zaire, Museum of African Life (Musée de la Vie Indigene). (American Geographical Society Collection, The University of Wisconsin-Milwaukee Library)

classical parti in most public buildings. The Auditorium Lovanium at the University of Kinshasa hides its classical intentions in modernist plane surfaces (Fig. C.30). The entrance gives a reformed look and meaning to classical gables and pediments, but its symmetry clearly betrays its origin as a classically inspired design. The symmetry and pro-

Fig. 9.9 Kinshasa, Zaire. Government housing projects. (American Geographical Society Collection, The University of Wisconsin-Milwaukee Library)

Fig. 9.11 *Kinshasa, Zaire. Catholic cathedral.* (American Geographical Society Collection, The University of Wisconsin-Milwaukee Library)

portions of the columns express verticality common in neo-classical buildings. Belgian and French architects emphasized this mix of modernism with a classical parti in some of the government buildings at the heart of Kinshasa (Fig. 9.12). Overall, Kinshasa is a modern city surrounded by African urban layouts. Land is scarce in the Brazzaville/Kinshasa cornubation due to the immense Congo River, which fostered the growth of the cities. Despite this problem of land scarcity, the population of both cities is on the increase because of the high level of rural to urban migration.

Fig. 9.12 *Kinshasa, Zaire. Customs office.* (American Geographical Society Collection, The University of Wisconsin-Milwaukee Library)

Fig. C.30 *Kinshasa, Zaire. Auditorium at Lovanium University. 1970s.* (American Geographical Society Collection, The University of Wisconsin-Milwaukee Library)

4

SOUTH AFRICA
AND THE EAST
AFRICAN
ISLANDS

10 THE ARCHITECTURE OF ANGOLA, MALAWI, MOZAMBIQUE, MADAGASCAR, MAURITIUS, AND SEYCHELLES

chapter

ngola, a region of the former Congo, is an example of how Western contact with Africa has deprived a nation of the opportunity to express itself architecturally (Fig. 10.1). As developed in this area, the triple heritage culture now has more Western influence than Islamic. Belgian, British, and especially, Portuguese activities in the Congo were too destabilizing for the region to develop itself during the 16th century.

In Malawi, the early explorations of Dr. David Livingstone insured the evangelization and commercialization of the country. Its capital was transferred from Zomba to Lilongwe with the hope of correcting colonial mismanagement and planning, but the exercise resembles the Dodoma experience in that it has never been completed. Mozambique, a former Portuguese colony, shares the identical fate. Traditional architecture in Mozambique is explained in a later chapter in conjunction with the discussion of tradi-

tional architecture in Zimbabwe. In Madagascar, Mauritius, and Seychelles, the ancient trade in the Indian Ocean contributed to the formation of an Afro-Asiatic civilization. In each case, 19th-century European explorers played a significant role in determining the architectural heritage of these countries.

10.1 ETHNIC GROUPS AND HOUSE FORMS IN ANGOLA

Present-day Angola was once part of the greater Kongo (Congo) Kingdom. The inhabitants are descendants of the Bantu and Khosian language groups. It is believed that the Bantu speakers arrived in the region long after the Khosian were there. "Arriving from north and east, the Bantu settled in Angola between 1300 and 1600 A.D., and some have been there even earlier" (Roth 1979, 14). The Kongo Kingdom already had an elaborate and sophisticated bureaucratic governing mechanism before the arrival of the Portuguese in 1483. Roth (1979, 14) states that historical accounts of Angola are pieced together from Portuguese records and from African oral traditions. Jan Vansina based his historical accounts of Africa and Portugal on African oral tradition and

Fig. 10.1 Southern African countries.

Portuguese records concluding that an elaborate monarchial government was already in place before the Portuguese arrival.

The account of the formation of the Kongo Kingdom, which influenced the subsequent birth of Angola, goes as follows: In the late 14th century, a group of Kongo, led by the son of a chief from the area of modern Zaire, moved south of the Congo River into northern Angola, conquering the people they found there and establishing Mbanza Kongo, the capital of the kingdom. The victors absorbed the people they conquered into their community instead of isolating them. The success of the kingdom is often attributed to this assimilation of the aboriginals in the area. The kingdom continued to expand under the leadership of one monarchy and was large enough to be subdivided into six provinces by the early 16th century. Each province was governed by a chief or a governor who was subordinate to the king. The king had both religious and political powers; subordinate powers were in the hands of the regional governors and chiefs within each province. The provinces were further divided into districts,

ruled by district chiefs, and the districts were subsequently ruled by village headmen who reported to the district chiefs. Like many ancient African kingdoms, "the basic unit of the state was the village, at the core of which were members of a matrilineal descent group" (Roth 1979, 14), usually led by a headman or an elder, in most cases based on heredity. On the other hand, district officers and governors were appointed by the king who also had the power to remove them. The royal court was filled with numerous officials who specialized either in serving the king directly or in judging cases and counciling the king.

The king was elected from only the male descendants of the royal family, but another criterion was added after the death of King Affonso I, who was the first to convert to Christianity. The succeeding kings from the time of Affonso I's death in 1545 had to be traced directly to him.

The king raised his armies from his people in times of crisis, and the monetary system was strictly under his control. The currency was a type of shellfish that could be found only in the king's fisheries; thus, the king had absolute control over

Fig. 10.2 Luba, Congo. The king's reception room. 1608.

its circulation. He taxed the people to raise money for his huge bureaucracy, which included Portuguese advisers in the royal court, a tradition begun in 1512 due to the king's admiration of European technology and his desire to modernize his country. "By the 1530s, his capital [Affonso I's] Mbanza Kongo, had been renamed Sao Salvador" (Roth 1979, 16).

The cultural exchange of religious ideas between Christians and traditional ancestor worshipers in Mbanza Kongo influenced both the structures of European homes and commercial enterprises in the region. The cultural exchange emanates from the ideology of royalty, popularly known as *nkisi*. Nkisi is derived from a religious philosophy that embodies three important cults: the cult of ancestor worship, for which the holy place was the royal cemetery grave; the cult of the worship of territory spirits such as the spirit of Mbanza Kongo; and the worship of royal charms. The clergy who served in the territory cult shrine were called *mari kabunga*. As Vansina (1981, 554) points out, "the nkisi concept was funda-

mental, and the Christians were to adopt the term, using it to mean that which is sacred. The church was the house of the nkisi, the Bible the book of the nkisi, and the priest the *nganga* of the nkisi."

The union of African occult and Western religion produced a social class whose real intent was commercial exploitation. The majority of the people were left out of the resulting literary and commercial adventures except in that the people became commodities for export, as Portuguese plantations in Brazil needed laborers. The aristocracy lived luxuriously in large houses made of brick and timber. The taste for Western goods became part of the class systems and its privileges; houses, for instance, were adorned with chandeliers to match the status of the occupants (Figs. 10.2 and 10.3).

Angola was founded by a renegade Ndongo chief, Ngola, who declared himself independent from the supreme Kongo king at Mbanza Kongo. "Gradually the chiefdom spread in

Fig. 10.3 Mbanza, Congo. The king's reception room. 1850s. (Jan Vansina)

size and power, and in 1556 it gained its independence from Kongo with the aid of Portuguese arms" (July 1980, 191) and mercenaries. The Bobo, Bunda, Ndongo, Nbala, Suku, and Dende are some of the ethnic groups in Angola.

Traditional family structures and dwellings follow the forms found in many African societies. Of interest are the dwellings of fishermen found around the coastal towns of Angola and near the banks of rivers. These rectangular houses are made of palm frond mats and are carefully netted together to withstand the climatic elements. In recent times, some fishermen have roofed their houses with aluminum sheets. Settlement is along family lineage, and the extended family is an extension of the nuclear family. For centuries, the natives in this area resisted Portuguese domination, but the Portuguese used biblical politics to make inroads into the local population, which found itself continuously exploited by slave raids and forced labor from the 16th century onward.

By 1548, a Catholic church with a Portuguese bishop was already in place in Mbanza Kongo. The bishop's palace was built with sun-dried brick plastered over with cement. From then on, "European influence was strong and was reflected in the importation of European stone architecture (churches and palaces), symbols of authority (swords, crowns, flags and vestments)" (Vansina 1981, 546) first under the guise of Christian evangelism, but later as an absolute act of commercial and territorial control that was to be guarded closely and with brutal force. Several contracts were imposed on the natives by the Portuguese to give legitimacy to enforcement by the imperial military. The city of Luanda was begun as a trading port by the Portuguese in the 1600s. It was first called St. Paul de Loanda and "the Jesuits had set up a mission at Loanda by 1575" (Freeman-Grenville 1991, 77).

10.2 LUANDA

What began as a trading post under the Portuguese in the 1600s was to become a booming commercial center. Consequently, the need arose to defend and protect these commercial activities from other competing European powers. Usually, this was achieved by an accelerated settlement policy and by the construction of fortifications. Thus, Portugal's major attempt to consolidate its grip on the region and to monopolize the slave, ivory, and mineral trade dates to the construction of the Fort Sao Miguel (Saint Michael) in 1641 off the coast of Luanda.

Fig. 10.4 Luanda, Angola. Fort Sao Miguel. 1641. (American Geographical Society Collection, The University of Wisconsin-Milwaukee Library)

Fort Sao Miguel was a self-contained town built in the medieval European style (Fig. 10.4). Like most Portuguese forts in Africa, the plan is anthropomorphic with areas that symbolically represent human limbs and head. The wall is made very thick, with bastions for cannons. Within the walls of the fortress, there were many buildings, some of them homes, while the high structure was used as a slave depot and for administration. Fort Sao Miguel's location on a tiny island made it easily defendable and difficult for enemies to penetrate.

Unfortunately, it is not possible to identify some of the 17th-century Portuguese architects who worked in Africa and the Orient due to some inconsistency in the history of Portuguese architecture. "The history of Portuguese art and architecture before 1700 still consists only of two lists, between which the connections are regrettably few" (Kubler 1972, 6). One list names the buildings without connecting them to the architects, whereas the other names the architects without connecting them to the buildings. Hence, it is possible to identify the dates and styles of some Portuguese structures that were constructed before 1700 without knowing who and what inspired the designer to take a particular approach. The knowledge that there was a transfer of military

architecture to religious architecture by people like Diogo de Boytaca should help in the assessment of the influence of Portuguese architecture in Angola. If anything, Sao Miguel is a true manifestation of Portuguese plain architecture and a reflection of the ideology and trend of architecture in Portugal in the mid-17th century. This trend was more visible in the Luanda cathedral that was founded around 1628 (Fig. 10.5) and the Chapel of Nazareth that was constructed between 1644 and 1648 (Fig. 10.6).

One unmistakable point of departure in the search for the origins of Portuguese plain-style architecture is the realization that "after 1550 the Jesuits were the most prolific builders in Portugal, enjoying royal favors and gaining through their successful educational policies the support of rich citizens and powerful nobles in the cities everywhere..." (Kubler 1972, 56). The Jesuits exported their success to Brazil and to Africa as a major evangelical campaign to win new souls for Jesus. It is not certain, however, how many of the designs came from the Jesuits themselves or from hired architects. Non-Jesuit historians give credit to professional architects, but Jesuit historians believe these buildings were mainly the work of Jesuit masons and master builders. Whatever the case may be, the results were basically a transfer of architectural structures

Fig. 10.7 *Luanda, Angola. Skyline. (American Geographical Society Collection, The University of Wisconsin-Milwaukee Library)*

from Portugal to the colonies of Brazil, Angola, and Mozambique.

Another common point of departure for the plain style is the Italian church facade invented by Alberti, enriched by Palladio, and diversified in many baroque variants. It was not adopted as a style but as a point of departure in the process of searching for local Portuguese forms. Moreover, 17th-century Portuguese designers exploited the Italian style for the convenience of opening up several entrances separated by classical columns. The style also evolved into buildings with central parts of the facades higher and narrower than the aisles, which have clear and distinct expression. The upper story ties to the wide base with volutes capped with pediments. The Jesuit cathedral and the Chapel of Nazareth in Luanda can be

Fig. 10.5 *(Opposite, top) Luanda, Angola. Luanda cathedral. 1628. (American Geographical Society Collection, The University of Wisconsin-Milwaukee Library)*

Fig. 10.6 *(Opposite, bottom) Luanda, Angola. Chapel of Nazareth. 1644–1648. (American Geographical Society Collection, The University of Wisconsin-Milwaukee Library)*

studied from this perspective. Their plain surfaces clearly identify them as the Portuguese search for modesty after years of ostentatious decoration and lavishness.

Luanda (Fig. 10.7), the largest city and the capital of Angola, has several architectural styles, representing almost 500 years

Fig. C.31 *Luanda, Angola. General hospital. (American Geographical Society Collection, The University of Wisconsin-Milwaukee Library)*

Fig. C.32 Luanda, Angola. Bank of Angola. (American Geographical Society Collection, The University of Wisconsin-Milwaukee Library)

of Portuguese presence in the country (Fig. C.31). The general hospital makes no secret of its neoclassical realism. The entrance is approached by dual Palladian steps on the sides, with a pediment resting on six classical Renaissance columns. A row of Spanish balustrades supports the stair handrails from one side to the other. Government offices built in the 17th century are as Renaissance and Romanesque as their contemporaries in Europe. The Angola National Bank Building in Luanda makes no pretext about its classical intentions. The Roman arches forming the rusticated base give way to classical columns that carry the pediment on an axial second floor. Residential buildings echo Portuguese and Spanish influences (Fig. C.32). These buildings began with Palladian Italian dual access and ended with plain Portuguese surfaces. Obviously, the European influence cannot be underestimated.

10.3 ETHNIC GROUPS AND HOUSE FORMS IN MALAWI

Malawi, formerly known as Nyasaland, was under British control for more than 70 years beginning in May of 1891. It became independent from Great Britain on July 6, 1964. Malawi is located 350 mi (560 km) west of the Indian Ocean. The landscape is dominated by the East African highlands and the Rift Valley which give the country a varied topography. Malawi is a long, narrow country that measures about 530 mi (852 km) in length and about 100 mi (160 km) in width. It is the last stronghold of Islam on its journey to southern Africa. "The Yao now form the southernmost outpost of the Islamic world in Africa" (Agnew 1972, 14).

Malawi's early history dates to the prehistoric past, but the lack of records has been an obstacle in determining an accu-

rate history. Linguistic, cultural, physical, economic, and occupational studies done in the region suggest that Malawi has gone through many different phases of history. Pachai (1973) identified the pre-Bantu period, the proto-Bantu period, and the Bantu period. The pre-Bantu period refers to historical events of the late Stone Age beginning about 8000 B.C. The second period of the proto-Bantu peoples coming to Malawi represents a transition between the earliest and the latest settlements. There were Bantu-speakers moving from north to south who are identified by oral tradition as the Pule, the Lenda, and the Katanga. These groups engaged in agriculture and pastoralism. The latest group to arrive brought ironworking skills.

Again, as in many African countries, in Malawi the struggle between ancestor worship, Christianity, and Islam began in the 17th century and intensified in later years. The Arabs came to Malawi from the northeast with Islam, and the Europeans came from the southeast with Christianity. As in Uganda, the people were caught in between, having to choose their own religion or those of the Arabs and the English. Regardless, traditional family ties remained strong. The extended family, the village, and the clan were reinforced as centers of spiritual nourishment and as a way of guarding against the intruders. Settlement patterns reflected this desire to be together. In Malawi, it is not uncommon to find traditional dwellings of circular and rectangular shapes next to one another, as one would find in Tanzania and Uganda, and traditional building technology does not differ from that in Tanzania and Uganda.

The Yao ethnic group rejected Christianity in favor of Islam in southern Malawi, but Christianity managed to entrench itself in the other parts of the country, especially at Khondowe, Likoma Island, Blantyre, and Zomba, the former capital city. Anglo-Portuguese struggles for dominance did not interfere with the spread of Christianity in Malawi during the 19th century. "In East and Central Africa, by as late as 1850 only a single society, the church missionary society, was operating" (Boahen 1981, 40), but the death of Dr. David Livingstone in 1873 triggered a surge of missionary activities in the region.

Dr. Livingstone, based on his explorations in Africa, gave several speeches in Europe about the benefit of investing in Malawi, especially for cotton and sugar because of the favorable soil. "Livingstone saw two pillars for the operation of his scheme. These were Christianity and commerce, both of which had to be launched at the same time" (Pachai 1973, 71). Although by the time of his death in 1873, his plans had not materialized, Livingstone's death became a spiritual catalyst for commercialization of the region. Businessmen, politicians, and missionaries attended the burial of the Anglo-

Fig. 10.8 Blantyre, Malawi. Blantyre Mission Church. 1876. [United Nations Educational Scientific and Cultural Organization (UNESCO)]

Scottish explorer and donated funds to carry out his missionary work in Malawi. The Free Church of Scotland formed an organization known as the Livingstone Mission in 1875 and established the Livingstone Blantyre Mission in 1876.

The Livingstone Scottish Mission Church at Blantyre, the Livingstone Scottish Mission Church at Khondowe, and Saint Peter's Cathedral at Likoma Island were among the first Western structures in the country aside from British administrative buildings. There was of course no real separation among commerce, church, and state in the early stages of Western intrusion into Malawi. These churches are witness to that period (Fig. 10.8), and no church made its intentions more open, as a commercial venture rather than an evangelical pursuit, than the New Church of the Providence Industrial Mission, which was founded in 1900.

The Scottish missionaries brought a building tradition similar to what they were accustomed to in Scotland. Many 19th-century Scottish houses of worship were influenced by medieval and Renaissance Scottish tower houses, which often had towers at the entrances, corners, and in the case of castles, at strategic wall locations. Unlike the roof of the Roman watchtower, which covers the structure as a canopy, the Scottish superstructure is a conelike spire within the tower. In other words, the roof does not really cover the battlement section.

The towers of the mid-13th century Caerlaverock Castle on the shores of the Solway Firth and the entrance of Saint Machar's Cathedral, Aberdeen, are good examples of Scottish architecture. Unlike the conelike spires on the towers of Caerlaverock Castle gate, Saint Machar's twin tower spires are tall, pointed cones with sharp edges in three segments. However, all are positioned similarly on their respective structure. The twin domes on the towers of the main

entrance to the Blantyre Mission Church in Malawi have their precedent in this Scottish tradition. The Blantyre Church facade is garnished with 19th-century Renaissance English Georgian period ornaments. Symmetry is emphasized in ordered formalism. The windows and doors of the main entrance are Gothic inspired, but the side entrance is fashioned with Greco-Roman gables and pediments.

Unlike the Blantyre Mission Church, Livingstonia Mission Church at Khondowe and Saint Peter's Cathedral at Likoma Island did not adopt Renaissance elements, though their windows and entrances are Gothic inspired.

10.4 FROM BLANTYRE AND ZOMBA TO LILONGWE

The Malawi government decided to move the capital from Zomba to Lilongwe, an existing town in the north-central part of the country, shortly after independence in 1964. Prior to the move, Zomba could only accommodate half of the government departments of Malawi; the rest were located in Blantyre. As Agnew (1972, 1) states, "Lilongwe was selected as the site for the new capital, partly because of its central position in Malawi and partly to encourage economic development north of the southern region in which economic development has been concentrated." This reason is not surprising, as many African countries—Nigeria, Tanzania, and Cote d'Ivoire—used it later to engage in more ambitious capital city projects.

Unlike Abuja, Dodoma, and Yamoussoukro, all of which were founded on new sites without previous urban centers, Lilongwe was an existing city that received a new function. It was already the third largest city in Malawi before being designated the national capital, and the move was also designed to alleviate the inefficiency of managing a national government in a twin city (Blantyre and Zomba). Before the move, Lilongwe already had a population of 60,000, and the entire district had 500,000. The projected population increase for the city was 125,000 in 1980 and half a million people by the turn of the century. A moderate temperate climate due to its altitude 3400 ft above sea level and rich agricultural land are bonuses for the development of the new city.

Lilongwe River is a major physical feature in the old town and divides the city into east and west. This natural landmark posed a major problem because it gave the city dual focal points, one on either side of the river, and also created two major city cores that divided the city by class. According to Gerke and Viljoen (1968, 20), who prepared the document for the new city, "The better class shops and the regional government offices are located in the western sector. The business sector east of the river contains a greater number and variety of retail shops." This dual city center, with its unpleasant dual image based on social stratum, was to be resolved by the creation of a new city center. The commercial zone west of the river has an industrial concern that extends to the town, drawing undesired traffic that detracts from the less bulky retail shops. Several wholesalers occupy the commercial district east of the river. East and west of the river, there are several residential buildings with adequate room for future expansion. According to Gerke and Viljoen (1968, 28), the form of the new city is determined by the spatial relationship among the following five main components:

1. A new city core, comprising the government administrative buildings, a new shopping and commercial zone, a central city park and cultural center, and a special zone for embassies and other important buildings;
2. A recreation zone featuring a central sports and general purpose stadium;
3. The industrial zones;
4. The new residential sections; and
5. A "processional way" which, together with a main and secondary road network, connects the above elements with the existing town.

The focus of the city is now the new House of Assembly and the executive and administrative buildings. The Malawi government selected a site 3 mi north of the center of old Lilongwe on a prominent, flat ridge for the Assembly Building. In the new plan, the processional way acts as a channel for government buildings along its sides, with generous open space and pedestrian alleys (Fig. 10.9). The objective was to group government office buildings into small units that enclose open spaces. The open spaces are subsequently linked to form pedestrian access roads. This plan helps in separating vehicular from pedestrian traffic. Every building faces a park on one side and parking spaces on the other. A large number of shops, the new central market, and office buildings are connected by pedestrian walkways. Civic buildings are located north of the shopping and business district, with a large open space between them as a buffer. Overall, this Johannesburg-based plan was unified by residential buildings around the four major lanes that define the city core, and 13 residential districts have been spread out with clear connections to the central city plan.

Lilongwe should not be compared with Abuja, Dodoma, Yamoussoukro, or Nouakchott because the latter are cities founded on nonurbanized virgin lands. Besides, the extravagance of Abuja makes it comparable only to Brasília. However, the new capitals are all motivated by identical political-economic goals intended to develop the underdevel-

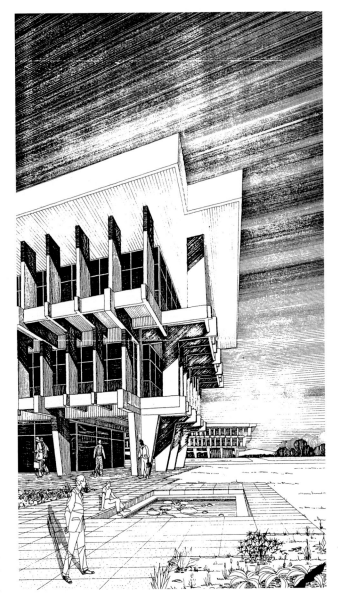

Fig. 10.9 Lilongwe, Malawi. Perspective of city center showing Government Building. (Gerke and Viljoen, 1968)

oped sections of the country. Political ends and interests by powerful elites were not ruled out, though. Potts (1985, 44) notes, "that Connell has speculated on whether Lilongwe was chosen as the result of regional or ethnic loyalty, as it is located near Kasungu where Banda was born, and it is also near the core area of his ethnic group, the Chewa."

The possibility of selfish concern deserves attention because it tends to be prevalent in the process of locating new capital cities in Africa. For example, in Cote d' Ivoire, the capital was moved from Abidjan to Yamoussoukro, the hometown of President Houphouet Boigny. On the other hand, centralization, neutrality, and national unity are the major factors behind the move of Nigeria's capital from Lagos to Abuja. Most African countries inherited capital cities that were located along the coast for the convenience of the excolonial lords in shipping goods to their homelands. Malawi is not along the coast, but its old colonial capital was situated as close to the periphery as possible to achieve the same sea-route convenience. As a consequence, development took place in the northern region where there were fewer people and a less educated elite available to run the government when the colonials left. This gives legitimacy to Malawi's desire to improve its interior. President Banda, however, used the opportunity to secure political interest over national interest. As self-declared president for life in Malawi, he needs to govern in a place where he will always have support, and no place provides that better than his ethnic home base, Lilongwe.

In spite of its modest plan and the desire to unify the social classes, Lilongwe remains a dream difficult to realize due to the enormous cost of the project, disastrous state of the Malawian economy, and President Banda's repressive iron-fisted approach to remaining in office for life. As Perl (1984) points out, it must be remembered that Malawi still has not moved its parliament and several government departments, even 20 years after building Lilongwe. It is also suggested that Lilongwe is President Banda's search for a prestigious national project for which he can personally take credit regardless of the financial cost. The new capital project entailed expenditures well beyond Malawi's financial capabilities, and eventually, loans were solicited from South Africa in 1968. The city is still far from completion, and today Malawi is still being governed from two separate cities.

10.5 ETHNIC GROUPS AND HOUSE FORMS IN MOZAMBIQUE

The aborigines of Mozambique come from various major language groups, such as the Bantus and Khoisani peoples. Today, the Cuabo, the Nyasa, the Tonga, and some Shona live in Mozambique. One of the largest medieval empires in southern Africa was ruled by the Shona dynasty, whose dominion covered most of the Zambezi River Basin (Mozambique, Zimbabwe, southern Malawi, and parts of Zambia). The Shona dynasties were centered at Great Zimbabwe, a vast, walled complex near the city of Maavingo in present-day Zimbabwe. According to Rhinehart (1985, 10), "More than 150 madzimbabwe (stone enclosures; sing., Zimbabwe) of this kind were constructed by the Shona over a period of several centuries in Mozambique and Zimbabwe as administrative centers, markets, and religious shrines."

These stone structures make up some of the traditional architecture of the Mozambiquan people. The kingdom was already in decline by the time the Portuguese arrived in the 15th century. Even then, early Portuguese, German, and other Western explorers did not believe that these were African civilizations.

Another dimension of pre-European Mozambiquan history that should not be overlooked is the high volume of trade between Africans and Arabs along the coastal towns of the Indian Ocean. "These towns, stretching from Benadir coast in Somalia to Sofala in Mozambique, became links in an extensive commercial network connecting East Africa with Southwest Asia and the Indies" (Rinehart 1985, 9). The arrival of the Portuguese in the 15th century changed the history of this region, beginning with Vasco da Gama who bombarded the town of Mozambique in 1497 and headed northward to raid the cities of Mombasa and Kilwa. The end result of the meeting of these three cultures—indigenous, Islamic, and Western—was a triple heritage that manifests itself in the sociocultural and architectural characteristics of the region.

One of the earliest Portuguese architectural structures in Mozambique is Fort Sao Sebastian, constructed of granite at Mozambique in 1552. The Dutch attacked several Portuguese outposts in 1604 and took them over, but Fort Sao Sebastian did not fall, although it was an occasion that marked the beginning of the Portuguese demise and overthrow by the English and the French. In 1776, the Portuguese regrouped in Lourenco Marques, but were expelled by an Austrian company who built a fortress there (Fig. 10.10). The Austrian design was primarily for defense against other marauding European powers of the time. The Portuguese returned to Lourenco Marques in 1781, but again were expelled, this time by the French during the Napoleonic wars.

Fig. 10.10 Maputo, Mozambique. Portuguese fort. 1552. (American Geographical Society Collection, The University of Wisconsin-Milwaukee Library)

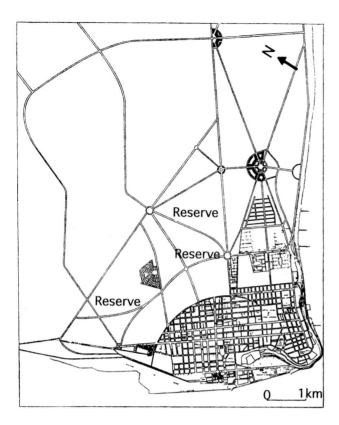

Fig. 10.11 Maputo, Mozambique. City plan. 1952.

10.6 MAPUTO

Maputo (formerly Lourenco Marques), the present capital of Mozambique, was planned as a European city by the Portuguese colonial administration (Figs. 10.11 and C.33). It had become a bustling, prosperous city by the turn of the 20th century and especially during the years after World War II. As in Luanda, Angola, public and private buildings took on European styles. Government office buildings were predominantly of a colonial Renaissance style. For example, the central railway station is a mix of 20th-century industrial steel construction on a 19th-century baroque facade. It is a slight deviation from the usually less ostentatious plain Portuguese style of architecture. However, the interior construction of the industrial warehouse, with skylights that let adequate sunlight into the waiting space, compensates for the exterior baroque tendencies. The arches that open the doors to individual rooms and the simplicity of the smooth surface echo the simpler Portuguese style. The Catholic cathedral is a beautiful building in neo-Gothic style (Fig. C.34), while homes (Fig. 10.12) reflect the spirit of Portugal in their plain facade and modest ornamentation on window and door openings. Finally, the spirit of the modern movement with Le Corbusier's influence manifests itself as it does in many European cities.

Fig. 10.12 Maputo, Mozambique. Private home in Portuguese style. (American Geographical Society Collection, The University of Wisconsin-Milwaukee Library)

Fig. C.33 Maputo, Mozambique. Skyline. (American Geographical Society Collection, The University of Wisconsin-Milwaukee Library)

Fig. C.34 Maputo, Mozambique. Catholic cathedral. (American Geographical Society Collection, The University of Wisconsin-Milwaukee Library)

Fig. 10.13 Madagascar. Traditional architecture.
(American Geographical Society Collection, The University of Wisconsin-Milwaukee Library)

10.7   ETHNIC GROUPS AND HOUSE FORMS IN MADAGASCAR

Madagascar, formerly known as the Malagasy Republic, is the largest African island in the Indian Ocean. There are many ethnic groups in Madagascar: the Antankara, Antandroy, Antambohoaka, Antanosy, Antemoro, Antesaka, Antefasy, Bara, Betsimisaraka, Betsileo, Bezanozano, Merina, Mahafaly, Sakalava, Sihanaka, Tanala, and Tsimihety. It is important to mention that all the Malagasy people speak the same language and have similar customs and religions, except for a few ethnic groups. "Thus, despite the existence of regional differences, the Malagasy were, and have remained, one people, with one profound cultural and ethnic unity" (Mutibwa 1981, 412). There are several views about the origin of the Malagasy people, in spite of their common customs and religions.

There is really no fine line that separates the various cultures from one another or their degree of influence upon one another; thus, it is dangerous to conclude that the culture uniquely belongs to a certain group. This cultural syncretism is also reflected in the architecture of the island. Brown (1978, 11) states that "it is more difficult to identify the sources of the different elements in that culture. One can say with reasonable certainty that the rectangular hut is of Indonesian origin, the typical African round hut is nowhere to be found." Brown does have a point in that the cultures have mixed so much that one cannot really separate them. However, it is presumptuous to conclude that the absence of round houses makes the architecture (rectangular houses) of the island essentially of Indo-Polynesian origin. Africa has a strong mix of round and rectangular houses all over the continent, and in many cases, they coexist within the same homestead or com-

pound, as is particularly true of many Bantu-speaking people of whom there are large numbers in East Africa. The realization that the Bantu speakers, for instance, migrated to East Africa from both Northeast Africa and West Africa to southern Africa helps to explain some of the cultural similarities among the African peoples.

The traditional architecture of Madagascar displays a strong Indo-Polynesian origin with influence from the African mainland. The Asian influence is more visible in the gables and roof treatment than on any other parts of the Malagasy house. On the other hand, the rectangular shape and the urban layout were highly influenced by Africa (Fig. 10.13). For example, traditional house orientation in Madagascar is strongly affected by superstitious beliefs about the spirits of ancestors. The Malagasy people pay respect to the spirit of their ancestors by ensuring that their tombs are much larger and grander than residential houses. Above all, houses have a north-south orientation to avoid winds that would bring unfriendly evil spirits.

10.8   ANTANANARIVO: THE CAPITAL OF MADAGASCAR

Antananarivo is a legacy of the historical periods and events that shaped the destiny of this world's fourth largest island. The triple heritage factor cannot be ruled out on Madagascar, especially the Western influence. The attainment of political supremacy by the Merina dynasty of the heartland and the move to center the power in Antananarivo ushered in unprecedented contact with the Western world later in the 19th and 20th centuries.

Madagascar's contact with the West began much earlier, though. Diogo Dias left Portugal in 1499 as part of a 13-ship Portuguese fleet bound for India. The fleet encountered a storm that claimed four ships and left the rest scattered around the South African cape. Diogo Dias's ship was pushed to the east, but when the storm subsided, he sailed to the north until he sighted land. He thought he was along the coast of Mozambique, but the land ended in the north. He then realized that he had come upon a large island. He called the island Sao Laurenco (Saint Lawrence) after the saint on whose feast day he came across the island. Two years later, the name was changed to the Island of Marco Polo when the Portuguese learned of its discovery. From then on, Madagascar and its inhabitants ceased to be isolated from the West. Shipwrecked sailors, pirates, and other European treasure-seekers turned it into a port of call with a considerable amount of traffic. This island, located less than 250 mi off the East African coast, was later bombarded and occupied by the French in 1895.

The history of modern Madagascar cannot be told without mentioning the great modernizer, King Radama I, who succeeded his father in 1810 at the age of 18. "He is regarded, indeed as he saw himself, as the Napoleon of Madagascar" (Mutibwa 1981, 416). Up to this time, Madagascar had been closed to Western ways of life. This young king, however, not only subdued other smaller independent groups on the island, but also signed friendship treaties with the English and allied missionaries to establish churches and schools in Madagascar. Mutibwa (1981, 419) writes that "following this agreement on 3 December 1820, David Jones of the London Missionary Society (LMS) arrived in Antananarivo. Radama welcomed British missionaries for they brought with them not only education (although tied to Christianity) but also technical assistance." The first school was opened on December 8, 1820, with only three pupils, all the king's nephews. James Cameron arrived in Antananarivo in 1826 and initiated technical training in building construction, carpentry, tanning, tin-plating, and weaving. Above all, he designed many buildings himself, one of his most prominent works being the addition to the Queen's Palace at Antananarivo.

Queen Ranavalona I hired Jean Laborde, a French treasure-seeker and adventurer who arrived in Antananarivo in 1832, as her minister of works. This ambitious Frenchman first established a factory at Ilafy, about 10 km north of Antananarivo, before establishing an industrial complex at Mantaseo where he employed some 20,000 workers, most of them as forced laborers. The complex produced a variety of goods ranging from guns and cannons to glass products and soap. In 1839, the queen commissioned Laborde to design a palace. The three-story wooden palace was built in the traditional style and oriented north-south as the rest of the houses in the village (Fig. 10.14). Traditional wood construction was maintained but amplified, with an enormous ebony post some 130 ft (39.62 m) high at the center, three stories of massive high walls with surrounding verandas, and a steeply pitched two-sided roof. The Laborde structure became a style that was adopted by the elite of the society and copied in Antananarivo and other parts of the country. Manjakamiadana Palace, meaning "where it is meant to reign" in the Malagasy language, received an adjacent neighbor for Queen Rasoherina who had a short reign lasting only from 1863 to 1868.

In 1861, James Cameron encased the original Laborde Manjakamiadana Palace in granite blocks, following a Romanesque Renaissance style. The ebony posts were then transformed into heavy Roman columns and arches. The original pitched roof retained its structure, but two dormers were added to each side of it. Cameron chose to clamp the arches with four Renaissance towers on the four corners of the building, thereby enhancing the vertical appearance of the building which had been overpowered by the strong horizontal rhythm of the arches. The protruding roof and the towers balanced each other as a uniform composition. One of the towers was fitted with a round Victorian clock, while the other three had round louvered occuli to match the clock. James Cameron completed his renovation in 1869.

Antananarivo would never be the same from then on. It must be remembered that this was a period of French colonial expansionism, and for urban designers, it was a time to experiment with new theories that were tested abroad on a large scale in French colonies such as Morocco. The French were further inspired to explore their new beaux-arts urban design theories in Madagascar because of increasing problems with malaria and urban degeneration during and after the years of World War I. "In addition, the colonial government needed to make a gesture to the local population, acknowledging that

some 40,000 Malagasys had gone off to serve in European combat, one in ten dying in the trenches" (Wright 1991, 273). The French responded with urban design policies that followed the examples of Lyautey in Morocco. Several urban design schemes were proposed for Antananarivo and other major regional cities in Madagascar from 1916 to the 1930s. Industrialization and national urban design were harmonized in Antananarivo in ways that pleased the colonial government.

Antananarivo is, therefore, a city of multiple personalities manifest in traditional pretext, colonial motives and definitions of modernity and progress, colonial commercial adventurism, and above all, competition between colonial powers for the loyalty of those they colonized. These multiple characteristics are all visible in the plethora of different architectural styles that adorns the city. Some pretend to be sensitive to tradition, but the majority echo the spirit of modernization. In the end, what was designed and built was what the colonials considered good for the Malagasy people, not by consensus of the Malagasy people themselves, but by domination and absolute disregard for their culture.

10.9 MAURITIUS

Mauritius Island was known to ancient Phoenician, East African, and Arab Malay sailors but was not urbanized until late in the 16th century. A Portuguese sailor, Domingo

Fig. 10.15 Port Louis, Mauritius. Legislative Assembly and Government Center. The building on the right with a flag and statue in front is the 18th-century Trade Building. The building on the left is the new addition by Fry, Drew and Partners. (Fry Drew and Partners and Fry Drew Knight Creamer)

Fernandez, was the first European to arrive at Mauritius in 1511. The Dutch settled it in 1598 but could not maintain a self-sustaining community and finally left in 1710. In 1715, the French East India Company claimed the island for France in the name of Louis XIV. The Napoleonic War and the events that led to the Anglo-French Treaty of Paris in 1814 finally gave the island to Great Britain. The treaty allowed France to keep the Island of the Reunion, while Mauritius, Rodriguez, and the Seychelles went to Great Britain. Port Louis, a convenient stop for sailors heading to the East Indies, became the capital of Mauritius.

Like Mauritius, Port Louis is a city of diverse faces and culture. The population of the country is a mosaic of Africans, Asians, Arabs, and Europeans. Hence, the urban character is very European, but the existence of traditional African structures, Hindu temples with pagodas, Renaissance-inspired and Victorian buildings, and above all, mosques with blends of Arabian and Hindu features, and modern architecture make it a universal city with a great deal of tolerance for diversity. Most of the buildings in Port Louis and other cities of Mauritius were executed by architects from the former colonial countries, particularly the United Kingdom.

The Government Center of Mauritius is situated in the capital and port of Port Louis where, at the head of a square open to the harbor, the 18th-century residence built by the French has long been the seat of government. According to Fry et al. (1978, 154), "In a country where architectural monuments are few, it was decided to retain this beautiful three-story stone and timber building and, by joining up several blocks of existing government offices, to create a nucleus." This nucleus incorporated a new Assembly Building and offices for the principal departments, with the possibility of extending this group in two directions as opportunity offered (Fig. 10.15).

The Assembly Building (Figs. 10.16 and 10.17) is freely modeled, reinforced concrete partly cased in green and black Indian marble. It accommodates an assembly of up to 100, with some 50 seats for the public in a separate gallery. The existing old French building has been completely restored and the old throne room preserved.

Phase Two of this project was on an adjacent site which centralized all major ministries in close proximity to the center of government. The building also includes a conference/banquet hall that seats 500 people. The restricted nature of the site and the constraints of the brief have, to a large extent, predetermined that the new building must be arranged on a northwest-south-east axis parallel with the existing buildings. This orientation gives reasonable sun protection to the long sides of the building without the use of extensive brise soleil.

Sun control has been designed to protect the northeast and southwest elevations from sun penetration until 4:00 P.M.,

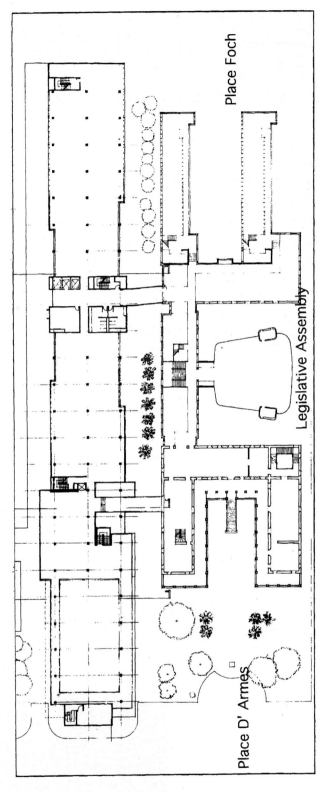

Fig. 10.16 Port Louis, Mauritius. Plan of the Government Center and Legislative Assembly. (Fry Drew and Partners and Fry Drew Knight Creamer)

when work normally ceases. This has been implemented by means of a series of cantilevers and downstand beams which

Fig. 10.17 Mauritius. Chamber of the Assembly Building. (Fry Drew and Partners and Fry Drew Knight Creamer)

give a variety of modeling to the building and provide welcome shade to the entrance courtyard at the second level. The building has been banked to take into account the slope of the ground and provide, economically, two areas of car parking under the buildings.

10.10 SEYCHELLES

The port city of Victoria is the capital of this former British colony. Seychelles has a small population. In 1985, 72,542 tourists visited the country, outnumbering the 65,244 inhabi-

Fig. 10.18 Mahe, Seychelles. Court and Treasury Buildings. (Peter Vine and Immel Publishing)

Fig. C.35 (Top, left) Victoria, Seychelles. Catholic cathedral. 1930s. (Peter Vine and Immel Publishing)

Fig. C.36 (Top, right) Victoria, Seychelles. Interior of Catholic cathedral. (Peter Vine and Immel Publishing)

Fig. C.37 (Right) Victoria, Seychelles. Sheik Muhammad Mosque. (Peter Vine and Immel Publishing)

tants. The projected population of the whole country by the year 2000 is 82,443. The nation's close affinity to the United Kingdom is fairly reflected in its architecture. The late 19th-century Court and Treasury Building at Mahe features a Victorian clock (Fig. 10.18) with a decorated steel column mounted on a square concrete base. Most houses are hybrids of the traditional architecture, like those of Madagascar, but with a Victorian cottage touch to roof gables and balconies.

A simple cottage style building served the Catholic community in Victoria from 1889, but a new building in the Renaissance style was erected in the 1930s (Figs. C.35 and C.36). Its portico is a two-story central tower with a Renaissance gable carried by round Roman Ionic columns and paced by two smaller aisle arches and a larger central arch. The traceries of the three windows on the upper story of the tower follow tropical themes and shades.

As one of the final frontiers of Africa in the Indian Ocean, Seychelles has a Muslim community and several mosques. The Mosque of Sheik Muhammad in Victoria (Fig. C.37) is more a hybrid of Afro-Asiatic Islamic architecture because of strong Hindu influence. Fancy concrete blocks are used to shade a section of the mosque from intense sunlight, and its location at the foot of a hill, together with its modest size, gives the building a tranquil environment for religious worship and meditation.

THE ARCHITECTURE OF BOTSWANA, NAMIBIA, ZAMBIA, AND ZIMBABWE

This chapter concentrates on the architecture of Botswana, Namibia, Zambia, and Zimbabwe. The triple heritage architecture of Africa becomes increasingly Westernized from central-southern Africa to the Cape. The objective here is to find meaning and to create a forum for further discussion in the field of architecture with the hope that an inclusive vision and identity can be found for the region.

The chapter reviews how major historical epochs have affected and conditioned the triple heritage architecture of the nations mentioned here. It also investigates the applicability of traditional architecture to contemporary design. The stage of development in Botswana and the works of Professor Julian Elliott are mentioned in particular. The final objective of this chapter is to open up a new dimension in the study of traditional African architecture, beyond academic spheres into practical application, by raising issues that have not been considered in the practice of architecture on the continent. One major advantage of the approach adopted in this chapter is that it returns to the grass roots and raises questions that are indeed applicable to all of Africa.

11.1 BOTSWANA

Botswana, formerly Bechuanaland, became an independent republic on September 30, 1966. Prior to that, it had no capital city because Great Britain, its former colonizer, governed the country from Mafeking, South Africa. Just 4 years before gaining independence, Botswana had to search for a national capital city and selected Gaborone, north of Mafeking and near the South African border in southeast Botswana. Gaborone (Fig 11.1) is a growing city, and most of the civic structures are just being put in place.

The people of Botswana are known as the Tswana. Theirs is a culture in which agriculture and cattle are the basis of wealth. Hence, cattle ranching is not uncommon, and the lives of the people are intricately woven into their physical surroundings. As a landlocked nation, Botswana depends largely on its own resources rather than trade for survival, except in recent times when diamond mining has become the

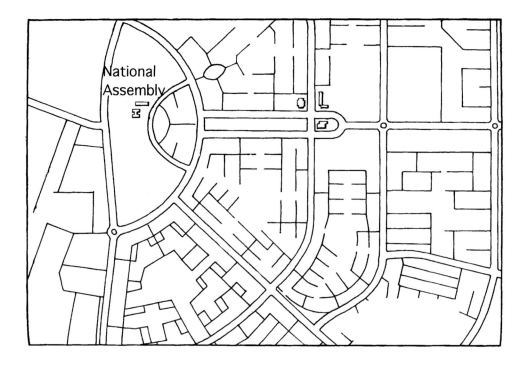

Fig. 11.1 Gaborone, Botswana. City plan. (Gabriel Okafor)

major source of national revenue. The country lies at the eastern edge of the Kalahari Desert, with annual rainfall ranging from 18–27 in in the northern region. However, dunes occur only in the extreme southwest, and it is erroneous to describe Botswana as a desert.

The country has a subtropical climate moderated by the average elevation of about 3300 ft. It is predominantly grassland that favors cattle rearing. The winter nights are cool, with occasional frost, but the summer nights are moderated by north-east winds in late evening. This climate encourages the intensive use of outdoor space.

The *kraal* was the most ideal form of settlement in Botswana when cattle grazing was the predominant occupation. Kraals can be seen as large oval compounds inhabited by many households tracing descent from the same ancestor. They serve as defensive enclaves for their inhabitants, and stones are the dominant foundation structures. The fortresses have provisions for living space, private space for households, and open or less intimate spaces for socialization and other items on the community agenda such as funerals and meetings.

The Tswana people also worship their ancestors who play a significant role both in the design and the spiritual functioning of the kraal. The ancestors are the mediators between the living and the Supreme Being, Almighty God. The central space or courtyard within the kraal is a major theater where burial ceremonies, marriages, and meetings take place. It is a

common practice to bury the chief in the kraal with his head facing west, the direction of sunset, indicative of a life that has symbolically set like the sun. The kraal is now used to refer to the open space or courtyard which unites the whole settlement (*kgotla*). Kgotla is a Tswana term for "getting together," a reference to the various households who form the entire compound.

11.2 NAMIBIA

Information is scarce on the architecture of this part of Africa because it has been a closed region due to political instability. Namibia was colonized by the Germans in 1890 but was annexed into South Africa in 1915. The country formally became independent in 1991, with its capital at Windhoek. Traditional architecture in Namibia varies from the grass house to the stone house. There are also clay houses with grass roofs. Distinct mural paintings with varied colors derived from differing shades of clay decorate the walls of the houses. Windhoek (Fig. 11.2) is a planned city with many buildings that reflect colonial taste. Generally speaking, the architecture of Namibia is highly Westernized with little Islamic influence. The triple heritage architecture in Namibia tilts toward the West with strong vestiges of indigenous architecture that are changing rapidly in the name of modernization.

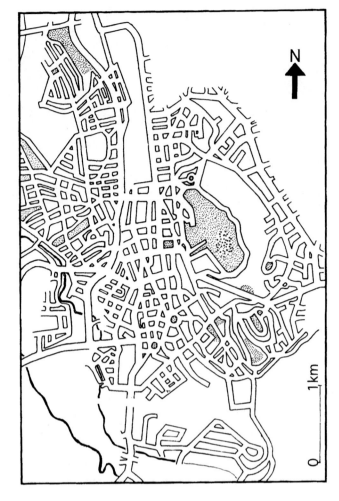

Fig. 11.2 Windhoek, Namibia. City plan from its early beginning. 1913.
(Gabriel Okafor)

11.3 THE REPUBLIC OF ZAMBIA

The Republic of Zambia is a composite of many ethnic groups whose origins stretch beyond the borders of the country. Some of the major ethnic groups in the country are: the Chewa, Bemba, Lozi, Ila, Kaonde, Ambo, Lala, Lamba, Lenje, Lima, Nsenga, Sala, Soli, Swaka, and Ushi. These ethnic groups belong to the Bantu language group. In the 15th and 16th centuries, this region was dominated by the arrival of the Maravi from the Congo and the rise of their state. Some historians place the arrival of the Maravi in the region as early as the 14th century. The kingdom of Kalonga, founded by the Maravi immigrants, was the earliest known kingdom in the region. The extension of cultural influence from the Luba and Launda states in Central Africa shaped the cultures of the people of Zambia. Trade along the east and west coasts of Africa with Arab and European traders also influenced events in the

interior of south Central Africa, as did the activities of British agent Cecil Rhodes. The introduction of Europeans to the gold deposits in the Transvaal in 1886 accelerated the process of Westernization of Zambia.

A series of forced treaties displaced the native population from arable agricultural lands and intensified land occupation by Europeans. "By 1930, some 60,000 Africans had been forced to move from lands that had been reserved for white settlers" (Smaldone 1979, 26). The rest is a history of pogrom as is the case in many episodes of the history of Europe and Africa. Zambia became an independent republic on October 24, 1964, with its capital at Lusaka.

11.4 LUSAKA: THE CAPITAL OF ZAMBIA

Lusaka is a colonial city that originally grew along a railway line. In 1931, it adopted the role of capital city of Northern Rhodesia, the colonial name for Zambia. Colonialism and treasure-hunting played major roles in this development. As Geoffrey Williams (1986, 72) puts it, "The location of Lusaka was determined by the need to establish sidings at 20 mile (32 km) intervals along the single-track railway which had crossed the Zambezi River at the Victoria Falls in 1905 heading for the Broken Hill mine" (Fig. 11.3). An indigenous village in the region was moved to accommodate the railway station, and then the station adopted the name of that village, Lusaka. European settlement in the region increased because Europeans were able to obtain land below market value or at no cost.

Farm settlements grew around the city. Father Torrend, a Jesuit priest, appears to have been in the midst of European settlement, founding Kasisi Mission northeast of Lusaka in February 1906, while Mr. J. J. Geldenhuys occupied the first European farm in November of the same year. Industry began to move in, and the town started to grow. By 1913, a village management board was established, along with an administrative area that extended 1 mi^2 around the railway siding and was subsequently enlarged in 1916. Several debates as to the suitability of the area as a government center for new settlers followed the 1913 regulation of the town. In fact, veterinary facilities, medical facilities, and administrative buildings erected in the new town were considered temporary until 1931 when other major government infrastructures were constructed there following the amalgamation of northwestern and northeastern Rhodesia. "In July 1913, after two years of debate and study, the Colonial Government took the decision to build a new capital city on the wooded ridge which runs from two to six km south-east of the old town of Lusaka" (Collins 1986, 95).

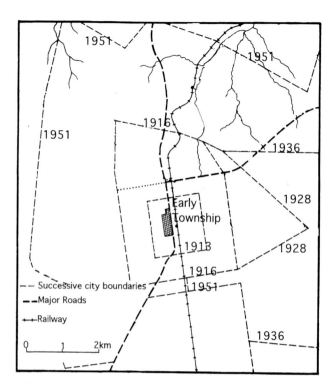

Fig. 11.3 Lusaka, Zambia. City development from 1913 to 1951. (Gabriel Okafor)

Fig. 11.5 Zambia. Attala House. (Julian Elliott)

From then on, the city was configured on a grid plan that spread out to the rest of the environs. Early European architecture in the city reflected its history. The British South Africa Company built Charter House as its corporate headquarters in Lusaka during the early years of its founding. This Renaissance building clearly exhibits its origin with four neoclassical columns. The material is mostly red brick fashioned by skilled masons. The State House (Fig. 11.4) was executed in the same manner, except for the raised concrete base.

This predominance of traditional Western style was to change in later years when European architects who were born and raised in Africa began to respond to the unique nature of the African environment. They held a sincere desire to find meaning and understanding in the African environment itself and to respond to it with a consciousness of the

Fig. 11.4 Lusaka, Zambia. The State House. (American Geographical Society Collection, The University of Wisconsin-Milwaukee Library)

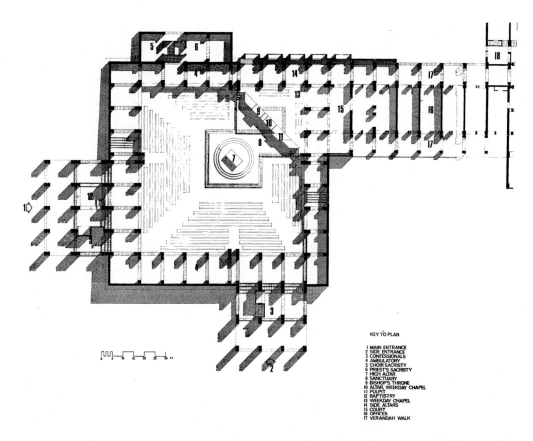

Fig. 11.6 Zambia. Plan of Kasama Cathedral.

(Julian Elliott)

Fig. 11.7 (Below) Zambia. Kasama Cathedral.

(Julian Elliott)

KEY TO PLAN

1 MAIN ENTRANCE
2 SIDE ENTRANCE
3 CONFESSIONALS
4 AMBULATORY
5 CHOIR SACRISTY
6 PRIEST'S SACRISTY
7 HIGH ALTAR
8 SANCTUARY
9 BISHOP'S THRONE
10 ALTAR, WEEKDAY CHAPEL
11 PULPIT
12 BAPTISTRY
13 WEEKDAY CHAPEL
14 SIDE ALTARS
15 COURT
16 OFFICES
17 VERANDAH WALK

fact that African architecture had not had the opportunity to grow, or flow through synthesis of study, evolutionary development, and refinement as its European counterpart.

Foremost among this group of architects is Professor Julian Elliott who is currently at the University of Cape Town. His works in Zambia and other parts of the South African region demonstrate that African architecture has a place in the modern world.

Arabisance in North Africa was a mechanism by which the Europeans appeased and made gestures to their colonies in

Fig. 11.8 *(Top) Zambia.*
Interior of Kasama Cathedral.
(Julian Elliott)

Fig. C.38 *Lusaka, Zambia.*
Kasama Cathedral. 1964.
(Julian Elliott)

*Fig. 11.9 Zambia. Plan of the
Pilcher House. (Julian Elliott)*

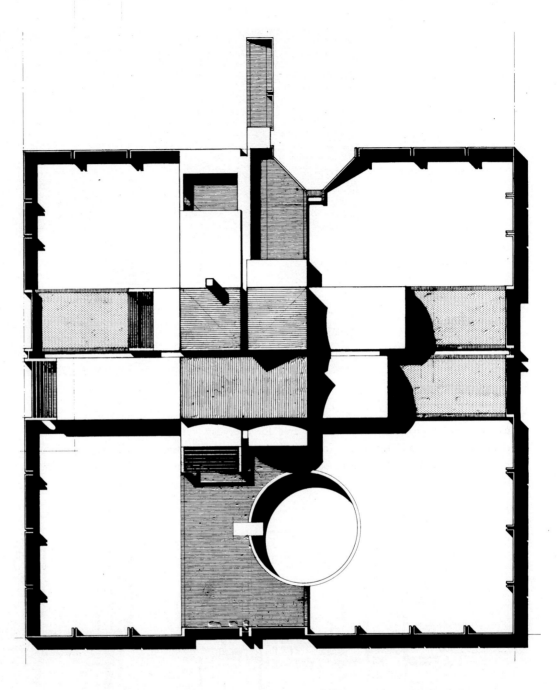

that region. Due to colonial chauvinism, no similar artistic synthesis was implemented in sub-Saharan Africa. It is not that a pure African form will be or could have been evolved through these studies and applications because there is nothing like pure form, just as there is no pure European, pure Chinese, or pure any form of architecture. Rather, as with other forms of architecture which evolve out of need and different stages of hybridization to meet contemporary needs, traditional African architecture could also evolve to meet contemporary needs if put into use by trained architects

instead of being abandoned as obsolete relics of native incompetence and primitiveness.

Julian Elliott executed several projects that tried to adapt to the African architectural repertoire. These creations of a roof-dominated architecture can be seen in several works, the most notable being the Attala House of 1960 and Kasama Cathedral of 1965, both in Zambia (Figs. 11.5 to 11.10 and C.38). Professor Elliott's work was further influenced by the ruins of Great Zimbabwe where he learned the functions of indoor and outdoor courtyards within large walls. The walled

Fig. 11.10 Zambia. Allen House. (Julian Elliott)

Fig. 11.11 (Below) Lusaka, Zambia. University of Zambia: (1) library, (2) assembly hall, (3) forum, (4) education, (5) African studies, (6) administration, (7) humanities, (8) natural sciences, (9) medicine, (10) residences, (11) student center, (12) book shop, (13) dining halls, (14) conference center, (15) car parking. (Julian Elliott)

external spaces provide an appropriate area for everyday domestic activities and also an environment that satisfies the intuitive demand for order and repose in a measurable setting. This fortress parti was adopted in the design of the University of Zambia in 1964 (Fig. 11.11). Here, the library, assembly hall, and student union form the core of the campus, and all the other structures symbolically create open spaces around them like enclosure walls.

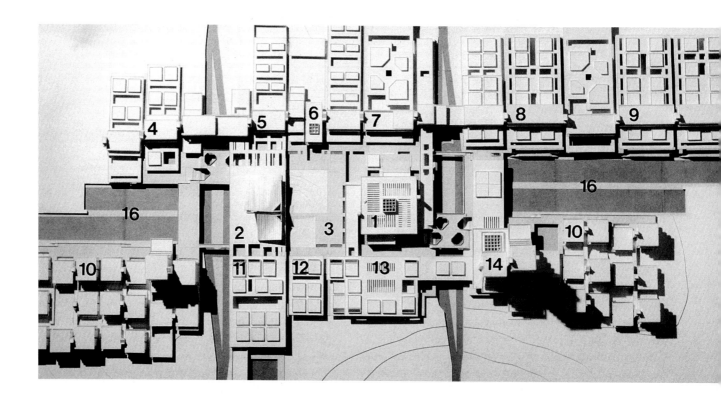

11.5 ZIMBABWE

Zimbabwe, formerly Rhodesia, finally achieved official independence in 1980 after several years of guerilla warfare waged by the disenfranchised African majority. Today, the country is one of the success stories of Africa, with the unification and national reconciliation between the black population of 8 million and the white population of 15,000. Zimbabwe is peopled by the descendants of the Shona civilization, a Bantu-speaking group that migrated from the north before the 10th century. The subgroups within the Shona civilization include the Kalanga, Karanga, Zeruru, Korekore, Manyika, and Ndau. The Shona civilization was headquartered at Great Zimbabwe. Other dynasties that once reigned in the region include the Munhumutapa dynasty and the Changamire dynasty. The Munhumutapa, shortened to Mutapa, and the Rozvi dynasties also evolved from the Great Zimbabwe culture. The Shona civilization extended from the interior area of the Kalahari Desert to the East coast of Africa in present-day Mozambique.

Great Zimbabwe's 12 clusters of stone structures, covering more than 40 ha on the top of a granite bluff and in the adjacent valley, housed a large population as well as the royal court, markets, warehouses, and religious shrines. European treasure-seekers in the 16th century later considered the structures imports from the Arab world or India. Some guessed that they were parts of King Solomon's gold mine.

The number of major stone ruins found in the South African region is substantial, although they are unevenly distributed: "There are over 600 listed stone ruins in Zimbabwe alone, between the Zambezi and Limpopo rivers, and nearly 7,500 further ruins have now been identified in northern areas of South Africa" (Mallows 1984, 5). Some of these ruins are very recent, but many others may be as old as 2000 years.

11.6 THE ARCHITECTURE OF GREAT ZIMBABWE

Great Zimbabwe is a group of fortress complexes located both on a hill and at the foot of the hill (Fig. 11.12). The hilltop complex, which dates from the 9th century, was called the acropolis of Africa by early European explorers. Its location provided a good defense for its inhabitants against enemy attacks. The choice of the site was probably due to abundant gold reserves in the region, good agricultural land, and surplus building materials, mainly granite. One major element in the construction of Zimbabwe is the huge walls. "Blocks were laid without mortar to make walls from 4–17 ft thick, whose height was about double their thickness" (Garlake 1973, 16).

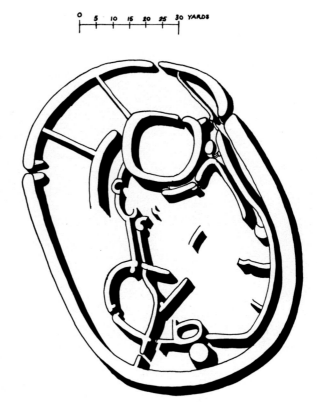

Fig. 11.12 *Zimbabwe. Plan of Great Zimbabwe.* (Julian Elliott)

Certain walls were skillfully decorated at the top edge with a chevron border and herringbone patterns. Some had evenly spaced ramparts (Figs. 11.13 and 11.14).

The most prominent structure at the Great Zimbabwe complex (Fig. C.39) is the Elliptical Building, which is identified by different names depending on the author. The Karanga ethnic group, whose ancestors built the structure, called it Mumbahuru, meaning "the house of the great woman," while the English called it the Temple. "The outer wall of this building, over 800 ft long and, at its greatest, 17 ft thick and 32 ft high, forms an irregular ellipse with a maximum diameter of 292 ft" (Garlake 1973, 27). An inner enclosure wall surrounded some houses on the southeast side of the wall. The focus of the entire building is the 18-ft-wide by 30-ft-high conical tower (Fig. 11.15). The Elliptical Building is surrounded by several building complexes and enclosures around the foot of the hill.

This architecture at Great Zimbabwe is unique in the world. While the regular coursed blocks suggest an offshoot from brick architecture, the absence of mortar, the irregularity of the walls, and the distinctive composition confirm that Great Zimbabwe is an indigenous response to a local building problem. Lack of mortar in the masonry work in spite of the

Fig. 11.13 (Above) Zimbabwe. The Elliptical Building of Great Zimbabwe. *(American Geographical Society Collection, The University of Wisconsin-Milwaukee Library)*

Fig. 11.14 (Right) Zimbabwe. Wall of Great Zimbabwe with ramparts. *(American Geographical Society Collection, The University of Wisconsin-Milwaukee Library)*

Fig. 11.15 (Opposite) Zimbabwe. The conical tower that forms the locus of the Elliptical Building at Great Zimbabwe. *(American Geographical Society Collection, The University of Wisconsin-Milwaukee Library)*

Fig. C.39 Zimbabwe. Aerial view of the acropolis. By architect Julian Elliott. (Julian Elliott)

abundance of clay materials that could have served that purpose indicates that Zimbabwe had not been influenced by Arabs whose buildings on the East African coast are very symmetrical and rigid.

A picture of the layout of the traditional African house has started to emerge. At Great Zimbabwe, the Elliptical Building was not designed as an object; rather, it was constructed as part of the natural landscape. The conical tower was not made to dominate the landscape but to fit into it. The hill provided protection as a fortress, but it did not isolate the building from its surroundings. In other words, the walls saved the people from enemies, formed an outdoor living space (kgotla), became part of the storage place for food and livestock,

served as a garden, formed a major enclosure for a house that provided privacy for individuals and families, and above all, formed a bridge or a gate between the built environment and the natural environment which still dominate and control the surroundings. The African house does not impose, but rather it finds a niche, a place for itself in recognition of the supremacy of the earth, the eternal and everlasting, that bears all fruits and takes all back when it wishes. The earth outlives all no matter what. It is there before a building rises, and it will be there long after the building is gone.

Moreover, the house is venerated in reverence to the ancestors. The compound or kgotla is a place where the descendants are called upon in constant communion with

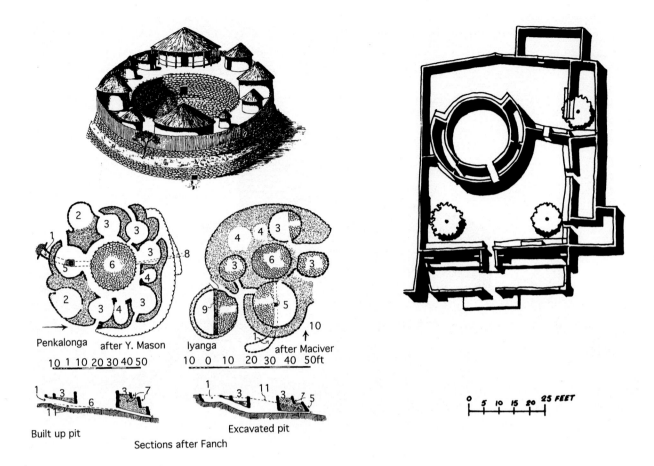

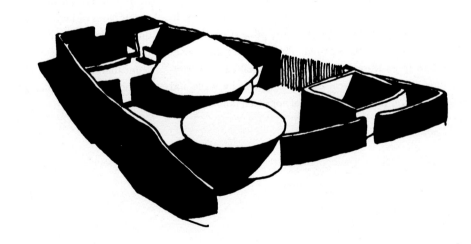

Fig. 11.16 (Above, left)
Zimbabwe. Pit Circles:
(1) tunnel entrance, (2) hut
mound, (3) hut, (4) store,
(5) shaft hut, (6) pit,
(7) revetment, (8) drain,
(9) mud wall hut, (10) ground
slope, (11) original ground
level.

Fig. 11.17 (Above, right)
Zimbabwe. Plan of a Ndebele
house. (Julian Elliott)

Fig. 11.18 (Right)
Zimbabwe. Sketch of a
Ndebele house. (Julian Elliott)

one another and with the ancestors. This is done in the name of, and for the sake of, the ancestors and everything they represent: oneness in blood, protection, good spirits, and mediation as spirits that have passed from the mortal world to the omniscient immortal world between the individual and the Almighty God. This calls for the presence of an ancestral shrine in every compound. Hence, the ancestral compound is by all accounts a spiritual institution no different from a

Fig. C.40 Bulawayo, Zimbabwe. Pentecostal church. *(David Hughes Photos)*

church or temple. Rather than going from separate and individual homes on specific days to a special place for worship and communion, daily living is itself the process of communion in the ancestral compound. Finally, Ndebele houses (Figs. 11.16 to 11.18) exhibit these communal and security-conscious designs with great clarity, amplified by walls and controlled entrances. This traditional approach differs greatly from the European urban designs found in Zimbabwe's major cities of Harare and Bulawayo. The application of traditional design concepts to modern buildings such as the Bulawayo Pentecostal church (Fig. C.40) underscores the point that traditional African architecture has a place in contemporary building design.

chapter

THE ARCHITECTURE OF THE REPUBLIC OF SOUTH AFRICA

To write about the Republic of South Africa one has to make a leap of faith that goes beyond the moment and looks to the future with optimism and the restoration of faith in humankind. This approach does not advocate ignoring problems of the Republic of South Africa. Rather it recognizes the enormous sociopolitical problems that face the country and believes that they will be resolved to the benefit of all concerned and humanity at large. The history of the Republic of South Africa cannot be discussed without looking at these problems because of the close ties of its economics, sociopolitical attributes, and architecture, the latter of which is largely reflected in settlement patterns and urban landscape. South African architecture will probably experience a period of construction boom as the government of the new South Africa under Nelson Mandela tries to provide housing and social infrastructures such as schools and hospitals for the whole population. There will be temptations to arrive at quick design solutions to meet political needs, but South African architects should exploit the traditional precedents around them and not let political expedience guide their design concepts.

The architecture of South Africa, as mentioned previously, draws more on European building style than any other. Islam ended its journey toward the Cape at Malawi; hence, there are fewer Muslims in this part of the continent and very few structures that reflect Islamic building designs. This does not imply that there are no Muslims in South Africa; rather, it signifies how little Islamic influence is in the region compared to North, East, or West Africa. The traditional architecture of the Republic of South Africa should not be isolated from the traditional architecture of Zimbabwe. For example, in Lesotho, South Africa, the conical beehive roof with a cylindrical structure made from pliable materials takes on a new expression to meet contemporary needs (Figs. 12.1, C.41, and C.42). Similar structures can be found in Swaziland, while both the conical beehive and the cone are readily seen in traditional Zulu kraals (Figs. 12.2 and 12.3). A significant element of traditional South African architecture is the mural paintings on the walls. The Ndebele excel in creating these paintings. Their houses radiate bright colors in images derived

215

Fig. 12.1 Lesotho, Republic of South Africa. Traditional
architecture. *(American Geographical Society Collection, The University*
of Wisconsin-Milwaukee Library)

Fig. 12.2 Swaziland, Republic of South Africa. Traditional
architecture. *(American Geographical Society Collection, The University*
of Wisconsin-Milwaukee Library)

Fig. C.41 Lesotho, South Africa. Traditional architecture
with modern material. Beehive type. *(American Geographical*
Society Collection, The University of Wisconsin-Milwaukee Library)

Fig. C.42 Roma, Lesotho, South Africa. Chapel of the
University of Lesotho. *(David Hughes Photos)*

Fig. C.43 South Africa. Traditional Ndebele architecture.
(American Geographical Society Collection, The University of Wisconsin-
Milwaukee Library)

Fig. 12.3 Republic of South Africa. Traditional architecture of the Zulu: the beehive type with modern material. (American Geographical Society Collection, The University of Wisconsin-Milwaukee Library)

Fig. C.44 (Below) Cape Town, South Africa. Entrance to Elliott's house in traditional form. (Julian Elliott)

from their surroundings and living patterns, including designs taken from blankets, tiles, alphabets, and traditional birds (Fig. C.43).

It is useful to take a look at the evolution of the traditional South African house from this point. The need to balance a nomadic life in which cattle symbolize wealth led to the creation of an outdoor room encircling the living space. The outdoor living space was shared by residents and cattle. Gradually, two separate outdoor spaces evolved: one for the people and another for animals and agricultural products. The outdoor space also became more specialized in meeting residents' needs.

It is noted in Chapter 11 that the fundamental parti of kgotla evolved from the intrinsic need and desire of the people to be together. The labyrinth of the village plan in the South African region evolved from similar needs. This village labyrinth has contemporary validity for Wilhelm O. Meyer, a Johannesburg-based architect, whose works we discussed in Part 1. Two main themes emerge in Meyer's work: the search for a strong geometric form on a fairly monumental scale and the attempt to capture the "genus loci." The Verwoerdburg urban plan, executed in South Africa in 1979, expresses Meyer's philosophy in a concrete format. This philosophy has also been pointed out in the distinctive works of Professor Julian Elliott (Figs. 12.4, and 12.5; C.44). These projects have demonstrated that the past does have a place in the future and that vernacular architecture is a model that should not be forgotten.

Fig. 12.4 Cape Town, Republic of South Africa. Lower floor plan, Elliott's house. (Julian Elliott)

Fig. 12.5 Cape Town, Republic of South Africa. Upper floor plan, Elliott's house. (Julian Elliott)

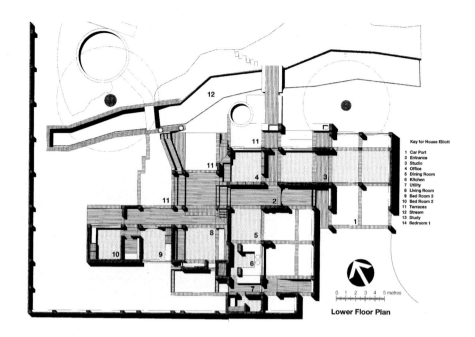

Key for House Elliott

1 Car Port
2 Entrance
3 Studio
4 Office
5 Dining Room
6 Kitchen
7 Utility
8 Living Room
9 Bed Room 3
10 Bed Room 2
11 Terraces
12 Stream
13 Study
14 Bedroom 1

0 1 2 3 4 5 metres

Lower Floor Plan

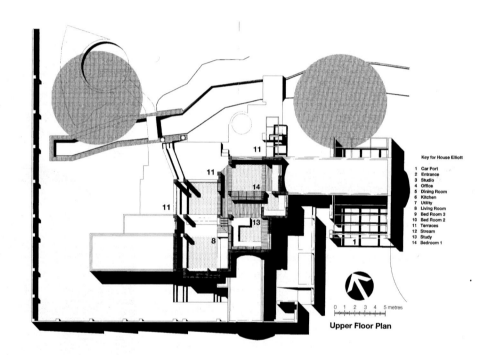

Key for House Elliott

1 Car Port
2 Entrance
3 Studio
4 Office
5 Dining Room
6 Kitchen
7 Utility
8 Living Room
9 Bed Room 3
10 Bed Room 2
11 Terraces
12 Stream
13 Study
14 Bedroom 1

0 1 2 3 4 5 metres

Upper Floor Plan

12.1 PRETORIA: THE CAPITAL OF THE REPUBLIC OF SOUTH AFRICA

As a national capital, Pretoria truly symbolizes the ambivalent and exclusive politics that threatened South Africa's existence as a republic. Formally incorporated into a city on November 16, 1855, "the new town was laid out upon the farmlands of President Martinus Pretorius and in 1857 Andries François du Toit surveyed the place" (Picton-Seymour 1977, 273). Originally founded by a group of Voortrekkers who had migrated to the Transvaal to escape British domination of the Cape colony, Pretoria was formally declared the capital of

Fig. C.45 Pretoria, Republic of South Africa. Skyline. (American Geographical Society Collection, The University of Wisconsin-Milwaukee Library)

Transvaal in 1860. The discovery of gold at Berberton, Lydenburg, and Witwatersrand gave the city and the republic great sums of wealth in the late 1800s, and the Transvaal republic then embarked on large building schemes that rivaled their counterparts in Europe.

The grand design and the economic boom that followed the reconciliation of the Boer and English communities in 1910 ignored the majority of citizens by official policy. Herbert Baker, the grand architect of major government buildings in the city of Pretoria, therefore excluded the majority of South African citizens from his plans. "South Africa's nonwhite population figured only peripherally in Baker's imperial vision, typified by an unexecuted design

for..." (Vale 1992, 69) a partly open, small place for native meetings.

Pretoria is located at the foot of a hill (Fig. C.45). In 1910, Herbert Baker chose the near top of this hill for the location of the Grand Union Building, with a temple in the background. The main facade of the Union Building is a neoclassical, semicircular arcade flanked by a colonnade of twin classical columns. This building of the Edwardian era was influenced by the works of Christopher Wren. As Vale (1992, 69) puts it, "Surely the strong influence of Sir Christopher Wren in the design left little doubt, at least among the architecturally initiated, about Baker's own cultural affiliations." An amphitheater, a pool, tubs with shrubs, spires, and a rotunda

Fig. 12.6 (Above) Pretoria,
Republic of South Africa. The
Union Buildings. (American
Geographical Society Collection, The
University of Wisconsin-Milwaukee
Library)

Fig. 12.7 (Left) Pretoria,
Republic of South Africa. The
city hall. (American Geographical
Society Collection, The University of
Wisconsin-Milwaukee Library)

Fig. 12.8 (Opposite) Pretoria,
Republic of South Africa. The
Administrative Building of the
University of Pretoria.
Designed by Brian Sandrock.
1969. (American Geographical
Society Collection, The University of
Wisconsin-Milwaukee Library)

landscaped the foreground of the semicircular facade (Fig. 12.6). The two wings of the building bind the semicircular arcade on either end. It was Baker's idealistic way of symbolizing democracy and, especially, the equality of the two races. "Baker claimed that his design symbolized the reconciliation of the two races of South Africa on equal terms, by which he meant, of course, not whites and blacks, but Boer and Briton" (Vale 1992, 69).

The city hall is another building (Fig. 12.7) with characteristics from many European architectural sources. It is highly influenced by Germanic and Dutch building traditions, but its fundamental parti is rooted in neoclassicism. The Raadsaal Province Administrative Headquarters in Church Square is a Renaissance-style building with magnificent stonework. The Transvaal Museum Building, on the other hand, was influenced by German neoclassicism, with a facade reminiscent of those in the homelands of some of the settler immigrants. From the middle to later 20th century, buildings reflect the modern movement, using strong modern symbolism. Topping the list of such modern symbolic buildings is the University of Pretoria Administrative Building (Fig. 12.8)

designed by Sandrock. This vast, four-story building echoes the feeling and imagery of early 1920s modernism with a strong Bauhaus influence. In this project, Sandrock was strongly influenced by the industrial age metaphors of Walter Gropius.

12.2 CAPE TOWN

Due to its strategic location between the Atlantic Ocean and the Indian Ocean, Cape Town is the oldest European town in the Republic of South Africa (Figs. 12.9 and 12.10). The Portuguese were the first Europeans to sail around the Cape in search of a trade route to India. A fortified castle built in 1666 is a reminder of early Portuguese activities in the region. The building now stands in the heart of the city, a symbol of Portuguese expansionism and its ambitious plan to control the maritime trade of the world in the 17th century. Like some of its predecessors along the West African coast, this castle in Cape Town was designed for internal fortification and self-sustenance. The walls and the surround-

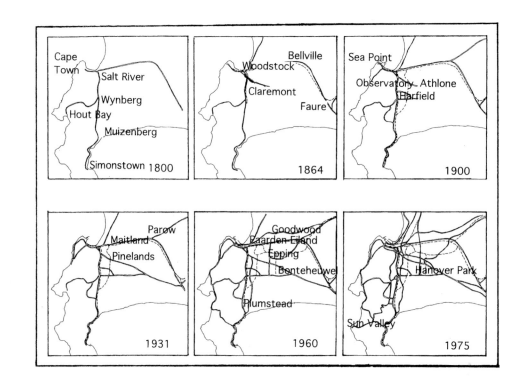

ings were manned with cannons ready to fire at intruders (Fig. 12.11).

A large influx of European immigrants—mainly Dutch, English, and Germans—flowed into this region, reaching a peak from the late 1800s up to the early 1920s. This steady pattern of migration brought about two distinct trends of settlement and urbanization in Cape Town. According to Dewar et al. (1977, 17), "The one type which dominated the development of the city before 1920 is that of the evolutionary developed areas." These evolutionary developments resulted from industrial growth and growth of the infrastructure, as roads were built and municipal services established. Consequently, the settlements were linear in structure, mainly along the paths of major roads. Cape Town and its inclusive suburbs such as Salt River, Wynberg, Hout Bay, Muizeuberg, and Simonetown evolved in this manner. A close look at the Salt River-Woodstock urban plan shows settlement largely following the two major roads that cross the town longitudinally.

"The second structural type of development, which has dominated the growth of Cape Town subsequent to 1920, is planned development" (Dewar et al. 1977, 19). This more for-

mal approach was motivated by a huge influx of European immigrants into the region between World Wars I and II. The objective of comprehensive planning of the metropolis was to achieve a coherent distribution of urban population. The advent of the automobile meant that people could live further away from the center of the city but still be a part of it and also that the railroad no longer dominated transportation. The development of planning as a profession further enabled the authorities to formulate a unified planning policy mechanism for the region.

Architecture in Cape Town is rooted in a tradition of mixing the old with the new and the past with the future, whether in public monuments, private homes, or commercial establishments. The Cecil Rhodes Memorial Monument embodies this concept. The building is situated on a hill to evoke images of the Greco-Roman past and of the pure form, a term associated with several Western shrines of antiquity. However, the fundamental parti of the Rhodes Memorial can be traced to ancient architectural elements originally developed in Africa. The horses and lions lining either side of the steps are recycled versions of architectural concepts derived from the Avenue of the Sphinxes, built by Pharaoh

Fig. 12.12 Cape Town, Republic of South Africa. Master plan showing upper and lower campuses of the University of Cape Town.
(Julian Elliott)

Fig. C.46 (Opposite, top) Cape Town, Republic of South Africa. Rhodes Memorial Monument.
(American Geographical Society Collection, The University of Wisconsin-Milwaukee Library)

Fig. 12.13 (Opposite, bottom) Cape Town, Republic of South Africa. The original buildings of the University of Cape Town. Designed by Jim Solomon, 1918. (Julian Elliott)

Major Open Space
Major Buildings

Plan Showing Current Development on the Upper and Middle Campus

UNIVERSITY of
CAPE TOWN
PLANNING
UNIT
Date: April 1990

Nectanebo during the 30th Dynasty, connecting the Luxor Temple to the Temple of Karnak. Similar comparison can be made between the lions on the Rhodes Monument and the rams along the Avenue of the Rams, Temple of Amon, at Karnak (Figs. C.7 and C.46).

Scholars who believe in the African origin of Western civilization via Greece see the Rhodes Memorial as a recycled expression of African architecture because "the Greeks merely continued and developed, sometimes partially, what the

Egyptians had invented" (Diop 1974, 230). Professor Bernal (1987, 118) confirms that Plato, Pythagoras, and Orpheus took their technological, philosophical, political, religious, and architectural ideas from Egypt.

In the field of architecture, African technology was sent to Europe in several forms. For example, the obelisk that stands in the square of Saint John Lateran, Rome, was placed there in 1588 by Pope Sixtus V, but it was brought from Egypt by Emperor Constantine II who placed it in the Circus Maximus

culture or sacred architecture because cultural exchange has been taking place between Africa and the West and between Africa and the East since ancient times. The Rhodes Monument was designed to implant a pure European heritage in a newly settled territory, while commemorating the achievements of a victorious colonialist, who removed "barbarians" and paved the road for "civilized people" to settle the land. The irony is that the civilized conquistadors unconsciously borrowed from the cultures of the barbarians to commemorate Rhodes's victory. Hence, the triple heritage has much broader implications because even Westerners adopt African traditions without thinking about or realizing it. One undeniable fact is the dominant Greco-Roman classical concept in the design of the Rhodes Memorial.

in 375 A.D. This cultural and technological dialogue continues to this day. History runs in cycles, just as the earth revolves around the sun and has different seasons. No nation can say that it has a monopoly on civilization and that it has a pure

There is a constructive lesson to be learned from this dialogue between classical African and European architectural concepts. It is the realization that European architecture has gone through several millennia of evolution without hesitat-

ing to borrow and experiment with foreign ideas, which it then accepts and proudly keeps as its own. Traditional African architecture has not had this opportunity since the end of classical times. It is paramount to approach traditional African architecture from a historical perspective, instead of using only tribalistic methods. The latter approach denies Africa its historical precedents and leaves almost nothing for the architect to work with. The importance of historical precedents in African architecture, therefore, must be emphasized because these precedents play the essential role of guiding the architect through the past in order to navigate back to the unexplored avenues of the present and the future.

Fig. C.47 (Opposite, top) Belville, Western Cape, Republic of South Africa. Library at the University of Western Cape. Looking through gateway to the entrance concourse and future west campus. (Julian Elliott)

Fig. C.48 (Opposite, bottom) Belville, Western Cape, Republic of South Africa. The University of Western Cape. Library atrium with a circular ramp enclosure. 1988. (Julian Elliott)

Fig. C.49 (Above) Belville, Western Cape, Republic of South Africa. The University of Western Cape. View of library from the west. (Julian Elliott)

Fig. 12.14 (Right) Belville, Republic of South Africa. Library for the University of Western Cape: (1) central open space, (2) west entrance concourse, (3) gateways, (4) main library, (5) administration, (6) student union, (7) assembly hall. 1988. (Julian Elliott)

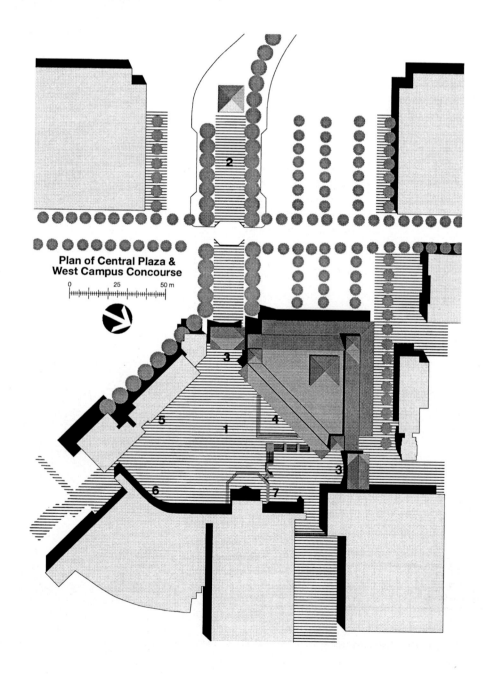

Plan of Central Plaza & West Campus Concourse

0   25   50 m

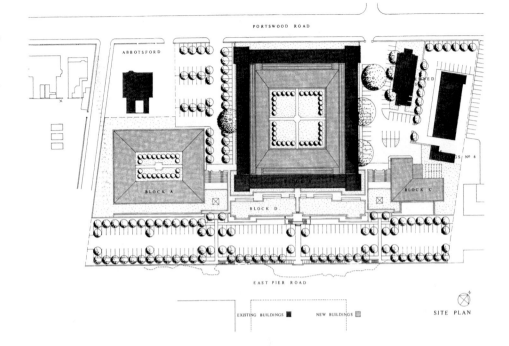

Fig. 12.15 Cape Town,
Republic of South Africa. Site
plan, Graduate School of
Business, University of Cape
Town. Revel, Fox & Partners.
1991. (Revel Fox & Partners)

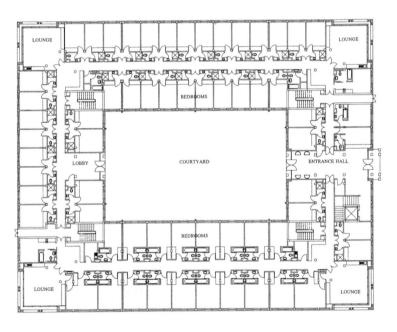

Fig. 12.16 Cape Town,
Republic of South Africa.
University of Cape Town,
Graduate School of Business,
ground floor plan. (Revel Fox &
Partners)

RESIDENCE BLOCK
BLOCK A GROUND FLOOR PLAN

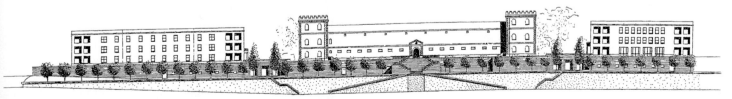

Fig. 12.17 Cape Town, Republic of South Africa. Graduate School of Business, east pier elevation. (Revel Fox & Partners)

Fig. C.50 Cape Town, Republic of South Africa. Graduate School of Business, University of Cape Town. 1991. (Revel Fox & Partners)

The other extreme of Western architecture in Cape Town is in its present-day expression, with its high-rise buildings, especially the mass produced low-cost housing projects. In Cape Town, the concepts of Mies van der Rohe provided the solution. In spite of the economic difficulties experienced by the country in the transition to democratic government, mass production based on beams and structural frame construction is convenient. Cape Town is a booming, growing commercial center for the Republic of South Africa. This fact is clearly reflected in the number of construction projects still going on in the city in both the private and public sectors. Moreover, the government of South Africa is expanding its educational infrastructures in anticipation of an influx of South Africans who have been denied access to higher education because of their ethnic background. This means an increase in the demand for infrastructure, such as the buildings in the expansion of the University of Cape Town (Figs. 12.12 and 12.13). In addition, works undertaken at the University of Western Cape are also in response to the anticipated influx of additional structures (Figs. 12.14 and C.47 to C.49). Julian Elliott and Grobbelaar, Revel Fox & Partners have been involved in such projects.

The decision to locate the Graduate School of Business of the University of Cape Town in and around the old Breakwater Prison was taken after the analysis of a number of alternative locations. The choice of The Breakwater Prison is regarded as beneficial to both the development program of the business school as well as to the overall develop-ment of the Victoria and Alfred Waterfront. The Breakwater Prison forms a significant element in the Portswood Ridge precinct, the second phase of development after the Pierhead precinct undertaken by the Victoria and Alfred Waterfront Company.

The use of The Breakwater Prison as the new accommo-dation for the Graduate School of Business is regarded as most suitable and appropriate. As opposed to other potential uses, for example, a hotel, the particular teaching approach of the business school allows the main structure to be main-tained intact. The fortresslike quality of the building, charac-terized by a dominant wall architecture with minimal open-ings, is thus preserved. The accompanying diagrams illustrate the plans (Figs. 12.15 to 12.17 and C.50).

12.3 DURBAN, PORT ELIZABETH, AND JOHANNESBURG

The architecture of Durban, Port Elizabeth, and Johannesburg could each fill a textbook of its own. Durban began its Western architectural history in 1497 with the arrival of Vasco da Gama on his way to India, although the city did not grow much until the middle of the 19th century. According to Picton-Seymour (1977, 233), "1840 was the year in which G. C. Cato laid out the original plan for the town-ship; this was known as the Dutch Survey." Several Victorian and Edwardian buildings were erected in the city from then

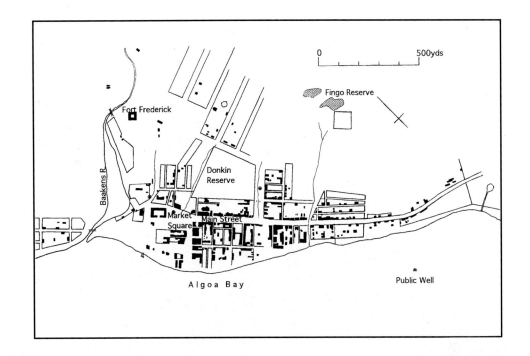

Fig. 12.18 (Opposite, top)
Durban, Republic of South
Africa. Town hall.
1903–1910. By Scott,
Woolocotti & Hudson.
(American Geographical Society
Collection, The University of
Wisconsin-Milwaukee Library)

Fig. C.51 (Opposite, bottom)
Durban, Republic of South
Africa. A Hindu temple.
(American Geographical Society
Collection, The University of
Wisconsin-Milwaukee Library)

Fig. 12.19 (Right) Port
Elizabeth, Republic of South
Africa. City plan. 1849.

Fig. C.52 (Below) Port
Elizabeth, Republic of South
Africa. Victorian terrace
houses on Donkin Street.

Fig. 12.20 (Above) Port Elizabeth, Republic of South Africa. City hall, Market Square. 1861. (American Geographical Society Collection, The University of Wisconsin-Milwaukee Library)

Fig. 12.21 Port Elizabeth, Republic of South Africa. Public library. 1901. (American Geographical Society Collection, The University of Wisconsin-Milwaukee Library)

Fig. 12.22 Johannesburg, Republic of South Africa. An impression of the early years.

Fig. 12.23 Johannesburg, Republic of South Africa. Market Square. Early years.

(Désirée Picton-Seymour)

Fig. 12.24 Johannesburg, Republic of South Africa. Saint Mary's Church. 1887.

(Désirée Picton-Seymour)

through the later years. The first city hall was built by the architect Dudgeon between 1881 and 1885 following an open competition. This early Renaissance city hall was surrounded by Corinthian columns, six of which held the pediment of the portico of the main entrance. By 1903, Durban was again inviting architects to submit designs for an even bigger and better city hall to be erected just across the square from the old town hall (Fig. 12.18). Scott, Woolocotti & Hudson of Johannesburg won the first prize. The building they designed

is crowned with a 48-m-high central dome. Smaller domes are stationed on each of the four corners. As in many South African cities, Durban architecture ranges from 19th-century Edwardian buildings to modern high-rise apartment complexes, as well as Hindu temples (Fig. C.51) as a reminder of the Indian population in the city and in South Africa as a whole.

Port Elizabeth presents less contrast with its Georgian Victorian-style architecture (Fig. 12.19). From the late 18th century, when the British constructed Fort Frederick to

Fig. 12.26 Johannesburg, Republic of South Africa. City hall. A Renaissance building. Designed by Hawke & McKinlay. 1910. (American Geographical Society Collection, The University of Wisconsin-Milwaukee Library)

defend their sea routes to the Orient and especially to keep the French away from the region, Port Elizabeth has favored European-style development and mirrored native settlements in the process. "After the erection of Fort Frederick but prior to the arrival of the 1810 settlers the small number of additional buildings which were constructed were mainly associated with the military" (Beavon 1970, 5). This military garrison grew into a sizable town by the mid-1850s following rapid settlements by European immigrants. Victorian terrace architecture, which is exemplified on Donkin Street, Donkin Reserve (Fig. C.52), was erected to serve this influx. These wooden houses were not built at the same time, but over a long period. The dominant material is wood, and the roofs descend the hill with broken, sharp edges in accordance with

Fig. 12.25 (Opposite) Johannesburg, Republic of South Africa. Skyline. (American Geographical Society Collection, The University of Wisconsin-Milwaukee Library)

the slope of the hill and distinguish the individual houses from one another. Each house has a balcony on the upper floor and two sashed windows on each floor. "Originally all the windows had twelve divisions in the Georgian tradition, but today many have been replaced by four larger panes" (Picton-Seymour 1977, 180). However, some of these houses are now preserved as a historic district.

The city hall of Port Elizabeth (Fig. 12.20) was built at the Market Square in 1861. This Renaissance building, with Corinthian columns, is symmetrically designed with two bays on either side of the main entrance. The clock tower was added in the 1880s. The Ritz Hall was built in the era of iron decorations; hence, its interior finishes are mostly with iron in the Victorian style. The highly ornate public library building was designed in the Flemish style by an English architect. It is a well-proportioned building, and the statue of Queen Victoria looking out across the city square unquestionably accentuates its Western legacy and impact on African triple heritage architecture (Fig. 12.21). In contrast, modern high-

Fig. 12.27 Johannesburg, Republic of South Africa. Middle-class house. *(American Geographical Society. The University of Wisconsin-Milwaukee Library)*

Fig. 12.28 Johannesburg, Republic of South Africa. Upper-class house. *(American Geographical Society. The University of Wisconsin-Milwaukee Library)*

Fig. C.53 (Opposite) Johannesburg, Republic of South Africa. IBM Headquarters. *(Arup Associates, London)*

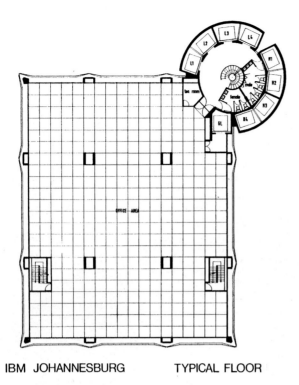

IBM JOHANNESBURG   TYPICAL FLOOR

*Fig. 12.29 Johannesburg, Republic of South Africa. Typical floor plan,
IBM Headquarters. (Arup Associates, 1976.)*

rise buildings dominate the central business district of the
city.

If San Francisco is the golden city of North America,
Johannesburg is the golden city of Africa. It, too, is a city that
grew out of a gold rush, in this instance in 1886 after George
Harrison, the first European to find gold in the area, had
announced his find to arriving European immigrants.
"Johannesburg came into being on 4 October 1886 when
President Krueger signed the proclamation of the form
Randjeslarte. Thus Johannesburg was created as a mining
town on proclaimed ground" (Picton-Seymour 1977, 302).
This tall city, with its huge, wide tracks of highways that
snake around its environs, still pays homage to its humble
beginning, the spot where the first European came across
some gold nuggets (Figs. 12.22 to 12.25). Several buildings
were built from 1886 onward as the population of the new
town grew rapidly. Twenty-four years after it was incorporated, the city needed a major city hall. Hawke and McKinlay
of Cape Town designed the building, and the foundation was
laid on November 29, 1910. This Renaissance building (Fig.
12.26) with its central dome and well-proportioned sides, heralds Baker's design for the Union Building in Pretoria. Later
public projects in the 20th century still invoke this neoclassical design. Private houses range from mansions, which of
course belong to Europeans, to medium income homes for
people of mixed ethnic heritage, to shanty towns for blacks,
the majority of the population (Figs. 12.27 and 12.28).
Regardless, Johannesburg is a major world metropolis,
though not as densely populated as Cairo or Lagos. Several
multinational corporate headquarters such as the IBM
Building (Figs. 12.29 and C.53) are located in the city. This
high-rise building is the epitome of a modern corporate
shrine, exemplified by height and grandeur.

5

WEST AFRICA:
THE SUDAN

13

THE ARCHITECTURE OF MAURITANIA, MALI, NIGER, AND CHAD

This historic architectural survey of African countries that began in Morocco completes its cycle in this part of the book. The focus of the discussion is Mauritania, Mali, Niger, Chad, Gambia, Guinea, Guinea Bissau, Senegal, Sierra Leone, Liberia, Cote d'Ivoire, Burkina Fasso, Ghana, Benin, Cameroon, Togo, Sao Tome and Principe, Equatorial Guinea, and Nigeria. The disputed territories of the western Sahara and its endless war are not discussed separately. This region, which has been at war with Morocco, has claimed the territory since the Spanish departed in the mid-1970s, a fact that has led to grave scarcity of information on the architecture of the region. The information on Morocco and Mauritania, however, should help in explaining the architecture of that territory.

The objective here is to establish and point out the forces that shaped the lives and the geopolitical history of West Africa before the second coming of Europeans to Africa via the Atlantic coast and of the Muslims via the Sahara Desert. The Sudanese style of architecture which dominates West Africa has been attributed to Islamic presence instead of indigenous genesis. It is therefore important to have a brief understanding of the history of the region to understand how its architecture has evolved. All of West Africa is also known as the Sudan, an Arabic name for "country of the blacks." This should not be confused with the Republic of Sudan, whose capital is Khartoum.

The current nations of West Africa are primarily the products of 19th- and 20th-century colonial imperialism; hence, it would be misleading to construct their history strictly on the geopolitical boundaries of today. This section reviews what the countries of this region have in common and how it affected their settlement patterns. The rise and fall of the major empires of the Sudan is very critical, especially in the case of Ghana, Mali, and Songhay. At their zenith, these empires were the paths and domains of cultural and intellectual exchange in West Africa. When Songhay, the last of the great empires, fell (1590 A.D.), several ministates developed in the Sudan and continued the process of cultural and intellectual exchange. A climate of uncertainty produced cultural hybrids that appear different, but essentially have common

roots. The cultural hybrids are reflected in language, traditional political structure, family structure, and architecture.

The region under discussion is immense (Fig. 13.1). "In all, it covers some 2.4 million square miles, or nearly five-sixths of the area of the United States. From its Western to its Eastern extremities the distance is some 1750 miles, nearly the same as between London and Moscow" (Mabogunje 1976, 1). The north-south distance of West Africa is over 1350 mi, nearly the distance from Oslo to Rome. Its location between the equator and the Tropic of Cancer keeps its temperature hot year round, with little variation. Unlike East and South Africa, where topological variation cooled the temperature and made it attractive for European settlement, West Africa has far fewer highlands, with the exception of the plateau where the year-round hot temperature is chilled yet still comfortable. This accounts for the sparse amount of European settlement in the region and explains their presence as purely economic and exploitative in nature. Hence, buildings were put up as temporary structures for commercial exploitation.

The people of West Africa can be classified into two major groups: the grassland zone people and the forest zone people. The grassland people inhabit the savanna and the regions with less rainfall. They tend to be brown in skin color and tall in stature. They include the Soninke, Malinke, Bambara, Mossi, Songhay, Hausa, and Kanuri. Some of these people speak Mande, for example, the Soninke, Malinke, and Bambara. The Ibos, Edo, Yoruba, Nupe, Fon, and Ashanti are all natives of the forest zone of West Africa. This zone has rainfall throughout the year. West Africa had great empires before the arrival of the Europeans in the 14th century and before the coming of the Arabs in the 7th and 9th centuries, including the Ghana empire, Mali empire, Songhay empire, Benin empire, the Hausa states, Oyo empire, and Bornu empire.

The area covered by each empire varied. The size and strength of these empires were partly influenced by local political events in the area and partly by external influences from the Mediterranean, especially the trade in gold and salt. Most of what is known about the Sudan before 1500 is from Arab scholars and traders. The earliest of the empires, Ghana, was already known in the Mediterranean and even in Baghdad as the Land of Gold. As Levtzion (1976, 114) points out, "The fame of Ghana reached beyond the Sahara, even as far as Baghdad," the original headquarters of the Islamic world. The 8th-century Arab writer al-Fazari, who lived in the court of the Abbassid caliph in Baghdad, may have been one of the principal authors of that fame.

To early Arab traders in Africa, Ghana was located in the Sahel, the shore of the huge sea of sand (Sahara Desert) in Bilad-al-Sudan, the land of the black peoples. The huge sea of sand was conquered by "the introduction of the camel into the Sahara, at the beginning of the Christian era" (Levtzion 1976, 114), causing a dynamic transport revolution in the area. Because of their limited ability to store water, horses and bullocks are not as well adapted to deserts as camels are. With the camel, the Berbers and the Sudanese in the south of the Sahara opened up a trade that brought gold to the north in exchange for salt.

The early inhabitants of the Sahara and North Africa were the ancestors of Africans who settled in the caves of the Fezzan and beyond before desiccation of the region began. The later arrival by Berbers and the Sanhaja nomads pushed these groups further south to settle in savanna and forest zones. Thus, while the Berbers fled southward from invading Romans in early Christian times, they pushed the savanna settlers and forest settlers further south. This was prior to the coming of Islam in the 7th century A.D. Once again, an imperial Western presence from the ancient times was established, and a new alien player was introduced into West Africa. Panikkar (1963, 22) states, "Slowly as various populations forced the population southward, a new element entered the desert. These were the desert nomads..." The ultimate outcome of such new migrations was the introduction of Islam into existing states in the region.

The seat of the triple heritage of African architecture in this area is in the Sudan, especially in Nigeria where the legacies of Westernization, Islamization, and yet indigenization and retention of tradition can be seen side by side. The origin of the Sudanese style of architecture which dominates the region remains an object of debate in academic circles. The myth of al-Sahili as the sole innovator of the architecture of the region has been disputed by scholars, including Prussin who suggests a Mandinka diaspora origin following the fall of the Ghana empire and several other empires in the region. Early descriptions of Ghana before the entrenchment of Islam and the fall of the empire indicate an urban center with a centralized government under a monarchy:

> The name of the country was Aukar and Ghana was the title of the king. The capital of the country consisted of two towns; the one inhabited by Muslims had twelve mosques and was very large....of stone and wood. The king's palace consisted of a castle and within an enclosure there were roofed huts....The king is adorned, as the women are with collars and bracelets; as head dress they wear several gilded bonnets, surrounded by very fine cotton clothes. When he gives audience to his people, to listen to their complaints and set them to right, he (the king) sits in a pavilion around which stand his horses caparisoned in cloth of gold; behind him stand ten pages holding shields and gold mounted swords; on his right are the sons of the princes of his empire, splendidly clad, and with gold plaited into their hair....At the death of the king, they build a large dome of wood which they place on the spot chosen for the grave, then they put near the dead man his ornaments, weapons, and the dishes and cups which he had used for his food and drink, and they shut up with him several of his cooks and drink-makers. The edifice is then covered with mats and clothes and all the crowd throws earth on the grave till it forms a large mound. They sacrifice victims to their dead and bring them inebriating drinks. (Panikkar 1963, 40)

Ghana was a gold mining country; all the nuggets belonged to the king. The people could take only the gold dust. Without that precaution, gold would have become so plentiful that it would have had practically no value.

This description of Ghana helps us establish when Islam became part of the triple heritage equation in West Africa. The mention of 12 mosques by al-Bakri indicates that Islam was already present in the region before the arrival of the Arab writers and gold-seekers. The exact date Islam entered the Sudan, particularly Ghana, is not known. The evidence that exists is paltry and often contradictory. The only approach is to take whatever pieces of evidence there are, put them together like a puzzle, and begin to interpret them based on what is known of the general history of North Africa, the Sahara, and the western and central Sudan from the 7th century to 1076 A.D. By that date it is known that an Islamic presence was definitely established in Ghana. Some scholars strongly propose that Islam may have begun its journey into West Africa soon after the Muslims conquered Egypt in 640 A.D. These scholars base their argument on the writings of Arab traders. While the authors give no specific date or confirmation of this proposal, Haskett (1984, 21) is of the opinion that "the total effect of all the comments and observations by the Arabic authors who wrote about the Sudan during this period is to leave one convinced that Islam did begin to make an impact there almost as soon as the Muslims conquered Egypt, let alone North Africa."

Further evidence of early Arab arrival is the fact that the detailed description of the burial practice highlights a much older practice of royalty burial from ancient Egypt, one not practiced in the Arabian countries. Al-Bakri would not have written about it as a different culture if such a burial custom were practiced in the Arabian gulf.

The impact of Islam on the indigenous art of the West African people has often been looked at from the orthodox viewpoint, which clearly indicates that Islam does not condone any form of idols and absolutely abhors pictorial imagery. The description of Ghana quoted earlier suggests a tolerance of indigenous culture and respect for the king and his people. Bravemann (1974, 28) believes that Islam has survived and prospered in West Africa because of its ability to adapt to the indigenous culture while trying to maintain its orthodox beliefs. This has made it easy for the people of West Africa to accept the religion with open arms, and it clearly means that traditional artforms survive and are easily inculcated into the Islamic religion by the believers. Hence, Islamization in West Africa is a two-way process: the process of religious indoctrination and the process of cultural adaptation of the religion to its new surroundings. This explains why several mosques and buildings for Islamic activities in West Africa are highly West Africanized in the indigenous style.

The syncretic nature of Islam in West Africa made it attractive to the elite of the region because it was no longer a threat to their status. Instead, it was lucrative socially and commercially. In this case, Mali empire and the glamorous, extravagant prince, Mansa Musa, must be mentioned as an example of an individual who used Islam to advance his social status around the world. The significance of Mansa Musa lies in his continuation of the tradition of the pilgrimage to Mecca by his predecessors. However, his trip marked the high point of the ancient Mali empire. "So great was his fame that his portrait figures on an early European map of West Africa, the Catalan Map of A.D. 1375. Here he sits in majesty, apparently presiding over the whole Sahara" (Haskett 1984, 29). The pilgrimage he made to Mecca in 1324 took his fame and wealth beyond Cairo and the shores of the Mediterranean to the heart of Europe, identifying his kingdom as the Land of Gold. This knowledge fueled the Portuguese desire to reach the Gold Coast in later years. Fernand Brandel explains: "Thus [Sudanic] gold played its part in the history of the Mediterranean as a whole, entering general circulation from the fourteenth century, perhaps after the spectacular pilgrimage to Mecca of Mansa Musa, King of Mali, in 1324" (Haskett 1984, 30). The major point in this discussion is that an Islamic pilgrimage by an African prince helped to create the conditions and circumstances that would later lead to the Westernization of the region. The Portuguese spearheaded the second phase of European intrusions in Africa in 1364, while the Romans were the initiators of Westernization of Africa in 146 B.C. However, it is important to look into what

made Mansa Musa's pilgrimage so special, famous, and significant to the process of Westernization in Africa.

First is the hypothesis that the Sudanese style of architecture came to the region with Mansa Musa upon his return from Mecca. This hypothesis is attributed to Abu Ishaq al-Sahili, an Andalusian poet turned architect, who accompanied Mansa Musa on his journey from Mecca. Ibin Khaldun, an Arab historian, was the perpetuator of this story. He said that the sultan, Mansa Musa, wanted an audience hall that was built and plastered because such things were not available in the country. Abd Ishak and Touedjin, the sultan's company from Mecca, built a square hall, surmounted by a cupola. The entire structure was plastered and ornamented in Arabesque style. The sultan was so impressed that he gave Touedjin 12,000 miguals of gold and a place in his court.

Delafosse, a French traveler in the region in the late 19th century, takes this story forward with the proposition that the mosques of Gao and Timbuktu were also built by these visitors. Leo Africanus, a 16th-century Arab merchant, makes reference to this Andalusian architect when he writes about his journey to Timbuktu between 1504 and 1505 A.D.: "the palace is not large, but of a very harmonious appearance; it was built nearly two centuries ago by an Andalusian architect known as Ishaq the Granadan" (Maalouf 1989, 169). However, no further detail was given about the palace, and other descriptions of Timbuktu by Africanus during his trip only confirmed stories about the wealth of the city and the generosity of its king. The Djenguere Ber Mosque has been identified and associated with the return of Mansa Musa from the *hajj* (pilgrimage to Mecca). It is suggested that "When Barth visited Tumbuctu in 1854, the inscription [Djenguere Ber—Songhay word for great mosque], while barely legible, was still in place" (Prussin 1986, 150). This mosque has been associated with the construction of an audience chamber for the returning emperor after a successful visit to Cairo, the center of the Western world during the Middle Ages. The commissioning date is believed to be 1324–1327 (Prussin 1986, 150). Caillie noted in 1864 that parts of the mosque were constructed with limestone and sun-dried bricks. He also noted the existence of vaulted arcades in dilapidated condition. However, it has been confirmed that the vaulted arcades to which Caillie referred were actually built of limestone, using true Roman arches. These vaulted limestone arches (rather than arcades) in the ancient ruins are unique to the West African architectural repertoire. It is possible that the arch and the dome of the Djenguere Ber Mosque are attempts to replicate North African mosque types, but this does not explain the uniqueness of the Sudanese architectural style as stemming from the genius of the visitors.

First, it is clear that Islam has been practiced in West Africa since shortly after the fall of Egypt to the Islamic movement in 640 A.D. The description of the empire of Ghana makes this succinctly clear. Al-Bakri states that "the capital of the country consisted of two towns; the one inhabited by Muslims had twelve mosques and was very large, while the King lives six miles away in a town called Al-Ghaba—the forest." This record was of ancient Ghana, and it does give a clue about the beginning of the twin city type of urbanization in West Africa: one city strictly for the king and his people; the other for the Muslims to practice their faith. According to Haskett (1984, 22), "Al-Batri tells of a city, built largely of stone and wood, not mud, divided into two quarters, a Muslim quarter and a quarter inhabited by the still polytheist Soninke." Aeradion (1989, 111) confirms that "long before the fourteenth century [when Mansa Musa visited Mecca], the pattern of twin cities was well-established whereby the Muslim traders were permitted to settle and trade maintaining their own life-styles on condition that they settle apart from royal town so as not to interfere with the traditional life-style." The major reason for the twin city was ancestor worship, which most of the African kings trusted more than they did Islam. However, they were tolerant of the Arab traders, and they let them live outside the royal cities to avoid religious and other cultural conflicts. It is also clear from historical documents that the first attack by an Islamic state against a West African state, Ghana, was by Morocco between 734 and 750 A.D. The attack was spearheaded by the Umayyads dynasty after they consolidated their power in Morocco.

The other dimension to Musa's visit to Mecca has to do with its overall significance and implications for the entire region. Mansa Musa's pilgrimage was made famous by the amount of gold he took with him and how he showered gifts on the royalty in Cairo and on other dignitaries along the way. There are various estimates of the amount of gold he took with him. By all accounts, it was enough to dazzle Egyptians, their Turkish Mameluke Sultan-Baybars, and the rest of the world, especially the European kingdoms. Ibn Khaldun, basing himself on Haj Tunis, the representative of Mali in Cairo, reports that he brought with him 80 loads of gold dust, each weighing 300 lb. The Masalik makes it 100 loads, and the Tarikh al-Fettah states that 40 mules were required to carry the gold. A moderate estimate would be that he had between 300–375 kg of gold powder.

The spirit of generosity espoused by Islam and a sincere need to perform the hajj as every pious Muslim would may have inspired Musa to give so much to the royalty and the poor, but he certainly had a hidden agenda of opening diplomatic channels and embassies with the world beyond his golden kingdom. The fabulous tales which he told the Easterners about his wealth and the extent of his kingdom would have taxed even the imagination of Baron von Munchausen. But due to his prodigality, the Careens readily believed all this. In his political objectives, Musa was extremely successful. Relations with Egypt were maintained, and he strengthened the bonds of Islam in his kingdom and the whole of the Sudan. With this in mind and the realization that Ethiopia had been surrounded and isolated from the Christian world in the 7th century, the foundations were laid for the second coming of the Western world into Africa. The unfinished business begun by Rome would be finished in a new way and on a massive scale that would have an adverse and lasting impact on the continent psychologically, historically, and economically. This time, the effects would be felt from Cairo to Cape Town. The simple laws of economics suggest that Musa's gold would have had him develop more wealth and construct his empire in accordance with the technology of his time. But this was not to be. Mansa Musa had gone on an economic campaign to advertise himself as the richest man in the world. His successful campaign was haunted by future events in Europe more than 100 years later.

England and France were embroiled in an endless war that threatened the whole economy of Europe and the stability of the region. "The long drawn-out war between France and England led to political instability which in turn resulted in monetary instability and a continuous devaluation of the currencies" (Panikkar 1963, 120). The French were desperate to fix their ailing economy. Jacques Coeur, a French financial expert of the time, advised the French monarchy to base its currency on gold like the Venetian ducat, which had remained stable regardless of the unrest in Europe. The Greek and Islamic nations consequently adopted the ducat. It was in these circumstances that a committee of experts met in Genoa, a city which was vitally interested in French currency and trade in 1447. Trade with the Arab world also drained the European gold supply. Both the spice trade from the Orient and the source of gold from Africa were in the control of the Arabs who charged high prices in gold for their supplies. Europe also feared being cut off from trade with the Arab world by a political error. All of these factors culminated in the European need to find a sea route to the Orient and a direct path to the heartland of gold in mysterious Africa. At this stage, the Europeans were ready to circumvent the Arabs to get to the sources of the gold and spices, and in so doing, they changed indelibly the direction of African history, first in West Africa.

13.1 MAURITANIA

Mauritania is a former French colony that became independent on November 28, 1960. Prior to that, Mauritania was

Fig. C.54 Oualata,
Mauritania. Courtyard of a
compound. Observe the
external stairs on the left and
the Arabic symbols of fertility.
(Jean-Louis Bourgeois and Carollee
Pelos—Spectacular Vernacular, The
Adobe Tradition 1989)

administered from Dakar, Senegal, as a member of the French Federation of West Africa. Modern Mauritania is not the same as the ancient Roman Mauritania Tingitana whose boundaries ended around the Draa River in the north. The land mass of Mauritania is large, but the population is extremely sparse because of the harsh landscape. For example, "Mauritania is larger than Nigeria [in area], yet the measure of the aridity of the former is its population of only 1,420,000 in 1976" (Church 1980, 234). Mauritania is a composite of many ethnic groups. The Neolithic people who inhabited this area, the Bafour as they are called by the Moors of today, are thought to have been the ancestors of Mauritania's Imraguen fishermen. It is believed that these African people gradually moved south as their once green valleys became desert. Regardless, Mauritania is still a composite of Berbers, Sanhaja nomads, and blacks. In French literature, Mauritanians are known as Maures (Moors) and are largely nomadic.

As nomads, the Moors move with the seasons in search of pasture for their cattle to feed upon. The landscape is dry, hot, sandy, and harsh, but the Moors have learned to live with these conditions. It is here in this landscape that the spirit of Islam and the nomadic life of the West African Sudan mix in a web of complex tradition that joins with ancestor heritage. In this case, ethnic lineage determines political loyalty to a large extent, and settlement is based along bloodline in extended family compounds. While the nomads and their livestock moved about in search of pasture, tent shelters were made within family circles. In addition, few settlements along the coast are permanent because of fishing grounds at the shore. A few settlements are in watered areas or oases in the desert.

Two types of traditional construction are found in Mauritania dictated by the desert climate and the livelihood of the people: the tent in its various types and adobe architecture made of clay. Like most Sudanic adobe buildings, the houses are highly colored, especially on the entrance and the inside. Because the clay material absorbs heat, it is a natural cooling mechanism and, therefore, most suited for local construction in the desert. Ancestor worship and the desire to build close to one's immediate blood relatives encourage the courtyard layout for compounds in Oualata (Fig. C.54). The courtyard is seen as an outdoor living space, and social activities take place there. Entrances and portals are carefully decorated with Islamic symbolism that reflects special meaning for the residents. Figure C.54, for instance, features arabesque symbols of fertility for the propagation of the ancestral lineage. The houses vary in height, but one and two stories are most common. Sometimes, though, three or more stories are utilized within a courtyard to house descendants of the same ancestor. This kind of architecture extends to the heartland of West Africa in various forms. However, from Khartoum in Sudan to the Hausa heartlands in Nigeria, the dry, hot days and cool nights have resulted in similar construction methods over this vast region. This is true in North Africa also, especially in Nubian Egypt.

13.2 CITIES OF MAURITANIA

Oualata is one of the oldest cities in the region. It is believed that Mansa Musa set out for his journey to Mecca from this city at the edge of the Sahara, the Atlantic Ocean, and North Africa. "Upon his return he commissioned an audience chamber at Oualata, and it was at Oualata that the Andalusian poet-architect resided" (Prussin 1986, 135). Oualata was a center of commercial and political activities for centuries before the encounter with Europeans.

In 1958, Nouakchott, the capital of Mauritania, was founded in anticipation of independence in 1960. By this time, French experimentation with urban design had reached a new climax following the proposal of Le Corbusier for a city of 3 million nearly 4 decades earlier. Nouakchott naturally followed the new urban design trend of its time on a limited scale due to financial constraint. The city was laid out in square grids, and government buildings were grouped in one area. The buildings are all in the modern style of the post-World War II era but with special treatment for the windows which are designed as shorters to minimize solar glare. A major disadvantage in the choice of material, concrete and brick, is that the buildings must be cooled by artificial mechanisms. The corrugated iron sheets utilized on the roofs were also problematic.

13.3 ETHNIC GROUPS AND HOUSE FORMS IN MALI

The Republic of Mali became independent from France in 1960. Its history reaches back long before becoming a French colony in 1892. In fact, most of the medieval empires of West Africa were centered in ancient Mali. Burial sites are some of the early architecture dating to the years of the empires. The tomb of Emperor Askia Muhammad, who reigned in 1493 when Islam was on the rise in western Sudan, is one of many medieval monuments scattered all over Mali. As a dedicated Muslim and as a tradition of the dynasty, the Askia went on a hajj. His tomb evokes images of the ziggurats found in Mesopotamia and the mastabas of Egypt. Often, the bodies of royalty were embalmed before they were laid to rest in peace, with most of their valuable belongings and slaves to equip them for the afterlife.

The Great Mosque of Jenne has surfaced as one of the monuments of the middle ages in the Sudan. The present mosque was not the first to stand on the site. "The present mosque is Jenne's third. Its first was probably built in the thirteenth century. Intense political drama marked the construction of its successors—the second mosque (built between 1834 and 1836) and the current one built between 1906 and 1907" (Bourgeois 1989, 127). The French have been conveniently credited as the architects and founders of the mosque, a subtle way of suggesting that Africans couldn't build such structures for themselves. The Great Mosque of Jenne is another victim of fabricated accounts designed, successfully until now, to obscure the real role of powerful political forces.

Davidson (1989, 128) mentions that "Jenne is the oldest known city in Sub-Saharan Africa. At a nearby site, Jenne-djenno (old Jenne) was established by the Third Century B.C., and had become a major urban center by about 850 A.D. The present city was founded between 800 and 1250 A.D." This early beginning is connected with the founding of the original mosque. Koi Konboro was the reigning king in Jenne in the 13th century, and he was also the first to become a Muslim, despite the fact that 25 predecessors were all ancestor worshipers. After his conversion, Koi Konboro demolished his palace to build a place of worship for God. This demolition marked the beginning of Jenne Mosque.

Islamic radicalism and conquest were often followed by mass destruction and internal dynastic struggles which erased records or ruins that would have been useful in reconstructing and understanding the design of the 13th-century Jenne Mosque. However, there are various accounts of its founding. Tarikh al-Soudan confirms that the first mosque at Jenne was built by Koi Konboro when he converted to Islam at the end of the 13th century. Unfortunately, he did not clearly describe the physical characteristics of the mosque. One of the early accounts of the structure of the mosque was from Caillie who visited Jenne in 1828. Caillie was obviously disappointed by what he saw: "There is at Jenne a large earthen mosque, dominated by two slight towers; it is crudely constructed, but very large; abandoned to the thousands of swallows who make their nest there...the infectious odor has led to the custom of performing prayer in a small exterior court" (Prussin 1986, 182).

Caillie may have observed correctly, but he was misled by the poor state of the mosque. Adobe architecture survives only if constantly replastered, especially after the rains; otherwise, a structure will dissolve. There is no doubt that it was a large mosque, as he had emphasized, but the lower towers may have been due to the several decades of abandonment. In those years, Sekou Amadou, the founder of the Peul empire of Mesina and who reigned from 1818 to 1843, pursued a fundamentalist Islamic policy and repressed the liberal version of Islam in practice at Jenne. Amadou feared that the neighborhood mosque of Jenne and Timbuktu would rouse anti-Peul domination, and he closed it down. Because Islamic law prohibits a Muslim from destroying a mosque, Amadou did not destroy the Jenne Mosque, and Caillie's accounts were no doubt influenced by the years of neglect which took place before he visited the region.

Felix Dubois, a French journalist who went to Jenne in about 1895, provided the next account. "He collected oral history about the mosque, examined its ruins, and suggested what the monument might have looked like" (see Fig. 13.2) (Davidson 1989, 133). From his observations and collections of oral history, Dubois concluded that the "long famous Mosque of Jenne is being considered more beautiful than the Kasbah of Mecca itself" (Dubois 1896, 154). He gave the dimensions of 183 ft (55–77 m) long by 39 ft high. He mentioned pylons and three groups of buttresses on each facade. The first group of pylons was about 32 ft (9.75 m) from the angle of the building, spaced 26 ft from each other. The orientation of the building facade in the direction of the cardinal points with the eastern part facing east, the direction of Mecca, was also clearly noted by Dubois. The sacredness of the eastern facade, emphasized by the lack of an opening and the enclosed adjacent courtyard, was precisely indicated as well. The marabouts (Islamic scholars) used the courtyard as a holy place for study and prayers. "With its ridged buttresses

alternating with pylons, and with no doors, no windows to break its uniform grandeur by a note of life, this eastern facade gave a very forcible impression of a mausoleum" (Dubois 1896, 156).

Finally, Dubois mentions the moat next to the mosque from which the clay material for its construction was obtained. Only wood and clay were used in its construction, in spite of the fact that it lasted eight centuries, and he blamed Amadou for ordering its destruction in 1830, about 60 years before he visited the city of Jenne." The mention of the sacred facade and the court indicates that the converted African monarch used special sections of the mosque as burial places, as a way of providing a link between ancestor worship and Islam. Prussin (1986) agrees with this view. In spite of this detailed account, Davidson (1989) suggests that Dubois's descriptions are problematic due to inconsistencies between the plan and the perspective sketch. In particular, Davidson singles out the fact that the buttresses at the corners of the perspective are absent in the plan; more important is the fact that Caillie's account may have influenced Dubois to underestimate the height of the mosque.

Another version of the history of Jenne Mosque states that Konboro's successor, Mahala Tanapo, who was not a believer but an ancestor worshiper, tore down the original mosque that Konboro built and put up another mosque on the west-

THE OLD MOSQUE RESTORED

Fig. 13.2 Jenne, Mali. Sketch of the original mosque built by Konboro. (Dubois, Greenwood Publishing, and Negro University Press)

Fig. C.55 Jenne, Mali. The Great Mosque. The projecting sticks are known as monkey-heads in ancient
Aksumite houses, Ethiopia. (Jean-Louis Bourgeois and Carollee Pelos—Spectacular Vernacular, The Adobe Tradition 1989)

ern site. This mosque was divided into two wings: one section for believers and the other for nonbelievers. This practice of having two sections was stopped by Askia Muhammad (1493–1528), successor of Emperor Sonny Ali (reigned 1464–1492), the man who tore the Tanapo Mosque down and built a new one. Both rulers used the eastern site as their official residence.

Another version of this story is that of the Moroccans, who supposedly destroyed Askia's Mosque and rebuilt Tanapo's Mosque. According to this, the Moroccan Mosque was too extravagant and unclean for Amadou who insisted on puritanical Islamization of the region and "in 1830, he removed its roof structure [the Moroccan Mosque] and had a more austere structure built on the site of the original Konboro Mosque" (Prussin 1986, 183). This gives irrevocable evidence that the present mosque was not the original mosque Konboro built.

Even in the absence of concrete evidence that the French had anything to do with the design or construction of the present mosque, it has been popularly advertised by scholars that the French did build it. One obvious fact is that the French were in Mali and Jenne when it was built (Fig. C.55). The French were busy constructing a madrasa when the mosque construction was in progress. According to Davidson (1989, 140), "In April 1907 when the mosque was inaugurated, no French attended the ceremony, not even Ernest Bleu, then

commander of the city." Aside from this, later sections show that the Sudanese style of construction had been employed by the people of the region thousands of years before the arrival of the French.

In addition, many great mosques in the region are built in the Sudanese style: the mosque near Niono Mali with its poetic sculpture that makes it look like a natural element growing out of the landscape instead of a planted object (Fig. C.56); Niono Mosque (Figs. C.57 to C.59) with its arched pillars and huge buttresses which have naturally adopted the function of the minbah, while maintaining their function as ancestral pillars guarding the shrine of worship; and finally, the main entrance of the Mosque at San (Fig. C.60) takes the mystical face of the ancestor spirits, the mask which is used in different traditional celebrations, including special ancestor

OVERLEAF:

Fig. C.56 Mali. Mosque in a traditional Sudanese (West African) style.

Fig. C.57 Niono, Mali. Mosque of Niono, 1957. (Jean-Louis Bourgeois and Carollee Pelos—Spectacular Vernacular, The Adobe Tradition 1989)

Fig. C.58 Niono, Mali. Courtyard tower of Niono Mosque. (Jean-Louis Bourgeois and Carollee Pelos—Spectacular Vernacular, The Adobe Tradition 1989)

Fig. C.59 Niono, Mali. South
entrance to Niono Mosque
with guarding pillars,
projecting doorposts, and
windowsills reminiscent of
ancient Egyptian domestic
construction. (Jean-Louis
Bourgeois and Carollee Pelos—
Spectacular Vernacular, The Adobe
Tradition 1989)

Fig. C.60 (Right) San, Mali.
Mosque with entry pylon as
ancestor mask, projecting
doorposts, and windowsills
reminiscent of ancient
Egyptian domestic
construction. (Jean-Louis
Bourgeois and Carollee Pelos—
Spectacular Vernacular, The Adobe
Tradition 1989)

rituals. These architectural motifs and repertoires have their origin in the architecture of houses, ancient palaces, and shrines in the region.

The houses and compounds of the Dongon peoples are among the unique architecture of Mali. These houses have their origin in Egyptian antiquity, and existing ones still have features similar to houses in ancient Egypt. Dongon resistance to the Islamic religion has preserved their building technology intact with features that echo their ancestors' homes. Contemporary or traditional Dongon houses have tapered pillars and hollow cylindrical pillars with apertures that serve the dual function of giving access to the roof and bringing diffused light into the sanctuary (Fig. 13.3). Similar roof ventilators have been found in ancient Egyptian houses from the Middle Kingdom (Badawy 1968, 22). The houses of Nebamun and Nakht have such ventilators.

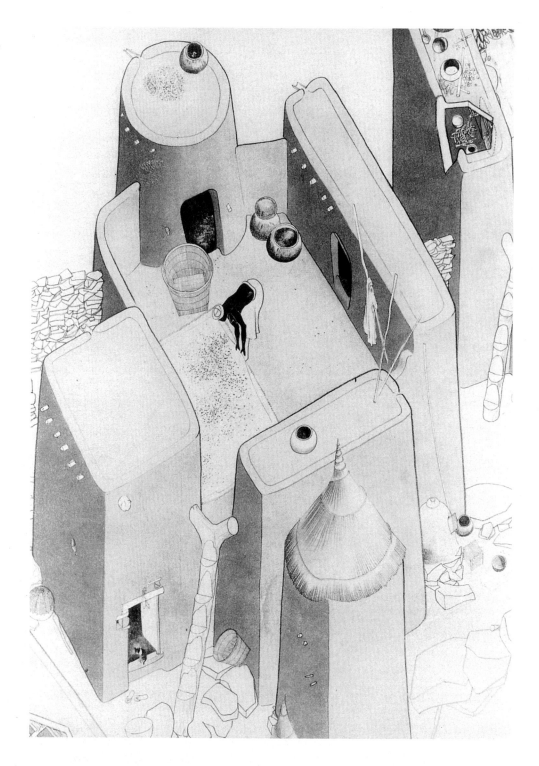

Fig. 13.3 Banani Mali.
Dongon rectangular houses
built like ancient Egyptian
domestic houses. (Jean-Paul
Bourdier)

Bamako (Fig. 13.4), the capital of Mali and the largest city in the region, was planned like a French city, with many diagonal streets, a characteristic of late 19th-century urban design. The major landmark in the city is the River Niger, which forms the terminus of the streets. Most of the early buildings are in adobe style with clay materials, but concrete buildings have become very common in both private and civic buildings. As a city located in the sahel, Bamako is given life in many forms by the River Niger, which supplies transportation, fishing, water, a focus of tourism, and a recreational landmark. Not all the districts of Bamako are formally planned. Some areas have the winding streets and houses

Fig. 13.4 Bamako, Mali city
plan. (Gabriel Orator)

close to one another of the typical African city plan. These narrow streets minimize solar heat and provide shade for the buildings adjacent to one another. They are also gathering places that serve as markets and plazas for local neighborhood activities.

13.4 NIGER REPUBLIC

Niger, a former French colony, should not be confused with its neighbor Nigeria, a former British colony. The existence of ethnic groups like the Hausas, Berbers, and Fulanis in these countries does make the colonial boundaries more artificial and convenient mainly for political reasons. For example, the

Hausa population, the largest ethnic group in Nigeria, is also the largest group in Niger, though in much smaller number. Both groups keep in close contact with relatives on either side of the border, and occasionally, they exploit the border whenever there is a price difference on farm and manufactured goods such as petroleum.

Niger presents another form of Sudanese architecture that extends further south to Nigeria, from where it derives the name Hausa architecture, which should be regarded as one of the varieties within the Sudanese style. In this case, every fenced compound has an entry house that keeps the visitor from having immediate access to the compound proper. The entry houses are often rectilinear but with domes. In northern Nigeria, this is one major element in the compounds of

chiefs, aristocrats, and the emirs. Prussin (1986) has indicated that most Hausa building technology and terminology come from the Mali and Songhay lexicon. Early in the 20th century, the largest houses in Hausaland were called *tafafara*, a term related to the Songhay *tafafara* and used specifically to designate the first entrance chamber and its distinctive ceiling structure. In Tahoua, Niger (Figs. 13.5 and 13.6), there is indication of the various forms of the dome and their use in the entry house (Fig. 13.7). The entry house serves other func-

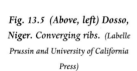

Fig. 13.5 (Above, left) Dosso, Niger. Converging ribs. (Labelle Prussin and University of California Press)

Fig. C.61 (Above, right) Affala, Niger. Granaries. (Jean-Louis Bourgeois and Carollee Pelos—Spectacular Vernacular, The Adobe Tradition 1989)

Fig. 13.6 (Right) Dosso, Niger. Intersecting ribs. (Labelle Prussin and University of California Press)

Fig. 13.7 Tahoua, Niger. Entry house (pylon) to a compound. (Labelle Prussin and University of California Press)

tions such as reception room, special meeting place, and prayer room. One major difference between Sudanese domes and those in North Africa is the choice of technology. While most of the North African domes are built with baked, kiln-dried brick, the Sudanese domes depend mostly on sun-dried clay similar to the technology employed in granary and pottery construction in the region (Fig. C.61).

13.5 NIAMEY: THE CAPITAL OF NIGER

Niamey became the capital of Niger in 1926. It was selected mainly because of its proximity to a major river in contrast to the dry inland city of Zinder. Niamey was planned by the French, and most of the buildings in the city were designed by French architects. Unlike major colonial cities in North Africa or Senegal in West Africa, the French did not have the intent to develop Niamey as a major urban center. All structures were temporary, for administrative functioning and the maximum extraction of resources. Unfortunately, no viable natural resource was found and mined in Niger until 1971, when the country started exporting uranium to France. By then, Niger had been independent for 11 years.

The infrastructure built in Niamey after independence was handled by French architects and was mainly for tourism, the Niger Hotel, for instance. This hotel, located on the bank of the River Niger, was one of the most modern hotels in the

country in the mid-1950s. The architects of the project, Daniel Badani, Michael Ducharme, and Pierre Roux-Porlut, were concerned with the hot temperature and dry weather. The first floor of the four-story building was made as translucent as possible by the use of several windows to encourage cross-ventilation. This helped to keep the three upper floors of the building cool. The building has wonderful panoramas of nature from its windows due to its location on the bank of the River Niger. This hotel remains one of the landmarks of modern Western architecture in the country. The combination here of the Islamic presence, the activities of the French, and the indigenous building tradition once again confirms the triple heritage of African architecture.

13.6 CHAD

The region of the Sudan now known as Chad has a history that dates back several millennia B.C. Some of the oldest evidence for Neolithic activities in Africa has been found in this region. According to Collier (1990, 5), "Many of the pottery-making and Neolithic activities in Ennedi date back further than any of those of the Nile Valley to the east," confirming the fact that the desert was one of the earliest settled parts of Africa, especially in the Tassili. Later history of the region suggests that present-day Chad was shaped to a large extent by some of the Sudanese empires of West Africa, the most

Fig. 13.8 Chad. Mousgoum castle.

influential of them being Kanem-Bornu which also shaped events in northern Nigeria.

The 19th century brought Europeans in large numbers, and with that the gradual colonization of Chad by the French. The French regarded Chad as the least important of all their territories and refused to modernize it. Ndjemena, the pre-sent capital, was the seat of colonial government and former-ly called Fort Lamy before its name was changed in September 1973.

As in many African countries, the three religions that rep-resent the triple heritage dominate Chad: ancestor worship, Islam, and Christianity. Ancestor worship was indigenous, and Islam became strong during the 14th century, although there are scholars who date its arrival in the 9th century or earlier. Christianity came to the region in the 19th century.

Like many African countries, Chad is a composite of numerous ethnic groups. These include the Bangadgi, Shuwa Aahs, Teda, Mousgoum, and the Massa, to name a few. Nomadism is a major lifestyle for many of the people because of the extensive grasslands of the savanna. However, there are also sedentary communities. While the nomads move according to the seasons with their extended family mem-bers, the sedentary communities settle according to their ancestral lineage. The tent is the major house form for the nomads, but those in the sedentary agricultural communities build homes. The Bangadji and the Mousgoum are famous for their unique clay castles sculptured on the landscape like natural ornaments (Fig. 13.8). These free-standing round cas-tles are constructed with wet clay that dries in the sun. In some cases, stumps of trees are inserted in the wall to improve its rigidity. Compound layout is on a group basis, according to ancestor lineage.

chapter 14

THE ARCHITECTURE OF GAMBIA, GUINEA BISSAU, GUINEA, AND SENEGAL

ambia, Guinea Bissau, Guinea, and Senegal are African states formed in the latter part of the 19th century by colonial European powers that were constantly competing for territorial control, trading one part of the land for another. Gambia today is populated by a number of diverse peoples brought into the Gambia Valley probably in the last 600 years as a result of pressures exerted in their former homeland of the Sudan (West Africa). Some of the major groups are the Wolof, Mandingo, Fipa, Jola, and Serahuli. Because of its location at the Gambia Valley, the Senegambia region retains a unique identity from the rest of the Sudan.

14.1 SENEGAMBIA

The countries of Gambia and Senegal tried to form a confederation of Senegambia, but it collapsed in 1990. If

the ancient Roman intrusion into Africa and the Punic Wars which sacked Carthage were undertaken to keep the European monopoly over the wealth of the Mediterranean, the later European intrusions into the interior of Africa were likewise undertaken with an economic and political motive, that of possessing the trade routes of the Sudan (West Africa), particularly of the Gold Coast, leading to a Western contribution to Africa's triple heritage architecture. Now several European competitors had to defend themselves from one another through the creation of spheres of influence jealously protected by "fortified trading posts along the coast at Arguin, Saint Louis, Goree, Fort Lamy, St. James, Cachen and Bissau" (Barry 1981, 268). These forts were very significant in two major ways. First, they were ministates extended from parent states in Europe. Second, they grew from fortified island enclaves along the Atlantic coast of Africa to expanded territories on the African mainland. In both stages, their major purpose was to serve the growth of capitalism. This occurred simultaneously with the growth of the sugar-cane industry in the New World, which had an increased demand for labor as a result. The wider implication was the need to secure as much of each territory as possible and to expand it as widely as possible. The ensuing combination of commercialism and territorial expansionism resulted in the final partitioning of Africa in the late 19th century. Senegal and Gambia became two different states as colonies of two separate European powers, the English and the French.

The Fort of Saint Louis (1659), at the Senegal River mouth to the Atlantic, gave the French a trading advantage along the Senegal River Valley. The construction of Fort Saint Joseph at upper Senegal River toward the end of the 17th century consolidated the French grip on the territory. On the other hand, the English built Fort Saint James in 1651 where the Gambia River flows into the Atlantic. This set the stage for the creation of Senegal and Gambia as two independent countries.

The Portuguese, finding the English, French, and Danish competition too difficult, settled at Cadheu, Bissau, and the island of Cape Verde, their main base in the Senegambia region. Goree Island, off the coast of Dakar, Senegal, became one of the symbols of 17th-century European hostility to one another as they ventured to the outer world. "Goree Island, which held the monopoly of trade along the petite cote was first occupied by the Dutch [1621] and later taken by the Portuguese in 1629 and 1645, then by the English in 1667, and finally by the French in 1677" (Barry 1981, 269). The final result of this rivalry was a settlement that gradually evolved into colonial ministates.

14.2 THE WOLOF AND THE TOKOLOR OF SENEGAMBIA

The Wolof, sometimes called the Jolof or Djolof after the name of the ancestor king, are spread between Senegal and Gambia. It would be inaccurate to identify the Wolof as only traditional village dwellers. There are Wolof in urban centers such as Dakar and Banjul holding professional positions, but most are farmers or nomads. At the traditional level, the Wolof economy is dependent on agriculture and nomadism. The Wolof also weave and dye textiles. Gamble (1957) lists leatherwork, pottery, and blacksmithing (including silversmiths and goldsmiths) as other traditional vocations practiced by the Wolof. Like many traditional African societies, the main element of Wolof social organization is ancestor and family lineage, which can be either paternal or maternal. The Wolof take pride in ancestor identity, a fact that is also reflected in their settlement pattern.

One key element in the Wolof village layout is the central square that forms the locus of the village from all directions. This is facilitated by the main road which runs through the square formed by the enclosure of groups of houses. Each group represents a family lineage and members of the extended family. According to Gamble (1957), a Wolof village square, like those in Salum, has a dat or pencha in its center. A

dat is a roofed platform under which the men cool off in the heat of the day, travelers pause for a chat, and children play on moonlit evenings. Facilities such as blacksmith shops are situated on the edges of the square or outside the village square. The houses of the compounds are grouped in circles with the elder's or chief's house being very close to the entrance. Again, according to Gamble (1957), in Gambian Salum practically all the Wolof houses are circular; however, the urbanized and more affluent people who return to the village build square and rectangular houses. Each compound has a mixture of clay houses and modern houses. Compounds often have storage facilities for grains (millet) and stables for animals. The Wolof are mostly Muslims, but there are also ancestor worshipers and Christians among them.

Professor Jean-Paul Bourdier (1991) discussed how the spread of Islam in Senegambia influenced Tokolor mosque designs and education. According to Bourdier (1991, 61), "The Tokolor people living along the [Senegal] river in northern Senegal are often referred to as the first Islamized blacks, and Futa, the first society in Senegambia to make Islam specifically its religion and culture." Islam is a successful religion in West Africa because it adapted to the lifestyles of the people, and the people of Tokolor were not exempt from this adaptation. As a result, various aspects of social, religious, and technical life were blended with Islamic prescriptions and West African cultural heritage. Early mosques built in the region, especially those built in the 17th, 18th, and 19th centuries, demonstrate the application of foreign elements to West African buildings and also the various phases which Islam underwent in the region: mainly from a militarist, conquering, coercive, rigid, religious force to a modest, flexible, adaptive, less confrontational, and compromising religious culture.

The impact of conquering, ambitious precolonial military officers in the region should also be taken into account when the mosques of the Tokolor are studied. One of the significant impacts of the French wars from the 1850s is the disposal of thousands of Tokolor citizens to different parts of the West African sahel, including the Dongon country. The collapse of the Tokolor empire and the return of the fleeing citizens brought various architectural elements from the sahel. The new elements were subsequently incorporated into building construction in the futa.

The Mosque of Seno Palel (Fig. 14.1) was built during the era of Islamic reform and it demonstrates "the interplay between several cultures" (Bourdier 1991, 64); in this instance, the mosque adapts both African and Islamic building traditions. Bourdier (1991, 64) suggests that "with a few exceptions, the square plan (recommended by Malekite law), the portico or abour to the east (opposite the qibla wall), and the three

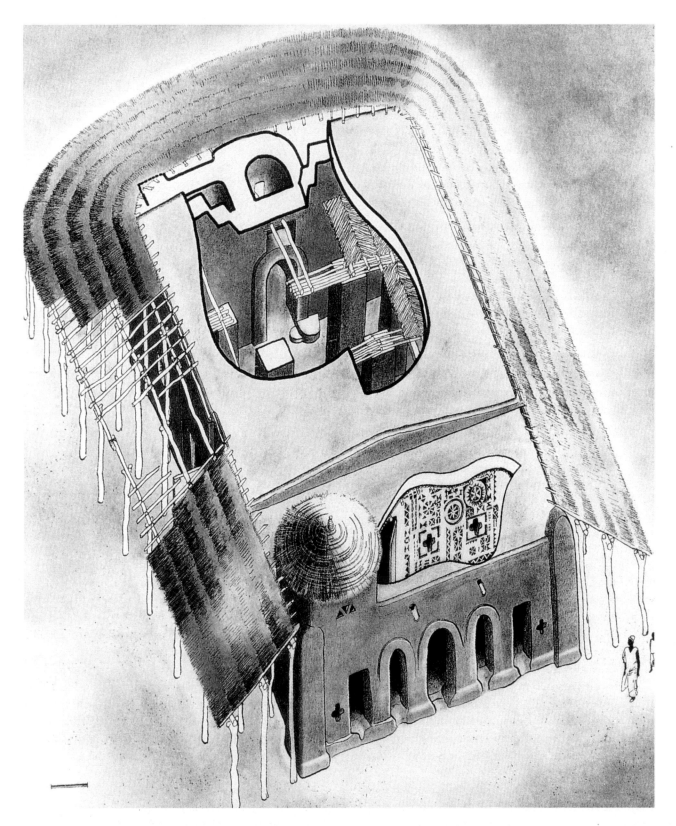

Fig. 14.1 Senegal. Seno Palel Mosque. 1770s. (Jean-Paul Bourdier)

entrances of the Prophet's courtyard seem to be a constant in futa mosques throughout history. What changes most noticeably is generally the outer wall of the building." This form of syncretism results in the modification and transformation of several building elements, spaces, and functions. Roofing systems, lighting systems, corridors, and other transitional spaces, doors, windows, and other openings in buildings are susceptible to such modifications. Bourdier (1991, 64) calls our attention to the impact of interplay between Islamic building recommendations and the African culture on the corridor space added to the front entrance of the Seno Palel Mosque:

> The original square plan of the praying place is kept, but it is supplemented with a transitional space which brings to mind both the late-comers gallery associated with Ottoman architecture, and the antechamber-like space (bafe) common to the (rectangular) dwellings of Futa. Unique to the bafe of these houses is the elaborate claustra work of the front wall, which shapes the penetrating sunlight and moderates the temperature of the interior."

The Seno Palel Mosque has demonstrated the depth of the triple heritage architecture in Africa. Buildings influenced by the fusion of indigenous elements and foreign elements are in large number in West Africa. It is very important to highlight indigenous contributions when such studies are conducted.

14.3 BANJUL, GAMBIA

Gambia is the smallest country in West Africa with an area of 11,295 km² (4361 mi²) and a population of 538,000 in 1976. It has been established (Church 1980; Gailey 1965) that the first European to visit Gambia was Alvise Ca'da Mosto, a Venetian who sailed up the Gambia River in 1455. In 1494, the Portuguese secured the exclusive right to trade on the coast. Present boundaries of Gambia and Senegal clearly reflect colonial competition gone awry. Gambia was carved along river banks by the British by going 15 mi on either side of the Gambia River. "The goal of the British at that time was to exclude the French from political control of any part of the river" (Gailey 1965, 1). However, British occupation of the river banks was given less importance during the endless Napoleonic Wars. As long as the French were kept out of the valley, the British were satisfied with the river valley boundaries.

In 1815, Captain Alexander Grant was authorized to reoccupy the Gambia River banks for the purpose of checking the unwanted slave trade in the area. Banjul (formerly called Bathurst) was thus established at the mouth of the river by Captain Grant, primarily as a military garrison. "His [Grant's] first objective had been to build a suitable military establish-

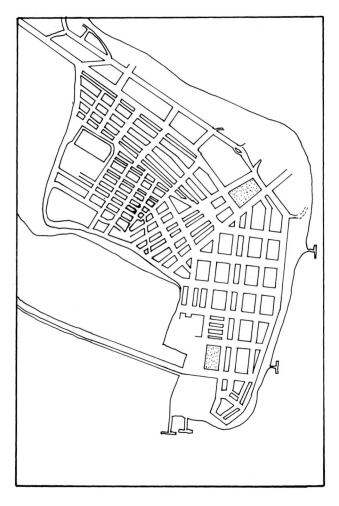

Fig. 14.2 Banjul, Gambia. City plan.

ment from which he could control the mouth of the river" (Gailey 1965, 62). The site he chose at the mouth of the Gambia River was originally called Saint Mary's Island.

The British colonial engineer of Sierra Leone was in charge of laying out Bathurst, the new town on Saint Mary's Island, named after London's colonial secretary of that time. The River Gambia provided the parti for the town's plan. Two parallel main streets were laid next to the river, the closest being Wellington Street. The main streets opened onto a square named after Colonel Charles MacCarthy, who was governor-in-chief of West African British territories in 1815. Six other streets linked the two main streets, all named after Wellington's assistants, while Government House was located beyond the square at the waterfront (Fig. 14.2). By 1821, the completed public buildings of Banjul (Bathurst) included Government House, barracks, officers' quarters, judicial buildings, and a hospital. Cannons were mounted near the Government House for protection and to regulate the river traffic.

Like many coastal West African cities, Banjul received both settlers and returning freed slaves, mostly from England. Part of Banjul is known as Portuguese town, after slaves set free from Portuguese slave ships in the 19th century. These emancipados brought building skills with them, and they erected buildings in the plain Portuguese style, now identified as Creole style. These buildings were two and three stories tall and were multifunctional. The ground floors were usually shops and warehouses, while the upper floors were used for residential purposes.

Banjul has had an eventful history. The choice of the site was based mainly on military reasons, not for purposes of colonial administration. Captain Grant sited Banjul at the choke point of the River Gambia mouth where it is narrowest (3.2 km, 2 mi), so that he could track slavers easily. In Captain Grant's view, he was establishing a military fort, and what mattered most was strategic efficiency. Little did he know that he was creating a center that would eventually become the capital of Gambia. Additionally, the fort is located on a swampy sand dune that is susceptible to annual flooding during the raining season. This increased sanitation problems and, consequently, the incidence of malaria. The problem was so bad that United States President Franklin Roosevelt described Banjul to Prime Minister Winston Churchill as "that hell-hole of yours" after Roosevelt caught fever there in 1943. Drainage systems to solve the flooding problem were completed in 1949.

14.4 DAKAR: THE CAPITAL OF SENEGAL

Dakar, like other West African cities, held its share of great colonial ambition. Each successful advancement of colonial power to the mainland and along the Atlantic coast meant the collapse of an indigenous empire. In 1758, almost 100 years after the French established Fort Saint Louis, the English captured it.

The French return to Goree Island and Fort Saint Louis in 1817 opened two opportunities for them. The first was the replacement of the slave trade with other products such as gum, hides, and beeswax; the second was the ability to invade and conquer the mainlands with little resistance. In other words, the extension of the citadel coastal ministates was achieved with less difficulty. In the case of Dakar, wars between indigenous warlords helped the French occupy the state. For example, customs duties paid to the Wolof aristocracy by the French precipitated power struggles within the Wolof leadership for control of the kingdom's lucrative trade. For a time, the French increased the "customs" paid to Wolof aristocracy, but this aggravated the succession wars normal to their political system. The resulting disorders, as well as the increased development of puritanical orthodox Islamization in the region by the Marabouts, made the governor of French Saint Louis nervous. Hence, he adopted an imperialist policy of conquer and rule.

Governor Fudherbe's first act was the complete annexation of Waalo in three military campaigns from January to June 1855. He himself moved from Goree Island and occupied Dakar in 1857. Soon, plans were in place to connect Dakar and Goree by telegraph and Dakar to Saint Louis by railroad which were completed in 1885. Peanut (groundnut) and other commercial export plantations were developed in the hinterlands along the coast to be sent to Dakar via railroad for shipment to Europe. With its natural deep harbor, the wide estuary of the Senegal River, Dakar began to assume the role of a central French outpost in the region, where all activities were coordinated.

The French made Dakar a naval base in 1898 when the British were having problems with the Boers and the natives in South Africa, and Anglo-French relations were again strained due to territorial competition. Dakar became a stopping point for French ships en route from Europe to South America. By 1914, the population of Dakar was 23,833. World War I brought increased prosperity and importance to French administrators in Africa because Dakar was designated the federal capital of French West Africa (the Sudan) (Figs. 14.3 and C.62). The French were then confronted with the unforeseen problem of what their policy should be toward the colonies. The resolution of this problem has a great impact on the final outcome of French-built colonial cities all over Africa and throughout the world. The principal debate was whether to assimilate Africans into the French culture, and if so, how far they should go to implement the policy in urban development.

The French policy of assimilation was rooted in the notion of the equality of all human beings and of the superiority of the European culture and civilization, with the French culture and civilization considered the finest. "Advocates of this policy believed that there were no racial and cultural differences that education could not eliminate" (Crowder 1967, 2). Hence, the French believers in this doctrine considered it their responsibility to convert barbarians into civilized people like themselves. For Africa, this implied accepting the African as an equal human being, but since, to the French, the African had neither culture nor history, he needed to be completely re-educated as a cultured Frenchmen, and the Frenchmen would be responsible for civilizing him. "Thus French books describe the French conquest of Africa as the establishment of 'la paix Franchaise' and her early administration as l'oeuvre civilisatrice" (Crowder 1967, 2).

Fig. 14.3 Dakar, Senegal. City plan: (1) Grand Mosque, (2) Office of Foreign Affairs, (3) Palais du Grand Conseil de L'Afrique Occidentale Francaise, (4) Presidential residence, (5) Prime Minister's residence, (6) Palais de Justice.

The other side of the equation was spearheaded by colonialists like Lyautey in Morocco. They advocated a policy of association which held that Africans could never be assimilated into the French culture because they are culturally different. However, unlike the British, who believed in the Luguardian policy of indirect rule, that is, of ruling the people through their own leaders and chiefs, the French regarded rule through indigenous leaders as totally inefficient for colonial exploitation of resources. Hence, they adopted direct colonial rule of the African as a form of assimilation and paternalism.

Crowder (1967) is of the opinion that in spite of the high number affected by the policy of association, assimilation remained an important element of administration in French West Africa. Some elites in the colonies, especially in Senegal, were assimilated into special communes. Still, the French abandoned the policy of assimilation in West Africa mainly because of cost and political implications. It would have led to the political, cultural, and economic assimilation of 20 million Africans to the same standards enjoyed by metropolitan French. In principle, the French believed in assimilation, but they were reluctant to pay the economic price. They preferred assimilation as a concept that would have no economic price tag, especially since they had no intention of settling in the region.

In Algeria, the French invested heavily in urban development from the 1850s on because they were intent on settling the area. However, they maintained the same policy of direct rule, in actuality a policy of unimplemented assimilation, as they did in West Africa. Crowder (1967, 17) mentions a French ministerial instruction of 1859 which explains why the French chose to settle and invest little in West Africa. "Nothing similar to Algeria could be undertaken in Senegal. The climate is against it." This meant that the Europeans should have been content with the business of governing Senegal and extracting resources. In a way, limited development was implemented. The French actually practiced full-scale assimilation in four communes in Senegal. Crowder (1967) points out the following characteristics of the assimilation: political assimilation to the metropolitan court (France) through the representation of Senegal in the Chamber des Deputes; administrative assimilation by creating a counsel

Fig. C.62 Dakar, Senegal. Waterfront. (American Geographical Society Collection, The University of Wisconsin-Milwaukee Library)

Fig. 14.4 Dakar, Senegal. Palace of Justice. Designed by Daniel Badani and Pierre Roux-Dorlut. 1948–1950.
(American Geographical Society Collection, The University of Wisconsin-Milwaukee Library)

general for Senegal modeled on the Counsel's Generaux of Departments of France; and by the establishment of municipal counsels on the model of France, the personal assimilation of Senegalese by according them French citizenship.

The French left eternal legacies and vestiges of Parisian urban design in Dakar, in spite of their reluctance to invest in the territory. This was mainly because Dakar was conceived as the capital of Federal French West Africa, a large area. Cote d'Ivoire, Guinea, Mali, Chad, Niger, Senegal, Togo, and Benin were all governed from Dakar. Its location at the Cape Verde Peninsula gave it little room to expand because of marshy land, and the Atlantic Ocean provided the overall parti of the city.

The basic format of the Dakar plan was derived from a 19th-century European Renaissance urban design model based on the use of avenues and boulevards that meet at 30° angles to form roundabouts and squares. Among these is Avenue Jean Javres which establishes a vista with the Palais de Justice. Avenue Andre Peytavin, Boulevard de la Republic, which terminates at the Palais du President de la Republic, and Avenue Courbet intersect with Avenue Jean Jaures to form the major

roundabouts of the city. The widest section of the city, which extends east, is laid out on a rectangular grid of 120-m blocks. A winding highway wraps around the city, giving it unlimited access to the beaches. Dakar is famous for these beautiful sandy beaches that have made tourism the second largest industry in Senegal after peanut (groundnut) exports.

Fig. C.63 Dakar, Senegal. Office of Foreign Affairs. (American Geographical Society Collection, The University of Wisconsin-Milwaukee Library)

Fig. C.64 Dakar, Senegal. Presidential residence. *(American Geographical Society Collection, The University of Wisconsin-Milwaukee Library)*

The Ministry of Foreign Affairs (Ministere des Affaires Etrangeres), the Presidential Palace (Palais du President de la Republique), the National Assembly (Assemble Nationale), and the Supreme Court (Palais de Justice) represent a wide spectrum of French influence on Senegalese architecture. The Ministry of Foreign Affairs has a neoclassical facade that forms a screen in front of a 20th-century building. Two pillars with twin pilasters support the gable on the main entrance. One wing of the symmetrical building has blind arches, while the other forms a colonnade with steel bars. The third story is recessed and partially hidden from view. The Presidential Palace is a hybrid of Renaissance architecture with a symmetrical facade. The emphasis here is on cooling the building and controlling sunlight with shutters. The compound is fenced with Victorian steel bars. The Palace of Justice is typical of the modern French movement which was distributed around the world, especially in the colonies during the years following the end of the World War II (Figs. 14.4, C.63, and C.64).

The culmination of this transfer in Senegal is in the Assembly Nationale Dakar. The building was begun in the early 1950s as part of the experimental French policy of political assimilation in West Africa, cultivating leaders elected to the Council de L'Afrique Occidentale Francaise. Daniel Badani, Pierre Roux-Dorlut, and Michel Ducharme were in charge of the architectural project. The building is oriented in an east-west direction. The plan called for an assembly chamber, library, offices for the deputies, grand reception room, restaurants, and bar (Fig. 14.5). However, the French were not the only foreign influence in Dakar.

Islam does coexist with Christian cathedrals in Senegal. Senegal has by far more Muslims than Christians. Their conversion to Islam can be traced to the years of medieval empires and the subsequent Islamic revolutions following

Fig. 14.5 (Opposite) Dakar, Senegal. Palais du Grand Conseil de L'Afrique Occidentale, Francaise. Designed by Daniel Badani and Pierre Roux-Dorlut. 1950.
(American Geographical Society Collection, The University of Wisconsin-Milwaukee Library)

Fig. 14.6 (Above) Dakar, Senegal. Grand Mosque.
(American Geographical Society Collection, The University of Wisconsin-Milwaukee Library)

Fig. C.65 (Right) Dakar, Senegal. Bank of Economic Community of West African States (ECOWAS). Pierre Goudiaby Atepa-Architects. 1990. (David Hughes Photos)

European intrusion into the region. Twentieth-century Islam in Senegal originates from ancient holy wars that moved eastward in the Sudan (West Africa) and the forest zone to shape the destinies of other states in the region. The Great Mosque of Dakar (Fig. 14.6), located in the northern suburb of the city, features all the elements of North African mosques. The main entrance has three wide horseshoe-shaped arches similar to those in Morocco and other North African countries. The minaret is decorated with Islamic designs which are also of North African origin. A few buildings created in the 1980s evoke images from African antiquity. A good example is the

Fig. 14.7 (Opposite, top) Goree Island, Senegal.
Seventeenth-century fort. (American Geographical Society
Collection, The University of Wisconsin-Milwaukee Library)

Fig. 14.8 (Opposite, bottom) Goree Island, Senegal.
Creole houses. (American Geographical Society Collection, The
University of Wisconsin-Milwaukee Library)

Fig. 14.9 (Above) Kabe, Futa Jallon, Guinea. Oldest
mosque in beehive style architecture. 1730s. [United Nations
Educational Scientific and Cultural Organization (UNESCO)]

Headquarters of the Bank of Economic Community of West African States, which was designed by Pierre Goudiaby Atepa-Architects. The building takes the shape of a pyramid and is lit with cathedral windows (Fig. C.65).

Like the City of Dakar, the architecture of Goree Island also tells the story of slavery and colonialism. The Fort (Fig. 14.7) which the Dutch established in 1621 is the dominant edifice on the island and the trade links between the island, Portugal and Brazil also influenced its architecture a lot—mostly Creole-style buildings (Fig. 14.8) with plane surfaces. The Senegalese government has put the fort into different uses in recent times, and some of the mansions have been renovated to house tourists.

14.5 GUINEA AND GUINEA-BISSAU

The republics of Guinea and Guinea-Bissau have a unique history that shaped them into two independent states. The Portuguese were the first to arrive in the region in the 15th century. They set up trading posts and began to export slaves, gold, and ivory to Portugal. However, hostility from coastal states with Muslim populations minimized Portuguese penetration into the interior. Increased European presence in the area in the 17th century and the fierce European competition that followed reduced Portuguese activity to the region of Guinea-Bissau, with the capital at Bissau. The French established themselves in Guinea after the Germans had been expelled. French control of the region began in 1849, but the relationship between France and Guinea changed in 1958 when the people of Guinea voted to break out of French West Africa. The French removed all equipment from the country, destroying buildings, roads, and bridges as a lesson to the other French West African states and as a way of keeping them under France's domination. Guinea would have collapsed if it had not been for immediate financial help from Kwame Nkrumah, then president of Ghana, and aid from the former Soviet Union and its allies.

Conakry is the capital of Guinea. Today, both Bissau and Conakry are well planned and highly urbanized. The culture of the people in this region was greatly influenced by the 15th-century Islamic reaction against Western intrusions in the area. However, the mosque in Guinea took on a new form, different from what the Sudan (West Africa) had given it (Fig. 14.9). This is a clear indication of Islam's ability to adapt to the culture of the West African people and to be innovative concerning its dogma, including building codes, when necessary. The transformation of the mosque in Guinea occurred largely because the natives maintained their orthodox Islamic faith and continued to build their sacred places of worship on the models of both their ancestors' places of worship and ancestor compounds. This supports the assertion that the mosques in Mali evolved as indigenous products rather than because of a revolution brought by one man from the northeast.

Several mosques in the Futa Jallon have beehive roofs that cover square clay structures. Usually, the beehive roof comes very low to the ground and obscures the inner clay structure. Most have radiating roof rafters supported by a set of wooden pillars that circle the square earthen structure. The square earthen structure usually has flat ceilings. In a sense, the mosque in the Futa Jallon is made up of two buildings: an adobe structure encased within a beehive roof structure. It is a roofing solution that arises out of the sacred nature of the mosque and the need to protect it from the torrential rainfalls of the region. This adaptation of a building type to local technology explains how many Muslim communities in Africa recycle foreign ideas and religions to serve their needs and purposes.

chapter

15

THE ARCHITECTURE OF SIERRA LEONE, LIBERIA, COTE D'IVOIRE, AND BURKINA FASSO

This section concentrates on the architecture of Sierra Leone, Liberia, Cote d'Ivoire, and Burkina Fasso. The circumstances leading to the founding of Sierra Leone and Liberia are discussed, and the architectural imports from the New World are mentioned. French colonial policy in West Africa, the emergence of Cote d'Ivoire when the empire disintegrated, and the two contemporary cities of Abidjan and Yamoussoukro in Cote d'Ivoire are also discussed, along with the continuity of an ancient building tradition that surfaces in the Gourounsi architecture of Burkina Fasso.

15.1 SIERRA LEONE

The name Sierra Leone seems to have been derived from Latin, through the Spanish or Portuguese *serra* for "saw" and *leiona* or *leona* for "lion." Pedro de Cintra, a 15th-century Portuguese explorer, called the jigsawlike rugged mountain along that part of the West African coast Sierra Leone or Lion Mountain in 1462 because the landscape reminded him of lions.

Two principal factors induced the English to establish Sierra Leone. The first occurred when black soldiers who fought for the British during the American Revolutionary War were not received in England due to legislative laws of 1765 and 1772, "which had made it a living and active principle in the Legislature of the British Empire that slaves cannot breathe in England" (George 1968, 19).

At this point, a group of English philanthropists began to look for a way out of this dilemma, realizing also that slaves who fought on the British side could not return to their American masters after they had lost the war. Mr. Sharp published a plan to settle some of the free disenfranchised slaves near the coast of Sierra Leone in 1786. Sharp entrusted Dr. Smeathman, who was already familiar with the region, with the responsibility of establishing the new colony. Many blacks quickly seized upon the opportunity to leave England, and by 1787, some of the emancipados had already resettled in Sierra Leone, and Freetown, the capital, was founded in 1792.

Freetown has many different sections (Fig. 15.1), among them Kru Town for the natives, Portuguese Town with a large Portuguese influence, and Maroon Town where

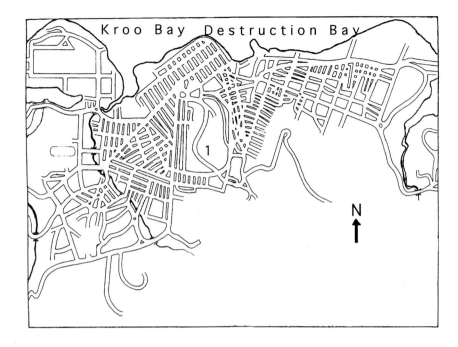

Fig. 15.1 Freetown, Sierra Leone. City plan: (1) Parliament House.

Kroo Bay   Destruction Bay

N

Jamaican maroons established themselves in the 19th century. Thus, the architectural character of Freetown ranges from the plain Portuguese style to hybrids of Creole West Indian style and Victorian-influenced structures. The original building of Fourah Bay College (Fig. 2.19) was built in the mid-19th century and is a good example of Victorian architecture. Basic cast-iron work of the Victorian era adorns the portico of the building. It is also important to note that the population of Sierra Leone is not just composed of emancipados who resettled in Africa. There are also indigenous groups with strong ethnic attachments such as the Mende, Lokko, Tenne, Limba, Susu, Yalunka, Sherbro, Bullom, Krin, Kono, Vai, and Koranko.

The Mendes are predominantly farmers who trace their origin to the Mende-speaking people of Guinea. They are one of the groups that moved southwest along the coast as the Fulani and Islamic fundamentalists made more excursions into the forest zone. Some of these Mende-speaking people eventually converted to Islam, and their culture became a mix of Islamic and indigenous African customs. This mix was subsequently integrated into the building traditions that they brought with them from the savanna. Some of the traditional houses built by the Mende have special buttressing pillars and pylons that differ from most of those found in Mali. Mosques were built within the specifications of Islam, but with the technology and the forms provided by the indigenous building tradition. In a way, the triple heritage is more highly mixed in the architectural traditions of West Africa than it is in other parts of the continent.

15.2 LIBERIA

Liberia has had a history similar to Sierra Leone, except that it was founded by freed American slaves who decided to return to Africa, a place they regarded as the promised land. This promised land was founded by the American Colonization Society in 1817. The society received United States government patronage when some ex-slaves began to return to Africa. This group also regarded itself as American Liberians and refused to be part of the indigenous population. Their flag has one star and some red stripes, and their government was fashioned after that of the United States. Monrovia, the capital of the new colony, was founded in 1822 (Fig. 15.2).

Life in the southern United States influenced the built environment of the returnees to Africa. They were a people living in two worlds: a world of indigenous Africa with all its traditions and people and a world highly influenced by the southern plantations of the United States. The Liberian experience is clearly an expression of the dominant culture of the large plantation owners, one touched and shaped in all aspects of material life by the African culture of the slaves. For example, in textiles, foodways, and agricultural practices, it is easy to discern contributions of both the black and the white cultures, although in matters of housing, and especially with regard to the plantation owners, "big houses and surrounding out buildings and quarters, white cultural attitudes prevailed" (Holsoe and Herman 1988, 3).

The house of President Roberts in Monrovia (Fig. 2.18) is a good example of the influence of the American south. This

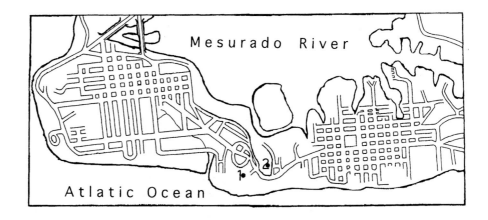

Fig. 15.2 Monrovia, Liberia, city plan showing the Presidential Palace and city hall.

house is in the tradition of the Victorian architecture that permeates North and South Carolina, Georgia, and the Virginias. Most striking is the transfer from farm churches in the southern United States. For example, the Methodist Church in Fortsville, Liberia, takes its form from the Carolinas. Residential buildings follow prototypes found in the Carolinas. The June Morre House in Arthington, Liberia, resembles a huge Carolinian plantation house such as Cove Grove built in 1830, in Perquimans County, North Carolina.

The Liberian House dates from mid-19th century and is certainly a carry-over of American influence. The roofs, front elevation, and arrangement of openings clearly exhibit their Carolinian origin. This is no coincidence since most of the settlers in Liberia came from the Carolinas and the Virginias. "The largest out-migration from any one county in the United States was from Southampton County, Virginia, in 1831–32" (Holsoe and Herman 1988, 3). The immigration of American blacks to Liberia was also the largest single out-migration from the United States.

15.3 COTE D'IVOIRE

The issues of French assimilation and association discussed in connection with Senegambia also apply to Cote d'Ivoire. The Senufo, who founded the trading center of Kong, were one of

Fig. 15.3 Korghoso, Cote d'Ivoire. Chief's house. 1925.
(Labelle Prussin and University of California Press)

Fig. 15.4 Palacca, Cote d'Ivoire. Chief's house. (Labelle Prussin and University of California Press)

the minigroups to emerge from the ashes of the West African empires of the Sudan.

The Senufo took advantage of the fall of the Mali empire to advance northward from the coast. Their settlement pattern was in clans which included the Korogho, Seguela, Odienne, and Kong. The Senufo were mostly peasants who worked the land around their villages efficiently. They had a centralized government dominated by religious rituals. Relationships within family reflected kinship and ancestor lineage. Byrnes (1991) points out that kinship groups were relatively resistant to change through modernization. As a result, one traditional descent group, the lineage, is so commonly used by all that it can be discussed in general terms without making specific distinctions among the various Ivoirian cultures.

In most traditional African settings, there is little distinction between religion and government. In fact, government at the traditional level is often an extension of ancestor theocracy administered by elders. This also manifests itself in the built environment because the house borrows from the elements that adorn the sacred houses of ancestors. Prussin (1986) has

mentioned that ritual imagery characteristic of traditional West African society finds its architectural counterpart specifically in the facade of its built forms. Prussin also identifies the incorporation of religious motifs into housing among the Senufo (Figs. 15.3 and 15.4): the lintel with its triangulated brickwork and an enlarged pyramidal shrine-vestibule. These elements were incorporated into the Sudanese terrace housing. The Senufo did not limit their creativity to architecture, but also produced some of the African symbolist-style artworks.

15.4 ABIDJAN

Abidjan (Fig. C.66) is one of the cities of West Africa that grew out of colonial French ambition. Since the collapse of Federal French West Africa in 1960, Cote d'Ivoire has become France's largest trading partner in West Africa, and Abidjan is the center of this commerce. Abidjan is one of the cities planned by colonial France in the 1950s as part of the policy

Fig. C.66 Abidjan, Cote d'Ivoire. Waterfront.(American Geographical Society Collection, The University of Wisconsin-Milwaukee Library)

Fig. 15.5 Abidjan, Cote d'Ivoire. Place de la Republic. Designed by Daniel Badani. (American Geographical Society Collection, The University of Wisconsin-Milwaukee Library)

to build a greater France. The city reflects French urban planning practices. Today, the heart of the city as well as its main focal point is established by the Place de la Republic (Fig. 15-5), which is centered with the Georges Leygue Monument. The monument is flanked on one side of a roundabout by the Hotel des Postes and its identical counterpart, the Post and Telex Office, on the other. Place de la Republic is also the terminus of Point Houphouet-Boigny, the bridge connecting Abidjan proper to Treichville.

This multipurpose bridge was also supposed to convey a railway line across the lagoon within an interior cavity. Its major significance, besides connecting Abidjan proper to Treichville, is the continuity with Avenue de la Republic. Architects Daniel Badani and Roux-Dorlut must be given credit for their contributions to what Abidjan is today. Badani's 1947 master plan for Abidjan has not changed greatly. He also planned Sassandra and Bouake in the same year.

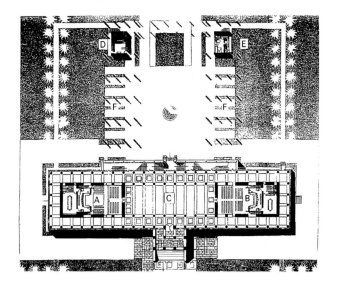

Hotel des Postes and the Telex and Telecommunication Building that surround Place de la Republic were completed in 1957. Badani's taste for classicism shows in both buildings. His genius is revealed in his ability to take classical partis and transpose them to contemporary times. That genius was also influenced by his partnership with Roux-Dorlut. Badani's love for symmetry and classicism shows once again in the Palace of Justice in Abidjan (Fig. 15.6), completed in 1953. In this instance, the rhythmic columns that make the turn at the roundabout in Hotel des Postes and the Telex and Telecommunication Buildings are replaced by four forms of symmetrically lined columns on either side of the parking lot.

Fig. 15.6 Abidjan, Cote d'Ivoire. Plan of the Palais de Justice: (A and B) court rooms, (C) concourse, (D and E) service facilities, and (F) parking. Designed by Daniel Badani. 1948–1950. (Keith Brown)

Fig. 15.7 Sassandra, Cote d'Ivoire. Banque de l'Afrique Occidentale. Designed by Daniel Badani. (Keith Brown)

Fig. C.67 (Opposite, top left) Abidjan, Cote d'Ivoire. Riviera complex. Designed by Roger Taillibert. 1983.
(Roger Taillibert)

Fig. C.68 (Opposite, top right) Yamoussoukro, Cote d'Ivoire. Golf resort. Designed by Roger Taillibert. 1982.

Fig. C.69 (Opposite, bottom) Abidjan, Cote d'Ivoire. A hotel built with concrete in the Mousgoum castle style. 1980s. (Jean-Louis Bourgeois and Carollee Pelos—Spectacular Vernacular, The Adobe Tradition 1989)

THE ARCHITECTURE OF SIERRA LEONE   277

These columns lead into a double level atrium with two courtroom chambers on either end. His design for French West African Bank (Banque de l'Afrique Occidentale) at Sassandra, Cote d'Ivoire, is an offshoot of the Palace of Justice in Abidjan (Fig. 15.7).

Numerous French architects worked in Abidjan, including Roger Taillibert whose latest work there is the Riviera golf complex, completed in 1983. The Riviera complex occupies 100 ha and has two golf courses, one eighteen holes, the other nine. The major structures in the complex are a public clubhouse and the Golf Hotel Residence together with other sports and recreational facilities (Figs. C.67 and C.68). Taillibert is a master at conceiving projects that work with the landscape. The hillside complex of Riviera is a classic example of this. He arranged the major structure to fit into and complement the landscape. The main access is located on the intermediate level of the building which is linked to a concealed parking structure that holds 250 cars.

Three horizontal levels reveal layers of amenities: lounges, restaurants, and bars with views of pools, fountains, and decorated waterfalls. The entire structure is constructed with reinforced concrete and situated on the edge of a hill.

Tourism is a major source of revenue for Cote d'Ivoire, and the government has invested in it heavily. Experimentation with traditional architecture is limited to the tourist industry, as exemplified by a new hotel in Abidjan (Fig. C.69) completed in the mid-1980s. This hotel took the parti of the traditional Gourounsi sand castles that are common in the savanna regions of the country.

15.5 FROM ABIDJAN TO YAMOUSSOUKRO: THE NEW CAPITAL CITY

Yamoussoukro, the new capital city of the Cote d'Ivorie, is President Houphouet-Boigny's hometown, and it has made headlines not because of major international events taking place there nor because of a grand master plan but because of its excesses in all aspects. As of today, the boulevards of the city are completely underutilized, as are the international airport and the university. The magnificent Hotel President, in which President Houphouet-Boigny himself has a financial stake, is utilized less than 40 percent. Thus, there is no doubt that the infrastructure now in place in Yamoussoukro is out of all proportion to the needs of the present population of about 90,222, a figure that has grown from 1300 in 1955.

This is another developmental African pursuit of utopia bought at a high cost to the economy. It is a utopia founded on materialism, without any tangible fruit for the Ivoirians. The tragedies of Brasília and Chandigarh repeat themselves in Yamoussoukro, as if modern cities are destined to fail. The excessive consumerism of Yamoussoukro can also be found in the town hall. Proudly situated on the Palace Jean-Paul 11, Yamoussoukro town hall boasts a conference hall the size of a football field, magnificent marbled corridors, glass chandeliers, and conference tables the length of train cars. These extravagances garnish the little village where President Houphouet-Boigny was born several decades ago.

Topping the list of excesses in Yamoussoukro is Our Lady of Peace Basilica (Basilica Notre Dame of Peace). The cost estimates ranged from $500–$900 million but the official government figure is $200 million. The entire structure was rushed to completion in fewer than 3 years and presented to the Vatican in 1990 as a gift from President Houphouet-Boigny. This gigantic edifice is the second largest church building in the world, after the Vatican, and there is no doubt that it is the tallest basilica in the world when the height of the cross on top of its 489-ft dome is factored in. Saint Peter's dome, with its cross, measures 452 ft, Saint Paul's in London measures 353 ft, while Our Lady of Peace measures 489 ft. It has been suggested that the Vatican asked for the basilica to be scaled down so that it would not be bigger than Saint Peter's in Rome (Bourke 1990).

The cathedral has a seating capacity of 7000 people, with enough room for 14,000 to stand. The mega-courtyard, with its 276 Doric columns, is capable of holding 400,000 pilgrims. The entire structure is completely air conditioned, making it the most expensive church building in the world to maintain due to cooling costs. The Vatican was not happy about accepting a gift that would cost nearly $10 million to maintain annually, most of this in cooling bills. The basilica has 80,000 ft^2 of glass, the most ever used in a church, and several tons of Italian marble columns. The surrounding landscape mirrors the classical French gardens of Versailles. All these were designed and personally supervised by the 47-year-old architect Pierre Fakhoury who took the opportunity to display his skill in classical architecture.

Houphouet-Boigny has built a monument for himself to cap his 30-year grip of power over Cote d'Ivoire. He was buried in a modern family necropolis in Yamoussoukro in February 1994. Only 11 percent of Ivoirians are Catholic; the majority are Muslims. However, President Houphouet-Boigny ignored the Muslim majority in the country. He quickly completed a mosque in Yamoussoukro when the city was still taking shape, but the mosque is very modest compared to the basilica. Unfortunately, the Muslim community had no knowledge of what he was doing. Their mosque was a pacification gesture which they couldn't refuse at that point.

If Yamoussoukro is the home of the tallest cathedral in the world, Casablanca, Morocco, is the home of the largest and most expensive mosque in the world, the King Hassan Mosque, completed in 1993 at a cost of $1 billion. Africa is, therefore, the home of two major shrines for two major world religions. But nobody remembered to build one for the ancestors. The answer may be that the Pharaohs have already done so, thousands of years ago, when they constructed the pyramids and the mortuary temples for themselves.

15.6 BURKINA FASSO

Burkina Fasso, formerly known as Upper Volta, was part of the main Mossi empire, one of the small empires to emerge out of the ashes of the collapsed medieval Sudanic empires. France began controlling the region in 1896, but formally declared the territory a colony in 1919. Burkina Fasso became independent in 1960 following the dissolution of Federal French West Africa. Ouagadougou, the present capital, dates to the 15th century as one of the capitals of the Mossie empire. Its growth was primarily from commerce and trade in gold. Ouagadougou has moved from a medieval structure to a planned city (Fig. 15.8), but it is threatened by the expanding and uncontrollable Sahara Desert, and its future as an urban center is uncertain.

The triple heritage is alive in Burkina Fasso as manifest by both Islamic and Christian activities in the city. The unifying element here between these two alien religions is the indigenous religion of the people and their building traditions. Situated on a dry, windy plateau, Ouagadougou has wide, windy, treeless streets; the houses are made of both cement and clay, with a mix of reed and flat clay roofs. Only about 10 percent of the population are Christians, the majority being Muslims. The Christians use indigenous techniques to represent Christian nativities which are displayed in their front yard, sometimes painted on the walls of the houses where they can be seen by passers-by. The round house with straw and reed roof, which is common to the Mossi people, is often integrated into a nativity. In fact, the level of syncretism between indigenous architecture and Christian symbolism reinforces the Western aspect of Africa's triple heritage. This is not limited to Christianity.

Burkina Fasso has more than residential compounds and buildings. Other religious buildings take their precedence from the ancestor shrine. The Bobo-Dioulasso Mosque (Fig. C.70) comes to mind. No exact date has been given for its founding, but it is generally accepted that it postdates 1879 when the French military explorer Binger visited the region. Ancestor pillars are the major elements of this mosque, and they form a rhythm that has no relationship with the mosques in North Africa. The Bobo-Dioulasso Mosque also

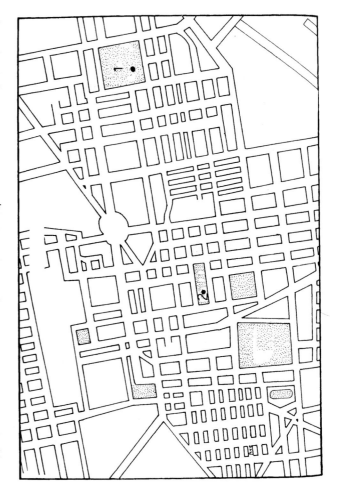

Fig. 15.8 Ouagadougou, Burkina Fasso. City plan showing the Presidential Palace and mosque.

varies in its buttressing methods from those commonly found in Mali because of the conical shapes. The hotel in Abidjan (Fig. C.69) has been influenced by this traditional method of construction, though the materials are all concrete.

Contemporary buildings in Burkina Fasso also use modern materials such as cement and aluminum roofing sheets. A few architects are beginning to find ways of integrating traditional African designs into their buildings. The mayor's office in Ouagadougou (Fig. 15.9) borrows its design precedent from the houses of the Gourounsi (Figs. 15.10 and 15.11). The slanted walls and parapets that characterize the ancient building tradition in the region are all well represented in the mayor's office, and punched windows are used for lighting and cooling. In a much more ambitious design, the Headquarters of the Central Bank of Economic Community of West African States takes its parti from the ancestral pillar, as one shaft that was broken into multiple vertical segments. The base is lined with traditional designs that take after Gourounsi

*Fig. C.70 (Above)
Bobo-Dioulasso, Burkina
Fasso. Mosque. (American
Geographical Society Collection, The
University of Wisconsin-Milwaukee
Library)*

*Fig. 15.9 Ouagadougou,
Burkina Fasso. Mayor's
office, 1956. (American
Geographical Society Collection, The
University of Wisconsin-Milwaukee
Library)*

Fig. 15.10 Koena, Burkina
Fasso. Axiometric view of a
Ko compound. (Jean Paul
Bourdier and Trinht Minh-ha)

Fig. C.71 Ouagadougou,
Burkina Fasso. Bank of
Economic Community of West
African States. (David Hughes
Photos)

Fig. C.72 (Far left)
Ouagadougou, Burkina
Fasso. Bank of Economic
Community of West African
States. (David Hughes Photos)

pyramidal housing types with parapets, tapered walls, and little openings at the upper levels (Figs. C.71 and C.72).

Many ethnic groups inhabit Burkina Fasso, for example,
the Bobo, Somo, Lobi, Gourounsi, Gourmantche, and
Dagari. It should be noted that ethnic classification in Africa is
a complex issue because each group has a subgroup, and
there are always traces of relationships among the various
groups and subgroups. For example, Bourdier and Minh-ha
(1985) confirm that the Gourounsi are a culturally homoge-
neous group that includes the Lela, Nuna, Ko, Piguli, Sisala,
Kassena, Nankani, and Kusasi.

The extended family and the compound are two major
ingredients of the Gourounsi housing layout. The extended
family provides the social structure that shapes the architec-

ture, while the compound is the manifestation of the needs of the social structure of the Gourounsi family. The objective here is not to go into a detailed account of a Gourounsi compound, but to briefly show that there is continuity in the architecture of the sahel Sudan. Several scholars have written extensively about this, including Bourdier and Minh-ha.

Bourdier and Minh-ha (1985, 27) identify the love of freedom which necessitates the need for defense as one of the prime factors that influences Gourounsi architecture. This is not surprising in a region plagued by war and invasion since the beginning of the desiccation of the Sahara to the period of colonialism. The compounds and homes of Gourounsi people are also very elaborate and carefully planned to meet the needs of the extended family (Figs. 15.10 and 15.11). Gourounsi architecture was problematic to early European explorers of the region because they could not accept the notion of a socially backward people constructing houses which they described as fortresses, castles, and citadels. Louis

Tauxier was one of those who confronted the issue in his book *Le Noir du Soudan* (1912). In his opinion:

> *How can these populations, so primitive in many senses—these Nounoumas, Menkieras, Kassonfras, and the Bobos and Sankouras, as well as the other populations residing around Leo, since they all have this architecture—how can these populations, in which women still dress in leaves and men, not long ago, went naked, without shorts, a single piece of goatskin on their backs, turn out to be so advanced architecturally? (Bourdier and Minh-ha 1985, 27)*

Tauxier addressed his question by looking back at the Songhay empire, which, he wrote, may have arrived in the region from Egypt and dominated the region for 6 centuries, until about the 10th century. There is an element of continuity in the traditional form of house from antiquity to the present, and the integration of these traditional elements into Christian, Muslim, and other civic buildings in contemporary times is an expression of the triple heritage architecture of Africa.

16

THE ARCHITECTURE OF GHANA, BENIN REPUBLIC, CAMEROON, TOGO, SAO TOME AND PRINCIPE, AND EQUATORIAL GUINEA

hana, Benin Republic (formerly Dahomey), Cameroon, Togo, Sao Tome and Principe, and Equatorial Guinea are the subject of this chapter. The focus, however, is primarily on Ghana and Cameroon.

Benin, in the years of the Dahomey kingdom, was notorious for its role in the slave trade. The kingdom and its slave trade enterprise survived until 1885, when the last Portuguese slave ship sailed from the country, forced to leave by its huge battalion of women soldiers known as amazons. Most of the slaves from Dahomey were shipped to Brazil. The present capital of Benin is Porto Novo (Fig. 16.1), a modest town whose plan is influenced by Porto Novo lagoon. Boulevard Exterior is the dominant street in the city, and it forms a ring around the edge of the lagoon.

Togo was a German colony until after World War I when the French and the English seized the territory. The major ethnic group in Togo, the Ewe, has about two-thirds of its kin in Ghana. Both sides have remained separated because Ghana and Togo became independent states. President Iyasingbe Eyadema engaged in an intensive office construction program in the late 1970s and early 1980s in the capital city of Lome (Figs. 16.2 and C.73). Most of the projects were executed by French engineers and architects. The most impressive landmark in Lome is the Headquarters of the Bank of Economic Community of West African States (Fig. C.74). The fundamental parti of the bank is derived from the egg as a symbol of life that can grow into something special if hatched and nursed.

Sao Tome and Principe lie south of Nigeria and west of Gabon in the Gulf of Guinea. This is one of the least known independent states in the world. The island was the largest producer of cocoa in the 16th century, until Brazil and the Caribbean took over the production. The majority of the people on the island have their roots in the mainland from countries such as Nigeria, Gabon, and Cameroon. The remainder are descendants of migrants from the Caribbean who came to work on the plantations, causing at the same time a strong Creole influence on the culture. Their language is also Creole as is their architecture, a hybrid of plain Portuguese style. Sao Tome and Principe became independent from Portugal in 1975.

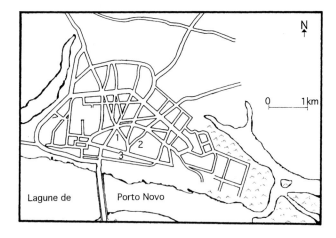

Fig. 16.1 *Porto Novo, Benin. City plan: (1) Government House and Palace Kokoye, (2) grand mosque, (3) market*

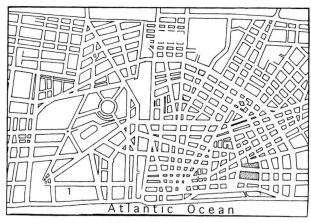

Fig. 16.2 *Lome, Togo. City plan: (1) National Assembly and Presidential Palace.*

Equatorial Guinea, with its rocky, troubled, dictator-ridden leadership, was first visited by Lope Gonsalvez and Fernao do Poo in 1409–1424. Both the Spanish and the Portuguese did much to control the destiny of this island nation, which covers an area of about 28,000 km². Ceded by the Portuguese, the Spanish converted this island state into plantations for cocoa, oil palm, coffee, and timber plantations toward the end of the 18th century. Because of migrant workers from Nigeria, Liberia, and the Cameroons, the territory lacked no labor to work the plantations. Equatorial Guinea became independent from Spain in 1968, with its capital at Malebo. Creole, a modified form of Portuguese and Spanish architecture, dominates the island. In addition, all these islands utilize traditional African buildings situated around courtyards. Houses are roofed with raffia, but the primary building materials are clay and timber. A lattice of square grid forms the structure of the wall, and the square openings are about 6 to 12 in. Wet clay is stacked in the squares from inside and outside the house until the wall is built up. A wet brush or sponge is then used to smooth the surface, the finished layer of which may use various hues of clay. Different geometric designs are sometimes used as decorations on the walls.

16.1 CAMEROON

Cameroon has many ethnic groups, including the Bamileke, Bamoun, Dourou, Fulani, Yako, and Yaunde. The family is often held together by the fabric of a long string of relatives that constitutes an extended family. The Bamileke, for example, group their houses around the homestead of the chief, something typical of many traditional African societies where leadership is by elder and seniority. This traditional housing

Fig. 16.3 *Cameroon. Colonial Lutheran church. 1906.* (Dipl-ing Wolfgang Lauber)

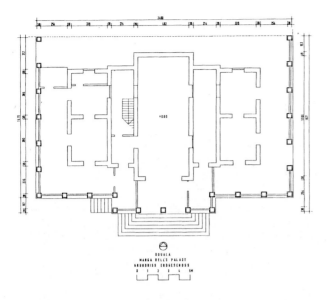

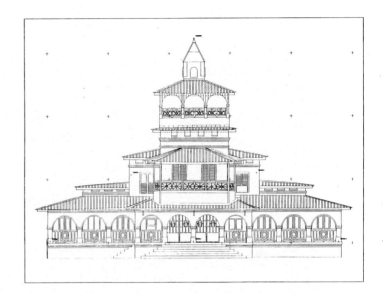

Fig. 16.4 (Above) Duala, Cameroon. Plan of Manga Bell's Palace.
(Dipl-ing Wolfgang Lauber)

Fig. 16.5 (Right) Duala, Cameroon. Southwest elevation of Manga
Bell's Palace. (Dipl-ing Wolfgang Lauber)

Fig. 16.6 (Below) Duala, Cameroon. Manga Bell's Palace. (Dipl-ing
Wolfgang Lauber)

Fig. C.73 (Opposite, top) Lome, Togo. Government office complex. 1980s. (Terri Plater)

Fig. C.74 (Opposite, bottom) Lome, Togo. Headquarters of the Bank of Economic Community of West African States. Pierre Goudiaby Atepa-Architects. (David Hughes Photos)

Fig. C.75 (Above) Buea, Cameroon. German colonial building. 1897. (Dipl-ing Wolfgang Lauber)

Fig. C.76 (Right) Cameroon. German colonial Lutheran church. 1890. (Dipl-ing Wolfgang Lauber)

Fig. 16.7 (Above) Bamenda, Cameroon. Courthouse. (Dipl-ing Wolfgang Lauber)

Fig. 16.8 (Left) Bamenda, Cameroon. Entrance to a German colonial fort. (Dipl-ing Wolfgang Lauber)

Fig. 16.9 (Right, top) Bamenda, Cameroon. A colonial fort. (Dipl-ing Wolfgang Lauber)

Fig. 16.10 (Right, bottom) Bamenda, Cameroon. German colonial house, governor's residence. (Dipl-ing Wolfgang Lauber)

pattern truly contrasts with the architecture brought by the Germans in 1884 and continued by the English and the French.

Some of the most striking colonial architectural landmarks left by the Germans in Cameroon are the Presidential Summer Lodge, still in use, and the Pagoda in Duala. Governor Puttkammer wanted to move the colonial capital to a less humid spot that would be more suitable to his health and that of future German settlers. Buea, at the foot of the Cameroon Mountain, was an ideal location. It was cool and had all the climatic conditions tolerable for a European in the tropics. Puttkammer transferred the administrative headquarters of the Kaiserliche Schutzruppe (police force) to Buea in 1897 after obtaining permission from Berlin. The Governor's Mansion was built on the highest hilltop overlooking Buea, and it remains the commanding landmark of the city. Catholic churches built in the 1890s and the beginning of the 20th century resemble those in the homelands of the missionaries, especially Alsace and southwest Germany, from which many of the missionaries came (Figs. 16.3, C.75, and C.76).

Manga Bell's Palace (Figs. 16.4 to 16.6), built for official use in Duala, represents the romanticized image of a colony in an exotic location far from Europe. There is no doubt that the Germans brought skilled workers and artisans to the colonies and built most of the projects in accordance with their construction methods at home. Another good example of this is the Magistrates' Court at Bamenda. The superstructure of the building was executed with burnt brick in excellent workmanship, while a wooden frame structure held the roof which was finished with shingles (Figs. 16.7). The first establishment in Bamenda was the fort, in 1912, before it was made a regional headquarters with a governor (Figs. 16.8 to 16.10). Thirty years of German presence in the Cameroons left indelible colonial marks, in spite of English and French efforts to erase German presence completely. Nevertheless, the German contributions should be seen as part of Africa's triple heritage culture.

16.2   TRADITIONAL ARCHITECTURE IN GHANA: THE ASHANTI FETISH HOUSE

In 1957, Ghana gained independence from Britain after 55 years of colonial rule. This was accomplished through the leadership of the charismatic leader, Kwame Nkrumah, Africa's greatest anticolonial warrior, a man educated in the United States. The new country was named after the ancient empire of the Sudan (West Africa). Ghana is not immune to the ethnic complexity that makes up African countries. It has its own share of numerous ethnic groups, ranging from the

Fig. 16.11 Banjwiasi, southern Ghana. Plan and section of a fetish house.

Ashanti, Fante, Ewe, and many others. This section focuses on Ashanti fetish houses.

It would be difficult to understand Ashanti architecture, especially the designs and decorations on the walls of the fetish houses, without taking a look at the meanings that inspired them. For the Ashantis, there is a direct connection between materialism, ancestor worship, and the house in which the shrine of the ancestor is located. These factors come together to form the mystical festival that the Ashanti celebrate annually. Ghana was not called the Gold Coast in vain. The Ashanti golden stool and the associated conspicuous golden jewelry, which are still celebrated annually, bear witness to this. No other ethnic group around the world displays so much wealth in gold during a single celebration. The whole exercise commemorates the greatness of the ancient Ashanti state.

One of the earliest descriptions of Kumasi, the major town of the Ashanti, was by T. Edward Bodich, an Englishman who published a book about his mission from Cape Coast

Castle to Ashanti in 1819. According to Bodich, the Ashantenes (King's) Palace was located in the center of the town, overlooking a central playground. The palace consisted of several buildings surrounding a number of courtyards, a tradition typical of many African palaces. The walls were well decorated, and the main entrance of the palace led to a court 200 yd long. This first court was surrounded by rooms occupied by the Ashantenes' captains. Other courts followed for the wives and for special occasions. The royal bed chamber was enclosed by a 30 ft² court. Overstuffed pillows and wooden window shutters garnished in silver and gold were in the royal chamber. The town itself was well laid out, with wide streets flanked by houses and trees.

A royal mausoleum in the town of Bantama contained separate rooms that housed the coffins and skeletal remains of eight Ashanti kings. These skeletons were held together with golden wires. Swithenbank (1969) states that the sacred nature of the Ashanti kingship and the absolute link between living and dead made the mausoleum the most venerated building in Ashanti. Swithenbank also mentions that Baden-Powell burned the mausoleum in 1895, after being unable to locate the golden skeletons. He wanted the gold that held the bones together, but the skeletons were hidden from him by the people.

The composition of fetish houses reflected the lifestyle of the Ashanti people. The courtyards were centers of outdoor activities, where children played, food was prepared, and meetings were held. Construction was done communally and the materials were mostly traditional. However, in recent times, aluminum roofs have largely replaced the traditional thatched roof (Fig. 16.11). The shrine, known as *abosom,* serves as the oracle, a place where disputes can be settled, advice given to individuals, sickness cured, and the village guarded, among other functions. The shrine is also closely tied to the Ashanthene, the Ashanti king, and each shrine or abosom has a chief priest and several other priests. There are, of course, seances, prophets, and prophetesses. The shrine ceremony is accompanied by music and celebrations, all in accordance with ancient traditions.

This is just part of the Ashanti's culture. Other ethnic groups in Ghana also have unique cultures and architecture that reflect the way they view their society. One of the aspects of Ashanti architecture that fascinated Western travelers is the gables and the tracesories that decorate the windows and walls of the houses. These designs came out of the mix of Islam and indigenous culture of the Ashanti people. Colonial activities in Accra and other Ghanaian cities demonstrate that the triple heritage is complete in Ghana.

16.3 ACCRA

Accra, on the Gold Coast, is the capital of Ghana. Most of the former British West Africa, such as Lagos, was governed from there as part of the British Gold Coast. Being centered at Gold Coast, Accra was planned as a capital for British West Africa,

Fig. 16.13 Accra, Ghana. General Post Office. 1930s. (American Geographical Society Collection, The University of Wisconsin-Milwaukee Library)

Fig. C.78 Lagon, Ghana. Library at the University of Ghana. 1950s. (American Geographical Society Collection, The University of Wisconsin-Milwaukee Library)

Fig. C.79 Accra, Ghana. Arch of Independence. 1957.
(American Geographical Society Collection, The University of Wisconsin-Milwaukee Library)

and the British built several structures there. Some of these buildings reflect the British desire for an imperial headquarters that would rival the headquarters of French West Africa. The essential elements of the architecture were of English influence.

The Customs House and the General Post Office buildings are two examples of British construction. Both buildings are executed in modest Renaissance styles, with Roman arches and symmetrical compositions (Figs. 16.12 and 16.13). Influences of the Portuguese plain style and North African horseshoe arches are also present. The Parliament Building, completed in the 1950s, has a modern look with classical influences clearly expressed in the portico of the main entrance (Fig. C.77). When Nkrumah assumed the presidency upon independence, he moved quickly to build universities, factories, and low-income housing. Ghana University campus at Lagon, completed in the 1950s and 1960s, has a series of courtyards surrounded by modest one-, two-, and three-story buildings. The facade of the main library at Ghana University Lagon has a courtyard and a central pagoda that are very inviting (Fig. C.78). The choice of organizing the buildings around courtyards comes from the traditional Ashanti compound, but other foreign influences on the composition as a whole are readily visible.

Perhaps the most contradictory of all structures in Accra is the Arch of Independence which celebrates the freedom of the Ghanaians from British imperialism. If nothing else, it represents the irony and identity crisis that surround African politics. For a Pan-Africanist and anticolonial warrior like the late President Kwame Nkrumah, the arch should be a reminder that the world is forever bound to a common destiny of give and take. The arch (Fig. C.79), finished in beautiful stonework with inscriptions of "Freedom and Justice," could be standing in Rome, Paris, London, Berlin, or any other Western capital. It is clearly an adoption of the imperial Roman triumphal arch to express Ghana's triumph over the British. Unconsciously, the Western legacy of Africa's triple heritage architecture is at work.

In this case, a Western trophy in stone has been borrowed to celebrate an African victory over a Western imperial power of the 20th century. In Cape Town, South Africa, ancient African architecture and progenies of the Great Sphinx and Avenue of the Rams were adopted to celebrate the Rhodes Memorial and the Western victory over Africa. This crossroads of cultural exchange is the reality of African politics which has shaped the continent since ancient times. But above all, these monuments are unconscious expressions of the truism of Africa's triple heritage culture.

chapter 17

THE ARCHITECTURE OF NIGERIA

igeria, with its 30 states and the federal capital territory of Abuja, presents an excellent opportunity for a discussion of the emerging urban centers throughout the continent of Africa. Additionally, in its architecture, Nigeria offers many examples of the triple heritage culture of Africa due to its ethnic diversity and the interrelated influences of indigenous, Islamic, and European culture. Accordingly, this chapter briefly examines the house forms of the Hausas, Ibos (Igbos), and Yorubas, and looks at the Nigerian cities of Kano, Zaria, Kaduna, Ibadan, Lagos, Abuja, Port Harcourt, Calabar, and Enugu.

Islam did not come to the region until at least the 10th century. During the 11th century, the 12th king was the first Muslim leader in the northern part of the country. By then, Nigeria already had strong connections with North Africa through Bilina and Zawila in the Fezzan. The vast region was under the Kanem Bornu state. There is little doubt, howev-er, that the mosque as a building type was introduced in the region as the ruling aristocracy became Islamized. The Mosque at Bornu, estimated to be 1000 years old (Moughtin 1985; Prussin 1986), is one of the earliest Islamic structures in the region.

European contact in Nigeria probably took place earlier, but the first well-documented contacts are with the Portuguese in 1472, who expanded the slave trade in the region in the 15th, 16th, and 17th centuries, and gradually introduced Western architecture, first as trading infrastructures and then as colonial administrative facilities. English pressure in the region to counter French presence came early, and the English began penetrating the interior by 1807. Sir Frederick Lugard, director of the Royal Niger Trading Company, unified northern and southern Nigeria into a federation in 1914 and became the country's first governor general. If India was the pride of British colonial acquisition in the Orient, Nigeria was the pride in Africa.

17.1 HAUSA ARCHITECTURE

The region in question is mainly in northern Nigeria, though Hausas can be found in Niger and the Mali republic. This

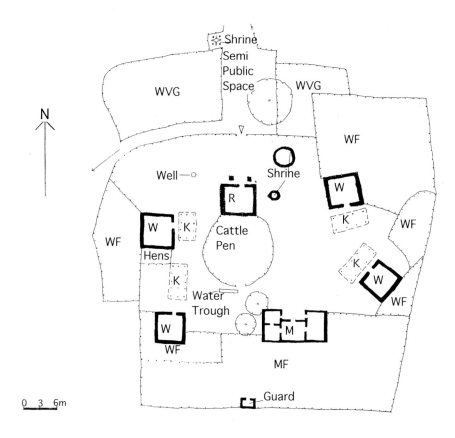

Fig. 17.1 Hausaland, northern Nigeria. A traditional compound: (W) women's room, (WF) woman's food store, (WVG) woman's vegetable garden, (K) kitchen, (R) reception room, (M) man's room, and (MF) man's food store. (J. C. Moughtin)

Fig. 17.2 (Opposite) Kano, Nigeria. Aerial view of Great Mosque.

region, known for the wealth of its agricultural produce, leatherwork, iron, gold, and kola nuts, is problematic to discuss in historical terms because of the conflicts of opinion and record about the origins and spread of the Hausa culture. Some scholars have suggested a northern, perhaps Saharan, origin for Hausas. However, more recently, the view has been advanced that Hausas spread not southward from the Sahara in the north but from east to west across the savanna belt of northern Nigeria. Several relationships between the architecture of Hausaland and that of Songhay suggest that they had a common origin in Egyptian antiquity and the disintegrated western Sudanic empires of Ghana, Mali, and Songhay.

For the purpose of this brief study, Hausa architecture should be seen as the traditional dominant architecture of cities that were under the medieval Hausa states. Cities such as Banely, Kano, Katsina, Bornu, Sokoto, Kaduna, and Zaria, to name a few, would fall in this category.

According to legend, Hausa states were founded by a man who killed a snake that prevented people from getting water from a well in Daura. Bayejida, as the man was called, then married the queen of Daura, and his sons founded the seven states of Hausaland. This legend is seen by some scholars as evidence of external intrusion from the north by a politically organized group who defeated the aborigines and set up a

political structure that led to the urbanization of the region.

Prior to urbanization, Hausas lived in small agricultural communities. Moughtin (1985) agrees with Abdullahi Smith that these early agricultural communities were likely to have been independent family groups practicing communal shifting cultivation. This agricultural community explains the emphasis upon extended family, with all its influences upon the social life of the people, including economic and production methods. According to Laya (1981, 453), "from 1500 to 1800 Hausaland remained primarily a region of manoma (farmers) who made judicious use of the agricultural potential through a variety of techniques, including fertilizers and crop rotation and association."

Moughtin (1985) also suggests that urban centers may have developed in Hausaland during the first millennium A.D., before the formation of states. He considered specialization in ironwork, leather, pottery, and goldsmithing as stimuli for the growth of such centers. Hence, the independent agricultural communities were representatives of a trade specialization by the majority who supplied food to the urban population. The practice of the indigenous African religion of ancestor worship and the belief in spirits predates the coming of Islam. There are two major types of Hausa settlement patterns: the indigenous settlement pattern and the pattern influenced by the coming of Islam after the Uthmadan Fodio

Holy Wars, or the *jihad*. This second pattern, formed by the influence of Islam, is actually a modification of the indigenous settlement pattern with the major gathering place, the emir's palace adjacent to the market square, replaced by a mosque.

Traditional religion, regardless of Islam and Christianity, plays a significant role in the life of the people and affects the building tradition. Moughtin (1985, 57) reports that the "Hausa house plan for both Muslim and non-Muslim families follows the traditional African pattern having rooms arranged within or surrounding a courtyard" (Fig. 17.1). The four cardinal points of the compass determine Hausa spatial schema, which goes in east-west, north-south, north-west-south-east, and north-east-south-west directions. These points meet at a center with a vertical axis linking heaven and earth, and it is this schema that also defines the relationship between people and the cosmos.

In Hausa mythology, the eastern and southern cardinal points are masculine, whereas the western and northern are feminine. These cardinal points become personified in ritual (Moughtin 1985, 34). For example, the priest in traditional religion believes that the gods reside in different sections of the cosmos, each corresponding to cardinal points. He therefore invokes them as "you gods of the East, West, North, South." The gods assume personalities according to their locations, "sometimes varying the formula to: sons of the East, sons of the South, sons of the West, sons of the North;

as though addressing a common father Dodo and four children" (Moughtin 1985, 35). The east, the direction of light or the sun, holds the key to life. In addition, the psychological impact of indigenous religion on the life of the people should be considered when evaluating their physical environment. The orientation of several Hausa cities, such as Kano and Zaria, gives credence to this proposition.

17.2 KANO

Kano had a humble beginning as demonstrated by the following poem:

Grass-hut after grass-hut, Kano was founded.
Thanks be to Allah and the Prophet, whose heart,
split, its anger cut out, emptied of all but deeds of light.
Tell of the mahogany tree where hunters first cooked and camped sharing lion
and elephant. Vapors rose, men soon came, a few with women trailing...
Came one who saw Kano had no wall,
another added fourteen towers, only the tallest crumbled in a flood....
Thus was Kano built, grass-hut beyond grass-hut
with thirteen ramparts on the outer wall.

Omar S. Pound (1971)

Fig. C.80 (Left) Kano, Nigeria. Great Mosque. Paid for by the emir and the citizens. Designed by Public Works Department. 1950. (American Geographical Society Collection, The University of Wisconsin-Milwaukee Library)

Fig. C.81 (Below) Kano, Nigeria. Before prayer time at Great Mosque during Ramadan. (American Geographical Society Collection, The University of Wisconsin-Milwaukee Library)

Fig. C.82 (Opposite, top) Kano, Nigeria. Prayer time at Great Mosque during Ramadan. (American Geographical Society Collection, The University of Wisconsin-Milwaukee Library)

Fig. C.83 (Opposite, bottom) Kano, Nigeria. Wall and entry pylons to emir's palace. (American Geographical Society Collection, The University of Wisconsin-Milwaukee Library)

THE ARCHITECTURE OF NIGERIA 301

Fig. C.84 Kano, Nigeria. A decorated Hausa house with indigenous and Western motifs. (American Geographical Society Collection, The University of Wisconsin-Milwaukee Library)

Fig. C.85 (Opposite, top) Kano, Nigeria. Traditional Hausa architecture reminiscent of ancient Egyptian house types. Roof is aluminum.

Fig. C.86 (Opposite, bottom) Kano, Nigeria. Governor's residence showing influence of Hausa and European styles. (Arieh Sharon, Eldar Sharon, and Egboramy Company Nigeria Limited)

Islam was already in Kano by the middle of the 14th century. The Kano Chronicles state that, in Yaji's time, the Wangarawa came from Melle (Mali) bringing the Muslim religion (Clarke 1982). In ancient Ghana, a twin city 6 mi distant developed with the rise of Islam to allow the Arab travelers to practice their religion, while the king and his people practiced their traditional religion in the royal city. Additionally, Kano had a region reserved for non-Hausa immigrants who were also non-Muslims, and the arrival of Europeans transformed that region, adding another city to the twin structure of Kano. Therefore, the triple heritage city is, without reservation, a fact in West Africa, especially in Kano, Nigeria, which has the walled Islamic city, the non-Islamic city occupied mostly by non-Muslim Africans, and the highly Westernized European quarters that later became government reserved quarters. In Kano, the walled city and the areas settled by non-Muslims, mainly Sabon Gari and the wealthy enclaves of Fagge and Tudun Wada (Wealth Hill), are quite visible. Fagge and Tudun Wada are occupied by merchants, mostly Nigerians, Lebanese, and Indians. Both sectors are, however, innovations of colonialism as a way to justify the existence of the European quarters. In the traditional city (Figs. 17.2, C.80 to C.83), the fundamental structure of the Hausa city is visible. The mosque, the palace, and the market concretely define the city square (Fig. 1.7).

Hausa cities were always surrounded by walls with gates, and Kano is no exception. As Moughtin (1985) points out, Barth, a German traveler, did comment on the size and scale of the defensive structures of Kano. The wall was estimated at 12-m-high, with high battlements and moats around its approximately 16-km outer circumference. The main mosque in the middle of the square and the endless wall of the emir's palace are two major objects that define the main square, the locus of the old city. Everything else spreads out from this square, which looks like a no man's land when it is not being utilized.

The main square is largely utilized in the early morning hours and in the evening, before the intense sun and after sunset. People hold meetings at different locations within the square, bringing their mats with them, and children play in the moonlight. However, on Fridays, the Muslim holy day, the situation is different, as it is on major Muslim festivals such as Ramadan and during other traditional ceremonies that the square belongs primarily to the mosque. As on regular days, the mosque blends with the surroundings, and any individual in the square is almost rendered invisible by the large open space. Gradually, the space begins to fill with people, on whom the intense sunlight seems to have no impact. In fact, people wear two to three layers of clothing, mainly light shades of silk that deflect the sun's rays. By the time the ceremonies begin, the entire area is packed with people seated on personalized spots covered with rugs, mats, and carpets. The ancient walled city of Kano still provides privacy for the Muslims during their celebrations by ensuring that a ritual designed to be private and sacred remains so within a public domain.

Kano retains a major architectural repertoire of detail and construction method (Fig. C.84) that has inspired varying interpretations from different scholars. The suggestions range from that of ancient Egypt as the origin of Hausa architecture to its source as a purely Islamic influence brought to the region by a few individuals who had been in contact with North Africa. In any case, as part of the savanna, Hausaland provides an ideal environment for the construction of adobe architecture. Hausa construction techniques are derived from the ancient Sudanic states of West Africa. Prussin (1986) points out that the similarity of several Hausa and Songhay construction terms demonstrates Songhay origin. For example, *soro* and *bene*, which mean "square clay house with an upper story or terrace," are common terms in Hausaland as well as in Songhay. The Songhays and Hausas have ancient connections to Egypt, and these are reflected in their architecture.

Wall decoration is an important aspect of Hausa architecture. Clay is a suitable material for the manipulation of colors. The most common method of applying clay plaster is by natural movement of the builders' hands, sometimes with the aid of a sponge or other soft materials that help to produce the desired effects. Ornamentation of exterior and interior walls derives primarily from traditional themes and motifs of animals, but Koranic and mechanical motifs have been incorporated into the vocabulary, as confirmation of both Islamic and Western influence. Heathcote (1976) writes that some of the wall paintings include bicycles, airplanes, and verses from the Holy Koran. The transition from the use of purely clay and adobe construction method is quite visible. The wall that surrounds the emir's palace is built mainly of cement and quarried stones. Most buildings in the complex and the rest of the city have also made the transition from the traditional material. The governor's residence in Kano, for example, combines Hausa vocabulary with modern forms to achieve balanced composition (Fig. C.85).

Kano also has a planned modern section outside the city walls testifying to the fact that the original master plan has changed considerably since 1903 when the British first occupied the city. A 20-year development plan was prepared for the city in 1963, and the city has grown with this plan as its major blueprint. Kano remains, since the 16th century, one of the major cities of Muslim Africa and will continue to occupy an important position for many centuries.

17.3 ZARIA

The city of Zaria also reflects the triple architectural heritage. In this case, the processional layout from the traditional city to Tudun Wada, the central business district, the European quarters (GRA), and Sabon Gari to the university is very clear. The living arrangement is similar to the living arrangement in Kano, but in a linear order from the old city. The locus of the old city is the palace, the mosque, and the market square (Fig. 1.7), which maintains a vista with the palace and the mosque. The market square is surrounded by artisans: leatherworkers, blacksmiths, goldsmiths, and fabric dyers. The wall that separates the emir's palace from the rest of the city forms a meeting point between the ruler and his subjects. The emir is not seen often, but when he emerges, the people rush to salute him and pay their respects in front of the palace. Both the front of the palace and the gate that creates it are symbols of power, and Nigeria's aristocrats do not hesitate to modify and enlarge it as time goes on. In Bauchi, Katsina, and Sokoto, the connection between Hausa architecture and the aristocracy is always very visible.

17.4 KADUNA

Lord Frederick Lugard's desire to mold a nation out of Muslim northern Nigeria and to divert the trans-Saharan trade from north to south where it would be seaborne to Europe motivated him to camp his military garrison next to River Kaduna. Several years later, the emirates which made up northern Nigeria were receiving orders from Camp Lugard. Kaduna was planned as the capital of the whole of northern Nigeria, an area about the size of France. The rail line that reached the city in 1927 helped to institutionalize its development as a regional capital. However, while the city continued to grow as a northern capital, other events overtook its destiny. These include: the joining of the northern and southern protectorates with the capital at Lagos; the division of Nigeria into four regions, and then into 12 states as it was sliding into war in 1967; the creation of an additional six states in 1975 by General Murutala Muhammad; and the final splitting of Nigeria into 30 states by General Ibrahim Babangida in 1991. In each case, a new capital was created for each state, and available resources were split into smaller parts. The objectives behind these partitions were to pacify disgruntled ethnic groups and to implement a development strategy through decentralization.

Because Lugard initially adopted a limited growth plan in 1915 (Fig. 17.3), Kaduna developed in stages. The city core was well established prior to World War II, but it was restricted to the government reserved area (GRA), parts of Sabon Gari, and Clarks Quarters. The villages of Makera and Kakuri, south of River Kaduna, were independent villages far from the city limits. Between 1932 and 1954, the city expanded

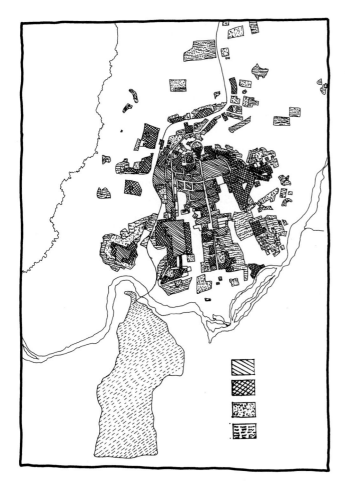

mostly north of the river, but it grew both north and south from 1954 to 1965, engulfing and bringing Makera and Kakuri into its limits. A proposal for future development of the city by Max Lock and Partners envisages Kaduna as a primary city in northern Nigeria. Different grades of housing were planned for the city, with the most luxurious set aside for Europeans in the government reserved areas.

Kaduna is one of the well-planned colonial cities of Nigeria. Its colonial buildings have left an indelible mark, with Lord Lugard Hall the most significant and the main locus of the original town (Fig. 17.4), testifying to Kaduna's original role as a colonial administration center. It is now the capital of Kaduna state, but its importance and industrial growth remain significant as one of the major cities of Nigeria. Because of its once booming textile industry, Kaduna has been described as the Manchester of Nigeria. Today, it is the home of Nigeria's growing military industrial complex, including petrochemical industries with oil shipped from the south to the north via pipeline. This will certainly ensure Kaduna's place as a major commercial center in the country.

17.5 IGBO ARCHITECTURE

The Igbos (Ibos) inhabit southeastern Nigeria, a forest zone with abundant timber and clay for building. Like many ethnic groups of Africa, Igbos live both in urban centers and in villages, and the extended family is the basic unit of social organization. The extended family house layouts are grouped in compounds. Most of the building material—clay, raffia palm frond ribs, and timber—is locally obtained. Raffia palm ribs and poles are used for wall construction. They are woven into a lattice of square grids and plastered over with clay, thereby forming a smooth surface. A similar lattice structure is used for roofing, with raffia palm fronds serving as matting. Most of the houses in Igboland are of the impluvium type because of the structure of the courtyards which they form, and each house is built to serve a specific function.

For example, meeting houses and spirit houses, which are variations of ancestor houses or houses of cults associated with specific deities, are common in Igboland. The Mbaris are one of the Igbo clans which has elaborate building traditions honoring their ancestors and gods. Mbari temples are dedicated to the supreme goddess, Ala. Ala temples are built in secrecy by special builders who are ordained to perform such

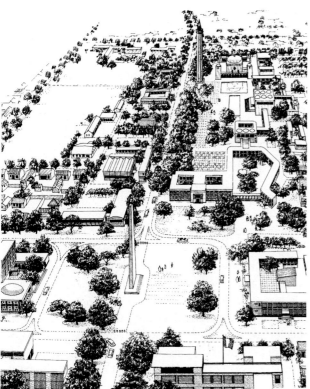

Fig. 17.3 Kaduna, Nigeria. City plan showing stages of growth. (Janel Hetland)

Fig. 17.4 Kaduna, Nigeria. Civic Center looking south. (Janel Hetland)

spiritual constructions. The temples are primarily rectangular and square in plan, and can be three stories tall. Serene locations, with trees and shade where the spirits of Ala and the gods will not be disturbed, are preferred. Typically, four major clay columns support the temple. Timber is used for the rafters and raffia palm as roofing mat. In recent times, aluminum has been applied as part of the roofing material, and the columns and walls are made with cement. Jones (1984) confirms that Mbari temples which were roofed with aluminum are modified to suit the new material.

A main entrance, determined by the direction of the deities portrayed in the temple, is a common feature; figurines of Ala, mother of the entire community, and her children are arranged around the edges of the main entrance. These figurines are molded in clay, and the entire edifice, the structure as well as the statutes, is painted. Sculptors who build Mbari temples are usually local artists and builders hired by the community. They are isolated from the rest of the community so that they have no distractions while working to produce special monuments for Ala and the deities of the town. It is not uncommon to have several carved and molded images in an Mbari temple.

Unlike the Mbaris who represent their ancestors with figurines and other images symbolic of the goddess Ala, the Igbo-Ukwu people built elaborate burial chambers for their departed chiefs. The chambers are lined with carved wood, and the corpse is laid or seated in the middle of the chambers. Some of the chief's precious earthly belongings are carefully arranged within the chamber so that he will not lack anything in the life after death.

House decoration is another essential aspect of Igbo architecture. Elaborate geometric patterns are painted on walls with clay plaster, and most finished walls have impressive smooth surfaces. In Igboland, clay is found in many different shades. The topsoil covering the clay is very dark. Thus, it is possible to obtain a wide range of hues for the wall painting, which is traditionally carried out by the women. Water is used to dissolve the clays, and the plaster is applied with sponges. In some cases, walls are painted in two separate colors, a dark color trimming the base, while the rest of the wall is whitewashed.

House decorations in Igboland also reflect the triple heritage of African architecture. In the past, most of the wall paintings portrayed images derived from daily experience and the way the people perceived the environment. Now, religious themes rooted in ancestor worship, mystical cults such as Ozo, morals which represent the achievements of notables in the community, and the symbols of fertility which ensure the continuity of the people are now indiscriminately mixed with nontraditional symbols in these house paintings.

Scholars and art critics call this form of mural expression *new functional art,* but it is appropriate to see it here as the continuity and manifestation of the triple heritage of African history. The incorporation of Western images into traditional Igbo architecture is indicative of a multifarious aesthetic expression (Vogel 1991). New functional art draws no distinction between manufactured goods, such as cars and airplanes, and natural objects, such as trees, birds, and animals.

Columns and portals are also decorated in traditional Igbo architecture. Iroko trees, *oji* in Igbo (*Chlorophora excelsa*), make excellent materials for carving. Some traditional houses in Igboland are embellished with carved columns, each usually carved from its capital to its base and thereby a sculpture by itself. Most have forked branches for beams, and animals, mythical creatures, masks, ancestors' images, and different kinds of geometric patterns are commonly represented on them. Carved doors and windows can also be seen in some traditional Igbo houses. Neaher (1981) says that the people of Awka, in Igboland, once decorated the portals of their houses with imposing carved door panels. Few of these remain today because most were destroyed during the Nigerian civil war. Neaher (1981) estimates that these doors are 1–1.5 m high and 1 m wide. Several panels may span the main entrance to a compound, one of which swings around a pivot for entry. *Mgbo ezi,* as they are called, meaning "the protector of the compound" in Igbo, differ from other portals both in dimension and in their intricate designs of delicately combined geometric patterns which may include circles, diamonds, rectangles, squares, and triangles; in most cases, other kinds of images are also represented on the panels. Mgbo ezi are significant not just as physical defense mechanisms but also because they protect the members of a compound from evil spirits and because they are carved and ordained only by men whose ancestors passed the skill of carving doors to them.

17.6 YORUBA ARCHITECTURE

The Yorubas are inhabitants of southwestern Nigeria. They trace their ancestry to Ife, where their great ancestor Oduduwa settled. Alagoa (1981) suggests that the primacy of Ife in Yoruba history is based on numerous factors. Its founder, Oduduwa, was supposed to have come from heaven or Mecca, and his sons to have founded all the Yoruba states. It is suspected that the oral legend referring to Oduduwa's migration from the east does not refer to any place in the Middle East, but rather to regions across the River Niger, north of present-day Yoruba territories. Similarities between Nok terra cotta in central Nigeria and the bronze art of Ife indicate a common origin in spite of a time gap of over 1000

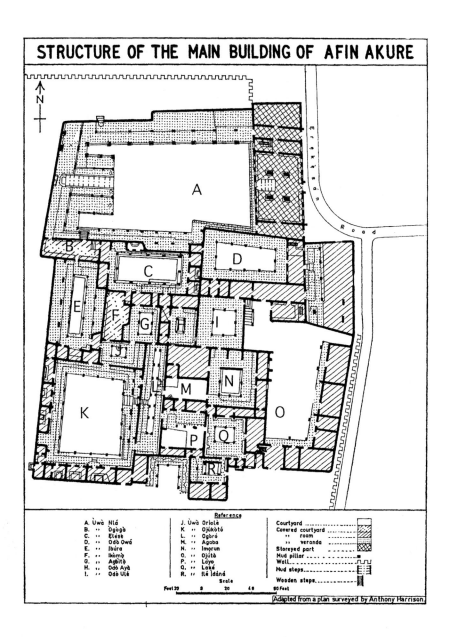

STRUCTURE OF THE MAIN BUILDING OF AFIN AKURE

Reference

A. Ùwà Nlá	J. Ùwà Orlolè	Courtyard
B. ,, Ògògà	K. ,, Ojúkòtó	Covered courtyard
C. ,, Elésè	L. ,, Ogbró	,, room
D. ,, Odò Owá	M. ,, Agoba	,, veranda
E. ,, Ibúra	N. ,, Imorun	Storeyed part
F. ,, Ikòmò	O. ,, Ojútà	Mud pillar
G. ,, Agbitò	P. ,, Láyo	Wall
H. ,, Odò Ayà	Q. ,, Loké	Mud steps
I. ,, Odò Ulé	R. ,, Ilé Idáné	Wooden steps

Scale

Feet 20   8   20   40   60 Feet

Adapted from a plan surveyed by Anthony Harrison.

years between the two cultures. Hence, the Yorubas may be descended from the much older Nok culture which settled north of the River Niger.

On the other hand, several vocabularies in the Yoruba language correspond and have similar meanings to ancient Egyptian vocabularies. If the Yorubas descended from the Nok culture, it follows that the Nok were one of the early groups to migrate from the Nile Valley to the River Niger area. This would explain the similarities in language, religion, and other cultural attributes passed down to the Yorubas from the Nile Valley.

The Yorubas are generally urban dwellers. Houses are grouped in compounds according to lineage, occupation, and position in town. The center and the most important part of

every Yoruba town is the *afin*, the *oba's* residence or king's palace. The afin occupied the largest area of land compared to all compounds in Yoruba towns. "By far the largest extant palace in Yorubaland is that of Owo. Extending over 108.5 acres, it is more than twice the size of the next biggest palace at Ilesha, which covers about 51 acres" (Ojo 1966, 23). The afin is usually a thickly walled, multiple compound within a walled town, and it is the cultural center of every Yoruba town. All roads lead to the afin, within whose grounds are the town hall, court of justice, theater, and sports arena.

The religious significance of the afin cannot be overemphasized. First, the oba (king) is restricted within the afin because he is sacred and must be present always to serve his people and his ancestors. This is where the wall surrounding

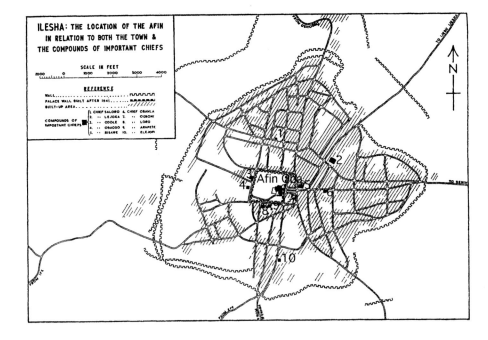

Fig. 17.6 Ilesha, Nigeria. The location of the afin in relation to both the town and the compounds of important chiefs. (G. J. A. Ojo, Oxford University Press, and Allison Crane, OUP)

the afin comes into play. This wall serves as protection because it was forbidden to see the oba, and whoever did so would die. The walls had miniwindows from which the oba could see everything happening in town without being seen. Confidential meetings were held within the walls of the afin in special courtyards and rooms exclusively reserved for such purposes. The oba could worship at the temples and shrines within the afin at his convenience, and special religious ceremonies and oaths were observed in the shrines in the witness of the gods, such as Sango, the god of thunder. In recent times, mosques and churches have become part of the religious shrines in a Yoruba afin.

The afin reflects a hierarchy and order of the city. For example, the wall that surrounds the town is often higher and wider than the walls of the afin, but all the other walls in the town are low in comparison to the walls of the afin. The walls around the town are for security, but the walls of the afin serve the purpose of keeping the oba from the sight of the general public because of his sacred nature and divine descendance from the gods. As the major focal point of every town, the main entrance to the afin always has highly decorated doorways and elaborate architecture. A series of courtyards opens onto one another for residence wives and special occasions (Fig. 17.5). Each house surrounding a courtyard has a front porch, which is usually almost enclosed by the low level of the roof.

The arrangement of the afin courtyards and surrounding buildings closely resembles the bureaucratic structure of the oba's government. This order is derived mainly from the

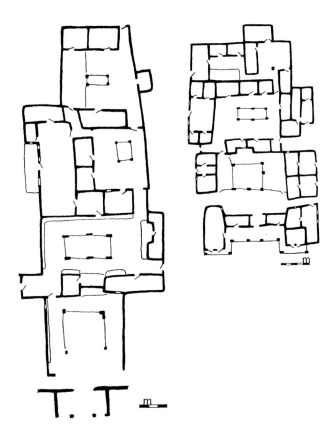

Fig. 17.7 Ife, Nigeria. Plan of the residence of Chief Fawole Onitiju Obalorun. 1974. (Arieh Sharon, Eldar Sharon, and Egboramy Company Nigeria Limited) or (Labelle Prussin and University of California Press)

Fig. 17.8 Ife, Nigeria. Plan of the Seru family compound. 1974.

sociopolitical structure of the Yoruba and is based on lineages, age groups, the title societies and cults such as Ogboni, the councils of chiefs, and the kingship. The afin is usually occupied exclusively by the oba and his wives who can number in the hundreds. In fact, the large size of the afin is primarily due to the number of wives. Surrounding the afin, as in Figure 17.6, are the residences of the oba's ministers and the king-makers. The oba's compound is not the only compound with multiple courtyards. Most Yoruba houses are laid out in a similar manner (Figs. 17.7 and 17.8).

Construction in early times was in clay adobe style with raffia and other roofing materials. However, the turn of the 20th century ushered in the use of modern building materials like cement and aluminum roofing. The style of the modern afin is of Portuguese origin and is now identified as the Brazilian style, probably because of the large number of emancipados who returned from Brazil and brought new building styles and culture with them. The smooth plain surface of the Portuguese architecture is quite visible. Sometimes, stairs are lined with handrails that have a series of balustrades. The afin remain major landmarks in Yoruba towns because of the role of the obas as spiritual and cultural custodians.

17.7   IFE AND IBADAN

Ancient African, European, and Muslim customs converge at Ife and Ibadan, the two most sacred Yoruba towns of Nigeria, to form a new kind of partnership in the triple heritage tradition of Africa. Here, myth mixes with science and 20th-century education to create a cultural maze that transcends architecture and manifests itself in the existential essence of both towns. Today, both Ife and Ibadan are not only homes to the spiritual leadership of the Yorubas but are also homes to two of Nigeria's premier universities.

The Yorubas trace their ancestry back to Oduduwa who is connected to Ife. In Yoruba mythology and history, Oduduwa, their founding god-ancestor, came from the east to settle at Ife, their most sacred town. Strangely enough, Yoruba religion still bears witness to this ancient myth with customs and sacred names that can be traced to Egyptian antiquity. For example, Orisa, the god of all gods in Yoruba religion, is a descendant of the Egyptian god Osiris. The same god features in Ibo (Igbo) vocabulary as Orisa. So *Orisa Emeka* ("God has done a lot") and *Ekene dili Orisa* ("Thanks be to God") are common Ibo expressions. The Egyptian sun god Ra survives in Yoruba as Rara. *Miri,* the Egyptian word for "water," is the same in both Yoruba and Ibo languages. Finally, the name of the spiritual head of the Yorubas who dwells in Ife as the custodian of Yoruba religion and culture is Oni. According to Diop (1974), Oni is another name for Osiris.

The blend between African architecture and the European and Muslim influences in both cities and in other Yoruba towns can be understood by looking at the personality of the Oni of Ife. The present Oni of Ife still obeys and enforces all Yoruba customs within his office, in spite of his university education. In his being is found an extreme multiple personality, that of conservative African culture intricately blended with the influence of colonial British Oxbridge mannerisms and lingual articulations. Architecture in Ibadan and Ife has taken these multiple characteristics, probably because this interrelationship is the inevitable destiny of the built environment in Africa. The Universities of Ife and Ibadan exemplify these complex relationships in African architecture.

Ife lies within the high-forest belt of Yorubaland, 800 ft above sea level. Its climatic conditions of rainfall, temperature, and humidity are mild year round. The town is located in an attractive, slightly undulating, wooded countryside, rich in agricultural plantations, which form the economic basis for the people's livelihood and also present an incentive for the development of the university's agricultural and biological departments.

According to Sharon and Sharon (1976), the architects in charge of the Ife University project, the main core of the university was conceived as a square, 240 by 240 m (Figs. 17.9 and C.87). This serves as the heart of the whole university complex, with its main piazza flanked on three sides by the secretariat, library, and assembly hall, and with all the main faculties grouped around this square. This core consists of a closely knit complex of buildings, gardens, and patios linked by covered walkways, ramps, and terraces, all progressing toward the main piazza. Bicycle and car parks are located on the verges of the building areas only, making sure that the main core remains a purely pedestrian architectural entity. This densely built campus is a modern hybrid of the traditional oba's afin where multiple courtyards are created to serve different purposes.

Maxwell Fry adopted a similar strategy in planning the University at Ibadan. One of the main planning considerations was to relate the building design to climatic factors. Most of the public buildings in Nigeria are oriented from east to west, their main elevations facing north and south, for protection from heat and glare. This also ensures cross-ventilation by prevailing breezes coming mainly from the south. Many of the buildings erected by English or local architects use either concrete canopies and frames around the windows or louvers and precast ornamental elements around the terraces as sun protection.

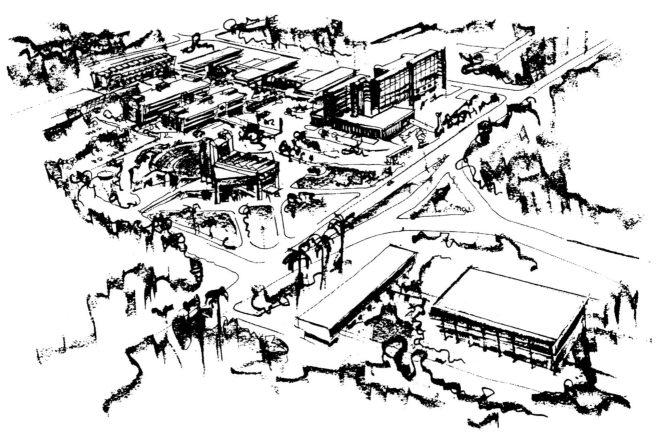

Fig. C.87 (Opposite, top) Ife, Nigeria. Aerial view of Obifemi Awolowo University (formerly University of Nigeria, Ife). Designed by Sharon and Sharon. 1969–1972.

Fig. 17.9 (Opposite, bottom) Ife, Nigeria. Obifemi Awolowo (Ife) University. Campus core. Designed by Sharon and Sharon. 1970.

Fig. 17.10 (Below) Ibadan, Nigeria. University of Ibadan. Campus plan. Designed by Maxwell Fry. (Fry Drew and Partners and Fry Drew Knight Creamer)

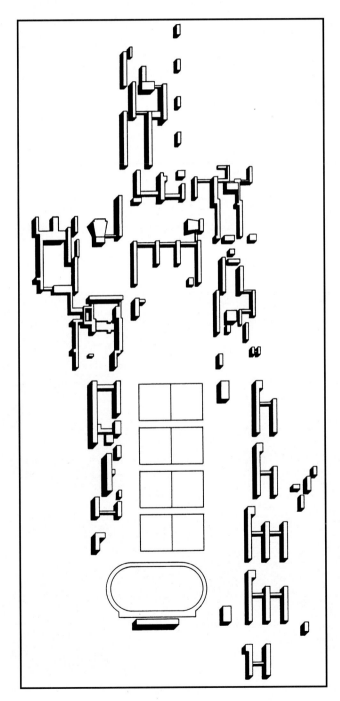

At Ibadan (Fry et al. 1978), the university nucleus is a highly concentrated nexus of connected buildings consisting of a ring of residential colleges about a center of teaching and administration. This concentrated layout is nevertheless strongly characterized by the accentuation of blocks of buildings running approximately east-west and receiving the prevailing south-west breezes at an angle that induces a greater penetration of the breezes into the quadrangles around which the residential colleges are planned (Figs. 17.10 to 17.13). The colleges and teaching facilities are rather closely grouped around the central administrative block, which is approached by a gently curving and descending double avenue from the main road.

17.8 LAGOS

Lagos, the former capital of Nigeria, was founded by Yoruba people. "At about six million people, Lagos is a metropolis by world standards and one of the largest cities in Africa" (Peil 1991, 1). The ambivalence of the Awori culture and the influences of the Awori people of Yoruba who founded the city as a fishing and trading port still feature conspicuously in the life of this vibrant and highly Westernized city. Awori people first settled in Isheri, then Ebute Metta, and later at Iddo Island. According to Church (1980), the Portuguese showed up in the mid-15th century and called the settlement at Iddo Island Lago de Curamo. Next, they changed the name to Onin and finally to Lagos, after one of their home towns. The Portuguese found the location suitable for trade in spite of dangerous sandbars that made it difficult for ships to enter the lagoon. Slave dealers, in fact, took advantage of this natural protection to expand on the illegal trade for several years after Great Britain had outlawed slavery.

The British seized the opportunity to occupy the city in 1851 in order to stop the slave trade and formally declared it a colony in 1862. But Lagos did not become an autonomous territory immediately in spite of the fact that more territories were being added to it. Between 1866 and 1874, it was governed from Sierra Leone, was under the governor of the Gold

OVERLEAF:

Fig. 17.11 (Top) Ibadan, Nigeria. University of Ibadan. Trenchard Hall. Designed by Maxwell Fry. 1960s. (Fry Drew and Partners and Fry Drew Knight Creamer)

Fig. 17.12 (Bottom) Ibadan, Nigeria. University of Ibadan. Courtyard of Arts Building. Designed by Maxwell Fry. 1960s.

Fig. 17.13 (Far right) Ibadan, Nigeria. University of Ibadan. Courtyard of Arts Lecture Halls. Designed by Maxwell Fry. 1960s.

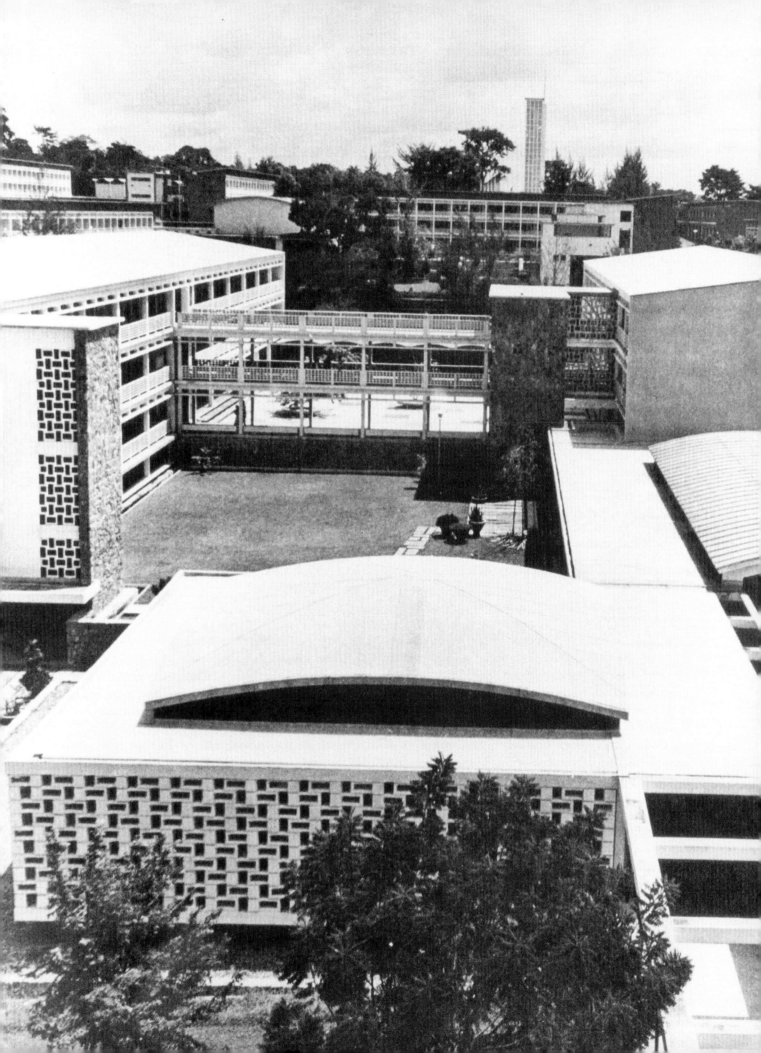

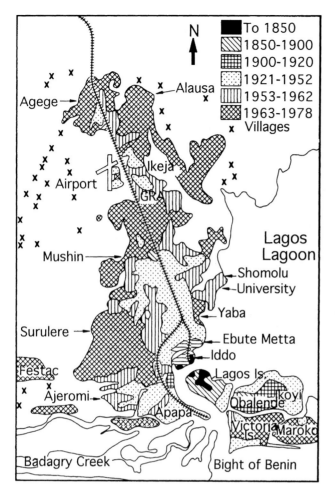

Fig. 17.14 *Lagos, Nigeria. City growth from 1850 to 1978.*

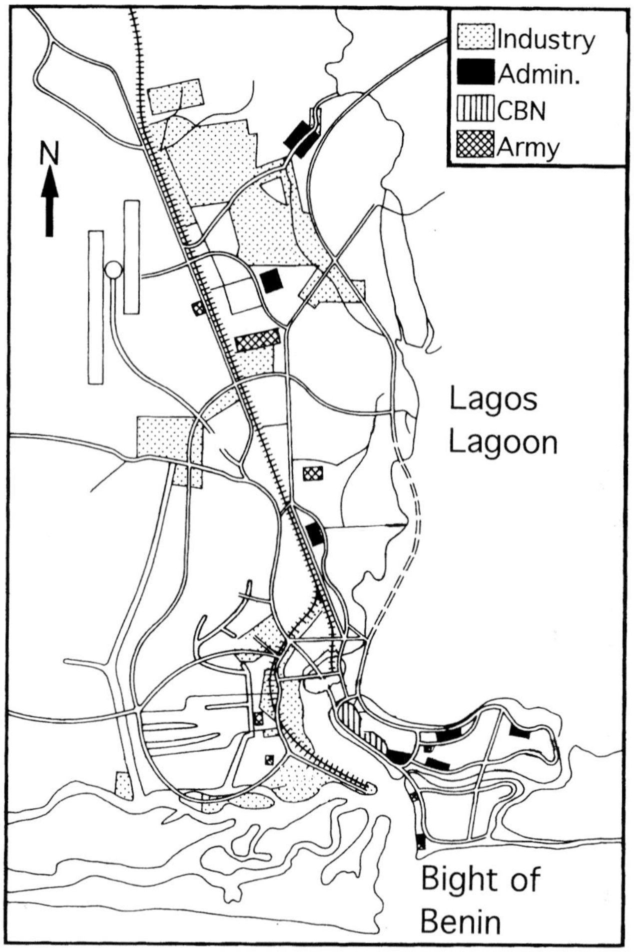

Fig. 17.15 *Lagos, Nigeria. Land use plan.*

Coast from 1874 to 1886, and finally under its own administration in 1886. Lagos became the headquarters of the protectorate of southern Nigeria in 1906, before Lord Frederick Lugard unified the northern and southern protectorates in 1912, when it became the capital of Nigeria.

Lagos is almost completely surrounded by lagoons, creeks, and marshes, which made it difficult for large expansion. Its location has been a benefit to land speculators since early times. Another difficulty for Lagos was the attitude of some of the British colonial governors who felt that Africans needed no protection; hence infrastructure, such as drainage and good roads, was built only in exclusive quarters reserved for Europeans (Peil 1991). In 1900, Governor Glover laid out a residential area in Ebute Metta. The colonial government was already developing Ikoyi by 1918 for reserved housing, while the rest of Ebute Metta and Yaba were developed between the 1920s and 1930s to minimize congestion on Lagos Island (Figs. 17.14 and 17.15). Other parts of Lagos—Surulere,

Ajoromi, Mushin, and Ikeja—were developed in the 1950s and 1960s for middle-class housing, while migrant workers settled in places like Shomolu, Bariga, and Agege.

The English left an indelible architectural mark in Lagos and in all of Nigeria. This ranges from special housing for colonial administrators to churches and office buildings. Two examples are the Catholic and the Anglican cathedrals in Lagos. Both churches wanted to outdo each other (Figs. C.88 and C.89). Each is finished in the Gothic style but with great differences in detail and approach. The Catholic cathedral has a visible Norman-period tower that rises from the narthex with Elizabethan Big Ben clocks on the four sides of the tower. Both churches have three aisles, but the flying buttresses in the Catholic cathedral are heavier, highly pronounced, and have additional vertical supports. The doors and windows are narrow, have pointed arches, and are without traceries. The vertical and overall composition is a Renaissance of heavy early English Gothic churches.

Fig. C.88 Lagos, Nigeria. Christ Church cathedral. (American Geographical Society Collection, The University of Wisconsin-Milwaukee Library)

Fig. C.89 Lagos, Nigeria. Anglican cathedral. (American Geographical Society Collection, The University of Wisconsin-Milwaukee Library)

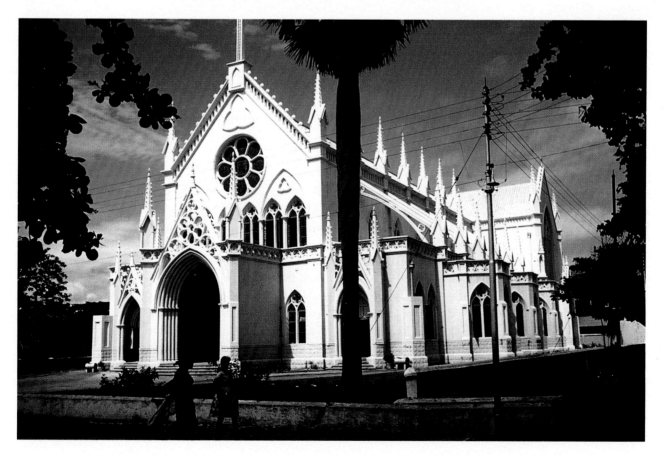

Fig. 17.16 Lagos, Nigeria. The State House. (American Geographical Society Collection, The University of Wisconsin-Milwaukee Library)

In contrast, the Anglican cathedral takes on the subtle, later Gothic revival style with camouflaged buttresses and windows with rose traceries. Each spire is well embellished and finished with pointed pinnacles. Windows are also wider and shorter with more naturalistic emphases. This church in Lagos is truly a hybrid of Selby Abbey in Yorks, United Kingdom.

For their administrative buildings, the British favored Italian Renaissance style which they transformed into Elizabethan structures. Figure 17.16 is the former Ministry of Justice, Lagos. This House has a Renaissance, two-story portico wedged between two Renaissance, three-story towers. Symmetry is a major factor in the design, and the columns are broken by a row of balustrades. Similarly the State House used to be the residence of Nigerian presidents and heads of state before the federal capital was moved to Abuja. It is a building with a dual political terminology depending on who

is in power. It is called State House when an elected civilian is the President of Nigeria, and the government is democratically elected. On the other hand, it is called Dodan Barracks when military dictators are in power in Nigeria. So far, only two elected presidents have lived in the building with its name as the State House, while seven military dictators have lived there with its name as Dodan Barracks. The military have ruled Nigeria for more than 25 years since the country became independent in 1960, so the State House has assumed the name of Dodan Barracks more than its real name—the State House. This change of name reflects the struggle for power and political dominance between the military and the Nigerian people.

The later years, especially the early 1950s and 1960s, ushered in new styles of buildings influenced mainly by the modern movement. Maxwell Fry was one of the architects who

*Fig. 17.17 **Lagos, Nigeria.** National theater. 1976. (Chioma Elleh)*

worked in Nigeria during this period. The headquarters of British Petroleum and Longman's Green House are two examples of his projects in Lagos. The British Petroleum Headquarters has shops and display rooms on the ground floor, with the office space located in the upper stories. Construction is of a reinforced concrete frame with reinforced concrete floors and roof slabs. The frame is exposed in the front elevation to hold adjustable, vertical sun screen louvers that help keep the building cool. As for Longman's Green House, the walls are load-bearing concrete blocks, while the floors are reinforced concrete floor slabs. The surface is treated with natural stone and colored cement. Servant quarters and a screened courtyard are included in the building. Maxwell Fry and his partners understood the requirements of building in the tropics, a fact that is discussed later.

Apartment buildings constructed by the Nigerian government in this period follow the new movement. These are high-rise buildings in a super-block layout. Reinforced concrete is the major construction material. The most prominent public building constructed in Lagos in the modern style during the 1950s is the Parliament House. The building does not incorporate any elements from the earlier Assembly Hall into its design. While

it emphasizes symmetry, it is designed to shade the interior from sunlight, so the cladding makes the building facade heavy. The material is mostly reinforced concrete, but the facade is finished with elaborate cement masonry block veneer.

Lagos experienced a period of financial boom during the 1970s. During this time, a multimillion dollar national theater was built by a joint consortium of Nigerian and European architects (Fig. 17.17). This high-tech building is expensive to maintain annually because all the major installations in it are imported from overseas. During the oil boom, Lagos was transformed into a major metropolis. Numerous overhead bridges and high-rise office secretariats were constructed by the government. The increasing expansion of the federal bureaucracy and an abundance of resources attracted many immigrants from rural areas and from neighboring countries as well, thereby swelling the city's population beyond manageable limits.

The oil boom and the population expansion resulted in growing congestion problems for the expanding metropolis of Lagos. Morgan (1983) points out that urbanization on this restricted site, together with rapid growth in the number of private cars and other vehicles in use, led to a crisis of traffic congestion in the 1970s, which was met in the short run by drastic restrictions and in the long run by heavy investment in overhead bridges and through roads. The traffic problem was so severe that cars with license plates that ended in even numbers could only run on certain days, while those with license plates that ended in odd numbers could only run on alternate days.

Lagos obviously was outgrowing its space for expansion. The problem was made more complex by the competition and struggle for dominance between the Lagos state government, whose headquarters is at Ikeja, a suburb of Lagos, and the federal government of Nigeria, which inherited the poorly planned Lagos as a national capital from the British government.

In 1975, the Nigerian head of state and commander in chief of the armed forces, the late General Murutala R. Muhammad, appointed the Aguda Panel to examine the dual role of Lagos as the capital of the federal republic of Nigeria and the capital of Lagos state. "That group reported to the military government on December 10, 1975, that Lagos could no longer cater adequately to the needs of its teeming population without unnecessary hardship to the people" (Ringing 1985).

The panel cited lack of housing, exorbitant rents, overcrowding, and many other urban problems and said that Lagos provided fertile breeding ground for delinquency, corruption, and other antisocial behavior. Indeed, the ills associated with urban sprawl are found in Lagos. Its population has grown from a mere 1.14 million in 1963 to over 5.62 million 25 years later (Rasaki 1990). Newly found oil wealth has made the problem more severe through overpriced real estate and land speculation ventures. Rasaki (1990) also notes that Lagos has some of the most expensive land and landed properties in the whole of Africa, side by side with some of the country's worst slums.

It was the panel's opinion that a new federal capital in a neutral territory would help to heal the wounds of the civil war. In support of this recommendation, they cited: (1) national security; (2) the need to develop interior Nigeria; (3) decentralization of economic infrastructures; (4) the development of indigenous Nigerian building industry; and (5) finally, the fact that Nigeria emerged from the ravages of the civil war of 1967–1970 not only a more united, stable, and confident country, but it also found much wealth and responsibility thrust upon it as the giant of Africa (Adekson 1981). This latter fact fed a national ego that increasingly demanded a new federal capital.

In selecting a site, the panel took the following factors into consideration: centrality, climate, land availability, water supply, drainage, and above all, ethnic neutrality. Lagos, though cosmopolitan, is still considered a Yoruba city, predominantly occupied by a population which derives from that group. On February 4, 1976, the federal government of Nigeria produced a schedule for implementing the panel's recommendations. Federal Government Decree No. 6 established for Nigeria a federal capital territory, an African version of the District of Columbia. The government took 8000 km² (over twice the size of Lagos state) out of three minority states—Niger state, Kwara state, and Plateau state—with the main objective in creating and designing Abuja of undoing everything the colonials had done wrong in Lagos.

17.9 THE LONG, PAINFUL JOURNEY FROM LAGOS TO ABUJA: CURING NIGERIA OF MAJOR NZEOGWU SYNDROME

Nigeria was ruled for 22 years by military leaders, while duly elected civilians have ruled for only 10 years since independence was gained from Britain in 1960. A series of successful and abortive military coups has plagued Nigeria since Major Nzeogwu took power in 1966, leading Nigerian leaders into thinking that architecture can be a solution to a political problem.

Besides being the most ambitious urban design project of the 20th century, Abuja is also a classic example of direct application of urban design and architectural solutions to sociopolitical problems. First, Nigerian mathematicians were given the task of determining an ideal location at the center of the country, both to achieve ethnic neutrality and to locate the national capital at an equal distance from all Nigerians.

A number of factors came together to manifest themselves in the built form of Abuja: the search for a democratic ideal; the desire to reconcile the country after the civil war; the need to undo the evils perpetrated on Lagos by colonial administrators who refused to plan the city properly and neglected infrastructure; the oil boom which increased Nigeria's revenue; the desire to develop Nigeria's interior; and finally, the hidden agenda of the aspiring bourgeoisie who took the spots left by the colonial masters and who are emerging like their counterparts in the West and the Orient. These aspiring bourgeoisie see the development of Abuja as a lucrative business that would enrich them to attain international status.

THE URBAN DESIGN OF ABUJA: A SYMBOL OF WHAT NIGERIA ASPIRES TO BE

Construction began in Abuja in 1981 under the leadership of President Shehu Shagari who was anxious to move from

Fig. 17.18 Africa and Nigeria showing the location of Abuja.
(Wallace, Roberts, and Todd)

Fig. 17.19 (Below) The genesis of Abuja master plan. Left to right: Abuja concept plan; Abuja urban design plan, Phase I; Brasilia master plan; and Tokyo circulation pattern.

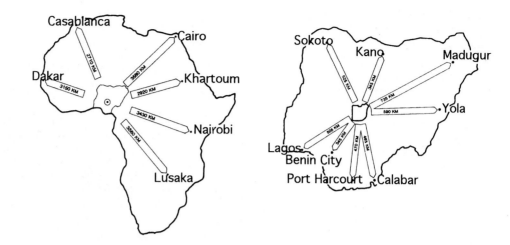

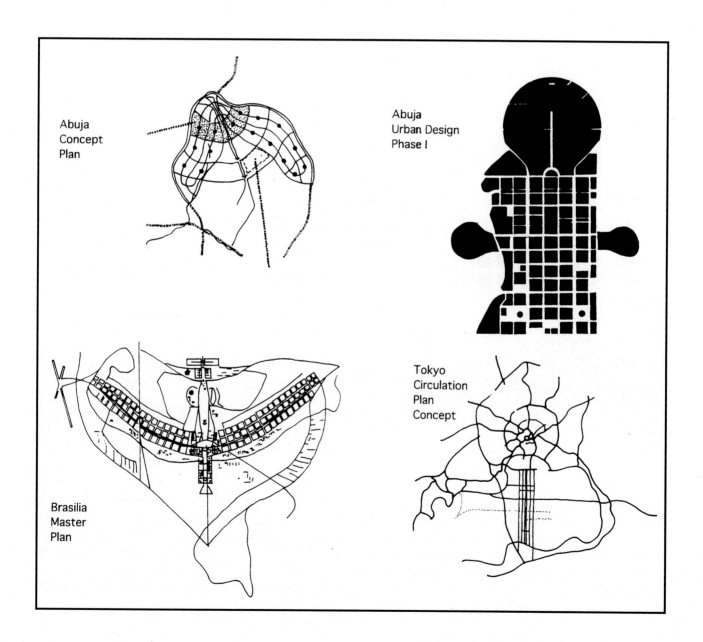

Abuja
Concept
Plan

Abuja
Urban Design
Phase I

Brasilia
Master
Plan

Tokyo
Circulation
Plan
Concept

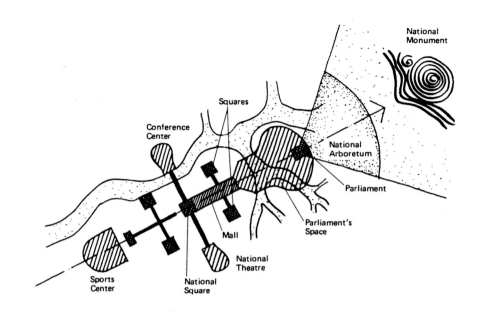

Fig. 17.20 Abuja, Nigeria.
Master plan concept. 1981.
(Wallace, Roberts, and Todd)

Fig. 17.20 Abuja, Nigeria.
Master plan concept. 1981.
(Wallace, Roberts, and Todd)

Fig. 17.21 (Below) Abuja,
Nigeria. Master plan showing
the Three Arms Zone: (1) Aso
Castle—The Presidential
Complex, (2) National
Assembly, (3) The Supreme
Court. 1981.

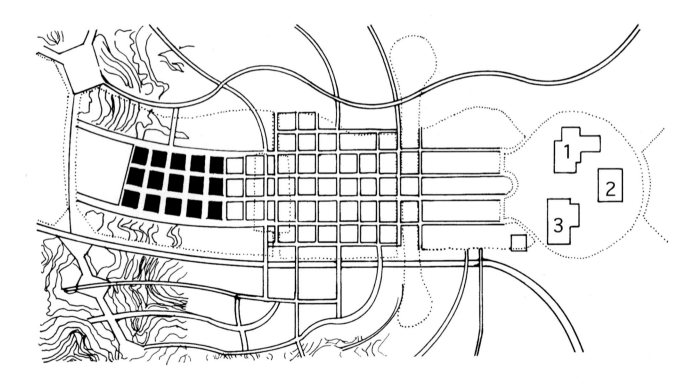

Lagos to the new capital. Abuja was conceived as a city for 1.3 million people, to be completed in 20 years, but President Shagari and his successors did not wait that long before moving to the new city. Whether or not the project will ever be executed on the scale conceived, especially the buildings, is a different issue.

Abuja is located on the Gwagwa Plains in the middle of Nigeria. The vegetation is predominantly savanna type due to centuries of destructive exploitation of the original woodland (Fig. 17.18). Its high elevation and numerous hills give the region a pleasant climate year round, one of the major attractions of the site as the venue for the federal capital of Nigeria.

Fig. 17.22 *Abuja, Nigeria. National mall (plaza) with Aso Hill in the background. The National Assembly
Building is at the foot of Aso Hill.* (Terri Plater)

Professor Lawrence Vale (1992, 139) writes that the
authors of the master plan constantly referred to the Nigerian
constitution in planning the new city:

> Its authors note that the new constitution indicates that the major
> elements to be housed in the New Federal Capital include the
> National Assembly, Legislative Offices, Executive Offices, the
> Judiciary and residence of the President and the Vice President. Other
> national government facilities would be the ministries and various
> commissions and parastatals. Any combination of these elements can
> be used—through urban design—to create the physical image of
> National Government.

Kenzo Tange, Urtec, and other planning agencies from the
United States had the solution. After looking at several
planned capital cities, especially Chandigarh and Brasília, and
including some begun in the 19th century, such as
Washington, DC, in addition to some of the new towns in
England, a bold plan focusing on the trilogy of the Nigerian
constitution which separates the power of the government
was conceived.

The plan borrowed wings from Lucio Costa's airplane plan
for Brasília, and utilized the circulation pattern from Kenzo
Tange's favorite city, Tokyo (Fig. 17.19). Tange (1986, 6)
makes no secret of the fact that the fundamental concept of
Abuja resembles the one on which Tokyo is based. The two
major concentric rings of highways that mark the outer para-
meters of Abuja are transplants from the Tokyo pattern.
Overall, the Abuja plan is in the form of a drawn bow, with
the outer ring expressway the bow, the inner ring distributor
the string, and the total city center an arrow aimed at Aso
Hill. A ceremonial highway connects the airport to the central area and to the centers of bureaucracy. Zoning is a major
functional catalyst in the outcome of the design (Figs. 17.20
and 17.21).

A democratic shrine called the Three Arms Zone sits at the
foot of Aso Hill (Fig. C.90), the commanding granite inselberg

Fig. C.90 Abuja, Zuma Rock (Aso Hill). The major focal point of the city. 1984. (Terri Plater)

that overlooks Gwagwa Plains. One of the planners' primary considerations was the government's desire to have Aso Hill dominate the city visually and symbolically. At the Three Arms Zone, the buildings of the National Assembly, the Presidential Palace for the executive, and the Supreme Court Building for the judiciary were located in a circle 1 mi in diameter (Figs. 17.22 and 17.23). The objective is to have the three branches of the government oversee one another, and the Three Arms Zone is a figurative rendition of the constitutional specifications for a government based on checks and balances. Lawrence Vale also suggests that the choice of locating the Three Arms Zone at the foot of Aso Hill was due to the hill's excessive height of over 1300 ft, and its sudden outcrop and steep slope. Hence, the Three Arms Zone may have been located on the hill much in the manner of Washington, DC, Canberra, and New Delhi.

The focal point of Abuja leads to a national mall patterned after that of Washington, DC (Figs. 17.24 and 17.25). However, Abuja's axial view is lined with high-rise buildings

on both sides. The Three Arms Zone contradicts the intentions for the city by being isolated in an exclusive zone of power. This makes the Three Arms Zone intimidating as a place of public gathering, different from the Plaza in Brasília. Vale (1992, 142) writes that "in this respect, Abuja's plan is more reminiscent of Lutyen's than of Mayer or Costa. Abuja's capital is the terminus of an axis, like Lutyen's Viceroy's Palace, with extensive gardens behind."

The greatest weakness in the Abuja plan is its extreme departure from traditional Nigerian cities in which the center of government and religion or shrines are the focus. Unlike Abuja, all other elements in the traditional cities radiate from the center, and the leadership (chiefs, kings, obas, emirs) is located at the center for easy access and interaction, especially during festivals. Walls often enclose the royal palaces to protect the divine nature of the king and ensure his mysterious powers. The walls do not protect the king from the people, but they ensure the continuity of the aura that surrounds the king, and the gates are always open to the people to bring

Fig. 17.23 Abuja, Nigeria.
Model showing the urban
design from Aso Hill to the
national stadium. (Kenzo
Tange) or (Chioma Elleh)

Fig. 17.24 *Abuja, Nigeria. Model showing the Three Arms Zone and the national mall flanked on both sides by high-rise buildings.* (Kenzo Tange)

Fig. 17.25 *(Opposite) Abuja, Nigeria. Model of national mall. Close view.* (Kenzo Tange)

their complaints to him. Abuja's Three Arms Zone does not give this feeling of an open-door policy to the people.

First, in Abuja, the river that runs down the hill forms a moat between the central part of the city and the shrine of power. This moat can only be crossed by a bridge, which is designed to be easily barricaded in times of disturbancs (Fig. 17.24). This is an advancement of Kenzo Tange's 1978 master plan for Morocco, which is governed by a monarchy. Thus, the possibility of marching to the shrine of power, as citizens can do in most democratic societies, has been neutralized by the urban design of Abuja. Any march in the city will stop at the national mall in the central district and be more than 2 km from the Three Arms Zone. This outcome is not accidental but a deliberate choice that ignores existing examples in Nigeria.

Abuja is a good example of symbolic architectural manifestations of national political ideology. Abuja's urban design does successfully represent a democratic government patterned after that of the United States and is indeed a symbol of the kind of government the people of Nigeria wish to have.

The desire to build a strong image for democracy without losing touch with nature also led to structures that evoke images of ancient African architecture. The authors of the plan were conscious of the pyramid as a symbol of power when they presented their first proposal for the National Assembly in the shape of a pyramid. In addition, the eternal power and visual presence of the mortuary Temple of Queen Hatshepsut at Deir al-Bahri carved into rocks during the 18th Dynasty are evoked at the foot of Aso Hill. The National Assembly Building is to be a modern version of this in grandeur and in cost. According to Vale (1992), the National Assembly alone was allotted 20,000 m², at a cost of $500 million, $100 million less than the cost of completing the first phase of the city.

Something irreparable, central, and fundamentally necessary for the genus loci of the African environment was lost in the mad rush to build a commercially lucrative capital for the bourgeoisie. Abuja represents a missed opportunity to study African urban forms and architectural repertoire(s) and to slowly apply the findings in Africa's grandest city. The likelihood of another capital city on the scale of Abuja in Africa in the near future is very remote because all of the countries are too busy trying to correct their economic problems. As for Nigeria, there is no turning back from Abuja because it has already been declared a federal capital city and the people are highly supportive of an ethnically neutral political center. So Abuja is an opportunity lost in the search for African architecture. The traditional walled city in which the oba's afin and the emir's palace become unifying spiritual and social centers is the opposite of the isolated and intimidating Three Arms Zone.

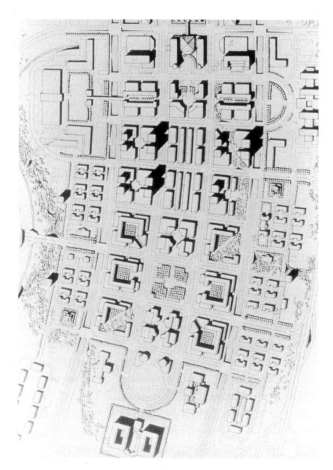

Fig. 17.26 Abuja, Nigeria. Urban design plan, Phase II. (Chioma Elleh)

The state-of-the-art highway engineering that uses a series of bridges to eliminate intersection traffic clearly designates Abuja as a city of the future, designed for automobiles and people of high status (Fig. 17.26). Abuja employed the most technically sophisticated approach of dealing with junction traffic by changing the grade at every intersection. This is an expensive, wholehearted embrace of the automobile instead of public transportation as the dominant mode of transport in the city. Vale (1992) also observes that transportation in Abuja is not planned for 70 percent reliance on public transport and 30 percent on private automobiles. Instead the master plan provides for 70 percent of both in anticipation of the fact that those who would work in this city will be men and women of status who will prefer private versus public transport.

The luxury villas and bungalows with six to seven bedrooms built for government officials underscore this notion of a city planned for the elite. This accentuates the segregation of the city government from the rest of the city. For example, the Presidential Complex has a villa for the vice president attached to it, and all other key ministries are provided with villas. In this case, Abuja has already cast a line between housing for the poor and housing for the rich and powerful (Fig. C.91). Housing segregation by status is an inherent part of the master plan. This is more of a social policy failure than an urban design failure because the master plan was indeed a reflection of the policies of the leadership.

Abuja does have a redeeming quality that makes it a unique city. Unlike Brasília, where ministerial super-blocks line the esplanade leading to the twin tower house of congress, Abuja's high-rise buildings and Three Arms Zone are fortifications designed to resemble the traditional courtyard. Despite its isolation from the city, the Three Arms Zone is enclosed to house the leadership as is the case in the palaces of the emirs and obas. The Presidential Complex, the Supreme Court, and the National Assembly essentially have courtyards (Figs. 17.25 and 17.26). The huge ministerial buildings and the central business district are all designed to take advantage of courtyards (Fig. 17.26). Hence, the 240-m-grid blocks of the city are mainly organized into courtyards.

The vista from Aso Hill and the National Assembly through the central area terminates at the national sports center, designed by American International Consultants. The vista essentially takes the viewer through a series of courtyards from Aso Hill to the sports complex. Two low hills on either side of the central area mark focal points that run in a north-south direction and define the institutional corridor along which the national theater, national mosque, national cathedral, national museum, and national square are located in a series of courtyards. A network of pedestrian linkages

Fig. C.91 *Abuja, Nigeria. Low-income housing. 1984. (Terri Plater)*

connects major centers such as the general market, general hospital, transportation center, and a host of open green spaces. The pedestrian pathways run parallel to the east-west expressways from Aso Hill. So the city is essentially oriented in an east-west direction, as most Nigerian cities are.

While the federal government of Nigeria allotted 20 million naira (about $40 million U.S. at the time of donation in 1982) to each of the buildings along the institutional corridor, the national mosque ended up as the most prominent structure because of an additional $40 million donation by Saudi Arabia to the Muslim community of Nigeria (Fig. C.92). The four major minarets of the mosque are visible from many places around the city. Located near the northern end of the institutional corridor, the mosque occupies a whole block within a series of courtyards and is already a major Islamic landmark in the new city. So, Abuja is a modern culmination of Africa's triple heritage culture, with architecture and urban design that try consciously to represent the history of the region.

It is too early to say whether Abuja is a success or a failure. However, its function as the national capital of Nigeria has been acknowledged since General Ibrahim Babangida declared it the national capital on November 23, 1991. In Abuja, Islam and Christianity maintain a fragile balance,

Fig. C.92 *Abuja, Nigeria. National Mosque. A.I.M. Architects. 1987.*
(Chioma Elleh)

something all Nigerians guard with apprehension. For now, police power is utilized to keep Abuja clean or free of squatter settlements. The increased population of migrant workers and the military government are already in collision. The war against squatter settlements is being won by the military because they demolish the settlements without recourse. However, the situation may change when an elected president assumes power and legal procedures govern the country rather than incontestable military decrees.

17.10 PORT HARCOURT: THE GARDEN CITY

Port Harcourt is a relatively new town, developed as a seaport at the delta region where the River Niger flows into the Atlantic Ocean through several tributaries. The town was founded by the colonial administration between 1912 and 1914 because of its convenient location near the sea and its natural harbors. It was named after a British military officer and a key player in the founding of the city. In 1967, when Nigeria was divided into 12 states, Port Harcourt became the capital of Rivers state and has grown from a relatively small population of 5000 in 1915 to over 1 million in a 1992 census. The petroleum industry with its refineries and associated industries is now the dominant force behind this town which began to gain importance as a significant industrial town in the early 1950s, when the Nigerian petroleum industry was still in its embryonic stage. The town was planned as two residential areas: the European quarters next to the golf course and the main town which is now the major commercial district. The growing importance of the city due to the petroleum industry encouraged the colonial administration to review the plan of the city. Professor Y. Ellon, an Israeli planner, was entrusted with the task of planning for future city expansion.

Professor Ellon's plan was based on a population of 250,000 people and included an industrial layout, two low density residential estates of 2500 acres each at Trans-Amadi and Diobu, and a major trunk road to join Aba Road and Owerri Road.

Fig. C.93 Port Harcourt, Nigeria. Private bungalow. 1988.

Fig. 17.27 Port Harcourt,
Nigeria. Colonial house.
1930s. (Chioma Elleh)

The recommendations of Professor Ellon were completed before 1960 because the city had money. Like many African cities, Port Harcourt has colonial European quarters which perpetuated segregation by class.

Shell-British Petroleum built a high-class and exclusive enclave for its engineers and executives, paralleling the colonial government's strategy of using housing as a means of social segregation. Ekpenyon (1989) notes that housing in colonial regimes, was the mechanism by which social groups were distinguished and separated. This practice continues today in a competitive form among the well-to-do. Bungalows with fortifications are the trend of residential housing for the elite (Fig. C.93).

Governor Alfred Diete Spiff embarked on office building programs during the oil boom years. Today, some of the buildings remain empty, and a few that were begun in the late 1970s have yet to be completed because of poor management, political instability, increasing costs, and dwindling oil revenue. The relationship between the administrative and commercial districts of the city is still not clear, in spite of the concentration of high-rise office building construction in one section of the town during Governor Diete Spiff's regime. This is primarily because the British planned Port Harcourt as a suburban town rather than as an administrative center. Most of the colonial buildings constructed in the 1930s and 1940s are still in excellent condition, and they readily reflect their European taste (Fig. 17.27).

In 1983, an elevated bridge was constructed in the center of Port Harcourt to help traffic congestion at the intersection of Aba Road and Ikwere Road next to the golf course. This was more of a political decision than shrewd planning policy. In the process, the beauty of the central roundabout with Azik Boro Monument in the center was destroyed. Today, the beautiful park is barely visible because the traffic is too fast and mostly overhead. The rapidly moving traffic through the heart of the city via the new elevated bridge could have been successfully diverted by the expansion of a new road that goes from the harbor to Port Harcourt Aba Road at the outskirts of the town near Eleme Road junction. Port Harcourt is still growing because of increasing migration to the city, but housing scarcity and exorbitant rents are helping to strain the resources of the city's low-income residents.

17.11 CALABAR AND ENUGU

Enugu and Calabar are also southern Nigerian cities with enormous colonial influence. Enugu was founded by the colonial administration for the purpose of extracting coal from the hills of Udi. Prospecting began in 1909, and mining started in 1915. A rail line joined Enugu from Port Harcourt in 1916, giving the coal mine access to the sea. Hence, the town grew with the mine.

Calabar was an ancient slave trading center used by the Ibiobio and the Efik along the Cross River. The British seized the territory in the mid-19th century, and missionaries were attracted to the region immediately to begin Christian activities. The triple heritage factor is expressed here by the

Christian march from the coast northward and the reverse journey taken by Islam from the north toward the south. The middle-belt of Nigeria is a watershed where neither Christians nor Muslims dominate. In each area, the indigenous culture is present, thereby completing the cultural triangle of Africa. It should not be surprising, then, that southern Nigeria is predominantly a Christian region, though there are Muslims in the south, just as there are Christians in the predominantly northern Islamic parts of the country.

At Calabar and Enugu, English cottage housing and Victorian houses were built for the Europeans and Nigerian colonial civil servants. In public buildings, the colonials combined their understanding of tropical architecture with 20th-century English Georgian architecture to meet their needs. Here, the major characteristics of this Western influence are delicate, refined ornaments and elements that can be traced easily to Greek and Roman origins, like the arches and the columns. Indigenous influence is expressed in slanted roofs that almost cover the upper story and in the use of a screen in front of a building for cooling purposes (Figs. C.94 and C.95). Sometimes, the buildings were pivoted above the ground with columns to allow cross-ventilation.

Fig. C.94 (Opposite, top) Calabar, Nigeria. Victorian house in government reserved area (former European quarters). 1930s.
(Daniel Iyang)

Fig. C.95 (Opposite, bottom) Calabar, Nigeria. Government secondary school. 1930s.
(Daniel Iyang)

6

MODERN
ARCHITECTURE,
URBANISM, AND
URBANIZATION
IN AFRICA

18

URBANISM IN AFRICA

he focus of this chapter is on urbanism. The term is used here to describe the distinct way of life created by the city. In Africa, urbanism is a complex issue that has evolved out of the three distinct factors of the triple African heritage: the indigenous culture, Western intrusion and influence, and Islamic legacies. Together, these factors combine to form cities different from those in any other part of the world. The uniqueness of African cities does not mean that they are excluded from the problems facing many developing countries. In fact, those problems abound and make it difficult to sort out the true social structures that form urbanism in Africa. It is important to mention that very little has been written on this subject from an architectural perspective, and like most of the material covered in this book, it represents a new field yet to be investigated. To date, geographers, ethnologists, anthropologists, and sociologists have contributed most of the available literature on African urbanism.

18.1 THE NATURE OF THE ENVIRONMENT IN AFRICA

At present, the African environment is in continuous transition both in the rural and in the urban areas. No part of Africa is immune from this trend of the times. Economic conditions of the past few decades have put enormous stress on the environment, from the most isolated village background to the most urbanized centers. But, of course, the extent of the effects varies from place to place.

Kibuka (1990) identifies population, general pattern of social deprivation, imbalanced rural-urban growth rates, illiteracy, health, lack of social security, land tenure systems, and social policy as some of the major elements influencing the African urban situation. He further acknowledges that political conditions and other unidentified social factors intensify the effects of these elements on the African continent. For a continent struggling to develop, the distance between the jungle and the city is very short. A place can be rural today and in 6 months be the location of an industry such as mining or refining; or in a few cases, a new city transforms the area and claims the jungle. Sometimes the passage of a two-lane highway near the perimeter of a small village transforms the village in a very short time, as gas stations, electricity, shops, and other businesses move in to service travelers along the road. It is indeed an unstable environment with many factors competing for attention and realization. This instability spills over into the built environment.

18.2 THE BUILT ENVIRONMENT IN AFRICA: THE ORGANIZATION OF THE AFRICAN CITY

It has been mentioned that some of the earliest built environments were in Africa. According to Clarke (1975, 263), "the first urban revolution took place along the Nile Valley five millennia ago, but a much greater phase of urban growth occurred in classical times when cities like Alexandria, Cyrene, Leptis Magna, Carthage, and Constantine and many others flourished in North and North-East Africa." Hull (1976) suggests that Neolithic stonemason villages dating as far back as 3000 B.C. have been located in southwestern Sahara regions, and he attributes the growth of towns and villages partly to agriculture and the acquisition of iron technology. Towns began as a casual activity of mutual interest at the Nile Valley.

Smith (1938) states that the embryonic town in Egypt was a casual grouping of clan, tribal, or more frequently, communal huts around the totem house of the high priest and chieftain, as can be seen in many villages around Africa today. The embryonic town evolved into ethnic or tribal spiritual centers which were associated with the tribal leader and totems.

> It is important to recognize that the taboo characters of certain animals and plants, and their veneration within tribal communities in Africa, is an ancient culture of totemism that has been passed down from ancient Egypt, and most totems that are still worn by Nigerian chiefs and those in other parts of Africa correspond to those worn by ancient Egyptian Pharaohs such as the ox-tail on Narmer's tablet. (Diop 1974, 78)

So the town has always been associated and defined as a place where a venerated chief lives. For example, Clarke (1975, 263) writes that "in many parts of Africa a settlement is called a town if a chief lives there; it is the seat of power and authority rather than an agglomeration, and inevitably may have no more than a few houses." Hull (1976) supports this notion with the view that most towns in Africa began as spiritual centers like Kano, in northern Nigeria, and Ife, the cradle of Yoruba civilization in western Nigeria.

The earliest geometrically planned towns in Africa were largely cities of the dead for the Pharaohs during their stay in the afterlife. A common practice since the First Dynasty, the towns accommodated the graves of the king's servants and dignitaries so that they would be with him and continue to serve him as they did when he was alive. This concept was later extended to the planning of towns for the living, such as in the planned towns of Kahun and the worker's town of Tell Amarna. The city of Alen (at Tell-Amarna), which Pharaoh Amenhotep IV built during the 18th Dynasty, should not be forgotten because it was inspired by the king's devotion to the sun god. The dynamics that shaped the destinies of these ancient towns must be traced to the growth of civilization along the Nile Valley, the rise of the First, Second, and Third Dynasties, the migration of Africans from the Nile Valley to the rest of the continent, the Assyrian-pioneered invasion that ended with Alexandria, and finally to the Ptolemies. In addition, Roman conquest of North Africa, the breakup of the Roman empire, the arrival of Islam in the 7th century, and future Western imperialism have in one way or another shaped the built environment in Africa, most conspicuously in cities that are influenced by Muslim culture.

Islam is a force that has shaped city life in Africa and subsequently influenced city structures that are identical in different parts of the continent. For example, medieval Cairo, Kano, and Fez have identical urban structures and compound layouts. The African cities influenced by Islam have all the characteristics of the medieval city, both in function and in structure, such as: compact labyrinth dwellings; high population density; wall or ditch that shows defense structure; uniformity of building height; and large civic buildings, mosques, churches, or palaces that break the uniformity of the buildings. The city square, which is often near the market or king's residence, is the central nerve of the city's social activities, and major roads lead to and from this particular square. There are special public and semipublic spaces that are fully utilized, such as in Kano and other medieval North African cities, where the bazaar or the souk become alleys of commercialism and other forms of social activity.

At the domestic level, the chief's, emir's, oba's, or king's palace stands out. These are usually walled and have many courtyards and houses for wives and royal courtiers. The procession from the public to the private space is ritualistic and often marked by a series of transitional passages. Residences in compounds are often determined by lineage, a characteristic that seems to be common among the traditional societies of Africa even where Islam is not the dominant religion. Other traditional groups have always used ancestry as a way of defining neighborhood, and the religious significance is quite obvious. While Islam specifically requires courtyards and secluded outdoor spaces for the women, ancestry also prescribes compound and lineage togetherness as an approach to settlement patterns. Thus, life patterns are influenced by religion and expressed in the built form.

In contrast, 20th-century Western-style housing produced a different kind of urban structure that reflects class distinctions. As a result, the educated, wealthy citizens can easily be identified by the type of housing and neighborhood in which they live. The major difference between this form of urban plan and the traditional urban plan is the separation of people based on class and lifestyle. This pattern has grown since the turn of the century when Europeans developed some centers for the convenience of administering and exploiting the colonies they had seized. New towns in recent times follow this pattern by developing special sectors called government reserved quarters (GRAs) for both the rich and government officials. Before the arrival of Europeans, non-Muslims were usually given their own quarters, while the king and his subjects lived in the ancestor city to practice their religions. Early Muslim leaders did the same by giving non-Muslims a separate town, so it can be said that some African cities were already divided by religious practice before the Europeans arrived. That division was not based on class or wealth, however, because the chiefs and their subjects lived together.

In general, most African cities are organized into the following composite sectors: (1) new town, developed during or after the colonial period, sometimes including the central business district; (2) the European quarters, reserved for Europeans only during the colonial periods; (3) the African

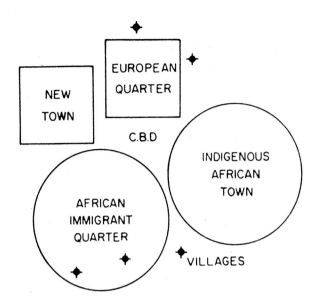

Fig. 18.1 A schematic of the triple heritage city showing settlement patterns.

immigrant quarter, found mainly in parts of Africa with strong Islamic influence such as Kano and Zaria; and (4) the indigenous African town where the chief lived before government or Europeans expanded the city. Ibadan, Benin City, and Ife are good examples (Fig. 18.1).

19

URBANIZATION
IN AFRICA

The goal in this chapter is to identify the major forces that are shaping the built environment in Africa. The roles played by agriculture, ancient empires, religion, conquests, and colonialism in the development of urban centers in Africa have already been discussed. The focus now is on the effects of sociopolitical and economic factors on rural-urban migration, class, and housing policies.

19.1 HOUSING POLICIES AND RURAL-URBAN MIGRATION IN AFRICA

Modern African cities are greatly affected by rural-urban migration and housing policies. Today, the cities of Africa are dense population centers, as people constantly leave their farms and rural areas to seek better lives in the cities. The problems thus created are multidimensional and range from inadequate housing to increased food prices due to falling agricultural output.

Kibuka (1990) points out that colonial policies excluded the local people from housing benefits because they were not government employees. The colonials used African towns as administrative and exploitation centers and housed only their employees with taxes collected from the citizens. Housing for the masses was not taken into consideration during the colonial era. The newly independent states initially had to struggle to build stable governments and manage social activities. In later years, the cities became centers of light industrial production, resulting in the concentration of amenities in cities at the expense of rural areas.

The concentration of amenities in urban centers has devastating effects on rural areas and on a country as a whole because of the dismal economic imbalance thereby created between the rural and the urban sectors. This explains why many African countries have cities equipped with basic utility services and rural sectors with no infrastructure at all. There is no electricity or running water, not to mention paved roads, schools, hospitals, and services such as police and banks. The amenities draw people from their farms to the cities to seek a better life. But the "urban factories," so to speak, unfortunately cannot absorb all the immigrants, and those who are absorbed are poorly paid. This results in high unemployment and generates slums, even in new cities like

Abuja. Additionally, the effect of this rural population drain on agriculture is devastating to the economy of African countries.

Until the 1960s, Africa was able to meet its food needs and had excess agricultural products for export to Europe. Today, African countries import food from the Americas, Australia, and Europe. Modern city planning succeeded in destroying Africa's agriculture by luring people away from their villages, only to dump them in shanty towns. That is why development in agriculture is particularly weak, especially in the poorest countries, and why living conditions do not improve for the most destitute people. Furthermore, this pattern has a much more adverse effect on countries like Nigeria which completely neglected their agriculture during the oil boom years. Today, a large portion of Nigeria's foreign debt is caused by the import of agricultural products.

Nigeria is caught in a vicious cycle of poverty. Kamrany (1978) states that the bottlenecks to development of the region can be conceptualized as a set of interacting problems or vicious cycles incorporating resources, sociocultural variables, and institutional factors. Some of the institutional factors arise from physical planning that includes urban policies alien to the traditional economies of Africa, while other factors are external trade and political considerations beyond the control of these countries.

For those who end up in the shanty towns, life is harsh and unkind. Unhealthy living conditions, open sewers, poverty, little education, poor diets, and perpetual segregation from those better off are constant realities. All the dreams end up in shanty towns, and residency according to class is reflected in the cityscape. Whether in a colonial city such as Port Harcourt or in an indigenous one such as Cairo and Kano, this segregation by income is quite visible. In fact, the case is so severe in Cairo that a cemetery with tombs was taken over and has become a town in itself (see Fig. 6.9). This is an indication that housing is still one of the most pressing needs in developing countries.

Almost every country in Africa falls within the category of nations termed developing countries. This categorization includes industrialized South Africa where more than 85 percent of the population live in economic conditions worse or similar to those of most people in other African countries.

A large portion of the least economically fortunate citizens of the world includes the more than 700 million people who make up the African population. The only exception here is in Libya, where petrodollars have comfortably housed, clothed, educated, fed, and provided other luxury goods such as television sets and cars for fewer than 3 million people under an Islamic-Socialist People's government. Once again, the apartments in Libya are high-rise buildings that give no consideration to indigenous Libyan architecture. These high-rise apartments are characteristic of the skylines of contemporary Benghazi, Tripoli, and other urban areas. Libya is so rich that it has more armored tanks than people who know how to drive them, more military airplanes than people who can fly them, and in addition, more of every other type of military hardware than any other country in Africa.

Some of the problems facing African countries are inadequacies in shelter, educational infrastructures, hospitals, cultural and ceremonial buildings, and bureaucratic and commercial buildings. Some African countries are trying to resolve these problems by building new cities and infrastructures, but their approaches have many shortcomings because of their serious economic implications. Social scientists and politicians have tried to solve Africa's development problems since the late 1950s to the present by using different development models. It was becoming clear to social scientists all over the world that the post-World War II economic boom was not happening in the former colonies of most European countries and that underdevelopment is a global problem, especially in African countries where rapid population growth in urban centers is prevalent. The result is increasing urban poverty and poor living conditions.

MODERN ARCHITECTURE: NEW TOWNS AS NATIONAL DEVELOPMENT STRATEGY FOR AFRICA

chapter

buja, Dodoma, Lilongwe, Nouackchott, and Yamous-soukro have been mentioned as some of the new towns of Africa. Nigeria created an additional nine states in 1991 and is working on a new master plan for the capitals of the thirty states of the country. Eleven of the new towns that have just become state capitals have very little or no infrastructure. This approach has several implications in the African context. It means that many cities are yet to be built and that more will be built as a means of decentralization and quick development. Professor Wole Soyinka dramatized this quick approach to development in *The Lion and the Jewel*:

> *They marked the route with stakes, ate*
> *Through the jungle and began the tracks.*
> *Trade,*
> *Progress, adventure, success, civilization,*
> *Fame, international conspicuousity...it was*
> *All within the grasp of Ilujinle...*
>
> *Professor Wole Soyinka*
> *Nigerian Nobel Laureate, 1986*

In *The Lion and the Jewel*, a village teacher named Lakunle decides to get rid of the past by refusing to pay his bride price because it was not civilized. He wanted to be married to a beautiful village girl without paying the bride price. The village teacher thought he could win the girl he loved with kisses, "as all educated men—and Christians kiss their wives. It is the way of civilized romance." On the contrary, he turned the village girl away with this approach because she did not understand what kissing meant. It represented avoidance of the traditional responsibility to pay a bride price. So, the teacher couldn't win the bride. The teacher's dream to convert Ilujinle, a small village, into a conspicuous city like Lagos could only be done by divorcing the past and clearing the jungle for the railway tracks and every other thing that represented progress in the modern city.

The village teacher in Professor Soyinka's *The Lion and the Jewel* is analogous to those who made the decision to plan Abuja, Dodoma, Lilongwe, Nouackchott, and Yamoussoukro. They saw development as clearing the jungle and planting buildings, roads, and other architectural elements that completely ignore the past. The builders of these new cities were in love with development, a symbol of technology, and they felt that the only way to win their bride (development) was to court her without making any reference to

341

the past. Historical precedents, continuity, and syncretism with the modern world were completely ignored in the design of the new cities for the purpose of development and technological advancement. This approach to city planning in African countries led to the importation of the city of 3 million people to Africa—Abuja.

20.1 THE CITY OF 3 MILLION PEOPLE: LE CORBUSIER'S GLOBAL MACHINE FOR HUMAN HABITATIONS

Le Corbusier's city of 3 million people, the machine for human habitation, has had a strong impact on modern architecture and, consequently, on the architecture of Africa. Le Corbusier did not initiate the modern movement, but rather it evolved out of social reforms advocated by intellectuals prior to the Industrial Revolution. Early modernism meant a moral commitment to human betterment, as well as the use of certain architectural forms and the elimination of other unnecessary forms.

The moral commitment advocated by early modernism evolved from the growing inquisitiveness of the intellectual community of the 18th century. Several publications changed and influenced the tide of social commitment at both the individual and governmental levels. The growth and publication of radical philosophies influenced architectural thinking. In particular, in 1776, Adam Smith published his inquiry into the nature and causes of the wealth of nations. In 1798, Thomas Malthus published his essay on the principle of population. In his writings 2 decades later, the French socialist Saint Simon urged government by experts. The exceptional ingenuity displayed by Adam Smith and his colleagues heralded the dawn of a modernist socialist architecture that would attempt to solve the problems of humanity.

"Although the optimists' belief in an enlightened technocracy and in man's perfectibility was to be short-lived, by 1800 it had generated a strong social purpose in architecture" (McKean 1980, 201). Industrialists of the age such as Robert Owen (1771–1858) believed in the socialist view of architecture as a vehicle to solve human problems. Architecture began to assume a new meaning and some advocates of this new meaning, such as Jean-Nicole-Louis Duran (1760–1834), a pupil of Boullee and teacher at the new Ecole Polytechnique in Paris, advanced a utilitarian goal. In his lectures, Duran advocated plain and simple architecture. He also argued that the aim of architecture was suitability and economy. Architecture should be exempt from pointless decoration, he said, declaring aesthetic pleasure a myth and adding that what people appreciate is convenience and value for their money.

These socialist ideals heralded the birth of modern architecture, as well as the city of 3 million people. As McKean (1980, 201) observes, "The technological age ushered in by the iron architecture of the nineteenth century was to find expression in a functional style that turned its back on the past and on eclecticism." This new industrial age construction turned its back on history because of a primary construction technique, reinforced concrete, which utilized glass and metal to produce different structures and shapes.

The influence of Le Corbusier on city planning cannot be ignored at this point. Scholars, architects, and people from all walks of life have a love/hate feeling toward him. The popularity of modern architecture since the end of World War II, however, is not an accident, and Le Corbusier supplied many of its points of reference. Some of these points have gained world acceptance. This is true both for the building design conceived as a machine for human habitation and for his urban designs, especially his famous *A Contemporary City for Three Million People,* which he prepared for the Salon di Automne in Paris in 1922. Le Corbusier's proposal for the contemporary city received a mixed reception because it was unconventional, but he was confident of his design, primarily because he realized the industrial power of the age and had no doubt that his design could be built if accepted. He also wanted to establish design templates for modern cities that were then in the planning stage and for the future. Le Corbusier claimed, "My object was not to overcome the existing state of things, but by constructing a theoretically water-tight formula to arrive at the fundamental principles of modern town planning" (Evenson 1969, 7). These principles, once correctly formulated, could be adapted to any specific urban case. On the other hand, Le Corbusier's plan for the city of 3 million people was so ambiguous that a journalist remarked of its future inhabitants, "Poor creatures. What will they become in the midst of all this dreadful speed, this organization, this terrible uniformity?...here is enough to disgust one forever with `standardization' and to make one long for disorder" (Evenson 1969, 19).

Brasília, the created capital of Brazil, and Chandigarh, the created regional capital of the Indian Punjab state, brought Le Corbusier's dreams of what modern cities should be like into fruition. Both cities gained widespread media attention from the time they were conceived to the time they were completed. Each also derived from identical political-economic decisions by their two independent sovereign governments to improve their political stability, enhance their economic development programs, and upgrade the standard of living of their people.

Le Corbusier did not have the opportunity to build his city or carry out any of his idealistic building plans until after World War II when Europe was being rebuilt. He first displayed his building skill in the Unite d'habitation in Marseille. From then on, his model(s) became departure points for future city designers and architects.

The call for a new capital of Brazil began much before the 1950s. It only materialized then. Evenson (1973, 105) notes that "The first recorded advocacy of a new capital appeared in 1789 in a statement by a group of political revolutionaries in the state of Minas Gerais, who called themselves the 'inconfidentes Mineiros'." These were members of a radical political organization calling for independence from Portugal, their parent colonial country. Several advocates preceded the inconfidentes Mineiros before Brasília was finally put on the drawing board after an international competition in the 1950s. "In August 1956, as the initial step in developing the new capital, the Brazilian Congress authorized the creation of NOVACAP (Companhia Urbanizadora de Nova Capital), a government corporation charged with directing the construction of Brasília" (Evenson 1973, 105).

All the major buildings were designed by Oscar Niemeyer. The goal was to achieve a new city with uniform architecture, something that Brazilian cities lacked. A 7-mi-long axis terminates with the city's most important buildings. Political structures are the dominating landmarks in the new city. In this case, a twin, 25-story Administration and Congress building, the Supreme Court, and the Presidential Palace form the focus of the city.

If the need for political and economic development motivated Brazil to create a new capital city, similar and much more intense needs also motivated India to create a new regional capital city for Punjab. Indians decided to invest parts of the national development on the new city of Chandigarh. Prime Minister Nehru said: "Let this be a new town symbolic of the freedom of India, unfettered by the traditions of the past...an expression of the nation's faith in the future" (Kalia 1987, 21). Nehru's bid for the future meant new towns built in the Western tradition instead of trying to bridge the gap left between India's past and the future architectural heritage.

Today, Abuja, a city that owes its roots to Corbu's dream, is the capital of the federal republic of Nigeria. The reasons behind its construction, however, have nothing to do with Corbu. The issue here is that Abuja has been rushed at the expense of other climatic, economic, and contextual factors that define African architecture.

20.2 DEVELOPING INDIGENOUS BUILDING TECHNOLOGY FOR AFRICA

Economic considerations, as well as cultural and climatic factors, underscore the need to develop indigenous African building technology to meet modern needs. To begin with, African countries do not have the resources to import building materials from the West and Asia to satisfy housing needs. Moreover, some African cities, especially those influenced by Islam, are laid out differently with spatial orientation in an east-west direction. The random layout of the urban medieval African city allows for ventilation in a way that a rigidly planned layout does not. Moreover, the courtyard compound and subsequent open plan houses surrounding the courtyard make movement and ventilation in the house easier than does the modern plan which is very rigid. The choice of material and thermal functions such as cooling also play a role. The traditional adobe structure and pliable roofing materials keep the house cool, but nothing can be more miserable than the heat of the day in an aluminum-roofed house without air conditioning. On the other hand, poor energy supply and lack of resources make the cost of cooling by air conditioning very expensive. So, it is important to seek building materials other than brick and aluminum. This raises the question of how Africa can cope with the construction of houses that use expensive imported materials.

20.3 ARCHITECTURE AND INDUSTRIAL DEVELOPMENT IN AFRICA

Le Corbusier's design grew out of the technology that inspired it. Africa is designing and building ahead of its technology.

The relationship between architecture and industrial development is not just an African phenomenon, but a universal one. However, Western influence on the African continent has made it increasingly difficult for the African people to develop their architecture in accordance with the level of their industrial technology. As a result, the underdeveloped nations of Africa are constructing sophisticated buildings. There is nothing wrong with African countries imitating Western countries in pursuit of development, but the resulting products of this imitation are usually economically and functionally burdensome to African countries that cannot afford to maintain their buildings after tremendous construction costs. This anomaly stems from the fact that African countries lag far behind in the industrial stage of the Western nations, with African resources not yet maximized. Unlike traditional times when labor and materials could be obtained locally, modern buildings in Africa are built with financial, human, and material imports from industrialized countries. Prefabricated industrial building components are used without the support of a productive industrial base. Western countries did not begin industrial architecture overnight. They began with the consolidation of the Industrial

Revolution in Europe. Gloag (1958, 307) writes that "Western architecture throughout its history has been identified with the character of Western civilization, and has reflected the rise and decline of the Age of Reason, the rise and decline of the Age of Faith, the humanism of the Renaissance, and the scientific and industrial rationalism of the nineteenth and twentieth centuries."

Joseph Paxton was one of the pioneer architects who utilized prefabricated units of cast iron, wrought iron, and glass in construction. His application of industrial materials in the Crystal Palace at Hyde Park in London set the tone of Western architecture for several generations to come. "Built to house the Great Exhibition of 1851, this structure, with its iron and glass units and its `airy lightness,' gave a preview of the New Western Architecture that was to develop during the next hundred years" (Gloag 1958, 311). Paxton's creation did not just happen; it was an accent to the application of some Western building traditions refined from ancient Roman times to the years of the Industrial Revolution. It is, therefore, appropriate to say that the West was ready for high tech architecture, whereas Africa was not because it does not have the industrial base to support it.

The only way the nations of Africa can maintain modern architecture is by depending on Western countries for the supply of both prefabricated industrial materials and skilled labor. Some development economists describe this reliance and its implications through the dependency theory, which holds that developing countries are vulnerable to economic disadvantages by working with developed trading partners. The answer to this economic and cultural disadvantage lies in balancing Africa's triple heritage architecture. To do so would reduce the exposure of African countries to this economic vulnerability in the building industry because several types of building materials and techniques can be obtained locally. Thus, there would be fewer imports of high tech construction materials and techniques from the developed countries.

CONCLUSION: DEVELOPING THE TRIPLE HERITAGE ARCHITECTURE

rchitecture is the least developed aspect of African art. Visual arts, music, and other forms of art have received a great deal of attention since the era of independence in the 1960s, and museums around the world have collections and exhibitions of contemporary African art. In the case of architecture, every work has to go back to the grass roots to look for information and ways of including indigenous African concepts into contemporary building design. The mix of Islam, indigenous culture, and Western influence dictates that attention be given to various aspects of life and the way they are expressed on the continent. African cities currently have two broad architectural styles. In North African cities like Tripoli, Tunis, and Cairo, the blend between Western architecture and Islamic architecture is easily identifiable. In the East African cities of Nairobi, Kampala, Maputo, and Dodoma, the international skyline dominates, a phenomenon which attains its climax in the South African city of Johannesburg. Cities in West and Southwest Africa, such as Abidjan and Lagos, are also dominated by international architectural character.

International architectural style is also invading the most isolated areas of Africa. The emergent business elite traditionally build two homes, one in the city and a second in their native village where they spend weekends. In fact, more emphasis is given to the status of the home in the village because it is the home of the ancestors and eventually their final resting places. Contradicting this further is the fact that the villas built by the new bourgeoisie are completely Western in style. It is obvious that traditional African architecture is being driven to extinction.

There is nothing wrong with a new kind of architecture that overshadows an underdeveloped architecture, but architecture is more than buildings. It is also a reflection of the behavioral, historical, religious, political, and environmental existential life of a people. As such, the maintenance of a balanced cultural heritage by synthesizing architectural elements from the three broad categories of African architecture would be more helpful to the future development of architecture in Africa. All cultures need new ideas and incentives to maintain their vitality and growth. No culture can be perfectly integrated, and the process of infusing new elements, while nec-

essary and desirable for the advancement and development of old cultures, is not a smooth one. Architects who practice in Africa must, therefore, rely on their creativity and abilities to maintain an eclectic dialogue among the various components of the triple heritage architecture.

The trend that calls for *replacement* as a building tradition for Africa needs to be stopped. Replacing existing structures and styles with foreign styles results in *compartmentalization,* which limits the newly imported elements within a certain segment of the society and is based on class. Compartmentalization results in biculturalism and creates unnecessary competition between the old and the new. In this case, the new wins and gradually drives the old into extinction, as has been the trend of architecture in Africa. Rather, the old should be seen as a resource for the advancement of the new tradition and the maintenance of eclectic dialogue for the benefit of historical and sociocultural continuity. In Africa, the triple heritage architecture has been determined both by culture and climatology.

Naturally, climatology in architecture resolves itself into issues of regionalism. From the viewpoint of regionalism, architecture responds to climatic concerns such as solar radiation, humidity, moisture, temperature variations, topography, and culture, as demonstrated by the distribution of Islamic, Western, and various forms of indigenous architecture in Africa. A few European architects who have practiced in Africa should be acknowledged for recognizing this factor and following traditional design concepts to develop what is now referred to as *tropical architecture.* This includes, for example, the realization that cross-ventilation helps in internal environmental control of temperature. It is, of course, obvious that climatology is a significant factor that cannot be ignored, at least not by any architect who can contrast a temperate climate, where winters necessitate layers of clothing to preserve heat, to a tropical climate, where the need to dress lightly is more pressing.

Architects who practice in Africa should pay closer attention to the adaptation of traditional building techniques to climatic elements. Traditional buildings use lightweight materials that are of low thermal capacity, hold little heat, and cool easily at night. In contrast, aluminum roofing and concrete cement, which dominate modern buildings in most parts of Africa, are heat conductors and do not cool easily. Randomly

Fig. 21.1 (Top) Abuja, Nigeria. The original homes of the natives before government relocation. (Janel Hetland) or (Labelle Prussin and University of California Press)

Fig. 21.2 (Bottom) Abuja, Nigeria. Homes provided for the natives by the government after relocation. 1984. (Janel Hetland) or (Labelle Prussin and University of California Press)

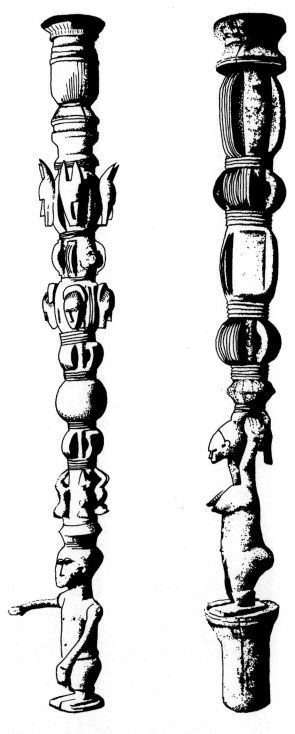

Fig. 21.3 Ghana. Application of Islamic design on columns. (Janel Hetland) or (Labelle Prussin and University of California Press)

Fig. 21.4 Grand Bassau, Senegal. Carved Columns. (Janel Hetland)

Fig. 21.5 Lagon region, Cote d'Ivoire. Carved columns. (Janel Hetland)

Fig. 21.6 *Yorubaland, Nigeria. Carved door.* (Janel Hetland)

Fig. 21.7 *Sahara Desert, Morocco. Traditional building method.*

arranged houses enhance the effectiveness of cross-ventilation, as opposed to the rigidly arranged houses in most modern housing estates in Africa. The layout of kraals, kgotlas, and other village plans should be studied and adapted to meet contemporary town planning needs.

It is also important to mention that understanding climatology and regionalism will not be enough in the development of the triple heritage architecture. Architecture is articulated by vernacular context and appreciation. Regionalism and vernacular are similar, but not identical. While regionalism covers a much wider area and provides a general concept, vernacular covers a much smaller area and provides the specific instruments of architectural articulation. For example, regionalism and Islam may give all of North Africa identical parties and architectural repertoire, but vernacular provides the specific tools of articulation in each of the countries in the region. The same principle applies in West Africa where Islam creates a need for the mosque as a building type, but regionalism brings about the articulation of the mosque in a different style compared to the styles in North Africa. In addi-

Fig. 21.8 Ethiopia. The application of modern building materials to traditional building methods.(American Geographical Society Collection, The University of Wisconsin-Milwaukee Library)

Fig. 21.9 Kano, Nigeria. The application of modern building materials to traditional building methods. (American Geographical Society Collection, The University of Wisconsin-Milwaukee Library)

tion, specific localities in West Africa have specific vernacular articulation for their mosques.

It is, therefore, critical that the vernacular identities of each region and locality be studied and coordinated with building function. Emphasis must not be on form, but on the ability of a people to relate to buildings functionally, physically, sym-

bolically, aesthetically, and technically. This is where eclectic dialogue between the past and the present is very important. If people misuse houses designed and built for them, it is not because they cannot relate to the forms, but because the spaces are woefully out of context to what they are used to. The primary goal should not be to duplicate traditional

Fig. 21.10 Port Harcourt, Nigeria. Middle-class homes. 1988.

Fig. C.96 (Left) Kolenz, Mali. Private house. Roman influences can be seen on the window arches, but a much older indigenous adobe construction method from ancient Egypt is also visible on the projecting timbers that form the terrace deck. (Jean-Louis Bourgeois and Carollee Pelos—Spectacular Vernacular, The Adobe Tradition 1989)

Fig. C.97 (Below) Mali. Decorated brick wall of a private house. (Jean-Louis Bourgeois and Carollee Pelos—Spectacular Vernacular, The Adobe Tradition 1989)

Fig. C.98 (Opposite) Mali. Entry to a private house. Observe the massive door post. Adobe construction. (Jean-Louis Bourgeois and Carollee Pelos—Spectacular Vernacular, The Adobe Tradition 1989)

Fig. C.99 (Left) Aore, Mali. Wall detail showing shades and shadows. Adobe construction. (Jean-Louis Bourgeois and Carollee Pelos— Spectacular Vernacular, The Adobe Tradition 1989)

Fig. C.100 (Right) Galasyne, Mali. External staircase to a roof. Adobe construction. (Jean-Louis Bourgeois and Carollee Pelos— Spectacular Vernacular, The Adobe Tradition 1989)

African architecture in modern materials and styles, but to create habitats that African people can relate to materially and technically.

The resettlement of the Kambri people during the construction of Kinji Dam in Nigeria is a good example of what architects should not do. The Kambris left their new "modern" houses and built themselves traditional houses less than a year after they were resettled by the federal government of Nigeria. Robin Atkinson successfully duplicated the traditional forms of Kambri houses with cement blocks and asbestos roofs, but the spatial aspects of Kambri architecture were not taken into consideration. The houses were too hot, the linear grid and streets disrupted Kambri lifestyle, and above all, the Kambri people could not maintain the materials, especially the asbestos roofs which broke easily. A combination of technical and sociocultural problems forced them out of the habitats before long.

Modernization is a good thing, but it should be achieved gradually. Indigenous people are skilled at incorporating foreign elements in their artworks and houses. Such modernizations are better adopted and adapted to than radical modern ones that are implemented rapidly. For example, the relocation of the natives of Abuja by the federal government of Nigeria is the right thing to do, but Abuja people should have been allowed to build their own houses with the money the government spent on their modern homes. There is something terribly wrong with a housing design solution that pro-

vides kitchens for modern electric or gas powered stoves, when the occupants of the houses use coal and wood in the kitchens. Such kitchens will not be utilized properly and the house will degenerate more rapidly (Figs. 21.1 and 21.2).

Vernacular articulation often includes the application of art deco to houses in addition to other structural peculiarities. Art deco can serve mainly aesthetic or symbolic purposes, with the symbols representing various aspects, events, memorials, and the religious and political heritage of a people. An unlimited, interdisciplinary approach that borrows from the whole culture of a people is often adopted in the application of art deco. For example, patterns found in *adinkra*, or the mourning cloth, are transformed into motifs that decorate walls and columns in Ashanti architecture. These motifs are also present in various leather artifacts, and some can be traced to their origins in Islamic calligraphy and art deco.

Structural elements that serve both aesthetic and structural values in buildings are abundant in Africa, as demonstrated by carved columns, doors, and intricate plasterworks on walls of Hausa houses, Swahili walls, and Zanzibar doors (Figs. 21.4 to 21.6). Art has been a convenient medium for cultural expression, and style, theme, and motif are the vehicles of this expression according to perceptions and representations. Hence, the themes expressed in art are those dominant and current in a culture for different purposes and times. Architects who practice in Africa must coordinate their efforts with African artists if they are to achieve meaningful levels of authentic indigenous architectural expression. One fact is certain: The triple heritage culture of Africa is a reality that will remain, but it has yet to find a harmonized expression in architecture. That is why more studies need to be done on Africa's triple heritage architecture.

Buildings that utilize indigenous elements such as columns, doors, and intricate plasterworks with foreign materials and style demonstrate that gradual syncretism is more manageable than rapid radical modernization (Figs. 21.7 to 21.9). There is also a significant difference in the way the emergent middle class and bourgeoisie utilize their buildings compared to the way the less affluent utilize theirs. The middle class and the bourgeoisie are more likely to furnish their homes with today's modern conveniences and are more likely to maintain their buildings than are the less affluent (Fig. 21.10).

GLOSSARY

Abu Simbel: The original sites of the two temples built by Ramses II, now submerged by the waters of Aswan Dam. 19th Dynasty (1304–1237 B.C.).

afins: The palaces of Yoruba kings.

aisle: A part of a church alongside the nave, choir, or transept, arranged by a row of columns or piers.

Amenemope: An African king who wrote several poems and verses that now appear in the Book of Proverbs of the Holy Bible (1405–1370 B.C.).

Amon: One of the ancient African gods of Egypt associated with life and reproduction, and later with the sun god Ra as Amon-Ra.

ancestor worship: The belief in the spirits of dead relatives—mothers, grandmothers, fathers, grandfathers, great-grandfathers—as guardian spirits and mediators between humans and God Almighty.

apse: A semicircular niche terminating one or both ends of the nave in a basilica.

arabisances: A new term for the process of converting European style buildings into Islamic buildings by the addition of Islamic motifs.

arcade: A series of arches supported by columns.

architrave: In Greek and Roman orders, the lowest member of the entablature, resting directly upon the capitals of the supporting columns.

balustrade: A railing supported by short pillars known as balusters.

baroque: Architecture characterized by irregular curves and ornamentations.

bazaar: A street of outdoor markets.

buttress: A projecting support built to reinforce walls.

canopy: A rooflike structure projecting from a wall or supported on pillars. An ornamental rooflike structure above a statue or similar object.

Carthage: An ancient city-state of Africa that was destroyed by the Romans in 146 B.C. after several Punic Wars. This marks the beginning of Western architecture in Africa as Roman imperialism increased around the Mediterranean.

chancel: A square or rectangular area between the apse and the nave or transept. Also known as choir.

Cheops: The African Pharaoh who built the largest pyramid during the Fourth Dynasty of Egypt. Also known as Khurfu at Giza.

chevron: The meeting place of rafters at the ridge of a gable roof; a zigzag pattern used as ornamentation in Romanesque architecture.

citadel: A fortification. A fortified place or city.

column: A cylindrical and slightly tapered pillar, serving as a support to some portion of a building.

Corinthian: The most ornate of the three Greek orders of architecture. It is characterized by the distinguishing features of its bell-shaped capital adorned with rows of simplified acanthus leaves.

courtyard: A space enclosed by walls or buildings.

dome: A vaulted roof of circular, polygonal, or elliptical plan formed with hemispherical curvature.

Doric: The oldest and simplest of the three Greek orders of architecture.

dynasty: The succession of rulers who are of the same family.

ethnography: Anthropological description of specific cultures.

facade: The face of a structure or a building. The exterior sides of a building or a structure. Also known as the elevation.

Falashas: A name given to Ethiopian Jews.

frieze: A continuous piece of painted or sculptured decoration. In a classical building, the part of the entablature between the architrave and the cornice.

gable: A triangular area framed by the cornice or eaves of a building and the sloping sides of a pitched roof.

Horus: Son of Osiris and Isis. The sun god.

hypostyle hall: Any large space whose ceiling is supported by columns. Mostly found in ancient African temples of Egypt. The large hall which preceded inner sanctuaries of the ancient African temples of Egypt. Hypostyle is a Greek term for "under columns."

Imhotep: The architect who built Zoser's Step Pyramid. Third Dynasty.

incantations: Holy words recited to ancestors, gods, and spirits during religious ceremonies.

indigenous: Existing or growing naturally in a region or country. Belonging to the place or region where it is found, not imported from an outside territory or region.

Ionic: One of the Greek orders of architecture characterized by the scroll-like ornaments of the capital.

Isis: Ancient African goddess of fertility; sister and wife of Osiris often represented with a cow's horns surrounding a solar disk.

Islam: The religion of Muslims as handed down by Prophet Muhammad and recorded in the Holy Koran. The Arabic name for God is Allah.

Judaism: The Jewish religion based on the principles of monotheism as handed down by Moses.

Karnak: One of the largest temple complexes in ancient African civilizations of Egypt. It is outside modern Luxor and dates from the Middle Kingdom to the Greco-Roman period. Several dynasties contributed to it.

kasr: A fortified enclave. Also a word used to describe a palace.

kgotla: An area where people live close to one another. A Tswana word for "large compounds." Derived from the kraal, the traditional Tswana compound. The kgotla represents a main central space for communal living and administration.

Kharidjites: A group of North African Berber Muslims who challenged the Arab ruling class and demanded to be part of the leadership during the middle of the 8th century A.D.

khekher: Reed parapet.

kraals: Traditional homesteads in southern Africa.

ksour: A fortification with many kasbahs.

labyrinth: A structure of plan with intricate passages.

lelapa: An inner private courtyard in a kgotla for family use or living area.

libation: A sacred ritual with a prayer to God, ancestors, gods accomplished by pouring holy water, wine, and/or special alcohols to the ground.

Luxor: A city along the Nile in southern Egypt with many ancient African ruins.

mace: A staff used as a symbol of authority.

madrasa: A theological school that provides students with lodging, prayer hall, and sometimes classrooms.

Maghreb: An area of Africa surrounded on the west by the Mediterranean Sea and on the south by a sea of sand, the Sahara Desert.

mastaba: A rectangular structure with a flat roof and sloping sides used as tombs in ancient Egypt.

mausoleum: Tombs or funerary monuments.

Menes: The first Pharaoh of Egypt. He unified Upper and Lower Egypt to a single state and began the tradition of wearing the double crown. Also known as Narmer. (3100–2700 B.C.)

mihrab: The small niche that indicates the qibla wall of a mosque showing the direction of Mecca.

minaret: A tower with balconies from which Muslims are summoned to prayer.

monotheism: The belief in one God which began with the worship of the sun god Ra.

mosaic: Decorative work for walls, vaults, ceilings, or floors composed of small pieces of colored materials set in plaster or concrete.

mose: An ancient Egyptian term for "is born."

Moses: The Jewish leader who founded Judaism and led the Israelites out of slavery in Egypt during the reign of Ramses II. He was the author of the Torah, especially the Ten Commandments.

narthex: The transverse entrance to a church. It is sometimes enclosed, but mostly open toward the atrium of the church.

nave: The central aisle of a basilica, which is different from the side aisle.

necropolis: A cemetery belonging to an ancient city. Old burial place for a family or a city.

Neolithic: The New Stone Age. From the Greek words *neos* meaning "new" and *lithos* meaning "stone."

obelisk: A free-standing masonry structure that represents shafts of sunlight in ancient African temples of Egypt.

Osiris: The Supreme God or Being in ancient Egypt. The giver of life and death. Also known as brother and husband of Isis. It is known among present-day Igbo (Ibo) and Yorubas of Nigeria as Orisa, the Supreme God or Being.

parapet: A low wall around a roof or platform that prevents people from falling over the edge.

patelo: The circulation spaces in a kgotla.

Pharaoh: The title of ancient African kings of Egypt.

pinnacle: A small decorative structure capping a tower and other architectural members. They are common in Gothic buildings.

pliable: Easily bent or flexible.

Proverbs: One of the books of the Old Testament, credited to King Solomon.

pylon: (1) The monumental entrance in buildings to Egyptian temples or forecourt. It is often defined by massive walls with sloping sides with entryways. From the Greek word for "entry gate." (2) A tall structure at the entrance of a gate or bridge that marks an entrance or a major passage.

qibla: The element that indicates the direction of Mecca in a mosque. It is marked by a mihrab, and Muslims face it during prayers.

Ra: The principal deity of ancient African civilization of Egypt known as the sun god. It was usually depicted as having the head of a hawk with a solar disk as a crown.

rafters: The sloping members of a roof, such as the ribs which extend from the ridge or from the hip of a roof to the eaves. They support the shingles and roof boards.

Renaissance: The rebirth and revival in art, architecture, and literature of classical ideals in Europe in the 14th, 15th, and 16th centuries.

ribari: Fortified Islamic holy place for monks.

Romanesque: A style of architecture which developed in Western Europe between the Roman and Gothic styles. It is characterized by decorative use of arcades, rounded arches, and vaults.

sanctuary: A sacred or holy place within a building.

Solomon: A Jewish king known in the Bible as the wisest king who ever lived (976–936 B.C.).

soule: An outdoor and open air marketplace in North African cities.

sphinx: A good example of this creature has a lion's body and the head of a human at the funerary temple of Chefren. Its African features clearly explain its indigenous origin. It evolved into a ram's head at Karnak during the Middle Kingdom. The sphinx was exported to other parts of the Near East and the Mediterranean in different forms.

sub-Saharan: Regions of Africa south of the Sahara Desert.

Sudan: An Arabic word for "black people" or "country of the blacks." Also the name of an African republic.

Sudanese style: The indigenous adobe building style of the savanna countries of West Africa.

sufi: An Islamic cult whose leaders were both teachers and mystics. They built grandoise tombs for their past leaders and made the graves holy shrines.

Symmetry: Similarity of form or arrangement on either side of a dividing line. Balance of form on all sides.

synagogue: Holy place of worship for followers of the Jewish religion.

terrace: An elevated level surface of earth supported on one or more faces by a masonry wall or by a sloping bank covered with turf.

thatches: Straw, reed, or leaf coverings for a roof.

totem: Animal or object adopted as the emblem of a tribe or family.

tracery: Ornamental stonework in Gothic windows.

transept: An open space that crosses the nave of a church, usually separating it from the choir or apse.

Tutthmosis III: The African Pharaoh of Egypt who founded the 18th Dynasty. He was born of a Sudanese woman and was also known as the Napoleon of antiquity because of his imperialist pursuit around the Mediterranean and the Near East.

vault: An arched roof or ceiling usually made of stone, brick, or concrete.

Western: Used in this book to define any culture, policy, art, or architecture of European origin found in Africa from the Roman times in 146 B.C. to the present.

zankwaye: The decorative pinnacle on the portals of Hausa and Songhay buildings. It is made with reeds as in most ancient Egyptian homes.

Zoser: The African king of the Third Dynasty of Egypt who built the Step Pyramid.

CHRONOLOGY

pre-6000 to 4000 B.C.

This is the period before the desiccation of the Sahara Desert. The Sahara was full of vegetation and wildlife. Lake Chad was much larger, and several rivers watered the region.

Primarily cave dwellings in the savannas of North, East, South, and West Africa.

Proto-Egyptian rock paintings in caves dominate African art, some dating as early as 10,000 years.

The beginning of desiccation and migrations from the savannas to different parts of Africa, especially the Nile Valley.

4000 to 3300 B.C.

Advancement of agriculture and settlement in the Nile Valley.

Experimentation with tent structures, beehive-type houses of reeds, and varying forms of adobe (clay) houses.

3200 to 2777 B.C.

The beginning of the Old African Kingdom of Egypt.

The First and Second Dynasties.

The First Dynasty began when a Nubian (Upper Egyptian) king (Pharaoh), whom archeologists and historians identify as Narmer or Menes, conquered Lower Egypt (the Nile Delta) and united both regions.

Pharaoh Narmer (Menes) founded his capital city, Memphis, which was named after him.

Narmer (Menes) began the practice of wearing a double crown to represent Upper and Lower Egypt.

The early stages of tomb burials and rock-cut graves.

Proto-pyramid tombs (mastabas) made of several steps were in their early stage of development, in addition to brick and timber construction.

2778 to 2723 B.C.

The Third Dynasty was begun by Pharaoh Neterikhet (Netjrikhe).

Pharaoh Zoser (Djeser) commissioned the first monumental brick building (the Step Pyramid of Zoser at Saqqara) in the world, designed and built by architect Imhotep.

2723 to 2563 B.C.

The Fourth Dynasty, the era of great pyramid construction.

The great triad Pyramids of Cheops, Chephren, and Mycerinius were built.

Pharaoh Chephren, the son of Cheops, built the Great Spinx to represent himself as a powerful African king.

2563 to 2423 B.C.

The Fifth Dynasty. The Pyramid of Unas was built at Saqqara, with the pyramid text inscriptions on the wall of the tomb chamber. The texts were some of the most ancient Egyptian texts, and they include descriptions of the "cannibal feast."

The Tomb of Ti was built.

2131 to 2000 B.C.

The Eleventh Dynasty. The Mortuary Temple of Mentuhotep III was built at Deir-al Bahri.

2000 to 1785 B.C.

Pharaoh Sessostris I built the Sanctuary of Amun at Karnak.

The Pyramid of Sessostris at Lisht was built.

1580 to 1346 B.C.

The Eighteenth Dynasty, and the sun god Amon-Ra was dominant in the whole kingdom. Many temples were dedicated to it by various kings and queens.

Amenhotep I built a small temple at Karnak (1557–1530 B.C.).

The Mortuary Temple of Queen Hatshepsut was built (1520–1484 B.C).

The Twin Obelisks of Queen Hatshepsut were erected at Karnak.

Thutmose III built the Great Festival Hall at Karnak (1504–1450 B.C.).

The colossal statue of Amenhotep III was erected (1408–1372 B.C).

Amenhotep III built his large pylon at Karnak.

Ramses I built a larger pylon at Karnak.

1366 to 1350 B.C.

The city of Tell el-Armana, originally known as Aten, was built by Pharaoh Amenhotep IV.

Amenhotep IV changed his name to Akhnenaten, meaning "He in whom Aten is satisfied." Akhnenaten also meant the "luminous mountain-horizon-of-Aten."

Amenhotep IV decided to build a city that would recognize only one God, Aten. It was the first architecture and city dedicated to a monotheistic philosophy, but the priests at the ancient city of Thebes hated it because it threatened their powers.

1314 to 1200 B.C.

Nineteenth Dynasty.

The rock-cut Temple of Ramses II and his colossal statues were built at Abu Simbel (1301–1250 B.C.).

The Temple of Seti I was built at Abydos.

1200 to 1085 B.C.

Twentieth Dynasty.

Mortuary Temple of Ramses III was built (1198–1166 B.C.).

950 to 730 B.C.

Twenty-second Dynasty.

At the Temple of Amun at Karnak, the rams in the Avenue of the Sphinxes were built.

600 to 525 B.C.

The Assyrians invade Egypt. It marks the beginning of foreign occupations of Egypt, and Egypt is no longer isolated.

525 B.C.

The Persians occupy Egypt.

350 B.C.

The consolidation of Carthage as a major trading port in North Africa, following Persian conquest of their homeland.

The rise of Meroetic civilization south of Egypt, as Egypt becomes more unstable due to outside threats.

Beginning of Aksumite civilization in Ethiopia.

Aksum: The Palace of Enda was built.

Aksum: The Palace of Taakha Mariam was built.

The beginning of Nok culture and art in central Nigeria. The production of terra-cotta masks which preceded Yoruba, Benin, and Igbo Ukwu arts of Nigeria began.

333 B.C.

Macedonians invade Egypt under the leadership of Alexander.

General Ptolemy usurps power following the death of Alexander and introduces the Ptolemaic dynasty, the last dynasty of Pharaonic Egypt.

Kom Ombo: The Temple of Haroeris was built.

Dendra: The Temple of Hathor was built.

Edfu: The Temple of Horus was built.

146 B.C.

Romanization of North Africa began after the defeat of

Carthage by the Roman army.

Roman cities and colosseums were built in North Africa.

50 to 40 B.C.

Rome invades and occupies Egypt under Mark Anthony and Julius Caesar, resulting in the defeat of Queen Cleopatra, who was the last Ptolemy to rule Egypt. It was also the end of dynastic Egypt before the Islamic conquest.

100 to 400 A.D.

Algeria, Libya, Tunisia, and Egypt have become Roman colonies, and the fusion of indigenous African Berber culture and Roman culture was in its early stages.

The emergence of the West African (Sudan) empires of Ghana with interest in long-distance trade across the Sahara Desert.

Consolidation of Roman building traditions in North Africa, while the Romans exported some indigenous African building traditions to Rome and applied them to Roman temples and palaces like the Temples of Serapis and Isis, Hadrian's Villa at Tivoli, and Diocletian's Palace at Split.

Ancient African building traditions such as the complex temples at Karnak influence the construction of Roman basilicas, some of which were used as houses of worship by early Christians in Rome and in North Africa.

The expansion of the trans-Saharan trade between North Africa and West Africa (the Sudan).

Ancient Egyptian house types of adobe and stone buildings, identified as the Sudanese style of architecture flourish in West Africa.

Egypt, Ethiopia, and Nubia (mainly southern Egypt and northern Republic of Sudan) were Christian states and adopted traditional adobe houses with both round and square plans as early Christian churches.

The migrations of Bantu-speaking Africans toward the Congo Basin and beyond.

Early foundations of Great Zimbabwe.

570 to 632 A.D.

The birth and death of Prophet Muhammad and the beginning of Islam.

640 A.D.

The fall of Eastern Byzantine empire to conquering Muslim Arabs.

The fall of Egypt to the Arabs.

The foundations of Islamic Fustat, Askar, and Katai in Cairo.

632 to 800 A.D.

Arabs conquer Ifriquiya (Tunisia).

Arabs reach Moroccan Atlantic coast and cross into Spain to establish the caliphate at Cordoba.

Arabs settle along East African coasts and Islamize the region as the fusion of Arab and African cultures evolved into Swahili culture.

Trans-Saharan trading cities like Kumbi Saleh, Audoghast, Gao, Bornu, and Kano boom with trade.

The rise of the Hausa, Kanem-Bornu, and Yoruba states of Nigeria.

Christian Ethiopia and Nubia are isolated from Egypt and the rest of the Christian world because of conquering Arabs' blockade.

794 A.D.

The Great Mosque of Qarawan was built.

796 A.D.

The Ribat at Sussa was built.

800 A.D.

Fez, Morocco, was founded.

The city of Kano, Nigeria, was in its early stages.

856 A.D.

Fez, Morocco: The Great Mosque of Qarawiyin was built.

876 A.D.

Cairo, Egypt: The Great Mosque of Ibin Tulun was built.

972 A.D.

Cairo, Egypt: Al-Azhar Mosque was constructed.

991 A.D.

Cairo, Egypt: Construction began on Al-Hakim Mosque.

1000 A.D.

Great Zimbabwe was built.

Ghana was very prosperous in the Sudan.

1013 A.D.

Cairo, Egypt: Al-Hakim Mosque was completed.

1070 A.D.

Marakesh, Morocco, was founded.

1080 A.D.

The Great Mosque of Tlemecen was begun.

1096 A.D.

Algiers, Algeria: The Great Mosque was built.

1100 A.D.

The early stages of the Mali empire.

1180 A.D.

The Great Citadel at Cairo was begun.

1190 A.D.

Rabat, Morocco: The Mosque of Hassan was begun.

1260 A.D.

Kilwa, Kenya: Husni Kubwa was built.

1312 A.D.

Mansa Musa became the emperor of Mali.

1327 A.D.

Djinguere Ber Mosque was built by Mansa Musa.

1356 A.D.

King Lalibela of Ethiopia began the construction of rock-cut churches.

Cairo, Egypt: Sultan Hassan Mosque was begun.

1375 A.D.

The rise of the Songhay empire in the Sudan (West Africa) and the beginning of the end of the Mali empire.

1400 A.D.

The foundation and growth of the Benin empire and Benin City, Nigeria.

1480 to 1482 A.D.

Ghana (Gold Coast): The Portuguese began and completed Elmina Castle.

1480 to 1500 A.D.

King Affonso I's capital city, Mbanza Kongo, had been established and was renamed Sao Salvador.

1520 A.D.

Katsina, Nigeria: The oldest mosque in the city was built.

1593 A.D.

Mombasa, Kenya: Construction work was begun at Fort Mombasa by the Portuguese.

1600 A.D.

The Portuguese began permanent settlement at Luanda (Loanda).

1640 A.D.

Gonda, Ethiopia: Facilidas Castle was built.

1641 A.D.

The Portuguese built Fort Sao Miguel.

1651 A.D.

Gambia, West Africa: James Fort was built.

1621 A.D.

The Dutch began settlement and construction at Goree Island, Senegal.

1659 A.D.

Dakar, Senegal: Fort Saint Louis was built by the French.

1666 A.D.

A major trading fort (castle) was built in Cape Town.

1791 A.D.

The foundation of the city of Freetown, Sierra Leone.

1815 A.D.

Banjul (Bathurst), Gambia, was established by the English.

1822 A.D.

Monrovia, Liberia, was established by the Americans.

1830 to 1900 A.D.

Years of colonization of African countries by the English, the French, the Germans, the Dutch, and other European powers.

Introduction of new forms of Western architecture to meet administrative, residential, trading, religious, and ceremonial needs of the colonialists.

1838 A.D.

Algeria: The town of Sidi Bel Abbes was laid out by the French.

1840 A.D.

The city of Durban, Republic of South Africa, was surveyed by the Dutch.

Pretoria, South Africa, was incorporated into a city, and surveying began in 1857.

1850 A.D.

Lagos, Nigeria: The British began a colonial settlement after occupation of the city.

November 16, 1855 A.D.

1869 to 1872 A.D.

Modern Cairo was designed and built under King Ismail by the French architect Baron Hausmann, who designed modern Paris.

1876 A.D.

Livingstone Blantyre Mission was established in Malawi.

1886 A.D.

Addis Ababa was founded by Emperor Menelik.

October 4, 1886 A.D.

Republic of South Africa: The city of Johannesburg was incorporated.

1891 to 1900 A.D.

The Germans started redesigning and constructing buildings in Dar es Salaam.

1898 A.D.

Modern Khartoum, Sudan, was being planned by the British.

1912 to 1915 A.D.

The city of Kaduna, Nigeria, was planned by Governor Lord Lugard.

1913 A.D.

Lusaka, Zambia, was founded.

1917 A.D.

Port Harcourt, Nigeria, was planned.

Enugu, Nigeria, was planned.

1926 A.D.

The French declared Niamey the capital of Niger Republic.

1950 A.D.

Kano, Nigeria: The Great Mosque was built.

1958 A.D.

Nouakchott, Mauritania, was founded and developed in anticipation of independence in 1960.

1960 to 1966 A.D.

Gaborone was selected and developed as the capital of Botswana.

1963 A.D.

Addis Ababa: The Organization of African Unity (OAU) Headquarters was planned.

1964 A.D.

Lilongwe was selected as the capital city of Malawi.

1975 A.D.

The Aguda Panel was set up to find a new location for Nigeria's federal capital, and Abuja was chosen.

1979 A.D.

Construction began at Abuja.

1980 A.D.

Construction began at Yamoussoukro, Cote d'Ivoire.

1992 A.D.

The tallest basilica in the world, Our Lady of Peace, was commissioned in Yamoussoukro, Cote d' Ivoire.

November 23, 1991 A.D.

General Ibrahim Babangida formally declared Abuja the federal capital of Nigeria.

1993 A.D.

Casablanca, Morocco: King Hassan Mosque, the largest and most expensive mosque in the world, was completed.

REFERENCES

INTRODUCTION

Andrews, John. 1967. *African Place (Place d' Afrique)*. Manual for the African Place Pavilion in International Exposition, Montreal, 1967. Sidney, Australia: John Andrews International.

Ayisi, Eric. 1979. *An Introduction to the Study of African Culture*. London: Heinemann.

Ben-Jochannan, Yosef. 1988. *African Origins of Major World Religions*. Ed. by Amon Saba Saakana. London: Karnak House.

Bernal, Martin. 1987. *Black Athenia. I*. New Brunswick, NJ: Rutgers University Press.

Buxton, David. 1967. *Travels in Ethiopia*. New York: Frederick A. Praeger.

Collins, Robert O. et al. 1968. *Problems in African History*. ed. Robert O. Collins. Englewood Cliffs, NJ: Prentice-Hall.

Davidson, Basil. 1992. *Africa in History*. London, Great Britain: Phoenix.

Decenimal, Jean-Paul. 1964. *Living Architecture: Egyptian*. New York: Grosset and Dunlap.

Diop, Cheikh Anta. 1974. *African Origins of Civilization: Myth or Reality*. Trans. from the French by Mercer Cook. New York: L. Hill.

Garlake, Peter. 1990. *The Kingdoms of Africa*. New York: Peter Bedricks Books.

George, Hart. 1986. *A Dictionary of Egyptian Gods and Goddesses*. London: Routledge and Kegan Paul.

Habachi, Labib. 1984. *The Obelisk of Egypt: Skyscraper of the Past*. Cairo: American University in Cairo Press.

Haberland, Eike. 1973. "Reflections on African Art." In Haberland, Eike (ed.), *Leo Frobenius 1873–1973. An Anthology*. (58) Weisbaden, Republic of Germany: Franz Steiner Verlag GmbH.

Hance, William A. 1975. *The Geography of Modern Africa*, 2d ed., New York and London: Columbia University Press, p. 52.

Henry, Paul-Marc. 1965. *Africa Aeterna. The Pictorial Chronicle of a Continent*. Text by Paul-Marc Henry. Translated by Joel Carmichael. Lausanne: Sed.

Jordan, Paul. 1976. *Egypt. The Black Land*. Oxford: Phaidon.

Lewis, James. Feb. 1987. "Architecture for the Third World." *Royal Institute of British Architects Journal*, 94(2), pp. 40–44.

Mazrui, Ali. 1986. *The African, A Triple Heritage*. Boston: Little Brown.

Mertz, Barbara. 1966. *Red Land, Black Land. The World of the Ancient Egyptians*. New York: Coward-McCann.

Meyerowitz, L. R. 1968. "The Divine Kingship in Ghana and Ancient Egypt." In Robert O. Collins (ed.), *Problems in African History* (p. 37). Englewood Cliffs, NJ: Prentice-Hall.

Lucas, Olumide J. 1968. "The Religion of the Yorubas." In Robert O. Collins (ed.), *Problems in African History* (p. 34). Englewood Cliffs, NJ: Prentice-Hall.

Pankhurst, Richard. 1992. "The Falashas, or Judaic Ethiopians, in Their Christian Ethiopian Setting." *African Affairs*, 91(365), 567–582.

Perham, Margery. 1968. "The Kingdom of Aksum." In P. J. M. McEwan (ed.), *Africa from Early Times to 1800* (pp. 290–305). London: Oxford University Press.

Pothorn, Herbert. 1982. *Architectural Styles*. New York: Facts On File Publications.

Seligman, C. G. 1968. "Egypt and Negro Africa." In Robert O. Collins (ed.), *Problems in African History* (p. 25). Englewood Cliffs, NJ: Prentice-Hall.

Ullendorff, Edward. 1960. *The Ethiopians. An Introduction to Country and People*. London: Oxford University Press.

Vansina, Jan. 1984. *Art History in Africa. An Introduction to Methods*. London: Longman.

CHAPTER I

Abu Bakr, A. 1981. "Pharaonic Egypt." In G. Mokhtar (ed.), *General History of Africa II. Ancient Civilizations of Africa*, pp. 84–111. CA: Unesco and Heinemann.

Ashe, Geoffrey. 1976. *The Virgin*. London: Routledge and Kegan Paul.

Badawy, Alexander. 1966. *A History of Egyptian Architecture. Vol. 2: First Intermediate Period, the Middle Kingdom, and the Second Intermediate Period*. Berkeley: University of California Press.

———. 1987. "Egyptian Colossal Monoliths: Why and How Were They Erected?" *Gazette des Beaux-Arts*, 109 (1418), 100.

Baines, John, and Málek, Jaromir. 1980. *Atlas of Ancient Egypt*. Oxford: Phaidon Press.

Barocas, Claudio. 1972. *Egypt. Monuments of Civilization*. Text by Claudio Barocas; forward by Oscar Niemeyer. New York: Grosset and Dunlap.

Ben-Jochannan, Yosef. 1988. "Moses: African Influence on Judaism." In Saba Saakana, Amon (ed.), *The African Origins of the Major World Religions*. p. 2. London: Karnak House.

Bernal, Martin. 1987. *Black Athenia I.* New Brunswick, NJ: Rutgers University Press.

Breasted, James Henry (ed. and trans.). 1962. *Ancient Records of Egypt. Historical Documents from the Earliest Times to the Persian Conquest.* Vol. 2. New York: Russell and Russell.

Budge, Wallis. 1959. *Egyptian Religion. Egyptian Ideas of the Future Life.* New York: Bell Publishing Company.

———. 1969. *Gods of the Egyptians or Studies in Egyptian Mythology.* Vol. 1. New York: Dover Publishing, Inc.

Cenival, Jean-Louis. 1964. *Living Architecture. Egyptian.* New York: Grosset and Dunlap.

Champollion, J. F. 1814. *L'Egypte sous les Pharaons: Ou recherches sur La Geographie, La religion, La langue, les critures et L'histoire de l'Egypte avant l'invasion de Cambyse.* Grenoble.

David, Rosalie Ann. 1982. *The Ancient Egyptians: Religious Beliefs and Practices.* London and Boston: Routledge and Kegan Paul.

Davidson, Basil. 1971. *African Kingdoms. Great Ages of Man. A History of the World's Cultures.* New York: Time-Life Books.

———. 1991. *African Civilization Revisited.* Trenton, NJ: African World Press.

Denyer, Susan. 1978. *Traditional African Architecture.* London: Heinemann.

Diop, Cheikh Anta. 1974. *The African Origin of Civilizations. Myth or Reality.* Westport: Lawrence Hill & Company.

Donahue, Benedict. 1979. *The Cultural Arts of Africa.* Washington, DC: Cultural Press of America.

Dubois, Felix. 1896. *Timbucktoo the Mysterious.* Diana White (trans.) (1969). New York: Negro University Press.

El-Nadoury, R. 1981. "The Legacy of Pharaonic Egypt." In G. Mokhta (ed.), *General History of Africa II. Ancient Civilizations of Africa.* (pp. 155–183).

Finch, Charles. 1988. "The Kamitic Genesis of Christianity." In Amon Saba Saakana (ed.), *Afrikan Origins of the Major World Religions.* (pp. 33–58). Britain: Karnak House.

———. 1988. "The Kamitic Genesis of Christianity." In Amon Saba Saakana (ed.), *Afrikan Origins of the Major World Religions.* (pp. 33–58). London: Karnak House.

Fitchen, John. 1978. "Building Cheops Pyramid." *The Journal of the Society of Architectural Historians,* 37(1), 3–12.

Guedes, Amancio de Alpoim Miranda. 1985. "Vitruvius Mozambicanus." *Arquitectura Portuguesa,* 1(5), 68.

Gustafson, Fred. 1990. *The Black Madonna.* Boston: Sigo Press.

Habachi, Labib. 1977. *The Obelisks of Egypt. Skyscrapers of the Past.* In Charles C. Van Siclen (ed.). New York: Scribner.

Haberland, Eike. 1973. "Reflections on African Art." In Haberland, Eike (ed.), *Leo Frobenius 1873–1973. An Anthology.* (58) Wiesbaden, Republic of Germany: Franz Steiner Verlag GmbH.

Hance, William. 1964. *The Geography of Modern Africa.* New York: Columbia University Press.

Hart, George. 1986. *A Dictionary of Egyptian Gods and Goddesses.* London: Routledge and Kegan Paul.

———. 1990. *Egyptian Myths.* London: British Museum Publication.

Henry, Paul. 1965. *Africa Aeterna: The Pictorial Chronicle of a Continent.* Lausanne: Sed.

Hinkel, Friedrich W. 1991. "Proportion and Harmony: The Process of Planning in Meroitic Architecture." In Davies, W. V. (ed.), *Egypt and Africa. Nubia from Prehistory to Islam.* London: British Museum Press.

Hornung, Erik. 1990. *The Valley of the Kings. Horizon of Eternity.* David Warburton (trans.). New York: Timken Publishers.

Horton, Mark. 1991. "Africa in Egypt: New Evidence from Qasr Ibrim." In Davies, W. V. (ed.), *Egypt and Africa. Nubia from Prehistory to Islam.* London: British Museum Press.

Hughes, David. 1993. "Afrocentric Architecture. A Concept/Theory." Paper prepared for the International Conference on (Post) Modernity and Difference in Architecture. Singapore, April 14–17.

Hull, Richard. 1976. *African Cities and Towns Before the European Conquest.* New York: W. W. Norton & Company.

Jordan, Paul. 1976. *Egypt: The Black Land.* Oxford: Phaidon Press.

Kulterman, Udo. 1969. *New Directions in African Architecture.* New York: George Braziller.

Macquintty, William. 1965. *Abu Simbell.* New York: Putnam's Sons.

Macquitty, William. 1976. *Island of Isis. Phidae, Temple of the Nile.* New York: Charles Scribner's Sons.

Mazrui, Ali. 1986. *The African, A Triple Heritage.* Boston: Little Brown and Company.

Mertz, Barbara. 1978. *Red Land, Black Land: Daily Life in Ancient Egypt.* New York: Dodd, Mead.

Meyer, Wilhelm. 1981. Statement on the Johannesburg Art Gallery. Meyer Pienaar and Partners, Inc., Architects and Urban Designers, 9a Sturdee Avenue, Rosebank, Johannesburg 2196, PO Box 52317, Saxonwold 2132, Johannesburg.

———. 1991. Lecture. University of Cape Town and Port Elizabeth. Meyer Pienaar and Partners, Inc., Architects and Urban Designers.

Moughtin, J. C. 1985. *Hausa Architecture.* London: Ethnographica.

O'Connor, David. 1991. "Early States along the Nubian Nile." In Davies, W. V. (ed.), *Egypt and Africa. Nubia from Prehistory to Islam.* London: British Museum Press.

Pankhurst, Richard, and Ingrams, Leila. 1988. *Ethiopia Engraved. An Illustrated Catalogue of Engravings by Foreign Travellers From 1681 to 1900.* London: Kegal Paul International.

Pothorn, Herbert. 1982. *Architectural Styles.* New York: Facts On File Publications.

Prussin, Labelle. 1986. *Islamic Design in West Africa.* Berkeley: University of California Press.

Rosalie, David. 1982. *The Ancient Egyptian Religious Beliefs and Practices.* London: Routledge and Kegal Paul.

Ryder, Alan. 1969. *Benin and The Europeans, 1485–1897.* New York: Humanities Press.

Sellassie, Sergew Hable. 1972. *Ancient and Medieval Ethiopian History to 1270.* Addis Ababa, Ethiopia: Haile Sellassie I University.

Shillington, Kevin. 1989. *History of Africa.* New York: Macmillan Publishers Limited.

Shinnie, P. L. 1991. "Trade Routes of the Ancient Sudan 3000 B.C.– A.D. 350." In Davies, W. V. (ed.), *Egypt and Africa. Nubia from Prehistory to Islam.* London: British Museum Press.

Smith, E. Baldwin. 1938. *Egyptian Architecture as Cultural Expression.* New York: Appleton-Century Company.

Ullendorff, Edward. 1960. *The Ethiopians: An Introduction to Country and People.* London, New York: Oxford University Press.

Vansina, Jan. 1984. *Art History in Africa. An Introduction to Methods.* New York: Longman.

Willet, Frank. 1971. *African Art.* New York: Oxford University Press.

CHAPTER 2

Blake, John W. 1969. *European Beginnings in West Africa 1454–1578.* Hartford, CT: Greenwood Press.

Church, Harrison. 1980. *West Africa*. Eighth Edition. London: Longman.

Coquery-Virdrovitch, Catherine. 1991. "The Process of Urbanization in Africa (from the Origins to the Beginning of Independence)." *African Studies Review*, 34(1), 1–98.

Donahue, Benedict. 1979. *The Cultural Arts of Africa*. Washington, DC: Cultural Press of America.

Giedion, Sigfried. 1971. *Architecture and the Phenomena of Transition*. Cambridge, MA: Harvard University Press.

Guedes, Amancio de Alpoim Miranda. 1985. "Vitruvius Mozambicanus." *Arquitectura Portuguesa*, 1(6), 68.

Hutchinson, L. Daniel. 1979. *Out of Africa. From West African Kingdoms to Colonialization*. Washington, DC: Smithsonian Institute Press.

Kubbler, George. 1972. *Portuguese Plain Architecture*. Middletown, CT: Wesleyan University Press.

Mazrui, Ali. 1986. *The African: A Triple Heritage*. Boston: Little Brown and Company.

Meyer, Wilhelm. 1984. Statement on the Johannesburg Art Gallery. Meyer Pienaar and Partners, Inc., Architects and Urban Designers, 9a Sturdee Avenue, Rosebank, Johannesburg 2196, PO Box 52317, Saxonwold 2132, Johannesburg.

———. 1991. *University of Cape Town and Port Elizabeth. Presentation of Major Projects (1987 to 1991)*. Johannesburg: Meyer Pienaar and Partners.

Panikkar, K. M. 1963. *The Serpent and the Crescent. A History of the Negro Empires of Western Africa*. Bombay: Asia Publishing House.

Picton-Seymour, Desiree. 1977. *Victorian Buildings in South Africa*. Cape Town: Balkema Rotterdam.

Prussin, Labelle. 1986. *Islamic Design in West Africa*. Berkeley: University of California Press.

Ryder, Alan F. C. 1969. *Benin and the Europeans, 1485–1897*. New York: Humanities Press.

Tasie, G. O. M. 1978. *Christian Missionary Enterprise in the Niger Delta, 1864–1918*. Leiden, The Netherlands: E. J. Brill.

Warmington, B. H. 1980. "Carthage." In Arthur Cotterell (ed.), *Encyclopedia of Ancient Civilizations*. p. 237. London: Rainbird Publishing Company.

Wright, Gwendolyn. 1991. *The Politics of Design in French Colonial Urbanism*. Chicago: University of Chicago Press.

CHAPTER 3

Ali Ibrahim, Laiha. 1984. "Residential Architecture in Mameluk Cairo." In Oleg Grabar (ed.), *Muqarnas*, Vol. 2 (pp. 47–59). New Haven, CT: Yale University Press.

Aradeon, S. B. 1989. "Al-Sahili, the Historians' Myth of Architecture Technology Transfer from North Africa." *Journal Des Africanistes*, 59 (1–2): 99–130.

Briggs, Martin. 1974. *Muhammadan Architecture in Egypt and Palestine*. New York: De Capo Press.

Clarke, Peter. 1982. *West Africa and Islam. A Study of Religious Development from the 8th to the 20th Century*. London: Edward Arnold.

David, James. 1974. *Islamic Art—An Introduction*. New York: Hamlyn.

Davidson, Basil. 1991. *African Civilization Revisited*. Trenton, NJ: African World Press.

Garlake, Peter. 1990. *The Kingdoms of Africa*. New York: Peter Bedricks Books.

Hoag, D. John. 1977. *Islamic Architecture*. New York: Harry N. Abrams.

Hiskett, Meryn. 1984. *The Development of Islam in West Africa*. London: Longman.

Hutt, Anthony. 1977. *Islamic Architecture, North Africa*. London: Scorpion Publications.

Kuhnel, Ernst. 1966. *Islamic Art and Architecture*. Ithaca, NY: Cornell University Press.

Moughtin, J. C. 1985. *Hausa Architecture*. London: Ethnographica.

Papadopoulo, Alexandre. 1979. *Islam and Muslim Art*. New York: Harry N. Abrams.

Powells, Randall. 1987.

Price, Christine. 1964. *The Story of Muslim Art*. New York: E. P. Dutton.

Prussin, Labelle. 1986. *Islamic Design in West Africa*. Berkeley: University of California Press.

CHAPTER 4

Abu-Lughod, Janet. 1980. *Rabat. Urban Apartheid in Morocco*. Princeton, NJ: Princeton University Press.

Ailland, Charlotte. 1989. "A Designer's Transformed Harem in Marrakesh." *Architectural Digest*, 46(7).

Allison, Philip. 1988. *Life in the White Man's Grave*. London: Viking.

Bonine, E. Michael. 1990. "The Sacred Direction and City Structure." *Muqarnas*, 7, 50–72.

Duly, Colin. 1979. *The Houses of Mankind*. New York: Thames and Hudson.

Hoisington, William. 1984. *The Casablanca Connection*. Chapel Hill: University of North Carolina Press.

Johnson, Katherine. 1970. *Urban Government for the Prefecture of Casablanca*. New York: Praeger.

Kay, Shirley. 1980. *Morocco*. London: Namara Publications.

King Hassan II, H. M. July 11, 1988. *Hassan II Mosque*. Washington, DC: Embassy of the Kingdom of Morocco.

Landau, Rom, and Swaan, Wim. 1967. *Morocco*. New York: G. P. Putnam's Sons.

Pothorn, Herbert. 1982. *Architectural Styles*. New York: Facts On File Publications.

Prussin, Labelle. 1982. "Tents: Lady of the Builders." *Mimar*, 4, 18–55.

Scharfenorth, Heiner. 1991. "Focus on Berber Architecture in Southern Morocco." *Architektur and Wahnen*, Feb.–Mar., 132–146.

Taylor, Brian. 1984. "Demythologizing Colonial Architecture, Forms and Models." *Mimar*, 13, 16–25.

Tourneau, Roger. 1961. *Fez—In the Age of the Marinides*. Besse Alberta Clement (trans.). Norman: University of Oklahoma Press.

Wright, Gwendolyn. 1991. *Politics of Design in French Colonial Urbanism*. Chicago: University of Chicago Press.

CHAPTER 5

Alexander, Margaret. 1983. "Design and Meaning in the Early Christian Mosaics of Tunisia." *Apollo*, Jan., 8–13.

Baudez, G. and Béguin, F. 1980. "Observations on French Colonial Architecture in North Africa Between 1900 and 1950." *Lotus International*, 26, 41–50.

Berry, La Verle. 1989. *Historical Setting: Libya, A Country Study*. Washington, DC: Headquarters Department of the Army.

Hoag, John. 1975. *Islamic Architecture*. New York: Harry N. Abrams.

Hutt, Anthony. 1977. *Islamic Architecture North Africa*. London: Scorpion Publications Ltd.

Lebbal, N. 1989. "Traditional Berber Architecture in the Aures, Algeria." *Vernacular Architecture*, 201, 24–37.

The Libyan General Committee for Participation in the World of Islamic Festival. 1976. *Islamic Art and Architecture in Libya*. London: The Committee.

Malverti, X. and Picard, A. 1991. "Algeria: Military Genius and Civic Design (1830–1870)." *Planning Perspective*, 6, 207–236.

Mathews, K. and Cook, A. 1963. *Cities in the Sand. Leptis Magna and Sabratha in Roman Africa*. Philadelphia: University of Pennsylvania Press.

McMorris, David. 1979. *Society and Its Environment. Algeria, a Country Survey*. Washington, DC: American University Press.

Rinehart, Robert. 1986. *Historical Setting. Algeria, a Country Survey*. Washington, DC: American University Press.

———. 1979. *Historical Setting. Algeria, a Country Survey*. Washington, DC: American University Press.

Samdon, Julia. 1985. *Nefertiti and Cleopatra. Queen-Monarchs of Ancient Egypt*. London: Rubicon Press.

Tange, Kenzo. 1979. "Concepts of Recent Works." *Japan Architect*, Jul.–Aug., 267 and 268: 10–26.

Taylor, Brian. 1980. "Planned Discontinuity, Modern Colonial Cities in Morocco." *Lotus International*, 26, 53–66.

CHAPTER 6

Aldridge, James. 1969. *Cairo*. Boston: Little Brown and Company.

Hoag, John D. 1977. *Islamic Architecture*. New York: Harry N. Abrams.

Mazrui, Ali A. 1986. *The Africans, A Triple Heritage*. Boston: Little Brown and Company.

Russell, Dorothea. 1962. *Medieval Cairo and the Monastaries of the Wadi Natrun. A Historical Guide*. London: Weidenfield and Nicolson.

Shellington, Kevin. 1989. *History of Africa*. London: Macmillan Publishers.

Smith, Baldwin. 1938. *Egyptian Architecture as Cultural Expression*. New York: D. Appleton-Century Company.

CHAPTER 7

Allen, J. de V. 1974. *Lamutown: a guide*. Lamu, Kenya.

Andersen, Kaj Blegvad. 1977. *Traditional African Architecture*. London: Oxford University Press.

Boxer, Charles Ralph and Azevedo, de Carlos. 1960. *Fort Jesus and the Portuguese in Mombasa*. London: Hollis and Carter.

Buxton, David. 1970. "Ethiopian Architecture in the Middle Ages." In George Gerster (ed.), *Churches in Rock. Early Christian Art in Ethiopia* (pp. 51–60). London: Phaidon.

Collings, R. and Deng, F. 1984. *The British in the Sudan, 1898–1956. The Sweetness and the Sorrow*. New York: Macmillan.

Davidson, Basil. 1971. *African Kingdoms. Great Ages of Man*. New York: Time-Life Books.

———. 1991. *African Civilizations Revisited*. Trenton, NJ: African World Press.

Fernea, R. and Gerster, G. 1973. *Nubians in Egypt*. Austin: University of Texas Press.

Gerster, George, 1970. "The Churches of Lalibela, a Wonder of the World." In George Gerster (ed.), *Churches in Rock*. pp. 107–108. London: Phaidon.

Haile, Sellassie I. 1976. *My Life and Ethiopia's Progress, 1892–1937*. Edward Ullendorff (trans.). London: Oxford University Press.

Hammerschmidt, Ernst. 1970. "The Ethiopian Orthodox Church." In George Gerster (ed.), *Churches in Rock. Early Christian Art in Ethiopia* (pp. 42–50). London: Phaidon.

Pankhurst, Richard and Leila, Ingrams. 1988. *Ethiopia Engraved*. London: Kegan Paul International.

Rinehart, Robert. 1984. *Early History. Kenya—A Country Study*. Washington, DC: American University Press.

———. 1982. *Early History. Somalia—A Country Study*. Washington, DC: American University Press.

Stevens, Richard. 1980. *Historical Setting. Ethiopia—A Country Study*. Washington, DC: American University Press.

"Sudan 1600 B.C. Kingdom Discovered." *West Africa*. No. 3911. Aug. 31–Sept. 6, 1992, p. 1498.

Thompson, Virginia and Adloff, Richard. 1968. *Djibouti and the Horn of Africa*. Stanford, CA: Stanford University Press.

CHAPTER 8

Dahinden, Justus. 1987. *Architecture. Kar Kramer*. Stuttgart: Verlag.

Davidson, Basil. 1969. *A History of East and Central Africa*. New York: Anchor Books.

de Blij, Harm. 1963. *Dar es Salaam*. Evanston, IL: Northwestern University Press.

Freeman-Grenville, G. S. P. 1991. *The New Atlas of African History*. New York: Simon and Schuster.

Gray, Robert F. 1963. *The Sonjo of Tanganyika. An Anthropological Study of an Irrigation-Based Society*. London: Oxford University Press.

Kaplan, Irving. 1978. "The People of Tanzania." In *Tanzania, a Country Study*. Washington, DC: American University Press.

Meister, Albert. 1968. *East Africa. The Past in Chains, The Future in Pawn*. New York: Walker and Company.

Mitchell, Robert C. 1969. *African Primal Religions*. Niles, IL: Argus Communications.

Nooter, Nancy I. 1984. "Zanzibar Doors." *African Arts*, 7(4), 34–39.

Nyerere, Julius. 1970. *Arusha Declaration Parliament. Freedom and Development (Uhury Na Maendeleo)*. Dar es Salaam: Oxford University Press.

Oded, Arye. 1974. *Islam in Uganda. Islamization Through a Centralized State in Pre-Colonial Africa*. Jerusalem: Israel University Press.

Room, Adrian. 1994. *African Placenames. Origins and Meanings of the Names for over 2000 Natural Features, Towns, Cities, Provinces and Countries*. London: McFarland & Company, Publishers.

Sathyamurthy, T. V. 1986. *The Political Development of Uganda: 1900–1986*. Vermont: Gower Publishing Company.

Sheriff, A. M. H. 1981. "The East African Coast and Its Role in Maritime Time." In G. Mokhtar (ed.), *African Civilization*, Vol. 2 (pp. 551–567). London: Unesco.

Sutton, John. 1990. *A Thousand Years of East Africa*. Nairobi: British Institute in East Africa.

Vale, Lawrence J. 1992. *Architecture, Power and National Identity*. New Haven, CT: Yale University Press.

Webster, Ogot, and J. P. Chretien. 1981. "The Great Lakes Region, 1500–1800." In B. A. Ogot (ed.), *General History of Africa*, Vol. 5, (pp. 776–824). London: Unesco.

CHAPTER 9

Barnes, James F. 1992. *Gabon: Beyond the Colonial Legacy*. Boulder, CO: Westview Press.

Crane, Louise. 1971. *The Land and the People of the Congo.* New York: J. B. Lippincott Company.

Mamdani, Mahmood. 1988. *Social Movements, Social Transformation and the Struggle for Democracy in Africa.* Dakar, Senegal: Publication Unit, codesria.

O'Toole, Thomas. 1986. *The Central African Republic. The Continent's Hidden Heart.* Boulder, CO: Westview Press.

Vansina, J. 1981. "The Kongo [Congo] Kingdoms and Its Neighbours." In B. A. Ogot (ed.), *General History of Africa,* Vol. 5 (p. 546). London: Unesco.

Vellut, J. L. 1981. "The Congo Basin and Angola." In J. F. Ade Ajayi (ed.), *General History of Africa VI.* London: Unesco.

CHAPTER 10

Agnew, Swanzie. 1972. *Malawi in Maps.* New York: African Publishing Corporation.

Boahen, A. A. 1981. "New Trends and Processes in Africa in the Nineteenth Century." In J. F. Ajayi (ed.), *General History of Africa,* Vol. 6 (pp. 40–63). London: Unesco.

Brown, Mervyn. 1978. *Madagascar Rediscovered. A History from Early Times to Independence.* London: Damian Tunnacliffe.

Egerton, Clement. 1973. *Angola in Perspective.* London: Routledge and Kegan Paul.

Freeman-Grenville, G. S. P. 1991. *The New Atlas of African History.* New York: Simon and Schuster.

Fry, Maxwell E. et al. 1978. *Fry, Drew, Knight, Creamer. Lund Humphries.* London.

Gerke, W. J. C. and Viljoen, Charl. 1968. *Master Plan for Lilongwe. The Capital City of Malawi.* Johannesburg: Purnell.

July, Robert W. 1980. *A History of the African People.* New York: Charles Scriber's Sons.

Kubler, George. 1972. *Portuguese Plan Architecture. Between Spices and Diamonds 1521–1706.* Middletown, CT: Wesleyan University Press.

Mutibwa, P. M. 1981. "Madagascar 1800–80." In J. F. Ajayi (ed.), *General History of Africa,* Vol. 6 (pp. 412–447). London: Unesco.

Pachai, B. 1973. *Malawi, The History of the Nation.* London: Longman Group Limited.

Peil, Margaret. 1984. "How Abuja Measures Up." *West Africa,* No. 3483, 1066–1067.

Potts, Deborah. 1985. "The Development of Malawi's New Capital at Lilongwe: A Comparison with Other New African Capitals." *Comparative Urban Research,* 10(2), 44.

Rhinehart, Robert. 1985. *Historical Setting, Mozambique, A Country Study.* Washington, DC: American University Press.

Roth, Mark. 1979. *Angola, A Country Study.* Washington, DC: American University Press.

Vansina, J. 1981. "The Kongo Kingdom and Its Neighbors." In B. A. Ogot (ed.), *General History of Africa,* Vol. 5 (pp. 546–587). London: Unesco.

Wright, Gwendolyn. 1991. *Politics of Design in French Colonial Urbanism.* Chicago: University of Chicago Press.

CHAPTER 11

Collins, John. 1986. "The Historical Development of a Planned Capital, 1931–1970." In Geoffrey Williams (ed.), *Lusaka and Its Environs* (pp. 95–137). Lusaka: Zambia Geographical Association.

Garlake, Peter. 1973. *Great Zimbabwe.* London: Thames and Hudson.

Mallows, Wilfrid. 1984. *The Mystery of Great Zimbabwe. A New Solution.* New York: W. W. Norton and Company.

Potts, Deborah. 1985. "The Development of Malawi's New Capital at Lilongwe: A Comparison with Other New African Capitals." *Comparative Urban Research,* 10(2), 44.

Smaldone, Joseph P. 1979. *Historical Setting. Zambia, A Country Study.* Washington, DC: American University Press.

Williams, Geoffrey. 1986. "The Early Years of the Township." In Geoffrey Williams (ed.), *Lusaka and Its Environs* (pp. 71–94). Lusaka: Zambia Geographical Association.

CHAPTER 12

Beavon, Keith S. O. 1970. *Land Use Patterns in Port Elizabeth.* Cape Town: A. A. Balkema.

Bernal, Martin. 1987. *Black Athena, The Afroasiatic Roots of Classical Civilization,* Vol. 1. New Brunswick, NJ: Rutgers University Press.

Dewar, David, Roelof Uytenbogaardt, Martin Hutton-Squire, Caren Levy, and Menidis. 1977. *Housing. A Comparative Evaluation of Urbanism in Cape Town.* Urban Problems Research Unit of the University of Cape Town. Claremont, Cape Town: David Philip, Publisher.

Diop, A. Cheikh. 1974. *The African Origin of Civilization, Myth or Reality.* Translated by Cook, Mercer. p. 230. Westport: Lawrence Hill and Company.

Picton-Seymour, Desiree. 1977. *Victorian Buildings in South Africa. 1850–1910.* Cape Town: A. Al Balkema Rotterdam.

Vale, Lawrence. 1992. *Architecture, Power, and National Identity.* New Haven, CT: Yale University Press.

CHAPTER 13

Aeradion, Suzan B. 1989. "Al-Sahili. The Historians' Myth of Architecture Technology Transfer from North Africa." *Journal des Africanistes,* 59(1–2).

Badawy, Alexander. 1968. *A History of Egyptian Architecture. The Empire (the New Kingdom). From the Eighteenth Dynasty to the End of the Twentieth Dynasty. 1580–1085 B.C.* Berkeley: University of California Press.

Bourgeois, Jean-Louis, Pelos, Carollee, and Davidson, Basil. 1989. *Spectacular Vernacular. The Adobe Tradition.* New York: Aperture Books.

Bravemann, Ren A. 1974. *Islam and Tribal Art in West Africa.* New York: Cambridge University Press.

Church, R. J. Harrison. 1980. *West Africa.* New York: Longman.

Collier, John L. 1990. *Historical Setting in Chad, a Country Study.* Washington, DC: Library of Congress.

Dubois, Felix. 1896. *Timbuctoo. The Mysterious.* Diana White (trans.). New York: Negro University Press.

Hiskett, Mervyn. 1984. *The Development of Islam in West Africa.* New York: Longman.

Levtzion, Nehemia. 1976. "The Early States of the Western Sudan to 1500." In J. F. A. Ajayi and M. Crowder (eds.), *History of West Africa,* Vol. 1 (pp. 114–195). New York: Columbia University Press.

Maalouf, Amin. 1989. *Leo Africans/Amin Maalouf.* Translated by Peter Slugbett. New York: Norton.

Mabogunje, Akin. 1976. "The Land and Peoples of West Africa." In J. F. A. Ajayi and M. Crowder (eds.), *History of West Africa,* Vol. 1 (pp. 1–32). New York: Columbia University Press.

Panikkar, Madhu K. 1963. *The Serpent and the Crescent.* Bombay: Asia Publishing House.

Prussin, Labelle. 1986. *Hatumere: Islamic Design in West Africa.* Berkeley: University of California Press.

CHAPTER I4

Barry, B. 1981. "Senegambia from the Sixteenth to the Eighteenth Century: Evolution of the Wolof, Sereer and Tukulor." In B. A. Ogot (ed.), *General History of Africa.* London: Unesco.

Bourdier, Jean-Paul. 1991. "Houses of Light." *Mimar,* June, 39, 61–67.

Church, Harrison. 1980. *West Africa.* Eighth Edition. London: Longman.

Crowder, Michael. 1967. *Senegal. A Study of French Assimilation Policy.* London: Methuen & Co. Ltd.

Gailey, Harry. 1965. *History of the Gambia.* New York: Frederick A. Praeger.

Gamble, David P. 1957. *"The Wolof of Senegambia." Ethnographic Survey of West Africa.* Ed. by Daryll Forde. London: International African Institute.

CHAPTER I5

Bourdier, Jean-Paul, and Minh-ha, Trinto. 1985. *African Spaces. Designs for Living in Upper Volta.* New York: African Publishing Company, A Division of Holmes & Meier Publishing, Inc.

Bourke, Gerald. 1990. "Beauty or Beast. Pope Paul Consecrates a Controversial $200M Basilica." *West Africa,* No. 3812, Sept. 17–23, 1990, p. 2480.

Byrnes, Riba M. 1991. *Historical Setting. Cote d'Ivoire. A Country Study.* Washington, DC: Library of Congress.

George, Claude. 1968. *The Rise of British West Africa.* London: Frank Cass and Co. Ltd.

Holsoe, Svend E. and Herman, Bernard L. 1988. *A Land and Life Remembered. Americo-Liberian Folk Architecture.* Athens, Georgia, U.S.A.: University of Georgia Press.

Little, Kenneth. 1967. *The Mende of Sierra Leone.* London: Routledge and Kegan Paul.

Prussin, Labelle. 1986. *Islamic Design in West Africa.* Berkeley: University of California Press.

CHAPTER I6

Boahen, Adu. 1974. "Politics in Ghana, 1800–1874." In J. F. A. Ajayi and Michael Crowder (eds.), *History of West Africa II.* London: Longman.

Crowder, Michael. 1974. "The 1914 to 1918 European War and West Africa." In J. F. Ade Ajayi and Michael Crowder (eds.), *History of West Africa II.* London: Longman.

Swithenbank, Michael. 1969. *Ashanti Fetish Houses.* Accra: Ghana University Press.

CHAPTER I7

Adekson, Bayo J. 1981. *Nigeria in Search of a Stable Civil-Military System.* Boulder, CO: Westview Press.

Alagoa, E. J. 1981. "Fon and Yoruba: The Niger Delta and the Cameroon." In B. A. Ogot (ed.), *General History of Africa. Vol. 5: Africa from the Sixteenth to the Seventeenth Century.* (pp. 434–452). London: Unesco.

Church, Harrison R. J. 1980. *West Africa,* Eighth Edition. London: Longman.

Clarke, Peter B. 1982. *West Africa and Islam. A Study of Religious Development from the 8th to the 20th Century.* London: Edward Arnold Publishing.

Diop, Cheikh Anta. 1974. *The African Origin of Civilization. Myth or Reality.* Westport: Lawrence Hill & Company.

Ekpenyon, Stephen. 1989. *Housing, the State and the Poor in Port Harcourt Cities.* London: Butterworth & Co. Publishers, Ltd.

Fry, Maxwell E. et al. 1978. *Frey, Drew, Knight, Cramer. Lund Humphries.* London.

Heathcote, David. 1976. *The Arts of the Hausa.* London: World of Islam Publishing Company Ltd.

Jones G. I. 1984. *The Art of Eastern Nigeria.* London: Cambridge University Press.

Laya, D. 1981. "Hausa States." In B. A. Ogot (ed.), *General History of Africa. Vol. 5: Africa from the Sixteenth to the Eighteenth Century.* (pp. 453–490). London: Unesco.

Morgan, W. T. W. 1883. *Nigeria.* London: Longman.

Moughtin, J. C. 1985. *Hausa Architecture.* London: Ethnographica.

Neaher, Nancy C. 1981. "An Interpretation of Igbo Carved Doors." *African Arts,* 15(1), pp. 49–55.

Ojo, G. J. A. 1966. *Yoruba Palaces. A Study of Afins of Yoruba Land.* London: University of London Press.

Peil, Margaret. 1991. *Lagos. The City Is the People.* Boston: G. K. Hall & Co.

Pound, Omar S. 1971. *Kano.* Birmingham, England: Migrant Press.

Prussin, Labelle. 1986. *Islamic Design in West Africa.* Berkeley: University of California.

Rasaki, Raji. 1990. "Managing a Cornubation Like Metropolitan Lagos. In Olusegun Obasanjo and Hans d'Orville (eds.), *Challenges of Leadership in African Development* (p. 227). New York: Crane Russak.

Ringing, AA. A. 1985, May 16. "Abuja." *New Nigeria Newspaper.* No. 958. Nigeria: New Nigeria Publishing Corporation.

Sharon, Arieh, and Sharon, Elder. 1976. *Master Plan for Obafemi Awolowo (Formerly Ife) University.* Ife, Nigeria.

Tange, Kenzo. 1986. *Japan's Architect,* Mar., 8605, 6.

Turner, Terisa. 1981/1982. "Commercial Capitalism in Nigeria: The Pattern of Competition." In Dennis L. Cohen and John Daniel (eds.). *Political Economy of Africa, Selected Readings.* Longman Group Ltd., p. 155.

Vale, Lawrence J. 1992. *Architecture, Power, and National Identity.* New Haven, CT: Yale University Press.

Vogel, Susan. 1991. *Future Traditions. Africa Explores 20th Century African Art.* New York: The Center for African Art.

Williams, Gavin. 1981/1982. "Nigeria: The Neo-Colonial Political Economy." In Cohen, Dennis L. (ed.) *Political Economy of Africa, Selected Readings.* Longman Group Ltd., p. 45.

CHAPTER I8

Clarke, J. I. et al. 1975. *An Advanced Geography of Africa.* Great Britain: Hulton Educational Publications.

Diop, Anta. 1974. *The African Origin of Civilization, Myth or Reality.* Translated by Mercer Cook. New York: Lawrence Hill and Company. p. 78.

Hull, Richard W. 1976. *African Cities and Towns Before the European Conquest.* New York: W. W. Norton and Company.

Kibuka, Eric P. 1990. "The African Social Situation: Major Elements." In *The African Social Situation: Crucial Factors of Development and Transformation* (pp. 18–46). London: Hans Zell Publishers.

Smith, Baldwin. 1938. *Egyptian Architecture as a Cultural Expression.* New York: D. Appleton-Century Company.

CHAPTER 19

Kamrany, Nake M. 1978. "The Case of the Least Developed of the Underdeveloped Countries: The Sahel Sudan Region of West Africa." In *The New Economics of the Less Developed Countries.* Edited by Nake M. Kamrany, Boulder, CO: Westview Press, p. 57.

Metz, Helen Chapin. 1979. *Libya, A Country Study.* Washington, DC: Federal Research Division, Library of Congress.

Mguyen, Q. Tri. 1989. *Third-World Development. Aspects of Political Legitimacy and Viability.* East Rutherford, NJ: Fairleigh Dickinson University Press.

Todaro, P. Michael. 1981/1982. *Economic Development in the Third World,* Second Edition. London: Longman.

CHAPTER 20

Benton, Tim. 1984. *Urbanism. Le Corbusier Architect of the Century.* London: Arts Council of Great Britain.

Collins, John. 1986. "The Historical Development of a Planned Capital, 1931–1970." In Geoffrey J. Williams (ed.), *Lusaka and Its Environs* (pp. 95–137). Lusaka: Zambia Geographical Association.

Curtis, William. 1987. *Le Corbusier: Nature and Tradition. Le Corbusier Architect of the Century.* London: Arts Council of Great Britain.

Evenson, Norma. 1969. *Le Corbusier: The Machine and the Grand Design.* New York: George Braziller.

Evenson, Norma. 1973. *Two Brazilian Capitals. Architecture and Urbanism in Rio de Janeiro and Brasília.* New Haven: Yale University Press.

Garlake, Peter. 1973. *Great Zimbabwe.* London: Thames and Hudson.

Gloag, John. 1958. *Guide to Western Architecture.* New York: The Macmillan Company.

Kalia, Ravi. 1987. *Chandigarh in Search of an Identity.* Carbondale and Edwardsville: Southern Illinois University Press.

Kibuka, Eric P. 1990. "The African Social Situation: Major Elements." *The African Social Situation: Crucial Factors of Development and Transformation* (pp. 18–46). London: Hans Zell Publishers.

Mallows, Wilfrid. 1984. *The Mystery of Great Zimbabwe. A New Solution.* New York: W. W. Norton and Company.

McKean, John Maule. 1980. "First Industrial Age." In Michael Raeburn (ed.), *Architecture of the Western World.* (p. 201). London: Obis Publishing.

Muschenheim, William. 1964. *Elements of the Art of Architecture.* New York: The Viking Press.

Potts, Deborah. 1985. "The Development of Malawi's New Capital at Lilongwe: A Comparison with Other New African Capitals." *Comparative Urban Research,* 10(2), 44.

Raeburn, Michael (ed.). 1980. *Architecture of the Western World.* London: Orbis Publishing.

Smaldone, Joseph P. 1979. *Historical Setting. Zambia A Country Study.* Washington, DC: American University.

Soyinka, Wole. 1963. *The Lion and the Jewel.* London: Oxford University Press.

Sturgis, Russell. 1906. *A History of Architecture,* Vol. 1. New York: The Baker and Taylor Company.

Williams, Geoffrey. 1986. "The Early Years of the Township." In Geoffrey Williams (ed.), *Lusaka and Its Environs* (pp. 71–94). Lusaka: Zambia Geographical Association.

INDEX